THE DICTIONARY OF
MIND AND SPIRIT

P9-DUH-763

Avon Books are available at special quantity discounts for bulk purchases for sales promotions, premiums, fund raising or educational use. Special books, or book excerpts, can also be created to fit specific needs.

For details write or telephone the office of the Director of Special Markets, Avon Books, Dept. FP, 1350 Avenue of the Americas, New York, New York 10019, 1-800-238-0658.

THE DICTIONARY OF
MIND AND SPIRIT

COMPILED BY
DONALD WATSON

AVON BOOKS ◆ NEW YORK

If you purchased this book without a cover, you should be aware that this book is stolen property. It was reported as "unsold and destroyed" to the publisher, and neither the author nor the publisher has received any payment for this "stripped book."

AVON BOOKS
A division of
The Hearst Corporation
1350 Avenue of the Americas
New York, New York 10019

Copyright © 1991 by Donald Watson
Cover photograph by Mark Tomalti/Courtesy of Masterfile and Pictor/UNIPHOTO
Published by arrangement with Andre Deutsch Limited
Library of Congress Catalog Card Number: 92-14193
ISBN: 0-380-71792-1

All rights reserved, which includes the right to reproduce this book or portions thereof in any form whatsoever except as provided by the U.S. Copyright Law. For information address Andre Deutsch Limited, 105-106 Great Russell Street, London, WC1B 3LJ, England.

Library of Congress Cataloging in Publication Data:
    The Dictionary of mind and spirit/compiled by Donald Watson.
        p.   cm.
Originally published: A Dictionary of mind and spirit. London: A. Deutsch, 1991.
Includes bibliographical references and index.
ISBN 0-380-71792-1
1. Parapsychology—Dictionaries.   2.   Religion—Dictionaries.
I. Watson, Donald, 1946-
BF1025.D53   1992   92-14193
133'.03—dc20   CIP

First Avon Books Trade Printing: October 1992

AVON TRADEMARK REG. U.S. PAT. OFF. AND IN OTHER COUNTRIES, MARCA REGISTRADA, HECHO EN U.S.A.

Printed in the U.S.A.

OPM   10   9   8   7   6   5   4   3   2   1

List of Illustrations

Acknowledgements

My thanks to Piers for the initial idea and to his circle of family and friends for their constant interest and encouragement.

The author also wishes to thank Hiroki Fujita and Wisdom Publications for the use of the photograph on p. 192 and Princeton University Press for the use of the photographs on pp. 3 and 192.

Introduction

The terms and concepts that are defined and discussed in this *Dictionary of Mind and Spirit* have been chosen because of their occurrence when considering an area of our thinking where mind and spirit seem to come close together − the area which is often denoted by the word 'psychic'. In Greek *psyche* means 'soul'. The *Oxford English Dictionary* defines 'psychology' as 'the science of the nature, functions, and phenomena of the human soul or mind', but our modern tendency towards reductionism and academic fragmentation has led to a narrowing of the field of psychology making of it a very partial, mechanistic science, dedicated primarily to the study of overt behaviour and relatively automatic responses. Parapsychology was created to consider some of the areas which modern psychology was neglecting, but even parapsychology, in an attempt to find favour with those in the psychology camp, has tended to study only what is measurable in the modern 'scientific' manner, ignoring what has been accepted for millennia by large sections of humanity as a 'spiritual science'.

Reconsidering some of that traditional knowledge with an awareness of modern psychological understanding, as many people are now doing, and recognizing the similarities in different traditions, can give us a more complete picture of our psychic reality. It has taken us a long time to understand the workings of the human body, and that task is still not complete. Our understanding of the human soul is even more partial, and it is also more difficult to define in the concrete terms for which our language is best suited. But more and more people seem to be realizing that this area of knowledge has been unjustifiably neglected in modern times. This affects more than our reflective view of ourselves. More and more people are also coming to the realization that our contemporary view of the world is very partial and that our *consensus reality* may be due for drastic change.

The gradual disintegration of religious dogma reveals to those who can escape its clutches, whilst still retaining a sense of the spiritual, far more common ground than was ever generally acknowledged. If this can happen between different religions, sooner or later it can also happen between science and religion. Orthodox scientists maintain that the separation of science and religion is one of the crowning glories of modern scientific progress, yet the major figures on whose work much of modern science is built — people like Albert Einstein and Niels Bohr — have always stressed the unity of the religious and the scientific impulse. It was Einstein who said, 'Science without religion is lame, religion without science is blind.' The paranormal has remained on the fringe of orthodox science in the same way that esoteric traditions have been marginalized by orthodox religion. Yet it is in just these areas that the scientific and religious come close together and may even overlap.

So this dictionary includes terms related to paranormal phenomena and esoteric religion, to modern parapsychology and spiritual traditions, and an attempt is made where possible to draw parallels between different traditions and different schools of thought. Look up a word like *bioplasma* in any English dictionary and you will be lucky to find any definition at all, let alone any reference to other concepts that are comparable. *Bioplasma* is an example of the kind of thing that seems to straddle the great science-religion divide. It is a hypothetical natural substance or energy that Russian scientists have postulated, investigated, even registered and measured in various ways. Yet as a concept its antecedents can be found in the area of religious beliefs, recognizable as some sort of etheric energy throughout the world in various guises: *prana, mana, ch'i, od, orgone, Qi Gong.*

For the sake of economy, instead of saying 'When people talk of *earth-bound spirits* they mean . . .' the dictionary states rather bluntly '*Earth-bound spirits* are . . .', since anyone who uses this term means exactly the same thing. No such definition should be understood as automatically conferring objective reality. If the reader senses what appears to be the author's personal attitude in any of the discussion of the concepts under consideration, this should not be interpreted as a partisan bias for or against any particular view. I am convinced that no one school of thought has all the answers for us on these matters. I am equally convinced that there is practically always a grain of truth or a useful pointer to be found in the reasoning behind even the most abstruse theories. No one has a monopoly on truth. Each of us creates our own version of the truth by recognizing certain statements as valid for what we regard as reality, and if at the same time we are open to some concepts which do not immediately accord with our world view, our version of reality may eventually expand and become more inclusive. I believe such growth represents evolutionary change within the individual. It is not a question of being converted to any particular point of view. It is rather the development of a greater awareness of a variety of views and an ability to consider them from a vantage point which allows us to see them in perspective, always remembering that changing our position also changes the perspective. Recognizing other people's classifications and definitions helps us to formulate our own world-view more comprehensively. Perhaps it is in this sense that, in the words of Socrates, 'The beginning of all wisdom is the definition of terms.'

Donald Watson
May 1990

NOTE Entries cover psychic phenomena and theories, mental concepts, spiritual ideas and systems of spiritual thought. People are not included as headwords but the Index shows under which entries they are mentioned. Superior figures refer to the publications arranged in alphabetical order by author at the end of the book.

A

ABRAXAS For the second-century Alexandrian GNOSTIC Basilides, Abraxas was the name of the Supreme Being, comparable with Menander's ENNOIA (Supreme Thought), although perhaps also one stage of divinity higher, since the Supreme Being first generated Mind, from which came LOGOS, Understanding, Wisdom, Power and a whole succession of powers, principalities and angels in a complex spiritual hierarchy. The name Abraxas converts by gematria into the number 365, and Basilides believed that there were 365 *Aeons*, personifications of the emanations from the Godhead which effected the creation of matter. The first of these aeons was Christ, also called Nous. Basilides differed from other Gnostic schools in his concept of God as being essentially unknowable, an idea that can be traced to Indian sources, whose notions of MAYA and NIRVANA he also included in his philosophy.

Jung uses the name Abraxas to refer to illusory reality (*maya*) in his neo-Gnostic text entitled *Seven Sermons to the Dead*.[98] This was written 'semi-automatically' in 1916 by a part of himself he happened to call Basilides. AUTOMATIC WRITING is more typical of spiritualist mediumship than of scientific method, but the result is a core text in depth psychology. The writing immediately followed Jung's break with Freud and his experiences of poltergeist phenomena. Unlike the Gnostics, Jung did not teach the return of human essence to the Gnostic PLEROMA, where individuality was lost, but individuation, which maintained the fullness of human individuality.

ABSENT HEALING In 1890 T.J. Hudson carried out experiments in distant HEALING in an attempt to prove that one person's SUBJECTIVE MIND could telepathically link with another's to effect a physical cure. This was a logical consequence of his theory that the subjective mind was fundamentally in harmony with the whole universe, and that illness was caused by a loss of harmony with nature. That harmony might be restored with the assistance of another subjective mind, reaching out to the subjective mind of the patient. Hudson found that the best time to experiment with this effect at a distance was on the verge of sleep, i.e. when the

1

healer's 'objective mind' was relaxed. He also found that the patient's objective mind was less of a hindrance when aware of what Hudson was trying to do, although in modern research this would contaminate results by allowing a 'placebo effect' to creep in.

Eighty years later, Lawrence LeShan tried to get first-hand evidence for Hudson's theory. In *The Medium, the Mystic and the Physicist* he describes how, after one hour, his own distant healing group restored feeling to the legs of a boy who had been diagnosed as permanently paralysed after breaking his back on a trampoline.[108]

Nowadays there are many healing circles which SIT regularly to send out healing to those who they know are in need. Some of the sitters may also be practising HEALERS, but this is not a prerequisite. When healers do sit in a healing circle, they will invariably provide their patients with a boost between visits in this way. (It is this kind of distant healing which is more often referred to as absent healing.)

Another technique of healing at a distance (one which is not, however, usually implied by the terms 'absent' or 'distant healing') is RADIONICS. With the aid of a sample from the patient, such as a dried drop of blood, and his radionics box, detector plate and pendulum, the radionics practitioner claims to measure, identify and repair distortions in the patient's energy field.

ACTIVE IMAGINATION This was the term used by C.G. Jung to refer to the faculty which he developed in himself to create an inner world of the imagination, peopled by beings who were completely independent of his own personality. One such character was evoked regularly by Jung, an old man who first appeared to him as Elijah, but whom he subsequently called Philemon. Philemon became a kind of guide and teacher to Jung, bringing to conscious awareness ideas that were inaccessible to his logical, conscious mind. 'Psychologically, Philemon represented superior insight,' Jung wrote. 'At times he seems to me quite real, as if he were a living personality. To me he was what the Indians call a GURU. ... Philemon represented a force which was not myself. ... I held conversations with him, and he said things which I had not consciously thought. For I observed clearly that it was he who spoke, not I. He said I treated thoughts as if I generated them myself, but in his view thoughts were like animals in a forest.'[97]

This sounds very similar to the conversations that spiritualists report having with their GUIDES, although Jung maintained that Philemon was part of his own larger psyche, normally inaccessible

Jung's drawing of his 'guide', Philemon

to conscious awareness and therefore seeming completely separate from it. He accommodated the phenomenon neatly in his theory of projections, at least in his public pronouncements.

In Psychosynthesis, a similar technique known as GUIDED IMAGERY has been developed, although in this case, as its name suggests, not all the images arise spontaneously from the unconscious — they are specifically invited, even though the actual form they take is not necessarily predetermined. The images that are evoked in psychosynthesis are not restricted to figures with whom the individual can carry on a discourse; various objects — usually from the world of nature — may also be held in the imagination in MEDITATION exercises.

Another school which has developed directly out of Jung's ideas on Active Imagination, also drawing upon other traditions such as astrology and the TAROT, is the Inner Guide Meditation. Specific exercises are followed to evoke scenes in which inner guides can be consulted.[182] It is interesting to note that in this case there are warnings about 'false guides' which may also arise, and suggestions are made regarding how the meditator will be able to recognize them. One characteristic of a so-called false guide is when they start telling the individual what to do rather than simply giving guidance when asked. This is also one of the traditional ways of separating the wheat from the chaff when considering the 'spirits' communicating through MEDIUMS.

ADEPT An adept is another name for a certain kind of MASTER, one who is 'of a far higher stage of development than those discarnate communicators who describe the SUMMERLANDS, personal "heaven-worlds" of their own Inner-Plane state.'[54] According to occult tradition, these adepts or Masters have developed beyond the need to incarnate. Certain people (e.g. Alice Bailey) have maintained that the Masters who have communicated to them intuitively are in fact in the body in another remote part of the world, although this has been denied by other communications, such as Fortune's *Cosmic Doctrine*. In this work, Masters are described as human beings like ourselves but older. 'They are not Gods, nor Angels, nor Elementals, but are those individuals who have achieved and completed the same task as you have set yourselves. What you are now, they were once. What they are now, you can be.'[54]

A Master communicating through Dion Fortune said, 'What we are you cannot realize and it is a waste of time to try to do so, but you can imagine us on the astral plane and we can contact you through your imagination, and although your mental picture is not real or actual, the results of it are real and actual.'[54]

AFTERLIFE From the evidence of cave burials in China it is thought that primitive humans already believed in an afterlife half a million years ago. The Neanderthals (100,000–25,000 years ago) buried their dead in graves containing food and flint implements that would be needed in the next world. We cannot know what kind of afterlife primitive humanity looked forward to, but we do know what people believed in classical times.

In the ancient world there was a general belief that the dead were consigned to a dim, shadowy world which they inhabited as thin insubstantial shades. The Mesopotamians referred to this place as 'Kurnugia', the land of no return. The spirits of the ancient Greeks enjoyed a rather joyless and aimless existence in HADES, and the Hebrews were similarly consigned to unwelcoming darkness in their subterranean SHEOL (the Pit), which Job described as 'the land of gloom and deep darkness, the land of gloom and chaos, where light is as darkness.' These realms of the dead were far away from any divinity: as the Psalmist says, 'The dead do not praise the Lord' (Psalm 115, 17.).

The idea of a heavenly existence after death took a long time to develop in the human belief-system, and when it did, it was at first regarded as a privilege for the chosen few, the exception rather than the rule. Thus the biblical prophets Elijah and Enoch were snatched up into HEAVEN at the end of their earthly lives. The most heroic of the ancient Greek heroes hoped to walk the Elysian Fields after death, if the gods so decreed, and the bravest Norse warriors killed in battle were likewise conveyed to Valhalla.

Modern Christianity seems ambivalent about the nature of an afterlife. People used to believe in purgatory followed by heaven or HELL on the Day of JUDGMENT, but Hell has definitely fallen out of fashion, and Purgatory and the Day of Judgment seem to be going the same way, leaving rather a vacuum. Even heaven, as understood by many today, has become more of a limbo existence.

According to traditional Spiritualists, the soul eventually wakes up in 'SUMMERLAND', a world created by the desires of the individual. Everything is idealized in this perfect world of wish-fulfilment, the plane of illusion. It is equivalent to, but generally far more pleasant than, the *Kamaloca*, the second stage of the *bardo* world in the Tibetan BOOK OF THE DEAD. It is generally from this level of post-mortem existence that messages are received through mediums. The communicators often refer to higher levels, higher planes, realms towards which they must strive, but communications from these higher realms are much rarer, perhaps because they must be transmitted via intermediaries on the lower level.

Hindus, Buddhists, THEOSOPHISTS and ANTHROPOSOPHISTS give much more detailed accounts of events after death, and these accounts are basically very similar. At death the SOUL, consisting of the astral BODY (the personal consciousness) and spirit body (soul or ego), finally leave the physical body. The etheric body survives only a few days longer than the physical body itself, during which time the soul reviews the whole of the past life. The soul then enters *Kamaloca*, where the past life is reviewed in depth: desires and emotions are re-experienced and the soul may inflict its own purgatory on itself. This suffering brings purification, after which the astral body too is allowed to dissolve away, a process which involves the abandonment of the personality, so that the purified spirit body (or ego) rises to the spirit world, where it can start to choose its next incarnation.

The spirit world is made not of matter as we know it, but of the material of thoughts. We must assume that there is an added dimension in the afterlife, another dimension of time. But the immediate afterlife is at a relatively low level of the spirit realms, and in that state we are not aware of eternity. We do, however, appreciate earth-time in a new way, in much the same way that as physical beings we appreciate earth-space visually: 'now' becomes equivalent to 'here', and we can 'see' a little distance in the directions of past and present, just as we can see in different directions around us now.

AJNA Sanskrit for brow centre. See CHAKRAS.

AKASHA/AKASA Akasha is a Sankrit word meaning 'space'. It was the first of the five natural elements manifested by BRAHMAN (the other four being, as in the West, earth, fire, water and air). The Hindu and Buddhist concept of space is different from the Western idea: akasha is not so much empty space as an all-pervading substance embracing the four dimensions of space and time. It also represents the boundary of the phenomenal world. It entered nineteenth-century THEOSOPHICAL and SPIRITUALIST literature as the ETHER, the bridge between the material world and the mind, which bore the impression of everything that had ever happened in it, the AKASHIC RECORD.

AKASHIC RECORD Everything that has ever happened is said to be recorded in a kind of cosmic memory bank, which is referred to in various esoteric doctrines as the Akashic record. Edgar Cayce described it as 'the record that the individual entity itself writes upon the skein of time and space'. This record is accessible to some mediums and clairvoyants when either in trance or in a state of heightened sensitivity. The term seems archaic to some people. They may prefer to regard the Akashic record as a UNIVERSAL MIND, or something akin to Jung's notion of the COLLECTIVE UNCONSCIOUS. Others use modern technological analogies, comparing the cosmic memory bank to a holographic video disk capable of storing an infinite quantity of data. Jane Roberts, an American CHANNEL, often referred to a sensation of being in a 'library' when ideas and knowledge came into her mind as if from another plane.

The essential idea is that the record of everything that has ever happened in the cosmos is not stored in matter, but on another non-physical level of reality. This is in contrast to other postulated means by which records of past events are stored in matter, for example the fears associated with certain HAUNTINGS, or the emotions imprinted on objects which PSYCHOMETRISTS are able to 'read'.

Some form of the Akashic record is sometimes put forward as a means of dispensing with discarnate entities when 'explaining' the origin of channelled information. In this theory the channel or MEDIUM simply taps into the Universal Mind: any personality which 'comes through' is then just a memory, rather than an individual with a continuing non-physical existence.

ALCHEMY There are basically two modern views of alchemy. Some believe that the main concern of alchemists was the study of the natural world, in particular chemistry. To varying degrees they were prone to certain superstitious notions concerning the transmutation of elements, specifically the creation of gold from base metals such as lead. Whatever the alchemists' own beliefs in the possibilities of turning lead into gold, they had no qualms about financing their investigations by duping wealthy patrons. The other modern view, particularly since Jung's research into the subject, is that the alchemical writings are symbolic representations of the individual's mental and spiritual work, striving to unify body, MIND and SPIRIT and thus achieve a human divinity, the perfected human being.

According to this view, the transmutation of base metal into gold symbolized the transformation of natural, material man into spiritual man. The catalyst in this process was known as the PHILOSOPHER'S STONE, and the search for the Philosopher's Stone was known as the Great Work. According to alchemists, the production of the Philosopher's Stone involved blending and treating three basic substances, salt, sulphur and mercury, which in the esoteric view corresponded to the body, soul or mind, and spirit. When brought together in the cauldron and blended in the element of fire (representing love) the threefold process began. The first stage of Blackness represented purgation, the second, Whiteness, represented illumination, and the third, Redness, the colour of alchemical gold, represented the marriage of Luna and Sol, the union of the human and the divine, the finite and the infinite.

The alchemists' search for the Elixir of Life can also be understood in the same terms as the search for the Philosopher's Stone, the search for the means of recognizing man's true nature and thus achieving eternal life. Each individual, belonging to both the material and the divine world, contained a spark of the universal spirit imprisoned in matter, as well as having a soul and a body. The

Great Work can thus be understood as a symbolic representation of how human beings might achieve insight into their own divine perfection by freeing the spirit from the bonds of matter. The Church was notoriously antagonistic to such GNOSTIC beliefs, so it was only natural that a doctrine of this kind should be couched in esoteric terms. The ROSICRUCIANS continued the tradition into relatively modern times. According to the symbolism, gold represented the state of perfection which could be achieved in the material world; it therefore also represented the perfected body and the perfected soul, towards which we should all be striving.

Another objective of some alchemists — or perhaps the same objective described with a different metaphor — was the creation of life out of non-living chemical materials. Such an artificially created human being was known as a homunculus. One practitioner who wrote of the process was Paracelsus (1493–1541). He stated that human sperm was a necessary first ingredient. After a forty-day incubation period with certain chemicals, and a further forty-day period of nourishment with the ingredients of human blood, a miniature child could be produced. In spite of such fanciful beliefs Paracelsus's main aim in studying alchemy was to cure disease, in connection with which he developed his doctrine of SIGNATURES. Although he also held the alchemists' belief in the transmutation of base metal into gold, this was not one of his aims in studying alchemy.

It is interesting to compare the apparent practical concerns of alchemists with the preoccupations of medicine and biological research today. The alchemists' search for the elixir of life still goes on, although we call it prolonging our lifespan or slowing down the process of aging. And on the surface the attempt to create the homunculus bears a striking resemblance to *in vitro* fertilization. Either the alchemists were basically concerned with the same practical questions as modern science, or they were intuitively aware of what scientists would be working on centuries later. Either way, alchemy and science form a continuity which modern scientists generally choose to ignore.

ALPHA BRAIN WAVES – See BRAIN WAVES.

ALTER EGO The alter ego (literally 'the other I') is a term often used to denote the 'body' which appears in another location during ASTRAL TRAVEL or OUT-OF-THE-BODY EXPERIENCES.

ALTERED STATES Everyone recognizes at least two states of CON-SCIOUSNESS: being awake and being asleep. Some may divide waking consciousness into two types: normal everyday consciousness, in which most of what we do is relatively automatic, and a more focused form of concentrated awareness in which we are fully conscious of ourselves as autonomous individuals. Besides these there are other so-called altered states of consciousness. These can be induced in various ways: by taking drugs, or by unusual mental activity such as MEDITATION, going into TRANCE, self-hypnosis, or submitting to HYPNOSIS by another. Some altered states of consciousness may apparently occur without any deliberate intent on the part of the person concerned, as in cases of POSSESSION or OUT-OF-THE-BODY EXPERIENCES.

ANAHATA – Sanskrit for heart centre. See CHAKRAS.

ANGELS Strictly speaking, angels and ARCHANGELS are spiritual beings which never incarnate in human form. They are primarily concerned with generating creative, life-giving energies. Since they are never human they are, of course, sexless. What are sometimes called GUARDIAN ANGELS are more usually understood as being spirits who have incarnated, but whose present task is to watch over and guide those who are leading earthly lives, although some prefer to regard them as higher spiritual aspects of ourselves – our HIGHER SELF.

ANIMAL MAGNETISM – See MESMERISM.

ANIMALS What psychic abilities do animals have? The ability of pet dogs to discern the mood of their owner may suggest that they are more sensitive to the human AURA than we are ourselves, although one cannot rule out the possibility that our scent also changes according to mood. However, it is commonly believed that animals are more likely to be aware of 'psychic activity' in the form of HAUNTINGS and POLTERGEISTS.

The American investigator, Robert Morris, (who later became the first person to occupy the Koestler Chair in Parapsychology at Edinburgh University) once took a selection of animals to a supposedly haunted house in Kentucky. The dog refused to cross the threshold; the cat went in but hissed and spat at an empty chair in the corner of one room; and the rattlesnake adopted an erect aggressive position in front of the same chair. The rat, which was also taken into the house, was unconcerned. It is interesting to notice that the animals which sensed the presence of the 'ghost' included a reptile: it cannot therefore be something peculiar to the superior mammalian brain which enables creatures to register such things.

This suggests further that this SIXTH SENSE is one of two things. Either it is simply an extension of existing senses, and the effects perceived are truly external and could therefore be picked up by recording instruments, a feat which has still not been achieved. Or if, as seems more likely, it is a separate faculty, it is one which belongs not so much to the next stage of human evolution as to the very distant past. It is therefore, as many occultists have claimed, a faculty of which all are capable, one that has been temporarily lost or forgotten by the majority of humanity in its present condition, but which we could recover.

The most widely acknowledged evidence of psychic (extra-sensory) ability on the part of animals is their ability to track down their mates or their owners when they have been separated from them, a phenomenon known as PSI-TRAILING. It has also been shown that dogs can locate boxes buried in the sand better when they are observed during their search by their trainers, who know where the boxes are (and who are of course out of sight and hearing of the dogs). Because of this, J.B. Rhine postulated 'a functional integration of man and dog mentalities', 'a kind of fusion between the two', which sounds similar to Lyall Watson's notion of SAMA.

ANTAHKARANA In Vedantic philosophy the antahkarana is the 'inner instrument' or MIND, which acts as a go-between for body and spirit. This definition of mind includes will and feeling as well as thought and imagination. Mental disciplines of YOGA and its various stages of MEDITATION are a means of bringing the body more in line with the spirit. CONSCIOUSNESS can also be regarded as encompassing both bodily and spiritual levels, and the antahkarana is sometimes referred to in occult doctrine as the umbilical cord or energy channel which connects the lower self, consisting of the everyday consciousness and the personal unconscious (or SUBCONSCIOUS), to the HIGHER SELF (also sometimes called the oversoul, or the SUPERCONSCIOUS). Jacob's dream of the ladder linking heaven and earth is regarded by many as a symbolic representation of the antahkarana.

ANTHROPIC PRINCIPLE Several contemporary physicists and cosmologists have commented on the fact that life is extremely improbable — a cosmic coincidence, or on the other hand that the laws of the universe seem to be geared specifically towards facilitating the evolution of life. Change a constant here or there and the whole cosmos would collapse or explode or otherwise be totally unsuitable for the production of stars with potentially life-generating planets around them. For example, if carbon and oxygen did not have precisely the atomic structure that they do have, these two elements essential for our form of life would never have been formed in stars at all. The British physicist Paul Dirac (1902—84) said 'something strange is going on'. The astronomer Fred Hoyle (1915—) thinks it looks like 'a put-up job'. 'A common-sense interpretation of the facts suggests that a superintellect has monkeyed with physics, as well as chemistry and biology, and that there are no blind forces worth speaking about in nature.'[85] It is from such responses to what science has learned about the universe that the so-called strong anthropic principle has been developed, which states 'that the laws of nature must be such as to admit the existence of consciousness in the universe at some stage. In other words, nature organizes itself in such a way as to make the universe self-aware.'[41]

This is still not part of mainstream science, but scientists do discuss the theory. It also fits in well with the EVOLUTION of the physical universe as presented in traditional occult teachings, and with more modern views such as Teilhard de Chardin's notion that CONSCIOUSNESS and its growth towards the OMEGA POINT is the purpose of the phenomenal universe.

ANTHROPOSOPHY The word *anthroposophy* (literally 'man-wisdom') was first used in the writings of the seventeenth-century mystic Thomas Vaughan. As a spiritual philosophy and set of teachings anthroposophy was founded by Rudolf Steiner (1861—1925). Steiner had started as a theosophist, but he felt that THEOSOPHY was developing too strong a bias towards eastern doctrines at the expense of western faiths. (It has been said that Annie Besant, who was the President of the Theosophical Society at the time of Steiner's separation from it, disliked the prominence Steiner gave to Christianity because of her own too-close attachment to the east, derived from a recent incarnation in India by which she was still being influenced.)

Steiner was perhaps closer to the ROSICRUCIANS. He firmly believed that Christianity was of unique significance in the evolution of humanity; the Christ of history and the Christ in the human heart were more than religious tenets, 'they are planetary facts'. Without Christ, humanity might well have brought about its own destruction, whilst as a result of the incarnation the Christ-consciousness is potentially in the hearts of all human beings.

Much of Steiner's teaching was already part of Western occultism. The central concept in anthroposophy is the cycle of involution/evolution beginning and ending with spirit. Spirit becomes dense and solidifies until the material nadir is reached. This was reached and could have been irreversible without the incarnation of Christ. The Second Coming is a metaphorical way of alluding to the situation when more and more human beings will have evolved to the point where they perceive Christ spiritually.

Consideration of the words themselves suggests that Theosophy ('divine wisdom') places God at the centre, whilst anthroposophy places humanity at the centre, or at least humanity is the obvious starting point. Steiner defined anthroposophy as 'a path of knowledge, leading from the spiritual in man to the spiritual in the universe'.[185] The individual aspires to 'higher knowledge': the lower self is made aware of the HIGHER SELF through intuition which is achieved by concentration and meditation. Steiner expounded three forms of higher knowledge: Imagination, the ability to perceive the spiritual world around us in form and colour; Inspiration, the ability to receive information from the spiritual world, information about the processes and order of creation; and Intuition, the ability to recognize and communicate intuitively with spiritual beings.

Steiner considered as unacceptable the idea of an impenetrable UNCONSCIOUS, inaccessible to self-observation and rational thought processes. He believed that nothing needs to remain inaccessible, below the level of consciousness. Humanity can perceive cosmic totality by using the faculties of Imagination, Inspiration and INTUITION, which refer to the perceptive modes of the etheric, astral and spiritual. These are the three 'worlds' in ascending order of separation from the physical. Steiner often referred to man as 'a citizen of three worlds'.

> The physical body, as the coarsest structure, lies within the others, which mutually interpenetrate both it and each other. The ether-body fills the physical body as a life-form; extending beyond this on all sides is to be perceived the soul-body (astral form). And beyond this again extends the sentient soul, then the intellectual soul which grows the larger the more it receives into itself of the true and the good. ... These formations in the midst of which the physical body appears as if in a cloud, may be called human AURA.

The reality of 'higher worlds', the 'super-sensible world' or the spirit-world is basic to Steiner's philosophy. 'As ice is only a form in which water exists, so are the objects of the senses only a form in which soul-and spirit-beings exist. If we have grasped this, we can also understand that as water can pass over into ice, so the spirit-world can pass over into the soul-world and the latter into that of the senses.' 'The lungs do not create the air for which they long, neither does the human soul create out of its longing the ideas of the super-sensible world. But the soul has this longing because it is formed and built for the super-sensible world, as are the lungs for the air.' Training oneself to become aware of this 'super-sensible world' was an essential part of studying what Steiner called 'spiritual science'. 'Through insight into what is hidden from the senses the human being expands his nature in such a way that he feels his life prior to the expansion to be no more that "a dream about the world".'[183]

APPARITIONS People who are emotionally close and temporarily apart have sometimes had simultaneous HALLUCINATIONS of each other. This happened to Rosalind Heywood. In 1918 she was in Macedonia while the man with whom she was emotionally involved was in Paris. They appeared to each other at what they later discovered was exactly the same moment. They did not deliberately 'will themselves' across the continent (see ASTRAL TRAVEL), neither were they aware of their presence elsewhere. The most plausible explanation in Rosalind Heywood's opinion is 'that both his hallucination and mine were self-created. But why did we create them? Was it merely frustration, or was this the only way that our conscious minds could be told of subconscious telepathic interaction between us?'[84]

Such phantoms (or phantasms) are sometimes called 'DOUBLES' or 'Doppelgängers'. They are a kind of thought projection which is transmitted accidentally more often than deliberately. The poet W.B. Yeats appeared twice one day to a fellow student for whom he had a message and had consequently been devoting some thought. The more urgent the situation, the more likely a projection of this kind is likely to be sent.

In view of their involuntary nature, 'projections' might be an inappropriate term. It is quite conceivable that the sensitivity of the person who sees the apparition is the crucial factor, in which case perhaps they should be regarded as hallucinations. In fact only certain people seem to have the ability to experience apparitions, yet these people show no particular proneness for fantasy when tested to assess their degree of imaginativeness. Support for this view is found in the fact that an apparition usually corresponds to what the percipient believes to be the appearance of a particular person, and is not a precise representation of them, suggesting that it has been conjured up by the percipient's mind. But this does not exclude the possibility that such apparitions may contain information which is unknown to the percipient. Such hallucinations would be the means by which messages from the unconscious mind are brought to conscious awareness, particularly in crisis situations.

There are countless well-attested cases of CRISIS APPARITIONS when people have 'seen' someone close to them in a strange situation. The usual pattern is that A is away from B and undergoes some crisis, often a fatal accident. B has no reason to expect this, but is made aware of it sometimes instantaneously, and generally within the next twelve hours, by experiencing a vivid hallucination of A. The apparition often includes aspects of the real situation, but need not necessarily be sad or frightening: the fear usually follows when B starts wondering how to interpret the apparition. (Fear is therefore a learned response of the conscious mind and may form a much less important role in the emotional make-up of the SUBCONSCIOUS.)

The simplest explanation for this phenomenon is that at a certain level the two people are unconsciously in telepathic contact with each other. The UNCONSCIOUS MIND of the percipient is aware of what is happening to the other person and creates a hallucination to convey this information to the conscious mind. The more senses involved in the hallucinatory process, the more difficult it is for some people to accept that all such apparitions must be mere constructs of the mind. It becomes even more difficult to accept this theory when, as sometimes happens, the apparition opens a door. If the percipient alone is responsible, this means that TELEKINESIS is also brought into play. The actual presence of a doppelgänger or projected double begins to look like the more economical explanation.

It is very common for figures which appear in apparitions to be reported as 'dressed in white'. This suggests that if they are 'real objects' they might contain their own light source, which against a dim background appears white rather than coloured. On the other hand, hallucinations would appear independently of any external light source and would in contrast with their surroundings also appear to shine with their own light.

There is an interesting link between apparitions and noisy movement as in many HAUNTINGS. Hallucinatory theories of hauntings and apparitions suggest that the amount of information apparently coming through the various senses should reflect the proportions of sensory input normally received by the brain. However, this is not the case: noise and movement are almost invariably noticed, if at all, before any visual stimulus. In fact it is the noise and movement which seem to attract our attention initially. It has been suggested that this 'earthquake sensation' accompanies the actual change in CONSCIOUSNESS when people enter the mode in which they are open to such experiences. (An example of this can be found in Matthew 28, in which 'a great earthquake' preceded the appearance of the ANGEL in the otherwise empty tomb.)

Another interesting point is that the act of looking away from an apparition is often sufficient for it to disappear. (The appearance and disappearance of APPORTS and the moving of objects in POLTERGEIST phenomena are also elusive when attention is maintained: they tend to occur when not directly observed.) This may be because such an act of redirecting one's attention involves a change in consciousness. A substantial proportion of apparitions occur when the percipient is waking up, which again suggests a particular state of consciousness, in this case HYPNOPOMPIC.

Hallucinatory theories cannot explain cases where several people witness the same apparition, unless there is mass hypnosis or telepathy on a grand scale. In the large-scale 1894 *Census of Hallucinations* a third of the apparitions were seen by two or more people and in more than half of those they were seen by all present. Such 'collective percipience' must surely have an external cause of some kind, unless we invoke some group mind like Lyall Watson's theory of SAMA.

Professor H.H. Price, holder of the Chair of Logic at Oxford University in the 1950s, considered it was unreasonable to declare that all apparitions were hallucinatory. He tended towards the view that an apparition was at least sometimes a 'real object' and claimed that as such it could easily be regarded as a 'vehicle of consciousness'.

Some time after a BEREAVEMENT the bereaved have been known to report suddenly seeing a ball of light which they know is a sign from the deceased, sent to reassure them that all is well. They may also hear the voice of their loved one. This usually seems to happen not long after death, at a time when the bereaved are at the lowest point of depression, and its effect is invariably to raise their spirits once and for all. Psychologists explain such apparitions away as hallucinations with no external cause whatsoever. But this is just the kind of apparition which suggests that there is an external cause — a 'real object' or 'vehicle of consciousness' as H.H. Price suggested. What makes these apparitions so evidential of some kind of survival after death is that the people who experience them are not usually aware of this type of occurrence at all until it actually happens to them. Although it is fairly common and follows the same pattern, it is not commonly known. This is seldom addressed by the sceptics who claim that the bereaved had been conditioned into expecting some such occurrence which they then hallucinated. The only other possibility (for the sceptics' case) is that we are *genetically* programmed to hallucinate in this way, so that we can emerge from our depression and get on with our own lives again, but that would not explain why the same rather peculiar form of hallucination is manufactured by our minds each time.

APPORT An apport is either an object that materializes in POLTER-GEIST phenomena or one which is believed to materialize in a so-called PHYSICAL CIRCLE. Very few mediums seem able to achieve these results; they are known as physical mediums. The objects (apports) which materialize usually have some significance for the sitters, although some physical mediums can only produce flowers, red roses being the most common. The process is said to involve a great deal of effort by those 'on the other side'. First they demateri-alize the object somewhere in the world and then cause it to be reconstituted in the darkened room where the circle is sitting. It is often said that the darkness must be absolutely total, as any light interferes with the process of materialization. When a sitter has touched an apport during its materialization, it has sometimes been recognized as being not yet fully formed: the stem of a rose, for example, may feel fatter and thornless, until it has fully materialized.

One of the strangest cases on record involves the medium Mrs Agnes Guppy. One day in 1871 a group of SPIRITUALISTS were holding a seance and asking the spirits to show them what could be done through spirit. Four miles away Mrs Guppy was sitting at home, doing her accounts, when she suddenly disappeared. She landed with an almighty crash (she was a heavy lady) on the table in the midst of the astonished group of spiritualists, still holding her account book. (This could also be called a case of TELEPORTATION.)

Less contestable evidence concerns apports that appear in polter-geist phenomena and cases of hauntings. In *The Link*[118] Matthew Manning describes his regular encounters with a ghost he met in his house in 1971. It seemed almost like a TIME-SLIP in that Robert Webbe, the ghost, regarded the situation as one in which Matthew Manning ('a ghoule of tomorrow?') was haunting him, albeit invisibly, but he left gifts for Manning — bread, a candle, pages from books. He also moved and hid other objects, so the mere brushing close together of two times would seem to be an inadequate explanation.

ARCHANGEL Most religions tell of spirit beings that have never incarnated. Such are the ANGELS who act as guardians and messengers between God and humanity. The highest of the angels are the archangels. Above the archangels there have been many other grades of spiritual beings. According to the spiritual hierarchy taught by Thomas Aquinas the closest to the Godhead are the Seraphim, who are in eternal contemplation of God. Next come the Cherubim who contemplate the Law, followed by the Thrones who implement it. Below the Thrones are the Dominions who prescribe action, the Powers who govern the operation of such action, and the Virtues who distribute energies. Then come the Principalities who are concerned with the welfare of nations, and eventually the archangels who guide the actions of the great and the movements of humanity that they instigate.

There are traditionally four main archangels, familiar to Jews, Christians and Muslims. Michael is the messenger of divine judg-ment — usually depicted with a sword. Gabriel is the messenger of divine mercy — often depicted holding a lily, as in representations of the Annunciation. (Mohammed was asleep in a cave on Mount Hira when Gabriel came to him in the form of a man with his feet astride the horizon and dictated the Koran to him. In Islam God is aways referred to first and foremost as God the Merciful.) Raphael is the bringer of divine healing — shown as a pilgrim with a staff and gourd. Uriel is the bearer of the fire of God, prophecy and wisdom; he is usually shown holding a scroll and a book. Other less well-known archangels are Chamuel, Jophiel and Zadiel.

In the Kabbalah each of the ten sephiroth is ruled by its own archangel. Malkuth, the mundane Kingdom, is ruled by Sandalphon, the Lord of the four elements. Gabriel rules Yesod (Foundation) and the etheric world, including the AKASHA, hence his rulership of clairvoyant faculties and his title of Lord of Dreams.

Hod (Majesty or Splendour) is also the sphere of magic and is ruled by the archangel Michael. Netzach (Eternity, Steadfastness or Victory) is ruled by the archangel Haniel who governs all relationships and expressions of sympathetic interaction.

Raphael is the ruler of Tiphareth (Beauty) as well as of healing. Khamael, ruling Geburah (Judgment), is both a Protector of the weak and the wronged and an Avenging Angel upholding the Law. Tzadkiel is associated with Chesed (Mercy) and represents a source of calm and security.

Tzaphkiel, the archangel of Binah (Understanding), has been seen as the instigator of all mystic cults and is sometimes called the archangel of the Temple. Ratziel, the archangel of Chokmah (Wisdom), is regarded as being behind the creative impulse in the early stages of evolution. Metatron is the archangel of Kether (the Crown) and is said to have been responsible for granting knowledge of the Kabbalistic TREE OF LIFE to humanity; his sphere of activity is felt to be rather remote from human concerns, except when someone receives a blinding flash of spiritual illumination through his influence.

Most occultists agree that there is a hierarchy of beings in the realm of the spirit, even if they differ in the details of their identification of particular archangels. Archangels are also sometimes called GUARDIANS. Rudolf Steiner taught that Gabriel was the ruling spirit of the age in the so-called ROSICRUCIAN period which ended in 1879, and that the present age is ruled by Michael.

ARHAT In Buddhism an arhat is one who has attained NIRVANA by following the Noble Eightfold Path and negating the separateness and illusory nature of self-hood, thus escaping the need to be reborn. The equivalent in English terminology might be an ASCENDED MASTER.

ASCENDED MASTER Ascended masters are highly evolved spiritual beings who have probably experienced many incarnations as humans, but who no longer need to incarnate for further spiritual growth. If they did incarnate in physical form again, they would do so not for their own evolution but to serve the spiritual advancement of all humanity. Their CONSCIOUSNESS is totally focused and integrated as their HIGHER SELVES. If we communicate with them it is probably through our own higher selves.

ASOMA The body is physical, part of material existence. All non-material aspects of our being are referred to as *asoma*, literally 'non-body' (Greek). Different cultures, traditions, religions and belief systems have different terms and classifications for the various asomatic elements of our nature. Words like SOUL and SPIRIT may have similar meanings in various orthodox religions, but the interpretation put upon terms like EGO, SELF, superego varies enormously according to the discipline (spiritual or psychological) in which they are used. It is noticeable, however, that most religions have identified three basic asomatic principles: an animating life-force or etheric body which is closely associated with the physical and with sensation and which governs the physical body; an emotional and/or intellectual element, an astral body, which governs an individual's desires, motivation, moral character and behaviour; and a soul, spirit or self which is the truly immortal part of our being, containing the 'divine spark'. Esoteric teachings go beyond these three levels, identifying three more (see BODIES), but it is said that we cannot experience at those levels while attached to the physical plane, even though we draw spiritual energy from them.

ASPECT PSYCHOLOGY This is a term invented by Jane Roberts (1929–84), who channelled several books dictated by an entity called SETH[163,164]. 'Seth' maintained that each of us is part of a greater 'oversoul' which gains experience by incarnating part of itself as a human personality. Different parts of the same oversoul may incarnate at the same time; they are therefore different 'aspects' of the same oversoul. When we recall past lives the information is mediated by our oversoul, since our present personality has no direct means of remembering other incarnations. The simultaneity of incarnations of parts of the same oversoul could also explain cases where individuals have glimpsed past lives which apparently overlap.

ASTRAL BODY – See BODIES.

ASTRAL CORD The astral cord is said to link the astral body with the physical body when the two temporarily separate. Because of its appearance it is also often called the SILVER CORD. It can stretch to any length, enabling the individual to visit any part of the world in ASTRAL TRAVEL. Some say that it is made of the same substance as ECTOPLASM.

The point at which the astral cord is thought to join the physical body varies according to the authority. Some say the solar plexus, some the navel, others the head (both brow and crown centres). The famous populariser of OUT-OF-THE-BODY EXPERIENCES (OBEs), Robert A. Monroe[127], usually felt the astral cord joining his physical body between the shoulder blades, where it branched out rather like the roots of a tree entering the soil. OBEs often end with a sudden tug on the cord which brings the 'astral traveller' back into the physical body with lightning speed.

If the cord is broken the body dies: 'When the silver cord is loosed, then shall the dust return to the earth as it was, and the spirit return to God' (Ecclesiastes 12, 6). Plutarch, writing at the end of the first century, describes the uncorrupted soul (or nous) as hanging like a cord above the head and attached to the crown, so that it can guide the astral body, which he calls the *psyche*.

ASTRAL PLANE/ASTRAL WORLD The astral plane or astral world is said to be another dimension of reality coexistent in space with our physical world, just as the astral body is (usually) coexistent with the physical body. We may temporarily inhabit the astral world during normal sleep (a form of ASTRAL TRAVEL) and during OUT-OF-THE-BODY EXPERIENCES. Rudolf Steiner referred to its as the 'super-sensible world'.

The astral world is also sometimes called the inner PLANE. Its objectivity may then seem somewhat compromised. 'The astral plane is ... a state of real being plus a world of illusory forms, created by man himself and by his imaginative creativity.'[6] 'The "astral sphere" from an ordinary point of view may be defined as the *subjective world*, projected outside us and taken for the *objective world*.'[140] Others recognize the experience which people claim to have had in the astral world as examples of VISUALIZATION, or in Jung's terminology ACTIVE IMAGINATION.

The discrepancy between these two types of definition — one apparently spatial, the other mental or psychological — is somewhat artificial. Jung regularly practised active imagination, and he reported meeting and consulting an old man called Philemon in this mental state. Jung maintained that this personality proved to him 'the objectivity of the psychic world'. In such a mental world everything is perforce made of thoughts rather than material atoms, and thoughts do not need space to occupy as physical matter does. The psychic, mental or astral world is not therefore a world in the three-dimensional, spatial sense. The use of the word 'plane' is perhaps an attempt to show this distinction.

Figures such as Jung's Philemon are not the only beings one can meet on the astral plane. In *Journeys Out of the Body* Robert Monroe described various strange non-physical entities that he encountered there. These included demons and goblins and other 'rubbery entities'[127] which seemed intent on making life miserable for him; he was constantly having to fight them off. One can accept Monroe's experiences as real without necessarily conceding the objective reality of his goblins and demons. The astral plane is a state where all emotions become immediately detectable, just as physical objects are visible in our world, but we detect them with our own astral faculties. They might then be 'clothed' by our own imagination in whatever form our consciousness chooses to see them, which will probably be influenced by our past cultural conditioning.

Nature spirits, ELEMENTALS, elves and fairies are also said to inhabit this astral realm. As well as being the home of such non-human entities, it is believed to be the first realm of existence through which an individual passes after bodily death. It is 'here' that one experiences HEAVEN and HELL in the AFTERLIFE. In Vedic and occult terminology the astral plane is also known as the Kama World, *kamaloca*, the second lowest of the seven worlds (the lowest being the physical), the world of emotions, desires and passions.

ASTRAL PROJECTION/ASTRAL TRAVEL OUT-OF-THE-BODY EXPERIENCES (OBEs) used to be known as astral projection or astral travel. In 1886 Edmund Gurney called them 'phantasms of the living' in his book of that title, which recorded 350 such cases. Muldoon and Carrington revived interest in the idea in the 1920s with *The Phenomena of Astral Projection* and *The Projection of the Astral Body*.[123,134]

The three terms — OBE, astral travel and astral projection — have often been used more or less indiscriminately. One distinction is that OBEs always involve looking at normal external reality from a different viewpoint, whereas astral travel may involve experiences of another level of reality, the ASTRAL WORLD. There are other differences in usage, even though the processes are similar. Astral travel is often said to occur during sleep. OBEs occur in other situations when the body naturally, spontaneously or accidentally falls into unconsciousness. And it seems logical to use the term 'astral projection' for the less passive acts of astral travel, for *deliberate* out-of-the-body experiences, when an individual projects his or her consciousness to another location, or to acts of astral travel in which the individual actually interacts with others. These are not as common as the more spontaneous out-of-the-body experiences typical of operating theatres, but they are well documented.

The usual type of out-of-the-body experience, in which a person sees external reality from a viewpoint outside his or her own body, is a spontaneous event, occurring at a time of crisis, in an accident, or when the body is for some reason extremely weak. Such an OBE is often presaged by a feeling of paralysis as consciousness detaches itself from the body. In pseudo-physical terminology, the astral body carries consciousness, so during separation of the astral body from the physical body the physical body is normally unconscious. During OBEs people have also reported seeing a thread or SILVER CORD, also known as the ASTRAL CORD, linking the travelling consciousness with the sleeping body. The astral body is perhaps superfluous. The mind, when viewing a scene, takes a particular viewpoint in space because it is accustomed to doing so, and it invents a human body around itself for the same reason. Some people who have had OBEs remark simply on being free from the body and fail to mention any other bodily form or silver cord. OBEs have been induced by pain — a clear inducement for unconsciousness to overtake the physical body: a prisoner who was regularly put in a wet straitjacket, which tightened on him causing great pain as it shrank, appeared to fall asleep, and on waking reported having been walking the streets of San Francisco.

There are different degrees of interaction between the astral traveller and people in the new location. One case of almost maximum interaction was recorded in 1774. Alphonsus Maria de'Liguori (1696–1787) was a moral theologian, preacher and mystic who founded the Redemptorist order. While resting before taking a service in a prison in Arezzo, he fell asleep and appeared at the death bed of Pope Clement XIV in Rome, where he talked and prayed with others present. When he awoke in Arezzo he was able to announce that he had seen the Pope die. Four days later news of the death arrived in Arezzo by more conventional means. Alphonsus's knowledge of the event was attributed to coincidence or a dream, until it was later learned that those present at the Pope's bedside had both seen and spoken to him. It is interesting to note that this occurred at the end of a five-day fast, when the physical body was presumably quite weak. The event seems to have been spontaneous: Alphonsus did not deliberately project himself to Rome.

The researcher F.W.H. Myers reported a case in which a woman was hypnotized and instructed to travel 'astrally' and report what she saw. On one occasion she correctly described changed circumstances which were in apparent contradiction to what the hypnotist was expecting, but which were completely true, thus ruling out telepathy between subject and hypnotist. Similar experiments were carried out by Charles Tart.[126] This 'travelling clairvoyance' has come to be regarded as a separate area of study known as REMOTE VIEWING.

Another case described by Myers is the so-called Verity case, in which a young man named S.H. Beard actually decided to project himself into the house of his fiancée, Miss Verity, while he was in a self-induced trance-like state in his own home. His PSYCHIC DOUBLE was seen by both Miss Verity and her sister, but on returning to normal consciousness he had no knowledge of whether his attempt had been successful or not. They had been made aware of him, but he was not consciously aware of having been with them.[135]

Awareness worked in the opposite direction in a more recent case described by Robert Monroe.[127] He deliberately projected himself into the study where his colleague Andrija Puharich was working. They had a brief conversation, of which Puharich was later totally unaware, although everything that Monroe remembered of Puharich's study was accurate. This could have been a case of simple TELEPATHY, but since Puharich apparently apologized to Monroe during their 'astral' conversation, it seems more likely that Monroe had been in communication with a part of Puharich's psyche which was below conscious awareness. Monroe also reports instances when he has been unable to attract anyone's attention during an OBE except by pinching someone. One such friend whom he pinched while invisibly calling on her later showed him the small bruise that had mysteriously appeared.

If such projection depends on a telepathic link between two people, what of the effect of astral projection on an animal? At Duke University, North Carolina, in a controlled experiment, Stuart Blue Harary claimed to have left his body and comforted a rather energetic kitten half a mile away on the other side of the campus. Harary was wired up to an array of instruments which detected and recorded any physiological changes during the experiment. There were also many different kinds of detectors in the room housing the kitten which Harary had been told to play with. The kitten became much more relaxed between the time when Harary said 'I'm going' until the time he announced 'I'm back'. The instruments in the room around the kitten registered nothing at all; in the crucial four-minute period the instruments attached to Harary showed some changes typical of arousal (increased rates of respiration and heart-beat) and some associated with deep relaxation (decreased electrical potential of the skin).[170]

Many researchers maintain that we need not invoke an externalized astral double to explain the phenomenon of astral projection. Even when full interaction takes place, it could be described as a mutually experienced telepathic HALLUCINATION. It may be achieved by a deliberate act of mental will, whereby the astral traveller activates those brain processes that give rise to the sense impressions in those who share the experience. But the actual traveller is often unconscious during these phenomena — we know from instances when such events have occurred while the individual is in the operating theatre that they are accompanied by no brain activity whatsoever. So how is the event perceived at all by the instigator of astral projection? It would seem to be an experience of the mind which by-passes the brain altogether.

Astral travel is often reported to be instantaneous, which supports the notion that actual passage through space is not involved. If the astral body does not actually travel through space, it is therefore unlikely that it occupies space in the normal sense, or even that anything actually detaches itself from the physical body. Rather the individual enters a state of consciousness in which awareness can be extended beyond the confines of the physical senses. This may be accompanied by the projection of a THOUGHT-FORM, an image of the physical body, simply because waking human consciousness is so used to seeing things in spatial terms.

The idea of astral travel during sleep has also been used to explain embarassing instances of 'spirit' communication from people who are still very much alive. Messages have been received through mediums, using the voice and mannerisms of a DISCARNATE, and including all kinds of verifiable information, but the professed spirit is still most definitely incarnate. In such cases people sometimes claim that the medium is tapping into the AKASHIC RECORD. An alternative explanation is a kind of astral travel: the astral body — or that part of an individual's consciousness which is released and still active while the physical body is asleep — somehow manages to communicate as its own personality through the medium. We generally have no conscious memory of what we experience when astral travel occurs during sleep, so the sleeper would not necessarily know that communication through a medium had taken place.

Astral travel during sleep may however be remembered as dreams, and it may also be deliberately induced. Oliver Fox agreed with two friends, Slade and Elkington, that they should all meet one night in their dreams on Southampton Common. As planned, Fox dreamed he met Elkington, but Slade did not appear. When asked later, Slade said that he had not dreamed at all that night, whilst Elkington's dream experience matched Fox's exactly.

ATLANTIS Plato was responsible for one of the earliest surviving accounts of a supposed sunken continent which he called Atlantis. In his *Timaeus* and *Critias* he wrote of what Solon had learned from the Egyptians two centuries earlier: that the Atlanteans had invaded Europe, that they had been repulsed by the Greeks, and that Atlantis itself had been destroyed by a cataclysmic earthquake.

Even among the staunchest believers in the Atlantean legend there is little agreement as to the exact location of the continent. Some maintain that the Azores and the Canaries are the only remaining vestiges of Atlantis, which originally stretched far west. Others place it closer to the Caribbean. Many historians consider that the legend grew up following the destruction of the Island of Thera, north of Crete, when the volcano erupted around 1450 BC despite the fact that Plato placed it west of the pillars of Hercules, the straits of Gibraltar.

Otto Heinrich Muck (1892–1956) placed Atlantis firmly in the middle of the Atlantic Ocean. The Austrian-born scientist and member of the Peenemünde rocket research team researched both the many traditions and the scientific considerations in an attempt to ascertain the truth or otherwise of the story of a lost continent. Taking Wegener's theories of continental drift into account, for example, he noted that the North Atlantic coastlines are not as neat a fit as the South Atlantic. In the end he was convinced of the existence of Atlantis and even dated its destruction by a stray asteroid as having taken place in 8498 BC, giving rise to legends of cataclysm and flood all over the world.[132] His conclusions have been supported, perhaps surprisingly, by evidence gathered by Soviet scientists from the Atlantic sea-bed.[217]

The trance psychic, Edgar Cayce, often spoke of Atlantis.[27] He reported the final cataclysm as having taken place about 10,000 BC but he tells of the roots of the Atlantean civilization going back to before 50,000 BC. Initially spirit beings projected themselves into matter: some of them remained truly Sons of God, or Sons of the Law of One, but others were seduced by physical existence, becoming trapped in matter and caught up in the round of cause and effect, KARMA. This resulted in the first destruction of part of Atlantis, where the Sargasso Sea is today. There followed a second period of destructive earthquakes, put by Cayce's communications at about 28,000 BC.

Even after these cataclysmic events the Law of One was still not followed by all: the so-called Sons of Belial, in defiance of the children of the Law of One, were still intent on self-aggrandizement and self-gratification, misapplying knowledge and exploiting the earth to satisfy physical desires. They achieved a high level of technological development, apparently manipulating atomic forces and inventing a death ray which used crystals and sounds reminiscent of our lasers. Many of those who could see how it would all end migrated to other parts of the world — North America, Yucatan, Peru, the Pyrenees, and of course Egypt, where some vestiges of Atlantean knowledge were preserved and incorporated in, for example, the Great Pyramid (which according to Cayce dates from 10,000 BC — seven thousand years earlier than the dating by most archaeological authorities).

Some have seen a parallel between the cataclysmic fall of Atlantis and the Fall of Eden: they both represent a precocious striving for knowledge which overturns the natural order. 'According to tradition Atlantis fell due to an abuse of priestly power which so disturbed the delicate balance of the environment that the continent was submerged in a mighty cataclysm. It does not matter whether we see Atlantis or Eden as geographically locatable in time and space, or as myths or lost knowledge, they remain states that have been withdrawn from us — golden ages which cannot return.'[124]

The primal perfection of Atlantis or Eden remains in our consciousness as inner potentialities. Jane Roberts, channelling the entity known as 'SETH', placed Atlantis not only in our far past but also in the future. Although 'Seth' maintained that there were many lost civilizations which formed the basis of the Atlantean legend (in the Arctic and the Aegean as well as in the Atlantic), it is also a reflection of our fears for the future. Atlantis is not so much a physical fact, 'Seth' said, as a 'psychic blueprint': while yearning for the ideal civilization which in some respects Atlantis represents, we also see in it the seeds of its destruction. Many who discuss reincarnation and who claim to be aware of people's 'past lives' say that many beings from Atlantis are reincarnating on earth now. This might suggest a growing awareness among people today of both the possibilities and the dangers for our present civilization.

ATMAN According to Hindu doctrine, atman is the eternal, essential self which is continuously reincarnated until separateness and illusion are transcended and spiritual release is achieved. Each SOUL is eternal and unchanging atman: in its deepest being it is identical with Paramatman, the one universal Self, the eternal spirit of All-that-is, or BRAHMAN. Each soul considers itself to be individual and separate, and remains so until it realises its identity with Atman. Then it is like a jar which is smashed: the space within the jar remains as sheer space, united with all space.

Atman can also be regarded as what many in the West refer to as the HIGHER SELF. In Upanishad art two selves are depicted as two birds in a tree: one is the temporary, empirical self, (what many would now call the ego of the personality), and the other is the atman, the real, eternal self, which observes the multitude of empirical selves in successive incarnations. The atman can observe all these empirical selves, these egos, but the egos are aware neither of the atman nor of each other. It would seem from this portrayal that the atman is an external observer and does not experience the incarnations from within as the empirical selves do, although they may ultimately be remembered rather as dreams are remembered on waking when the atman returns to total consciousness.

AURA The physical body is surrounded by electro-magnetic energy. KIRLIAN PHOTOGRAPHY has revealed this for all to see — it exists around plant and animal life as well as human beings, but clairvoyants have long spoken of the aura which surrounds an individual, changing according to health and mood, and varying from one to another according to character.

The aura was referred to by Plutarch as revealing the passions and vices of the soul by the variation and movement of its colours. The fact that purity of character and spiritual development can be seen in an individual's aura has led to the traditional representation of saints with white or golden halos. This may also be related to the development of the crown CHAKRA, centred at or just above the top of the head. Christian tradition uses the term *aureole* for the aura surrounding the whole body and *nimbus* or HALO for the part of it around the head.

In 1911 Dr Walter Kilner of St Thomas's Hospital, London constructed a specially treated glass plate (now known as a KILNER SCREEN) through which the aura, or 'human atmosphere' as he called it, became visible.[102] Kilner also discovered that one woman could change the colour of her aura at will and project auric rods from any part of her body. These projections are thought by some to be the means by which PSYCHOKINESIS operates. (THEOSOPHISTS refer to the aura as 'astral' matter.)

Dr Shafica Karagulla, a modern investigator of the aura as viewed by sensitives has remarked that three types of force field are observed around the human body: first a 'vital field' reflecting the physical condition, second an 'emotional field' which shows the state of the individual's feelings, and third a 'mental field' revealing the degree of mental activity.[99] This corresponds to the occult belief that the aura consists of emanations from all the 'vehicles of consciousness' not just the etheric BODY.

Rudolf Steiner referred to the aura as a spirit-sheath: 'The spiritual skin expands continually with advancing human evolution, so that the spiritual individuality of man (his auric sheath) is capable of enlargement to unlimited extent.'[183] 'The size of the aura differs in different people. But an idea can be formed of it by picturing that the whole man appears to be on average twice as tall and four times as broad as the physical man.'

Clairvoyants typically see the aura extending about eighteen inches all around the body like an egg-shaped envelope, more tenuous at the edges and thickest close to the skin. They see different colours, representing different emotions, physical conditions, and even degress of spiritual development. When considering whether or not these colours actually exist, it is as well to remember that in normal perception it is our brain that interprets various wavelenghts of light as different colours; the colours do not actually exist as separate qualities. So whatever mechanism of perception the clairvoyant employs, their descriptions of actual colours need not have universal validity. (Even in the normal perception of colours we may argue about whether a particular colour is blue or green.) Steiner always maintained that the aura cannot be investigated by physical means: it was perceived through spiritual sight, not the physical sense. 'It is a gross illusion that the spiritual aura can be one that may be investigated by the external means of natural science.'[183]

Steiner saw activity arising from animal life as producing irregular clouds of colour, whilst spiritual characteristics produce purer rays of colour from within. He interpreted his appreciation of some of the colours thus:

| brown and reddish-yellow | : strong emotions of an animal nature |

red streams	: violent anger
dark green clouds	: injured dignity
brighter reddish-yellow and green	: delicate emotions
green	: thinking
rose-pink, light violet	: noble sacrifice
blue	: devotional
brighter shades	: active

Clairvoyants see the colours ebb and flow according to the individual's inner life. They maintain that the colour-tones change and that auras vary in texture (fine or coarse) and blemishes (grainy, striped, spotted, and so on) as well as colour. Certain diseases may cause actual gaps in the aura in certain places, or it may bulge out in the case of other complaints. Auras also differ according to the sex and age of an individual. The more mentally active a person is, the more refined the aura will be, a more 'physical' person having a generally greyer aura.

AURIC FIELD – Another term for AURA.

AUROGRAPH Clairvoyants sometimes draw a pictorial representation of what they see in an individual's AURA. This so-called aurograph may be a symbolic MANDALA-like image of the person's life-path, where different positions on the disc as it is rotated represent different stages in the person's life, or it may be a picture of the aura itself – as seen by the clairvoyant.

AUTOMATIC WRITING A MEDIUM who has developed the ability to fall into trance or go under control may communicate by speech (also known as CHANNELLING) or in writing. These are examples of what Myers called motor AUTOMATISM. To start with, the individual holds a pen lightly on a pad of paper and moves it aimlessly until coherent words are formed, by which time he or she may be in trance, and the hand is moving apparently of its own volition without conscious control.

Automatists often write at an amazing speed, much faster than would normally be possible. The medium Geraldine Cummins, writing *The Scripts of Cleophas*, which purport to be a continuation of the New Testament Acts of the Apostles, could maintain a speed of 1500 words per hour, with each word running into the next without a break.[37] Mediums can not only produce another person's handwriting, they even write in languages of which they have no (conscious) knowledge, and which may bear no relation whatsoever to their own, as when an American medium produces Chinese. The Revd Stainton Moses (1839–92) was able to write with both hands simultaneously to produce two separate pieces of automatic writing on different subjects and in different languages.[131]

Psychotherapists have used the same technique to gain access to memories or fears which a person's conscious mind refuses to countenance. It has been used as a diagnostic and therapeutic tool in the study of mental illness and schizophrenia. In some cases patients have produced automatic writing with both hands simultaneously, each hand expressing a different personality, neither of which is identifiable as the individual's conscious personality. Similarly, the ideas which are communicated in this way through (or by?) a medium can seem quite alien to the medium's professed beliefs.

Even in cases where one cannot credit the claim that the communication comes from a DISCARNATE entity, there is often seemingly incontrovertible evidence for EXTRA-SENSORY PERCEPTION (ESP). More suggestive of discarnate control are cases where two or more mediums convey messages from one and the same purported source. In one instance a medium was writing in trance when she was disturbed by a sudden noise and returned to normal consciousness, whereupon another medium who was sitting in the same room immediately fell into trance herself and the writing resumed in mid-sentence.[197] At the very least this suggests that two minds can unite unconsciously and act in unison purposefully as one mind and one personality, which is almost more difficult to believe than that the controlling mind is actually a discarnate entity.

There are many accounts which have authenticated automatic writing as a valid means of gaining otherwise inaccessible information. One of the most impressive concerns the excavation of the ruins of Glastonbury Abbey by Frederick Bligh Bond. His friend, the medium John Allen Bartlett, using automatic writing, drew an accurate plan of the abbey which Bond followed and verified in his successful excavations. The Church of England authorities were naturally delighted – until Bond published his methods in a book entitled *The Gate of Remembrance*.[14] He was promptly dismissed. Even his guidebook to the Abbey was banned by the abbey bookshop. (See PSYCHIC ARCHAEOLOGY.)

If Bartlett's supposed communicator, 'William the Monk', was not a spirit entity, there must be some 'natural' process by which

Bartlett himself could in trance acquire otherwise inaccessible knowledge of the history of Glastonbury. There are several theories, each of which stretch the credulity rather more than the spirit hypothesis. The most biological is the memory-genes theory: memory resides in the genes; William the Monk must be an ancestor of Bartlett's. (Even if biologists accepted the idea that memory can reside in the genes, which they don't, how likely is it that a Glastonbury monk had an illegitimate child?) The most popular alternative to the spirit hypothesis is the SUPER-ESP THEORY: Bartlett is able to tune in to the history of Glastonbury using his own powers of clairvoyance. The question then remains, why would Bartlett's unconscious bother to create a personality to present this information? DOWSERS and PSYCHOMETRISTS don't need to invent personalities to communicate the information, so why should it be necessary in the case of automatic writing?

AUTOMATISM 'Motor automatism' was first coined by F.W.H. Myers to describe intelligent, purposeful actions performed without the person's conscious control. The 'automatist' is usually in a trance state, and the actions often involve either writing (also called AUTOMATIC WRITING) or speech (more commonly referred to nowadays as CHANNELLING). Communication is then made possible with a personality who appears to be a deceased person.

Other instances of automatism do not involve communication in the usual sense and perhaps for that reason have received less public attention, but they are none the less remarkable for that. There have been cases of automatic piano-playing, when a normally mediocre piano-player can play quite beautifully in trance. Rosemary Brown is exceptional in that she actually composes, rather than plays, and she identifies the source of each composition as a specific historical composer. Following the death of her husband Rosemary Brown suddenly found that she was able to play the piano much better than before. The pieces she played were also new, although they were in familiar styles. She claimed that composers such as Beethoven, Chopin and Liszt were taking her over and using her hands 'like a pair of gloves'.[20]

There are also cases of automatic drawing, the most famous in recent years being the young Matthew Manning (before his psychic gifts were channelled into HEALING). The young Matthew Manning found that he could draw 'automatically' in the style of Dürer, Leonardo da Vinci and Beardsley. In automatic writing he had produced a variety of scripts including Arabic. It is interesting to note that these automatic activities had been preceded by a period of intense POLTERGEIST activity, which stopped once the energy was channelled into the more creative enterprises. When asked how he could produce such expert drawing so quickly and with such apparent ease, he said 'It's not me. I simply switch on the energy.'[119]

In contrast to motor automatisms, F.W.H. Myers used the term 'sensory automatisms' to refer to phenomena such as dreams, HALLUCINATIONS, and intuitive visions which force their way into our consciousness through the senses without a conscious effort of will.

AUTOSCOPY In psychology, autoscopy is the technical term for the phenomenon of the Doppelgänger, when someone has the illusion of seeing their own image as a wraith-like figure completely separate from their actual body. For some reason this figure is usually described as a mirror-image, with right and left transposed, which perhaps supports the notion that it is a HALLUCINATION, rather than a psychic phenomenon.

In psychic terms, however, autoscopy has another meaning: it is the ability to view one's body not externally as a Doppelgänger, but internally and in minute detail. (It is not to be confused with PAROPTIC VISION, the ability to 'see' through the skin rather than the eyes.) Under hypnosis people have been known to diagnose their own physical ailments by apparently observing their internal organs in great detail. Usually the subject has no medical expertise and uses everyday language rather than specialist terminology, so no external agency needs to be invoked in such cases — no doctor 'on the other side'. When the hypnotist is a medical practitioner who can recognize the diagnosis, the subject may be told how to treat the condition while still under hypnosis, subordinating the autonomous nervous system to the control of the will.

An example of this was reported at length in a French medical journal in 1900. A patient suffering from HYSTERIA was being treated by hypnotherapy. At one point she also developed a fever accompanied by a pain in the region of the appendix. Under HYPNOSIS she described inflammation of the 'little skin' (her words for 'membrane') of the intestine. Changes of diet and regular treatments of ice-packs and cool baths brought only temporary relief, and the symptoms returned more severely with nausea, constipation, cramps and stabbing pains. So the hypnotherapist asked the patient to describe the area of her body where the pain was worst. She said that the 'little end' of the intestine was more inflamed than ever. When told to observe this more closely she said that it was full of a thick dirty liquid, and that buried in all this pus was something sharp. She was terribly afraid that this sharp point might pierce the intestine.

The patient was clearly describing the appendix where something had become lodged and was causing the inflammation. In the next consultation, under hypnosis, she was told to start moving her intestine in an attempt to dislodge the offending object. While reporting that her intestine was in motion, she pointed to the spot where the object was as it followed the path of the colon. She now described it more exactly as a centimetre long, like a piece of bone and pointed at one end. When it reached a certain point in the colon the doctor decided to try to wash it out with an injection of water, and he found a piece of bone which fitted the patient's description exactly. She was still under hypnosis at this point and said that the pointed object had gone out with the water.

AUTOSUGGESTION Emile Coué (1857–1926) met A.A. Liébeault in 1885 and developed his notion of SUGGESTION into one of autosuggestion. This was his explanation for all cases of HYPNOSIS. It also explained why different hypnotists and different subjects varied in their susceptibility to one another. According to Coué's theory the key element was not the will of the subject but the imagination.

AVATAR An avatar is an incarnation of the God-principle, like the Buddha and the Christ, sent to earth to bring ENLIGHTENMENT. Originally a Hindu term meaning 'descent' it was applied to Rama and Krishna as incarnations of Vishnu, but has since been used more freely. Some followers of Rudolf Steiner believed that he was an avatar. In modern times some say the same of Sai Baba.

AYAHUASCO The Conibo tribe in the Peruvian Amazon region make a sacred drink from the ayahuasco or 'soul-vine'. On drinking it, the anthropologist Michael Harner had visions of demons and bird-men, which he assumed must have come from his own cultural background, but which a Conibo SHAMAN later told him are always evoked by this drink.[81] However, when taken in another area with another tribe the drink produced images of different guides and animals appropriate to that tribe, suggesting that the DRUG allows us to dip into a specifically local part of the COLLECTIVE UNCONSCIOUS.

One of the alkaloids in ayahuasco has been called *telepatin* owing to its effects of apparently allowing the imbiber to read the minds of those around.

BA The closest we can get to the ba of ancient Egyptian religion is probably SOUL. The difference between the ba and the KA was something like the difference between the astral body (or the mortal soul) and the spirit or immortal soul. The ba was a spiritual entity which left the body at the moment of death, although its continued existence seems to have been intimately bound up with the physical body. During the day the ba was believed to assume various forms (facilitated by mortuary rituals) and engage in activities which were useful to the deceased; at night it returned to the tomb where the mummified body lay, comforting and reassuring the deceased of immortality. This suggests that some sort of CONSCIOUSNESS was thought to remain with the physical body; the ba did not encompass the mind of the individual, but was somehow subservient to it.

During the New Kingdom (1567−1085 BC) the ba was depicted in tomb paintings and carvings, on mummies, and in the BOOK OF THE DEAD as a bird with a human head. If this seems strange to us we need only remind ourselves of more recent conventions, by which people have acquired angelic wings (not to mention harps) when ascending to heaven, to realize that illustrations give a very partial and possibly misleading reflection of actual belief. The ba was often shown in this form perched in or under trees around the tomb, hovering over the mummy, or sitting on its breast.

In the earliest religious texts of the ancient Egyptians, nameless gods were referred to simply as ba − spirit, or spiritual energy. Later the word was used to refer to any manifestation of a god: for example Apis, the sacred bull, god of fertility, was regarded as the ba of Osiris. The word was also used to refer to the power and authority of the king. It was only at the end of the Old Kingdom (*c.* 2200 BC) that the term came to be applied to all people. Although the 'soul' is the closest equivalent concept we have, the ba was not so much a spirit-body or vehicle for continued existence as a spiritual power or force which guaranteed immortality to the individual after death. The individual still resided in the physical body and acted and experienced, as it were, by proxy through the agency of the ba.

BANSHEE Many old Irish families are said to have had warnings of imminent death given by a wailing female spirit, a banshee. (The word comes from the Gaelic for 'woman of the fairies'.) This disembodied soul usually had intimate connections with the family, which was always of pure Irish stock. She could be a tender, loving spirit, sent to warn and comfort those about to be bereaved, although more often she seems to have been a vengeful ghost, the spirit of a murder victim or a deceived lover, whose soul could not rest in peace until every last member of the family was dead.

The belief in 'wailing banshees' has been so widespread in Ireland that they cannot be dismissed as mere superstition. Either they are what popular belief maintains — supernatural harbingers of impending death, or they are hallucinatory creations of the UNCONSCIOUS human mind which itself has precognitive awareness of death. This latter theory has also been used to account for other APPARITIONS, in which the deceased themselves appear to announce their own demise to their survivors.

BARDO The *bardo*, according to Tibetan Buddhism (the Tantric branch of Mahayana Buddhism), is a state between death and rebirth. Literally, *bar* means between, and *do* means two. The Tibetan BOOK OF THE DEAD (*Bardo Thodol*) describes what happens to a person after death during the forty-nine days (probably a symbolic number) between death and rebirth in a new body.

It takes three to four days for the bardo body to detach itself from the physical body. The conscious mind then experiences the first bardo state, a radiant clear light of pure reality. This is the first chance for the self to attain NIRVANA, abandon ego-existence and become one with the Light, abandoning the need ever to return to earth again. But most are not willing to be united with the Light at this stage. The self then acquires a karmic body, formed by the action of past thought and deeds, and encounters all the deities that are projected by its own mind, both benign and vengeful, loving and judgmental, in accordance with its beliefs and conditioning whilst on earth. JUDGMENT and punishment follow. In the third, final stage of bardo life, the self prepares for its next birth, assuming the nature and adopting the tendencies that will be the hallmark of the next life.

This description of the AFTERLIFE process parallels that of other occult traditions, where the astral body creates its own reality until the desires and emotions which drive it have been purged. For the final stage of existence between lives the soul rises from the ASTRAL to the mental PLANE, there to prepare for the next incarnation.

BASE CENTRE — See CHAKRAS.

BEACON In REMOTE VIEWING experiments at California University's Stanford Research Institute, the person at the target site, which the 'viewer' perhaps thousands of miles away would try to describe, was called the beacon. In other experiments into TELEPATHY such a person might be called the 'transmitter'.

BEREAVEMENT Orthodox psychology describes bereavement as affecting the thoughts, actions and perceptions of the bereaved. According to this view the bereaved display an urge to search for the lost person, pondering constantly on the events leading up to the death 'as if they could find out what has gone wrong and put it right again'. They 'keep alive the memories of the dead' and treasure possessions that act as reminders of them. 'Sights and sounds are commonly misperceived as evidence of his or her return.' This last statement is apparently intended to dispose of the phenomenon of APPARITIONS and negate any suggestion that an individual might actually be made aware of the lingering presence of a departed soul. (Quotations taken from Colin Murray Parkes in *The Oxford Companion to the Mind*.)[70]

It is worth considering how much of this 'psychology of bereavement' is true of other situations where a loved one is suddenly absent but not through death. The recurrent thoughts and ritual actions probably still apply. There may even be a few so-called 'misperceptions' — mistakenly glimpsing the missing person in the street, for example. But such misperceptions are of a completely different order from actual apparitions, many of which occur in situations where bereavement as such hardly applies, either because the 'misperceiver' is not close enough to the dead person to be at all grief-stricken, or because the bereaved who see apparitions often do not yet realize that they are bereaved.

BETA BRAIN WAVES — See BRAIN WAVES.

BHAKTI *Bhakti* is a Hindu term for personal devotion and love of God. The word comes from a root meaning to share or participate, and the concept is close to what we understand by *agape*. According to the *Bhagavad Gita* this way is the highest form of YOGA. There are five aspects of bhakti: quiet contemplation, active service, friendship, filial attachment, and passionate love.

BILOCATION The power to appear in two places simultaneously, bilocation, has been attributed to mystics and ecstatics as well as psychics. Observers see a psychic or 'astral' DOUBLE apart from the person's physical body and sometimes without the person's knowledge. Bilocation has also been experienced by people in accidents: they apparently witness the accident in which they are involved from a completely different viewpoint, usually above the site of accident. This form of bilocation is often known as OUT-OF-THE-BODY EXPERIENCE, since consciousness is apparently outside the body, and indeed views the body with a strange sense of calm detachment. The individual who 'bilocates' is seldom aware of two viewpoints simultaneously, and awareness usually seems to reside in the 'projected body' rather than the physical body.

BIOENERGY/BIOENERGETICS This is a literal translation of a Russian word for the phenomenon usually known in English as PSYCHOKINESIS. It has been characteristic of the Soviets to prefer words which use elements such as 'bio-' over words with 'psi-' or 'psych-' with their less materialistic associations. In Czechoslovakia the same force is called PSYCHOTRONIC ENERGY.

BIO-INTROSCOPY – Another term for PAROPTIC VISION.

BIOLOGICAL INFORMATION This is a literal translation of a Russian expression for what we call ESP (extra-sensory perception). In English 'supernatural' sounds too close to the miraculous, so scientists investigate PARANORMAL phenomena. But for the Soviets paranormal also smacks too much of superstition and the supernatural, so they prefer to emphasize the natural basis of the phenomenon, even though the mechanism is not yet fully understood. Biological information is therefore information that a human organism becomes aware of without recourse to the usual five senses.

BIOPLASMA/BIOPLASMIC ENERGY Bioplasma is the equivalent of the Western PSI-FIELD, the hypothesized field of psychic force surrounding people and objects which is involved in such phenomena as ESP and PSYCHOKINESIS. When Russian scientists use the term 'bioplasmic body' they are referring to what occultists refer to as the ETHERIC BODY. Semyon Davidovich Kirlian, an electrical technician, invented a method of high-frequency photography by which in 1940 he succeeded in photographing brilliantly coloured radiations issuing from living tissue. These rays of energy have also been photographed by KIRLIAN PHOTOGRAPHY. In Czechoslovakia bioplasmic energy is called psychotronic energy.

BLACK BOX – See RADIONICS.

BLACK MAGIC – See SORCERY.

BODHISATTVA In Buddhism a bodhisattva, literally 'wisdom-being', is an individual who is so advanced spiritually that ENLIGHTENMENT is imminent. In one sense, it can be anyone who is well-advanced 'on the path', seeking enlightenment. More particularly it is one who is on the brink of NIRVANA but refuses to enter it until all other creatures are saved: he chooses to delay his own nirvana and incarnate again in order to teach and help humanity. Love and compassion have therefore replaced nirvana as the ideal (in Mahayana Buddhism). So a bodhisattva is as close to Buddhahood as it is possible to get without actually becoming a buddha. A bodhisattva remembers all past lives and is no longer born 'in a state of woe'. Other characteristics of such an advanced soul are that he is never born into a situation of poverty, never suffers defects of the body, and never incarnates again as a woman.

BODIES It is one of the most persistent beliefs of humanity that consciousness continues to exist after the death of the physical body. The Christian theologian Hans Küng maintains that 'belief in immortality has always existed'.[106] The vehicle of consciousness which survives death is most commonly referred to as the SOUL.

According to many religious systems the human being consists of at least three component parts: body, soul and spirit. (This trinity was accepted by the Christian Church until the year 869 when it was reduced to body and soul.) Many spiritual teachings speak of four bodies: the physical, built of atoms like those found in inorganic substances; the life-body, etheric or sensation body, built of 'higher vibrations' of matter; the astral or emotional body, which survives the death of the physical body (also known as the mortal soul); and the ego-body, spirit-body or (immortal) soul, which confers full self-awareness. All living creatures have physical and life-bodies, and higher mammals may be developing astral bodies, but the EGO or soul is unique to human beings.

In most esoteric schools the human being has not just four but seven bodies. Just as there are intermediate states between ordinary physical consciousness and pure spiritual consciousness, so there are also intermediate vehicles of consciousness. This is common to most religious systems including Christianity, Judaism, SUFISM, Buddhism, YOGA, THEOSOPHY, ROSICRUCIANISM, Zoroastrianism as well as the teachings of ancient Egypt and Greece. The *Upanishads* speak of seven bodies: the physical, the etheric, the astral, the mental, the ego, the ATMAN and BRAHMAN. Above the etheric level (which is the most subtle level of the physical world) these bodies coincide with equivalent levels of consciousness. The four bodies above the astral level sometimes go under different names: the mental body is sometimes called the ego, and the highest three levels are then the causal body, also known as MIND (MANAS), the intuitional body of intuitive or spiritual awareness (BUDDHI), and the spirit being or 'atmic' body (atman); these three comprise the MONAD.

These seven bodies are similar but not identical to the seven PLANES of consciousness or levels of existence. There is not an exact coincidence because in the physical sphere we have two bodies, the dense physical and the etheric. The astral body is therefore our third body (counting from the lowest level), but the ASTRAL PLANE is the second level. The highest monadic plane is consequently not the highest plane of consciousness, this being the domain of God as pure spirit.

The physical and etheric bodies coincide spatially and are considered to be inseparable. Etheric forces underlie and shape all animate matter. Rudolf Steiner described the etheric body as 'the principle which calls inorganic matter into life'. For this reason it is also called the 'life-body' or 'formative-force-body'. There are obvious parallels with various scientific theories of a LIFE-FIELD and a MORPHOGENETIC FIELD.

The etheric body ensures the well-being of the physical body by channelling vital energy from the cosmos. (See PRANA and CH'I.) Illnesses which arise from within the organism rather than from without arise first in the etheric body, although if their root cause is emotional or psychological this will be found at a more basic level still in the astral. It is primarily the etheric body which is directly affected by certain therapies such as homeopathy and acupuncture.

When the etheric body receives such treatment to restore the energy balance, it effects a cure in the physical body.

The etheric body is also sometimes called the sensation body. When there is no sensation in the physical body, the etheric is no longer in perfect synchronization with it. Some say that under anaesthetic the etheric is temporarily dislodged. When blind people have learned to detect or 'feel' colour and form through their fingertips or cheeks (PAROPTIC VISION, or 'bio-introscopy'), occultists have claimed that it is the etheric, sensation body which is actually perceiving the light. The most famous case of this was Rosa Kuleschova in Russia. It is interesting to note that she was also an epileptic, a condition associated with a lack of synchronization between the etheric and the physical.

The etheric body, or that part of it which extends beyond the physical body, is visible to sensitives as the AURA. It is permanently attached to the physical body until death. After death the etheric body also dissolves away, a process which some say takes three days (Steiner) and others up to forty days (Daskalos), and then the spirit and the astral body enter the ASTRAL PLANE.

Although the etheric body is not made of solid matter, its energy is basically physical. The astral body on the other hand is more 'ethereal', and not physical at all. The astral body is also known as the desire body or the feeling body (in the sense of 'emotional', not 'sensation') but it is also mental in that it houses the memory. It is sometimes called the dream body since it experiences dreams. As the agent of psychic phenomena it is also called the psychical body. Early spiritualists called it the perispirit since it houses the spirit (Greek *peri* = around), but as it also dies it has been called the mortal soul.

Some believe that the astral body (including ego-consciousness) may temporarily detach itself in ASTRAL TRAVEL. This is also said to happen in sleep. Then, and in other xenophrenic states such as OUT-OF-THE-BODY EXPERIENCES, the astral body seems to move out of alignment with the physical body, and the two bodies — physical and astral — are said to be linked by the ASTRAL CORD. Whether or not anything actually leaves the physical body is a moot point. It is doubtful whether the astral body is three-dimensional in space in the way that the physical and etheric are, or that it actually separates (except at death). The astral body is a mental construct rather than physical matter. Because our present consciousness tends to see everything in spatial terms, it may during what is known as astral travel create its own astral body, a

THOUGHT-FORM which apparently occupies space, a sort of psychic DOUBLE. In some cases of ASTRAL PROJECTION consciousness clearly stays with the physical body and the individual may not even know whether the projection has occurred. In such cases it is probably easier to accept that a thought-form has been projected rather than that part of the individual has actually split off.

In a few cases apparent separation of one body from another is achieved with the impression that consciousness flits between the two. Something of this kind happened once to Rosalind Heywood. She describes an incident when she 'split in two'. The two parts looked at each other with decidedly different reactions. 'Pink Me' (she was wearing a pink nightdress at the time) regarded 'White Me' (the figure at the foot of the bed) as impersonal, pious, priggish, but also the stronger of the two; 'White Me' regarded 'Pink Me' as silly, selfish, and composed entirely of appetites. They coincide exactly with what we are told of the mental and astral (emotional) bodies. The emotional body has no appreciation of true meaning, and the mental body being purely occupied with meaning does not experience emotion.[84]

When recovering from a near fatal snakebite which paralysed him, Jack Seale remarked that normal consciousness returned in layers — layer by layer. He had in fact died: monitoring equipment had registered brain death, but not his return to consciousness while still paralysed. Jack Seale was aware of what was going on around him for eight days while his body was in coma. This is a NEAR-DEATH EXPERIENCE with a difference: Jack Seale's awareness was focused constantly on this world, not the bridge from this world to the next, and whilst part of his consciousness was with his physical body almost constantly, full consciousness returned as he described layer by layer.

This gradual return to full consciousness has much to do with the various bodies we possess. They did not actually leave the physical body in the sense that they left one space to inhabit another. Rather they were dislocated, so that they were no longer working in synchronization with each other, just as in sleep the astral and mental bodies are free to have independent experiences when not so strictly controlled by the physical body.

Only when the finer bodies are around the physical body and joined to it (or 'in gear') is the physical body conscious. When they separate from the body (or 'step out of gear'), consciousness also withdraws. We usually remember little if anything from the exploits of our astral body during sleep, although with training we can recall more.

The astral body and ego-body (mental and above) have to be 'timed down' when linked together with the physical body. For this reason, we are told, the astral body is seldom made visible in the ASTRAL WORLD while an individual is in the body. But while the physical body is asleep, the astral and ego get out of gear with the earth's vibrations and slip into gear with those of their own spheres. They can then contact other beings on the astral plane. Some SENSITIVES and MEDIUMS somehow induce this 'gear change' at will while remaining conscious in order to contact and communicate with souls on the astral plane.

The form of the astral body is conditioned by all the individual's emotions and desires; they are imprinted on it and become the visible, external body on the astral plane after the death of the physical body. These emotions determine the nature of the astral body. Just as the physical body can be afflicted by disease, so too the astral body can be afflicted by emotions such as hatred and guilt. After physical death the astral body gravitates to the level appropriate to its makeup on the astral plane. It is for this reason that so many religions insist that right emotions are much more important than right actions. Consider the supreme importance St Paul attaches to 'charity'. 'Whoso hateth his brother is a murderer', is another instance which shows the crucial nature of the emotions.

Just as the astral body is developed by exercising the emotions, the *mental body* is developed by exercising the mind. The length of time that these bodies will persist after death is determined by their development during physical life. They do not decay, but they eventually dissipate when all their vital energy has been used up. The first to fall away is the astral body. In the case of great thinkers the mental body may persist for a very long time indeed. When the mental body has used up all its energy the soul is drawn back to the physical plane by the pull of unresolved desires and ambitions.

There is a gap between the mental sphere of the mental body or ego and the higher mental sphere of the *causal body*, between the lower levels of the concrete mind and the higher levels of the abstract mind (*manas*) which is part of the monad. In other words there is a gap between the soul and the monad. So the soul and the personality together try to build a bridge to the monad, represented in the Bible by Jacob's Ladder, and known in Hindu mysticism as the ANTAHKARANA or rainbow bridge. Others refer to it as linking with the HIGHER SELF. This is also the level of Christ-consciousness, which reminds us of Christ's saying that 'None cometh unto the Father but through me'. A common interpretation of the Second Coming is this achievement of Christ-consciousness within the individual.

BOOK OF THE DEAD *The Tibetan Book of the Dead* is not to be confused with the Egyptian papyri known collectively as *The Book of the Dead*. The two are completely different.

The Egyptian Book of the Dead is a collection of ancient Egyptian texts which date from about the sixteenth century BC (during the New Kingdom) although they incorporate earlier writings. The various chapters deal with life in the afterworld and contain invocations which are intended to be spoken by the deceased, not by a priest in any ritual. The papyri were consequently buried with the mummy in the tomb and served a very practical purpose from the deceased's point of view, being a valuable guarantee of protection and sustenance in the AFTERLIFE. Any particular burial contained only a selection of what we now know as *The Book of the Dead*, which was not a book as such. It was not scripture or dogma for the guidance of the faithful, although from it we can gain a great deal of information about what ancient Egyptians actually believed.

The Tibetan Book of the Dead, *Bardo Thodol*, is also concerned with the experience of the soul after death and separation from the physical body, but it is a book of teachings for the living as much as for the dying. The whole of human experience is regarded as persistent illusion and a complex system is described involving the formation of the world out of the five elements. Three stages of after-death experience in the BARDO world are described in the book: the first of transcendent ecstasy at the sight of the pure Light of Reality and loss of self; the second of visions, both pleasant and unpleasant — a kind of purgatory; the third stage is the process of rebirth into the physical world.

BRAHMA Although there are several branches of Hinduism they all distinguish more clearly than the monotheistic religions between two aspects of the Divinity. BRAHMAN is God as Absolute Being, whereas Brahma is God as creative impulse.

Buddhists do not believe in an eternal Creator God or a Supreme Being. Brahma is sometimes referred to as a creator god, but only because he is the first to emerge from chaos at the beginning of each aeon.

BRAHMAN In Hindu MYSTICISM Brahman is the transcendent and immanent Spirit of the cosmos; neutral, static, life energy; God as Absolute, Unmanifest Being; cosmic unity. It is close to what the NEO-PLATONISTS called Universal Mind. The aim of the mystic is to achieve union between ATMAN, the individual Self, and the divine Brahman, to realize as it states in the *Upanishads* that 'the "I" within me is one with Brahman'. 'This UNIVERSE before it was created existed as spirit, as Brahman. When spirit created the universe his inmost spirit entered into all that had been created. It is given to man, rare among created things, to know this. If a man dies without realizing the unity of the Self with Brahman he has not reached the true goal of life. He must return again.' (*Upanishads.*)

BRAIN In 1972 Robert E. Ornstein published *The Psychology of Consciousness* and popularized almost overnight the notion that there are two sides to the human brain.[137] It is now common knowledge that the left hemisphere of the cerebral cortex is the part of the brain which in most people controls their use of language when speaking. This is also the area where most logical thinking seems to be reflected in brain activity. The right hemisphere is more concerned with spatial concepts, aesthetic appreciation. This gross over-simplification has been degraded even further into characterizing intellectuals and logical thinkers as 'lefties' and artists and sporting people as 'righties'.

Because the left hemisphere is undeniably 'dominant' in most people (it controls the right-hand side of the body), it has been suggested that much of what has been attributed to the SUBCONSCIOUS might actually originate in the right hemisphere. Whilst the left hemisphere controls most speech, hearing is dealt with by both left and right, and Julian Jaynes believes that the right hemisphere is the origin of all inner voices. He considers our modern form of consciousness to have developed by to a certain extent suppressing the activity of the right-brain. Until the first millennium BC it was, he maintains, normal for people to hear the voices of the gods. 'The speech of

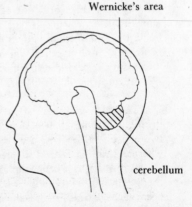

Cross-section of the brain

Wernicke's area

cerebellum

the gods was directly organized in what corresponds to Wernicke's area on the right hemisphere and "spoken" or "heard" over the anterior commissures to or by the auditory areas of the left temporal lobe.' In other words the right hemisphere was speaking to the left and this was understood as the voice of the gods. According to Jaynes, this ability to receive inner guidance was gradually lost as modern consciousness evolved, and people had to resort to prophets, oracles and shamans to tell them 'the word of the Lord' and the instructions of the gods who were rapidly receding further and further away from humanity. As the gods withdrew a variety of ANGELS and DEMONS stepped in to act as messengers between heaven and earth.[90] Without fully subscribing to Jaynes's theory, many have accepted that the right hemisphere might be the part of the brain which perceives para-normally, whether hearing voices, seeing visions or linking telepathically.

An alternative theory has been put forward by Stan Gooch, who attributes the paranormal faculties not to either part of the cerebral cortex but to the much older cerebellum. He notes that the cerebellum is larger in women than in men, and larger in Asiatics than in modern Europeans. This is presumably linked with women's aptitude for intuition and mediumship, and the Asiatics' predisposition for such practices as YOGA.[63,64]

BRAIN ACTIVITY/BRAIN WAVES The brain generates weak electrical impulses which because of the way in which they are recorded graphically by the EEG (electro-encephalograph) are popularly known nowadays as brain waves. Brain waves were for a time known as 'Berger waves' after a German psychiatrist who first recorded them in 1929, but electrical brain activity had already been observed in a dog by Richard Caton, an English physiologist, in about 1875. It was Berger who developed the idea of placing metal disc electrodes on the scalp, measuring the difference in electrical potential between them and recording the amplified signals as lines on a graph (the electro-encephalogram).

Brain waves have been recorded in the unborn foetus, proving that there is a great deal of brain activity, particularly dreaming, before birth. Despite the fact that EEG patterns are as individual as fingerprints, they also vary according to whether one is calm or excited and they are affected by conditions such as temperature, headache or even loud music. DRUGS such as morphine, chloroform and ether lead to decreased activity in the cortex, but barbiturates, which deaden activity in the thalamus lead to increased activity in the cortex.

Normal EEG patterns contain impulses at many frequencies, but various types of brain waves have been classified according to which frequencies predominate. However, no physiological basis for the different waves has yet been discovered and some investigators maintain that the apparent correspondences between specific frequency bands and brain states are inconsistent and too vague to be of value. Sometimes the two hemispheres of the brain have been seen to show completely different patterns and subjects have shown the waves associated with relaxation without actually feeling at all relaxed.

The electrical activity of the brain is greatest when there is mental effort, concentration or watchfulness: the electro-encephalogram records this activity in apparent waves at frequencies of thirteen cycles per second and above, up to about twenty-six cycles per second. This is the range of *beta* brain waves. These waves can also be evoked by a state of anxiety, and it has been suggested that they are associated with POLTERGEIST phenomena (where poltergeists are considered to be produced by a human agency, typically a frustrated child around puberty).

When in a state of relaxation the electrical activity falls: *alpha* brain waves range from eight or nine to eleven or twelve cycles per second. These are characteristic of a person at rest, and they usually disappear when the person's eyes are opened, but it is not the opening of the eyes which prevents *alpha* brain waves so much as the arousal of the person's attention. Sustained *alpha* rhythms in the frontal and central regions of the brain are characteristic of the state of deep meditation practised by adepts of YOGA, ZEN and SUFISM. In the 1970s biofeedback devices were marketed which indicated when *alpha* rhythms were prevalent, and this knowledge was sufficient for people to sustain this state of brain activity and achieve a deep state of relaxation.

It has been found that when mediums are in TRANCE, and when psychics are attempting to produce particular paranormal phenomena, their brains generate waves at eight cycles per second. This is on the borderline between *alpha* and *theta* brain waves. *Theta* brain waves are slower than the waves associated with relaxation (*alpha*) but not as slow as those of deep sleep (*delta*). They are in the range of four to seven cycles per second. They register typically when a person feels conflict, frustration, discomfort or embarrassment. It has been noticed that any of these emotions can hinder ESP. J.B. Rhine observed that even the experimenter's enthusiasm could cause embarrassment in the subjects, which would obstruct ESP.

Theta waves are also characteristic of creative reverie and a certain kind of problem-solving, not the less focused mental activity of normal thinking with all the sense channels wide open (with much faster *beta* waves), nor the relaxed but alert state characteristic of a feeling of well-being and serenity (with *alpha* waves).

MEDITATION can evoke both *alpha* and *theta* waves. They are accompanied by other physiological changes: oxygen consumption decreases, as does the consequent elimination of carbon dioxide; there is a reduction in the heartbeat and blood pressure; there is an increase in finger temperature and skin resistance. The difference between the two ranges seems to be that *alpha* waves encourage alert receptivity, whilst *theta* waves accompany the active use of the imagination. If one stays in a meditative state with predominantly *theta* rhythms the imagination will probably throw up images from one's own psyche in the manner of ACTIVE IMAGINATION, unlike the more passive, empty state typical of Zen meditation with characteristic *alpha* rhythms. (An overactive imagination could also obstruct receptivity to ESP.) Meditative practices often encourage stilling the mind (getting rid of fast *beta* rhythms) by first exercising and then disciplining the imagination (the slower *theta* rhythms) in order eventually to settle between the two with predominantly *alpha* rhythms.

Both *theta* and *delta* brain waves occur for short periods during normal sleep. *Theta* brain waves are characteristic of light sleep. In deep dreamless sleep or when the person is otherwise unconscious the electrical activity is further reduced: *delta* brain waves are below four cycles per second and can be as low as 0.5 cycles. It is in deep sleep during periods of *delta* brain waves that growth hormone is released. This is when we are least responsive to sounds or irritation on the skin and the body's oxygen consumption is at its lowest. These frequencies are also characteristic of damaged brain tissue. The term *delta* brain waves was chosen by Dr Grey Walter, who first classified them, because of the initial letter of disease, degeneration and death, with which he associated them.[205]

Research into brain activity continues. It has been discovered that a signal at 18,000 hertz fed into the brain induces mystical feelings. Russian scientists have measured differences in brain activity during telepathic and telekinetic experiments, more activity being at the back of the brain.

Despite the current preoccupation with identifying specific measurable brain activity with different states of consciousness it is worth remembering that the two may not be linked as causally as

47

mainstream scientists suppose. The neurosurgeon Wilder Penfield regards MIND not as an EPIPHENOMENON of the brain but as a different entity altogether. 'After years of striving to explain the mind on the basis of brain-action alone, I have come to the conclusion that it is simpler (and far easier to be logical) if one adopts the hypothesis that our being does consist of two fundamental elements.'[146] Others such as the philosopher and psychologist Henri Bergson (1859–1941) have regarded the brain as a filter whose purpose it is to reduce the amount of data which would otherwise invade our consciousness and to eliminate what is superfluous. This filter or reducing valve is bypassed in certain states when information is 'paranormally' perceived.

Table of brain wave patterns

Approximate frequency range	Main characteristics
delta 0.5–3 cycles	Oblivious deep sleep. Irregular *delta* rhythms are very common in the months before and after birth.
theta 4–7 cycles	Inspirational, HYPNOPOMPIC and HYPNAGOGIC (just before and just after sleep), anxiety, creative hallucinations, reverie but not day-dreaming, higher levels of awareness and creativity. Zen meditators pass from *alpha* to *theta* in trance.
alpha 8–13 cycles	Pleasantly calm, relaxed, disrupted by attention or emotion, increases in meditation. Rare in children under ten years old. People with a vivid visual imagination have fewer *alpha* rhythms; non-visualizers (who prefer auditory, tactile modes of perception) have stronger *alpha* rhythms.
beta 14–26 cycles	Normal waking states, active mind, concentrated tension, anxiety, focused attention, thinking.
gamma 27+ cycles	Not fully investigated, nor generally accepted as distinct from *beta*.

BREATHING We normally take about fifteen breaths per minute. The rate of breathing increases naturally with physical exertion, strong emotions or loud rhythmic music, but when consciously induced, rapid breathing (polypnea) or prolonged deep breathing (hyperpnea) can reduce awareness of pain, even producing anaesthesia, and can send the individual into TRANCE through a lack of carbon dioxide in the blood. The same result can be achieved by prolonged singing, shouting and dancing as practised by certain ecstatic cults such as the whirling DERVISHES.

Reducing the rate of breathing is a common method of stilling the thoughts and emotions for the purposes of MEDITATION. Slow breathing increases the carbon dioxide content of the lungs and blood and reduces the amount of oxygen reaching the brain. Carbon dioxide intoxication can induce a trance and cause hallucinations and visionary experiences. The normal fifteen per minute can easily be reduced to ten, and well-practised meditators may take as few as five or even four breaths per minute.

Breathing in and out through different nostrils, and the use of specific rhythms within one breathing cycle are also taught by certain spiritual disciplines. One rhythm thought to be conducive to general well-being has the simple ratio of 3−5−7−9 for time spent inhaling, holding the breath, exhaling, and waiting before inhaling again. In *pranayama* YOGA the so-called 'healing breath' follows a ratio of 1:4:2 (or 2:8:4, or 3:12:6, etc.) for inhaling, holding and exhaling. (See also PRANA.)

BROW CENTRE − See CHAKRAS.

BUDDHA A buddha is one who has become enlightened. A buddha can then enter NIRVANA and depart from this world, or stay in the world and teach. Gautama chose the latter course, using his memories of the twenty-four lives he had experienced while on the path as a BODHISATTVA to illustrate his teachings. The next bodhisattva to achieve buddhahood will be the teacher known as MAITREYA.

BUDDHI In Hindu teaching buddhi is the faculty of higher intelligence, wisdom rather than mere knowledge. It enables an individual to value everything in life as a means of advancing the Self. Occultists also equate buddhi with the faculty of INTUITION, the ability to know and discriminate without having to reason or exercise the 'lower mind' or MANAS.

BUDDHIC PLANE The fourth of the seven PLANES is known as the Buddhic plane or the intuitional world. It is through contact with the Buddhic plane that a few individuals achieve ENLIGHTENMENT.

CHAKRAS/CENTRES Many spiritual traditions share a common belief that the human body receives sustenance from the cosmos in a subtle form such as PNEUMA or PRANA and that it is this energy that gives both life to the body and power to the psyche. The energy is drawn in, converted and transferred through specific centres in the body. According to Indian tradition these centres are the focal points by which the human consciousness holds together its seven BODIES of manifestation.

The Sanskrit word, *chakra*, means 'wheel'. Clairvoyants who are able to see the centres see them as wheel-like vortices of energy; the higher an individual's spiritual development, the faster the centres spin, until they resemble spheres of radiant energy. When a person is not so spiritually developed, the centres resemble saucer-like depressions in the etheric body.

Western theosophists tend to place the centres on the front of the body, whilst Tibetans and Indians place them along the axis of the spine, but this is probably simply a reflection of the type of clairvoyant faculty which is used when observing them: an astral psychic will see their position in respect of the astral body (towards the front), and a mental psychic will see them in a more rarified form lying along the spine.

The number of centres is variable according to the tradition under consideration. In the West we have taken over the seven main chakras of Hindu teaching, although there are several other lesser chakras at other points of the body. In Tibet there are five main centres: brain, throat, heart, solar plexus, sex organs. To these is added a sixth in China and Japan: below the navel.

It is thought that St John refers to the centres in Revelation as the seven seals on the back of the book of life (perhaps reflecting their position along the spinal column). Hidden centres are referred to in ancient Greek texts, probably derived from Egypt. They passed into NEO-PLATONIST thought and into the beliefs of some

Christian sects such as the Hesychast monks who mentioned six: between the eyebrows, throat, heart, solar plexus, sex organs, anus.

The Kabbalists spoke of seven gates of the soul, and they equated four of the centres with points on the central pillar of the Sephiroth on the TREE OF LIFE: head (Kether — the world of emanation), heart (Tifareth — the world of creation), navel (Yesod — the world of formation), sex organs (Malkuth — the world of matter). For the SUFIS there were also four main centres: forehead, throat, heart and navel.

Starting at the lowest level the seven main Indian chakras are in ascending order the base chakra (*muladhara*), the sacral (*svadhisthana*), the solar plexus (*manipura*), the heart (*anahata*) the throat (*vishuddha*), the brow (*ajna*) and the crown (*sahasrara*). Each is usually associated with a particular organ in the glandular system of the body.

Other energies associated with individual centres vary according to the centre. The base and sacral centres are specifically linked with the physical body. The next three are more closely linked with the SUBTLE BODIES: the solar plexus with the lower activity of the astral body, and the heart and throat with the astral's higher activity. The crown and brow centres are intimately linked with the individual's spiritual life.

They can also be grouped as a lower triad (up to and including the solar plexus) associated with the personality, a higher, spiritual triad (heart, throat and crown) with the brow centre acting as the focus of the integrated personality. In this grouping each centre in the spiritual triad is said to receive the transformed energies from the lower triad: the heart from the solar plexus, the throat from the sacral, and the crown from the base.

During one's integration of the personality and one's spiritual development, the centres are said to be 'awakened' or activated in turn. Various practices in YOGA are in-

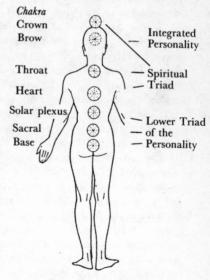

Position on the spinal column of the seven main chakras

tended to aid this. Awakening them prematurely is considered to be dangerous, as is the unsupervised or too ambitious arousal of the KUNDALINI.

It is from the lowest of the main chakras, the *base centre* (*muladhara*), situated at the base of the spine, that the kundalini power rises in a spiralling movement up the etheric spine. The base chakra is the polar opposite of the crown chakra, which is situated on the top of the head at the bregma, and it is often considered to be situated at the other end of the torso at the perineum. It belongs to the lower triad of chakras which powers the personality, and its energies are associated with an existential 'will-to-be'. Some also regard it as the root of sensual pleasure and the generator of power used in sex-magic, although the *sacral centre* (*svadhisthana*) is more specifically linked to sexual power (and the will to procreate rather than exist as oneself). In a spiritually evolved person the energies of the base centre and sacral centre are transferred to the crown and throat respectively.

The third chakra is the *solar plexus* (*manipura*), situated below the level of the shoulder-blades and above the diaphragm on the spine and just below where the ribs divide at the front of the body. Although it is sometimes called the navel centre it is usually placed above the navel. The plexus itself is the biggest nerve-centre in the body apart from the brain, and the glandular counterpart of the chakra is the pancreas, which governs the action of the stomach, liver and gall bladder as well as other functions of the sympathetic nervous system. As the solar plexus regulates digestion, strength in this area leads to general physical well-being. Blockages of energy in this centre can result in diseases such as diabetes.

The solar plexus belongs to the lower triad of chakras concerned with the PERSONALITY, and it is particularly concerned with the ego and one's self-image, with will-power and ambition. Energies usually pass freely between each of the chakras in the lower triad. When an individual is evolving spiritually these energies are passed to the upper triad and they all pass through the solar plexus centre before being transferred to the appropriate higher centre. Energy from the solar plexus centre itself is transferred to the heart centre.

Energy from the lower triad can actually be felt passing through the solar plexus when it is exteriorized either in physical phenomena such as RAPPING (the instance in which Jung experienced the sensation) and the creation of ELEMENTALS, or for the use of a MEDIUM. Mediums can utilize both their own solar plexus energy and that of others sitting in the CIRCLE (hence incidentally the frequent warning against eating shortly before a SITTING). Although ECTOPLASM has been seen emerging from virtually all orifices of various mediums, the generating power always seems to be focused at the solar plexus and this is the area to which it most often withdraws. Awakening the solar plexus centre can also precipitate a certain clairvoyant ability. Cesare Lombroso reported cases where mediums 'read' writing that was placed against their stomachs and this was explained by some as the work of the solar plexus centre which had been aroused.[113]

In the balanced spiritual evolution of an individual the energies of the solar plexus centre will be transferred to the heart centre, where they will be used for soul-enhancing work with a spiritual purpose. It is easy to see how the incidental psychic powers which can be evoked by activating this centre might prove to be a distraction from this purpose, a danger which yogis often warn against.

The *heart centre* (*anahata*) governs the heart, the blood and the circulatory system, and it is associated with the thymus and the vagus nerve. It is through this chakra that we radiate love, charity, compassion and self-sacrifice. The emotions are felt here both on a personal and transpersonal level. When the heart centre is awakened, one perceives the inner emotional state and physical condition of others literally 'sympathetically', feeling the joys and sorrows, aches and pains within oneself. It is the focal centre for an awareness of group consciousness. The heart chakra is the lowest centre in the spiritual triad consisting of heart, throat and crown.

It is not surprising that the *throat centre* (*vishuddha*), being close to the voice-box, is considered to be concerned with the spoken word, sound, singing and communication, but it is also involved in study and the search for truth. Scholarship and intellect are developed with the development of the throat chakra; it is the seat of intelligence and creativity. In the process of evolving spiritually, an individual transfers the energies from the sacral centre in the lower triad of the personality to the throat centre, thus converting energy associated with the reproductive system into higher creative energy. Sensitives sometimes claim that just as concentrating on the brow centre in meditation is thought to encourage CLAIRVOYANCE, concentrating on the throat centre can lead to CLAIRAUDIENCE.

The chakras should be awakened and develop naturally and harmoniously one after the other. If this development is unharmonious or irregular, too much energy in the throat centre could turn the love of science and scholarship into dogmatism. This could result from a lower chakra being too active, developing too strong an ego-sense in the solar plexus for example, or it could reflect resistance to opening up the next chakra, the brow centre.

The *brow centre* is often associated with the PINEAL GLAND, responsible for the production of melatonin. The pineal gland is sensitive to light and some believe it is sensitive to certain frequencies of light which are beyond the visible range, and which have been postulated as a possible carrier of information which is perceived 'extra-sensorily'. Activation of the brow chakra, opening the third eye, is accompanied by heightened perception such as 'seeing' what goes on inside a leaf, and increased psychic ability, particularly clairvoyance. The ajna centre also expresses imagination.

When clairvoyants report 'seeing' images or scenes, or the AURAS of their sitters, they usually describe the act of clairvoyance as taking place in the centre of the forehead using the third eye. Similarly PSYCHOMETRISTS often hold the object they are psychometrizing close to the forehead to facilitate their vision. But a worthier aim of working on this chakra in spiritual development would be greater discernment, since faculties such as clairvoyance are thought by true adepts to be a distraction from the spiritual path. Whether one is aiming for clairvoyance or discernment, focusing on the brow chakra during meditation seems to facilitate the evocation of intuitive images.

How can one actually use the brow chakra? After wrestling with a problem, viewing it from all angles and arguing with oneself about it in vain, one sometimes comes to the conclusion that logical reasoning seems futile. If one can then stop thinking logically and focus calmly on the brow chakra, one may be able to see the matter in a completely new light, perhaps uniting arguments that had appeared to oppose each other. This is the type of discernment that the brow chakra can help us to achieve. The Buddha is often depicted with a precious stone set in the centre of the forehead in the position of the brow chakra, representing the spiritual awareness and understanding that he achieved.

In traditional Indian teaching the ajna centre is represented by a lotus with two multiple petals, which it is said parallel the two lobes of the pituitary gland. (There is some confusion regarding the exact relationship of the brow centre to the glands in the head, some saying it is associated with the PINEAL and others with the PITUITARY.) Combining these two petals with the forty-eight petals of the lower five chakras gives the number fifty, symbolising the integrated, perfected personality. Further number symbolism is contained in the smaller petals which make up the two multiple petals of the ajna centre lotus: each petal is made up of forty-eight smaller petals. Combining these ninety-six with the forty-eight of the lower five chakras gives a total of one hundred and forty-four, a mystic number representing the transformation of the individual, the completion of the work to achieve the union of the lower self with the soul.[191]

The *crown centre* (*sahasrara*) is the highest of the seven main chakras, situated at the bregma, the meeting point of the bones on the top of the skull which only join in a child's second year. It is also sometimes known as the sacred thousand-petalled lotus and the Hole of Brahman, through which DEW from the 'Ocean of

Table of Chakras/centres

Centre	Position	Glands	Organs governed	Other attributes
base	perineum, below the sacrum	adrenal	kidneys spinal column	channels the 'will-to-be'
sacral	base of lumbar spine	gonads	reproductive system	
solar-plexus	below diaphragm	pancreas	stomach, gall bladder, liver, nervous system	channels energies from lower centres to higher centres
heart	between shoulder blades	thymus	heart, blood, circulation. (vagus nerve)	radiates love for the world from the soul
throat	first dorsal vertebra	thyroid	lungs, bronchi, vocal chords, alimentary canal	expressses higher creative faculties
brow	centre of head, and forehead	pituitary (and pineal)	lower brain, nervous system, ears, nose, left eye.	expresses idealism and imagination (and 'third eye')
crown	top of head	pineal (and pituitary)	upper brain, right eye	focal point of the spiritual 'will-to-be'

Nectar' drips and trickles down to energize the other centers (the reverse process of KUNDALINI), bringing spiritual illumination and enabling the individual to link with the invisible world of spirit and universal consciousness. For this reason the crown centre is a most important area of consciousness and a focus for meditation. Recognition of the crown chakra can be seen in many parts of the world, both in symbolic ornamentation — from top-knots to crowns and headdresses, and in pictorial representation in the form of HALOS.

CHANNEL A channel is a person who claims to be able to communicate information from the spirit world, from other dimensions of reality or from other levels of consciousness. Channels were formerly known as MEDIUMS and sometimes still are. The new term has probably been adopted to try to get away from certain characteristics or associations of traditional mediums which modern channels presumably regard as unflattering in some way. Where mediums were eccentric, fuddy-duddy, and occasionally fraudulent, channels are modern, up-to-date, often young, fashionable, and full of the latest New Age jargon. Otherwise there is essentially no difference between the two terms. If certain writers choose to treat one term as more inclusive or exclusive than the other, the choice is quite arbitrary. (One way in which the new term is simply more useful than 'medium' is that 'channel' is also a verb.)

Some people prefer to use the word 'channel' because they assume that all self-styled mediums believe implicitly that the communications they channel are from DISCARNATE spirits, but this has never actually been so: Eileen Garrett and Geraldine Cummins were among the many outstanding mediums who willingly conceded that some of the communicators were aspects of their own psyche. If the word 'medium' has been responsible for this mistaken assumption, implying that external ideas are being expressed via the medium, the word 'channel' might be equally liable to such an interpretation. If by 'channel' we wish to suggest that a person has opened up a channel to a higher level of spiritual awareness, then the term may be preferable to 'medium', but in that case the person should not really be referred to as *being* a channel — such a person has opened up their own channel to other (it is to be hoped higher) levels of their own CONSCIOUSNESS. Speaking of people as channels immediately invites the same assumptions that are made about mediums — that external entities speak through them. In the words of SETH as channelled by Jane

Roberts, 'If you understood to begin with that you are a spirit, and therefore free of space and time yourself, then you could at least consider the possibility that some such messages were coming to you from other portions of your own reality.'[166]

CHANNELLING Receiving information which purports to come from the spirit world and communicating it to others by means of automatic writing or speaking has become more popularly known as channelling recently, although the mechanism is much the same as traditional trance mediumship. The person who was formerly known as a MEDIUM is now called a CHANNEL.

It should always be borne in mind that the label 'channelling' is applied to a process by which other aspects of the person's own psyche may be manifested: use of the term is not in itself a guarantee that the communications are from other spirit entities. In cases where it is accepted that the communicators are DISCARNATE spirits it is still as well to remember what spiritualists believe is actually happening. Most mediums or channels work by establishing contact with the ASTRAL PLANE. This is where the recently departed individuals may be found. They usually show themselves either as they were towards the end of their earthly life, or as they like to remember themselves, perhaps as younger men and women, or sometimes in a way that they know they will be recognized. This is a form that they actually mould for themselves, based on their own wishes. (The astral body is also known as the 'desire body'.) When showing themselves in this way they can also assume any form they choose, even pretending to be someone famous, particularly if this makes them think that others may take more notice of them. This is one of the reasons why so many mediums and channellers apparently manage to contact either historical characters on the one hand or 'highly evolved masters' on the other. MASTERS are not very likely to manifest on the astral in order to speak to a few individuals through a channel. As Alice Bailey wrote (as inspired incidentally by a Tibetan Master), 'Some transmitters work entirely on astral levels and their work is necessarily part of the great illusion. ... Some receive teaching from discarnate entities of no higher evolution, and frequently of lower, than themselves.'[5]

To avoid the dangers of deception on the astral plane people who are spiritually aware have to train themselves to tune into a higher level, the mental PLANE (to which souls progress after they have 'purged' all their outstanding desires and emotions on the astral plane). Here one is more likely to be able to receive accurate

CLAIRVOYANCE and knowledge of a soul-level nature. But people who do have access to this level are not usually the kind who seek fame and fortune as channels.

It is worth remembering the biblical exhortation to 'Believe not every spirit, but try the spirits, whether they are of God: because many false prophets are gone out into the world.' (1 John 4, 1.) One way to 'try' or test the entities that are channelled by potential 'false prophets', apart from asking them point blank, is to notice whether they start giving their audience instructions. With a few historic exceptions no truly evolved spirit gives out orders, no true spirit gives information unless it is specifically asked for, and no true spirit even gives advice unless it is sought. The same caveats apply when dealing with spirits as with GURUS and self-styled gurus, particularly in modern times with our healthy scepticism of any demands for uncritical acceptance or unthinking obedience. It can be argued that the preferred teaching style, whether by modern gurus or in channelled communications, should resemble the Socratic method, by which the seekers discover their own answers to the questions posed or rephrased by the teacher.

CHARISMATICS A charismatic is someone who receives religious inspiration, which may take the form of experiences of ECSTASY, giving voice to spiritual (or spirit) utterances, SPEAKING IN TONGUES or the gift of HEALING. Various aspects of what was once considered to be the accepted behaviour of only a few saints and mystics became permissible to the ordinary people in sects such as the Quakers and Shakers. The gifts of charismatics are basically the same as mediumistic powers but in a deeply religious and devotional context. Some sects have been founded on the work of people with such gifts, such as Joseph Smith to whom was revealed the *Book of Mormon* and May Baker Eddy who founded the Christian Science Church.

CH'I The ancient Chinese held that a vital energy, known as ch'i permeated the whole universe. The higher up the scale one goes from the mineral kingdom, through plants and animals to human beings, the more concentrated and powerful this energy is. The human body receives ch'i both by ingesting food and air (partaking of the animal, plant and mineral kingdoms) and on an etheric level from planetary and cosmic influences. Acupuncture is a technique by which ch'i can be redirected when imbalances or blockages have arisen in the human organism. QI GONG practitioners restore balances by transferring some of their own energy to the patient.

Ch'i is comparable to the Hindu concept PRANA. In the ancient Middle East a similar type of HEALING energy was known in Greek as *dunamis*. There has been no real equivalent in the West, although there have been several less widespread concepts such as animal magnetism or MESMERISM (Franz Mesmer), OD (Karl von Reichenbach), VRIL (Louis Jacolliot), ORGONE (Wilhelm Reich), and BIOPLASMIC ENERGY (Semeon Kirlian), all of which bear similarities to ch'i.

CHOHAN Tibetan MASTERS are known as chohans. The Dhyan-chohans are masters of a higher order, the equivalent of ARCHANGELS or beings in the spiritual hierarchy who act as planetary rulers.

CLAIRAUDIENCE EXTRA-SENSORY PERCEPTION (ESP), which the percipient experiences as hearing, was formerly known as clair-audience, a term which is still used to distinguish this mode of ESP from other manifestations of PSI faculties. It has sometimes been used loosely to cover a form of hyperaesthesia or HYPERACUITY — the ability to hear actual sounds that are imperceptible to most people, as well as paranormal hearing involving sounds that are so far away that they are physically undetectable — a kind of 'remote hearing' comparable to REMOTE VIEWING, and the subjective hearing of sounds generated somehow in the SUBCONSCIOUS MIND. It is in this latter sense that the term is most frequently used, and this use still includes two possible interpretations. Either the voices heard are illusory, mental creations of the individual who has become subconsciously aware of information which is passed on to the conscious mind and then 'heard' in the same way that CRISIS APPARITIONS may be 'seen'. Or the speakers, heard clairaudiently, have a certain external validity, such that Joan of Arc's 'voices' actually belonged to entities outside her own psyche and may have reverberated somehow in some form of ETHER.

The latter interpretation resembles what is commonly regarded as inspiration. This is the traditionally accepted view of how Gabriel communicated the contents of the KORAN to Mohammed. Many CLAIRVOYANTS operate in this way and maintain that they hear 'with the inner ear' what their spirit GUIDES or the guides of their sitters are saying to them. Some say that awakening or de-veloping the throat chakra encourages the clairaudient faculty, although it is the brow centre, the so-called THIRD EYE, that is most closely associated with paranormal perception, and whether the information is translated by the mind into pseudo-visual or pseudo-auditory terms may be purely a matter of habit rather than an indication of which chakras are activated.

CLAIRVOYANCE 'If a person becomes aware of some event or circumstance in the external world, of which no one else is cognizant (as, for example, of a card in a shuffled pack), the faculty involved will be called "Clairvoyance". It is not to be inferred from this that anything analogous to "seeing" necessarily enters into the process.'[203] It is perhaps because of the apparent implication that something *is* seen in clairvoyance that J.B. Rhine's coinage EXTRA-SENSORY PERCEPTION (ESP) became more current, but this is much more of an umbrella term and includes many psychic or paranormal faculties including TELEPATHY. As Tyrrell made clear, true clairvoyance does not involve telepathy, and for this reason the word is still preferred by some to the more common term ESP.

Some people seem to be born clairvoyant, others become clairvoyant following an accident or a NEAR-DEATH EXPERIENCE (NDE). Accidents involving severe concussion are often cited in this context. The famous Dutch clairvoyant, Peter Hurkos, fell off a ladder during the Second World War and cracked his skull. In hospital he discovered that he intuitively knew all about the other patients around him, even to the extent of knowing that a particular man was an agent and would shortly be killed. When Hurkos tried to return to normal life he found it impossible to concentrate. Lawrence LeShan has called the mental mode which Hurkos involuntarily entered the 'clairvoyant reality' as distinct from our normal way of looking at the world which we regard as actual reality.[108] Our normal way of appreciating the world with our minds through the mediation of the senses may be partial, but it is easier to cope with. So many impressions came flooding uncontrollably into Hurkos's mind that he was unable to carry out any normal work. His solution was to become a professional psychic.

Many clairvoyants and psychics say that the experience of receiving intuition or 'tuning in' to clairvoyant information involves a shift of viewpoint, rather like viewing the world at a completely different angle. This change of state is often abrupt and is reminiscent of the different state of CONSCIOUSNESS achieved in MEDITATION by mystics. Considering that such mystics regard time as an illusion, and clairvoyants prove that time is certainly no obstacle to accessing information about the world, the two groups probably achieve similar states and have similar experiences. This theory has been put forward by among others Lawrence LeShan.[108]

Eileen Garrett, a remarkable clairvoyant who has been investigated by many interested scientists, maintained that to operate clairvoyantly one had to 'withdraw from the environing world', withdraw 'as far as possible from the impact of all sensory perceptions', and 'seek to focus awareness (to the best of our ability) in the field of the SUPERCONSCIOUS — the timeless, spaceless field of the as-yet-unknown'. One thing which was always guaranteed to work against this process was conscious effort — the shift of awareness must be effortless.

Eileen Garrett has said more than most about the experience of operating in a clairvoyant mode. 'In clairvoyant vision I do not look *out* at objects ... as in ordinary seeing, but I seem to draw the perceived object towards me, so that the essence of its life and the essence of mine become, for the moment, one and the same thing. Thus to my sense, clairvoyance occurs in states of consciousness whose relations exist as a fact in nature, on levels of being that transcend the present perceptive capacities of our sensory faculties.' 'I have referred to an inner condition of "alertness" which is *the* essential factor in many of these activities. It is a realization of superior vital living. I enter into a world of intensely vibrant radiation; I am extra competent, I participate fully and intimately in events that move at an increased rate of movement, and though the events that I observe are objective to me, I do more than observe them — I *live* them.'[57] This is perhaps what Colin Wilson is referring to when he says, 'Clairvoyance has something to do with being *more alive*.'[214]

Clairvoyance is usually understood in the sense of foretelling the future, but it is more accurately the ability to perceive all levels of reality. Most clairvoyants have a bias in favour of one or two levels, usually relatively low (See PLANES of consciousness), but as a SENSITIVE becomes more evolved, so awareness of more levels and the ability to discriminate between them should develop. At the lowest, but also extremely useful level, the sensitive person will be able to see the etheric BODY and diagnose illness. Since most ailments are present on the etheric level before they manifest in the physical body, this enables the clairvoyant operating on this level to warn of impending health problems, so that the individual can take pre-emptive action and perhaps restore the body's balance before the trouble actually manifests. By observing a person's AURA a clairvoyant can 'read character' and much more. On the one hand the aura can change according to temporary mood, and on the other it also bears the effects of past experiences.

The brow CHAKRA or THIRD EYE is the centre most intimately involved in clairvoyance. When observing a person's aura and etheric body a clairvoyant may also see the state of the individual's chakras, revealing to the clairvoyant how developed that individual is spiritually. As well as observing the individual a clairvoyant may also become aware of THOUGHT-FORMS, ELEMENTALS and deceased spirits at an ASTRAL level. Focusing on a higher mental level (See PLANES) is necessary for true spiritual clairvoyance, information of a soul-nature, concerning the individual's past, present and future in terms of their life-purpose, perhaps referring to past lives. This was the kind of clairvoyance that Edgar Cayce was able to give when in trance. Some would say that this is the only true clairvoyance, all lesser forms being mere 'fortune-telling'. The dangers of the 'fortune-telling' type of clairvoyance operating at auric or astral levels is that the information is basically conditioned by the subject's own emotions and desires. The clairvoyant is more likely to perceive the individual's hopes and fears than their true reality. (See also PREDICTION.)

COLLECTIVE UNCONSCIOUS The collective unconscious is usually conceived as a kind of group mind underlying individual consciousness. When trying to account for his wife's telepathic ability, Upton Sinclair postulated 'a common substratum of mind, underlying our individual minds, and which we can learn to tap'.[180] Samuel Butler spoke of a 'racial memory', and Alister Hardy of a 'psychic plan' or psychic blueprint'.

For Jung, with whom the notion of the collective unconscious is most closely associated, the term denotes the inherited unconscious, shared racial memories, the sum total of all the knowledge acquired by humanity. 'Our body has an anatomical pre-history of millions of years, so also does the psychic system.'[94] Jung saw UFOS as an expression of something in the collective unconscious, an updated version of 'the gods' of old and the 'little people' of popular folklore.

Jung's model of the psyche

Mind is by definition timeless and spaceless, so all minds can be regarded as part of one mind. Such a 'group mind' has the potential to include information about all things that have ever happened or will happen anywhere. (See AKASHIC RECORD) Jung again: 'The collective unconscious is common to all: it is the foundation of what the ancients called "the sympathy of all things".'

It is through the medium of the collective unconscious that information about a particular time and place can be transferred to another individual mind. This was how Jung explained to himself the feeling of restlessness one evening, and then the dull pain that woke him at about 2.00 a.m., passing from the forehead and to the back of his skull, the day one of his patients shot himself in the head.[97] It was in the area of the collective unconscious that Jung believed he met and talked with the 'intelligent entities' Philemon, Elijah and Salome during his periods of ACTIVE IMAGINATION.

An alternative view is that an individual mind has access only to its own store of memories from the past, i.e. all the experiences and knowledge that the SOUL has so far acquired in all its incarnations. According to this view, not until a much higher level of consciousness has been reached will an individual soul have direct access to all other parts of the Universal Mind, even though we are always part of it. This idea does not contradict any of Jung's theories about archetypes. In fact in some respects it makes them more vital because of a slightly different emphasis: instead of the archetypes existing outside the individual consciousness in a collective unconscious, to which one must first gain access before contacting them, they exist within the individual as real memories.

Sheldrake has postulated a MORPHOGENETIC FIELD, reminiscent of Hardy's 'psychic blueprint', which influences the structure and behaviour of a particular species. In the case of human beings this could be the method of transmission of otherwise unaccountable abilities (which one would expect to be learned) and phobias (which have been explained so far, albeit rather inadequately, as instinctive). The mental aspect of such a morphogenetic field resembles the collective unconscious. Sheldrake's theory of 'formative causation' maintains that anything that has been learned by one group of individuals will be slightly more easily learned by a subsequent group – the so-called HUNDREDTH MONKEY PHENOMENON.

To test this theory, English children were taught three nonsense rhymes. The rhymes were in fact Japanese, but one of them was an actual nursery rhyme (already familiar to millions of Japanese people) and the other two had been specially written for the experiment. As anticipated, the authentic nursery rhyme was learned more successfully than the other two. Whilst this seemed to validate Sheldrake's theory, he was not entirely satisfied: perhaps the ease with which the authentic nursery rhyme was learned could be accounted for by the sounds and internal structure of the rhyme itself, and perhaps this in turn accounted for its existence and survival as a nursery rhyme.

A further experiment produced less ambiguous results. It involved black and white patterns, rather like inkblots, within which one could see actual pictures. Very few people spot these images without first having them pointed out. One particularly difficult picture was successfully identified by thirty-nine out of a thousand people tested. The picture was then shown briefly during a regional television show (31 August 1983). Then a further set of people all over the world were tested and 6.4 percent saw the hidden image (as opposed to 3.9 percent the first time). None of these people could possibly have seen the television broadcast. These attempts to prove the reality of a mental morphogenetic field produced statistics which were suggestive of the validity of Sheldrake's theory without actually being conclusive, and the theory has not yet found much favour with orthodox scientists.

The biologist Lyall Watson has seen a need for a new term for the common awareness that can be shared by a group: SAMA (composed of two Sanskrit roots – 'sa' meaning together, and 'man' meaning think), 'something which links together or is of like mind'. 'SAMA describes those parts of an individual or society which share information, whether they be in the soma, the germ cells or the mind.'[207] He believes that this group mind is plugged into in many psychic phenomena – POSSESSION and XENOGLOSSY as well as TELEPATHY.

The thalamus and hypothalamus, part of the so-called old brain common to all animals, controlling the autonomic nervous system and instinctive responses such as appetite, has been thought by some to be the area responsible for memories, impulses and feelings which we attribute to the collective unconscious. This viewpoint suggests that many paranormal faculties are old skills that we have forgotten, rather than abilities that are now evolving in humanity. On the other hand, awareness and appreciation of the collective unconscious can be extended into a more transcendent experience of COSMIC CONSCIOUSNESS, an aspect of the unconscious which is also referred to as the SUPERCONSCIOUS.

COMMUNITY OF SENSATION Like many natural scientists in the nineteenth century, as a young teacher Alfred Russel Wallace (one of the first proponents with Darwin of the theory of evolution) was interested in HYPNOTISM. In his experiments with William Barrett he noticed that hypnotized subjects reacted to actions of the hypnotist as if they had been doing them themselves. For example if the hypnotist pricked himself, the subject would rub the appropriate part of his own body, if the hypnotist tasted something bitter, the subject would grimace. This became known as 'community of sensation' and has since been recognized by many researchers, although science has found no explanation for it. A further intriguing aspect of the phenomenon is that it still operates even when the hypnotized subject is half a mile away, as Leonie was when hypnotized by Dr Gibert and Pierre Janet. This gives as concrete evidence as we are ever likely to have that the MIND exists as an independent entity of some kind, rather than as a mere EPIPHENOMENON of brain activity, and that it transcends both time and space. It also suggests that at a SUBLIMINAL or SUBCONSCIOUS level minds can overlap or operate as a kind of group mind or COLLECTIVE UNCONSCIOUS.

CONSCIOUSNESS William James regarded normal waking consciousness as just one particular kind of awareness and believed that there were other forms of consciousness. 'Our normal waking consciousness is but one special type of consciousness, whilst all about it, parted from it by the flimsiest screens, there lie potential forms of consciousness entirely different. ... No account of the universe in its totality can be final which leaves these other forms of consciousness quite disregarded.'[89] Other possible types of consciousness are dreaming, hypnotic trance, mediumistic trance, the mystical experience of ecstasy. Even intense concentration could be regarded as a different type of consciousness. Normal waking consciousness consists of a series of separate moments of awareness which are given continuity by memory. Gurdjieff considered that this so-called normal consciousness is in fact a state of light HYPNOSIS, and he maintained that most people are hardly ever truly awake. There is a similar implication in William James's belief that we use only one tenth of our mental capacity. Aldous Huxley was another who believed that normal consciousness was a narrow segment of our potential consciousness: he regarded the brain and sense organs as a kind of reducing valve through which experience was funnelled to protect us from being overwhelmed.

Instead of regarding different types of consciousness as separate states, discrete ways of being aware, it is possible to think of consciousness as a spectrum of mental states which merge into one another, varying degrees of awareness. Colin Wilson has postulated at least eight degrees of consciousness, labelling them from Level 0 to Level 7. They are not so much types of consciousness such as dreaming and trance, as degrees of wakefulness and degrees of awareness, progressing from the UNCONSCIOUS state of sleep to the SUPERCONSCIOUS state of TRANSCENDENCE. They are very roughly deep sleep (Level 0), dreaming and the HYPNAGOGIC state (Level 1), 'mere awareness' − a blank, unresponsive waking state (Level 2), self-awareness that is dull, bored, heavy and meaningless (3), an essentially passive and reactive type of normal everyday consciousness with an element of regarding life 'as a grim battle' (4), an active, more spontaneous, happy 'spring morning consciousness' in which life suddenly becomes more interesting and exciting (5), a 'magical level' which can be equated with Maslow's notion of PEAK EXPERIENCES (6), and a more transcendent level where time ceases to exist, the level at which Wilson's FACULTY X operates (7). Wilson sees an increasing awareness of 'connectedness' as one moves from one level of consciousness to the next and abandons the 'Ecclesiastes effect'. ('Vanity of vanities, all is vanity.' − Ecclesiastes 1, 2.) He sees further levels of consciousness beyond his Level 7 as experienced by mystics, but these remain undefined.[214]

Colin Wilson's degrees of consciousness can be extended backwards as well as forwards, into the domain of non-human consciousness. Rudolf Steiner regarded animal consciousness as the experience of desires, hopes and fears without self-awareness and the ability to view the body and those emotions from the point of view of an inner observer. He thought plants too had a form of consciousness, albeit very physical, perhaps resembling human sleep. The German philosopher Friedrich von Schelling (1775−1854) wrote, 'Mind sleeps in the stone, dreams in the plant, awakes in the animal, and becomes conscious in man.' Teilhard de Chardin thought that every atom even of the mineral kingdom possessed a potentiality for consciousness and that through the process of EVOLUTION the manifest universe is gradually increasing in consciousness of itself. The idea that inert matter has consciousness of some kind is present in a wide and surprisingly varied range of sources, from Hindu and Theosophical thought, and the communications of SETH channelled by Jane Roberts, to the ideas of orthodox scientists. J.B.S. Haldane wrote, 'We do not find obvious evidence of life or mind in so-called inert matter, ... but if the scientific point of view is correct, we shall ultimately find them, at least in rudimentary forms, all through the universe.'[77]

In the occult tradition something like the different levels of consciousness proposed by Wilson are equated with the PLANES of being. By withdrawing attention from the external world SENSITIVES can become conscious of higher levels — the subtle but still physical etheric, then the astral, then the mental. Consciousness can expand enormously at the mental level, but few are aware of this level while in the body. ECSTASY may be experienced at the intuitional level, the highest level that any human can consciously reach while still in the body. Occultists believe that we progress through these same planes of being or levels of consciousness after death, changing our focus as we discard first the physical body, then the astral body, and so on. 'Discarding the astral body' is in fact easier to understand as a metaphor for changing one's focus of consciousness and abandoning the desires and emotions which constitute awareness at the astral level.

CONSENSUS REALITY To recognize that what we call reality is only a consensus reality, only what we have agreed to call reality, is to recognize that we can only perceive what we can conceive. Captain Cook's ship was invisible to the Tahitians because they could not conceive of such a vessel. Even most major discoveries in modern science are mental speculations long before they are proved as 'real' in the 'objective' external world. As Joseph Chilton Pearce has neatly put it, 'Man's mind mirrors a universe that mirrors man's mind.' 'If an imaginative seed, the gist of an idea, can be planted, even though contrary to existent evidence, the seed can still grow and sooner or later produce confirmation. Data can be found to bolster the conviction. The desire for conviction can produce its own data.'[143] This has obvious implications for researchers in parapsychology, and also for their detractors.

The philosopher Alfred North Whitehead drew attention to the fact that the way our conditioned mode of thinking affects our view of reality is impossible for us to appreciate. 'There will be some fundamental assumptions which adherents of all variant systems within the epoch unconsciously presuppose. Such assumptions appear so obvious that people do not know what they are assuming because no other way of putting things has ever occurred to them.'[209] Our language is partly responsible for some of these assumptions.

Most of them are absorbed during childhood, so that as adults 'We interact with a "mediated reality" and consider the artificial result our natural condition.'[144] The psychologist Piaget recognized this obliquely by referring to a period of 'reality adjustment' in the pre-adolescent child during which 'magical thinking' faded away. What he did not consider is that this 'magical thinking' is a kind of primary process of perception which is of value. Pearce maintains that the child adopts consensus thinking largely through fear. 'Somewhere after our sixth year we had to adopt the semantic universe in place of a real one, and by adolescence the cultural metaprogramme had assumed complete dominance.'[144]

To some extent consensus reality is a convenience: it is practical and enables us to survive relatively easily. But it is also a convenient fiction, and a symptom of laziness. If there is no expectation, nothing will come. There is a permanent veto on the totally unexpected, such that miracles never can happen in a world which does not allow them to happen. Another consequence of this programming is a denial of humanity's own creative role and the sense of being victims of a chance universe. 'We are always plagued with the idea that "out there" is a great, eternal, and *a priori* state of truth. That the "realness" of our lives might hinge on *our* choice is disquieting.'[143]

CONTROLS 'This word is used of the intelligence which purports to communicate messages which are written or uttered by the automatist, SENSITIVE or MEDIUM. The word is used for convenience's sake, but should not imply that the source of the message need be other than the automatist's own subliminal intelligence.'[135]

When a medium becomes the mouthpiece (or writing hand) for various spirit entities, one such entity, usually the first, seems to take charge and vet all those who want to communicate through the channel. This spirit is known as the CONTROL. Unlike real-life telephone operators (with which they have been compared), controls also do most of the talking, often commenting at length on the nature of what is being channelled. This entity is considered to be different from a GUIDE, in that it uses the medium for its own purposes, albeit with the medium's consent. A guide is concerned primarily with the individual's earthly life and spiritual development, whether that individual is a medium or not. Similarly, a so-called 'helper' will be concerned with one particular aspect of the individual's earthly activity, such as healing.

If controls are spirit entities they are not usually considered to be as important as guides and may not be at a particularly high stage of development. Some seem to be quite limited personalities, and the experience they gain as controls may be just as important for their progress as the communications are to the sitters. If these communications tend towards the emotional and sentimental, it is probably an indication that the control is confined to the relatively less advanced levels of the astral plane. As well as giving both mundane advice and information on the spiritual development of a sitter, controls often give philosophical discourses on such matters as KARMA, REINCARNATION, and the meaning of life and death.

Myers's definition includes the alternative viewpoint, also expressed by some mediums, that a control could be a fragment of the medium's own mind. William James investigated the medium Mrs Piper and favoured the view that her control, known as Phinuit, was not a spirit entity with an independent existence outside the medium, but rather a secondary personality of the medium herself. This has been called the UNCONSCIOUS FRAUD THEORY. Geraldine Cummins regarded 'Astor', the author of her AUTOMATIC WRITING, as an off-shoot of her own psyche.

The medium Eileen Garrett considered this as a possibility in respect of her own control, 'Uvani', whose main purpose seemed to be to act as a go-between for those sitting with her and their dead relatives, a preoccupation which she herself regarded as trivial and rather tiresome. As a result of this she gave up mediumship to concentrate on CLAIRVOYANCE. In 1934 she underwent HYPNOSIS in an attempt to discover whether 'Uvani' was a childhood creation of her own mind, since she had vivid memories of distancing herself from reality to escape the torment of a particularly harsh upbringing. Under hypnosis she successfully recalled many incidents from her childhood, but 'Uvani' apparently played no part in her life at that time and the hypnotist was unable to contact him in this way. Another of Eileen Garrett's controls, 'Abdul Latif', expressed a desire to stay in Britain when the medium was planning to go to America, because he had got to know so many of her sitters and wanted to remain available for them, whereupon Eileen Garrett actually handed him over to another medium.

COSMIC CONSCIOUSNESS Cosmic consciousness, a term coined by a Canadian psychologist, Richard M. Bucke, in his book of the same title, is a transpersonal mode of CONSCIOUSNESS, an awareness of the universal mind and one's unity with it.[23] It is a mystical experience in which one loses awareness of one's self and receives illumination and understanding of the significance of life in the universe. Cosmic consciousness is a higher form of consciousness, to be equated with the SUPERCONSCIOUS of other writers and psychologists and not to be confused with the COLLECTIVE UNCONSCIOUS.

'The prime characteristic of Cosmic Consciousness is, as its name implies, a consciousness of the cosmos, that is, of the life and order in the universe. Along with consciousness of the cosmos there occurs an intellectual ENLIGHTENMENT or illumination which alone would place the individual on a new plane of existence — would make him almost a member of a new species. To this is added a state of moral exaltation, an indescribable feeling of elevation, elation and joyousness, and a quickening of the moral sense, ... a sense of immortality, a consciousness of immortal life, not a conviction that he shall have this, but the consciousness that he has it already.'[23]

It was following such an experience that Thomas Aquinas declared that all his learning was 'as straw'. Jacob Boehme wrote, 'The gate was opened to me so that in one quarter of an hour I saw and knew more than if I had been many years at a university.' The illumination may be accompanied or immediately preceded by feelings of ECSTASY and RAPTURE, of being transported as if to another dimension. This notion of rapture should not be understood as being the preserve of certain religious sects which have tried to make it their own exclusive right. As Bucke wrote, 'In contact with the flux of cosmic consciousness all religions known and named today will be melted down. The human soul will be revolutionized. Religion will absolutely dominate the race. It will not depend on traditions. It will not be believed and disbelieved. ... Doubt of God and of eternal life will be as impossible as is now doubt of existence.'[23]

Bucke saw this as the next stage in human EVOLUTION, implying that it would develop naturally. P.D. Ouspensky was more sanguine, believing that such evolution depended on the effort of the individual. 'Further evolution, if it takes place, cannot be an elemental and unconscious affair, but will result solely from conscious *efforts toward growth*.'[139]

CRISIS APPARITIONS/CRISIS TELEPATHY APPARITIONS of people at the moment of death are usually interpreted in the West nowadays not as ghosts but as a means of bringing to conscious awareness information acquired at a SUBCONSCIOUS level. Similarly a mental cry for help in a life-threatening situation can be communicated telepathically, usually to a relative. So crisis apparitions can be understood as a particular kind of crisis telepathy. Sometimes the TELEPATHY may involve other sensory stimuli, such as when the percipient establishes telepathic empathy and feels pain in part of the body that is affected by the 'transmitter'.

Psychologists have been more willing to concede that there may be something worth investigating in this type of telepathy, since the existence of such a faculty would have obvious biological advantages, conferring greater powers of survival on those individuals who possessed it, and so traditional evolutionists can use existing theory to suggest how it arose. However they cannot explain how this sense operates, and the underlying implication that in communicating directly with each other minds are probably independent of brains undermines most basic tenets of contemporary materialistic science. Those scientists who try to investigate telepathy experimentally can never artificially reproduce the kind of situation which creates the right emotional need for communication to take place. In experimenting with sterile ZENER CARDS, empty of meaningful information as well as emotional need to communicate, they seem to forget their initial reason for taking seriously the claims of telepathy as a purpose-oriented faculty that has evolved biologically for use particularly in crisis situations.

CROSS-CORRESPONDENCES After the death of the researcher F.W.H. Myers (1843–1901) various mediums in different parts of the world received messages purporting to come from Henry Sidgwick (1838–1900), Edmund Gurney (1847–88) and Myers himself. Some of the messages were unusually fragmentary and full of classical allusions to no obvious purpose, but when they were studied by Alice Johnson at the London Society for Psychical Research they appeared to fit together like pieces of a jigsaw: one medium's cryptic AUTOMATIC WRITINGS would be rendered intelligible by writings produced by another medium and purporting to come from the same source. The entity claiming to be the deceased Myers said that he had devised these complex communications to eliminate the hypothesis that TELEPATHY was involved. This did not prevent the more sceptical from suggesting that one of the mediums, Mrs Verrall, who had had a classical education was responsible (unconsciously) for producing the whole phenomenon, but this seemed less likely when the communications continued after her death. The other main criticism has been that the connections or 'correspondences' between the scripts were patterns imposed by the reader, following a natural human tendency to establish order on what is essentially disordered, in order to extract some sense out of vague, inconclusive conundrums.

Many who had known Myers accepted the first examples of cross-correspondences as not only authentic but typical of the sort of intellectual exercise his deceased personality might be expected to engage in. His enthusiasm also shone through: 'If it were possible for the soul to die back into earth life again,' 'Myers' wrote through Mrs Holland in 1904, 'I should die from sheer yearning to reach you to tell you all that we imagined is not half wonderful enough for the truth.'

As is the general rule in matters of 'proving' SURVIVAL, those who are temperamentally inclined to accept such evidence find it convincing. Cross-correspondences have continued to occur, but there is no reason to expect them to be of such calibre that all who read of them will be convinced. It is logical that they should be tailor-made for the group of people around the individuals who receive them. Their purpose is to confirm the faith of believers and banish understandable doubts, rather than to convert disbelievers. In connection with proving survival William James suggested the existence of a Law, to the effect that evidence will always be strong enough to assure the converted, but never conclusive enough to influence the total sceptics. This accords with the general principles of self-fulfilling belief systems: we always succeed in finding data to support our own hypothesis. (See CONSENSUS REALITY.)

CROWN CENTRE – See CHAKRAS.

CRYPTAESTHESIA The French psychologist Charles Richet (1850–1935) used the word cryptaesthesia (literally 'hidden sensitivity') for all forms of TELEPATHY, CLAIRVOYANCE and PRECOGNITION. It was a general term for what was later called EXTRA-SENSORY PERCEPTION (ESP).

CRYPTOMNESIA Cryptomnesia (literally 'hidden memory'), sometimes called latent or unconscious memory, is the faculty to bring to mind information that we never realized we knew and cannot remember ever actually learning, information that was hidden in the unconscious. The initial observation as well as the retention in the memory may be unconscious. It has sometimes been exploited when a criminal investigation has obtained information such as a car registration number by questioning a hypnotized witness who would not be able to remember the number consciously. It is also one of the common explanations both for cases of hypnotic REGRESSION, when a person apparently recalls past lives, and for certain so-called spirit communications.

A 'spirit' spoke through a woman under hypnosis, calling herself Blanche Poynings. She claimed to have lived in the time of Richard II and Henry IV and gave very detailed evidence of her life in fourteenth century England. It later turned out, however, that as a child the woman had had a historical novel read to her, 'Countess Maud', and all the information that Blanche Poynings gave, including the character herself, originated in that book.

XENOGLOSSY is also sometimes explained by cryptomnesia. It is well-established that our memories contain much more information than we can ever consciously retrieve, perhaps everything that we have ever experienced. The neurologist, Wilder Penfield, discovered in 1933 that touching a point in the temporal cortex of the brain with an electric probe can cause a patient to re-experience a scene from their past in great detail, as if the whole scene were being played back on a video recorder. A child might by chance hear a philosophical discourse or even a foreign language and reproduce it word for word later in life in a hypnotic trance, and those listening might be led to believe that the speaker is a DISCARNATE spirit.

CRYSTAL-GAZING F.W.H. Myers defined crystal-gazing as 'the act of looking into a crystal, glass ball, or other speculum or reflecting surface, with the object of inducing hallucinatory pictures. ... The pictures, of course, exist in the mind and not in the crystal.'[135] The act of looking at a relatively empty space in which the eye does not easily find a focal point on which to rest, and giving the brain a uniform absence of visual stimuli, seems to encourage the evocation of images from the SUBCONSCIOUS (or the SUBLIMINAL SELF, to use Myers's terminology). When the conscious mind is in a receptive state these images may carry useful information of a precognitive or telepathic nature.

A similar process can be seen in various MEDITATION techniques which involve the use of water as a focus of attention with the intention of restraining the otherwise constant thought processes that have been called 'roof-brain chatter'. This similarity has been recognized in the various 'levels' of CONSCIOUSNESS proposed by Colin Wilson. In meditation the purpose is to 'raise' consciousness, but the shift in awareness that seems to facilitate and accompany clairvoyant perception is probably part of the same spectrum of states.

CURSES Curses are a part of reality in many societies, but in the West they are generally regarded as primitive superstitions. On the other hand, science recognizes that individuals can be influenced by SUGGESTION. Western society certainly seems to believe in the power of advertising which is based much more on suggestion than on the effect of rational argument. So if a taboo is broken and the miscreant knows the traditional consequence of such an action in that culture, that knowledge is probably sufficient to induce the requisite suffering as punishment. Similarly, belief that a powerful person has laid a curse on a place or object can result in the transgressor becoming the victim. Belief creates expectation and the individual's subsequent experience will reflect that expectation. It has even been suggested that a proportion of sufferers from the common cold are victims of this process rather than of the virus. The same effect of 'mind over matter' can work beneficially too, as has been demonstrated by the placebo effect. Good luck charms can work in the same way.

The effect of curses where the victim is in complete ignorance of the situation cannot be explained so easily by suggestion. If the accursed do not know that they have been cursed, why should the curse have any effect at all? Here it is worth remembering some of the attempts to explain how suggestion works and other phenomena which have similar explanations: suggestion works to the extent that the SUBCONSCIOUS has power over the conscious mind and the body, TELEPATHY is a process of sharing information at a sub-conscious level, and HYPNOSIS is a method of communicating directly with someone at the subconscious level and perhaps controlling their subsequent behaviour. Ever since Pierre Janet observed Dr Gibert send Leonie into a hypnotic trance from the other side of the town of Le Havre it has been well-known that hypnotism and telepathy are closely linked. So provided that a certain rapport has been established it should not be too difficult to accept that a 'curse' could be communicated to someone telepathically even without their knowledge. This could be how SPELLS of all kinds work.

A slight difficulty arises where a curse is laid on an object or place and the unwitting transgressor has no connection at all with the originator of the curse. For example, witches commonly cursed the sites on which they were brutally burnt at the stake. Why should later settlers on such a site suffer any effects of such a curse if they knew nothing about it? The implication is that the site itself became somehow so negatively charged that the activities of the newcomers were affected by the 'vibrations' of the place. Such vibrations might not be the result of just one individual's emotional outburst; many other people may have known about the curse initially and reinforced the 'field of negativity' with their own beliefs. Reinforcement by merely tapping into such an emotional field was hypothesized by Tom Lethbridge when accounting for apparitions and presences he referred to as GHOULS. For those who find such imprinting of emotions on the environment a difficult concept to accept a visit to a place like Buchenwald in its eerie silence, void of all birdsong, can be a chilling experience. Reverence may also be a strong enough emotion to imprint on surroundings. Laurens van der Post tried unsuccessfully to photograph cave paintings in the Kalahari, which the bushmen maintained were protected by resident spirits. This is reminiscent of the apparent JINXES that often cause problems to equipment when people try to film psychics and paranormal phenomena.

Another example of the detection of possible fields around concrete objects is in the phenomenon of PSYCHOMETRY, where a SENSITIVE apparently acquires information about people from the objects they have had close to them. This may simply be a way of establishing a link before operating clairvoyantly in other more direct ways using general ESP. On the other hand psychometrists have been able to read the history of objects apparently by sensing the 'field' around them.

D'AAT/D'AATH – See TREE OF LIFE, KABBALISM.

DAEMON To the ancient Greeks a daimon or daemon was a divine being which provided the individual it attended with advice and information. Some may see this as a personification of the 'voice of conscience', others may equate it with a guardian angel or spirit guide. Socrates spoke of his own inner voice or daemon in this way: 'By the favour of the gods, I have since my childhood been attended by a semi-divine being whose voice from time to time dissuades me from some undertaking, but never directs me what I am to do' (Plato, *Theagetes*). When Joan of Arc heard her voices, she interpreted them as directing her in no uncertain terms. In more recent times there are countless stories of people who have avoided potentially fatal action because 'something told me not to do it': in London during the Second World War Winston Churchill changed his mind while getting into his car and walked round to the other side. If he had sat in his usual seat he would have been blown sky-high moments later when the car ran over a bomb. The basic difference between this inner voice and a mere HUNCH is not simply that the voice might be 'heard' but that it is also accompanied by a sense of urgency or certainty.

Many creative people have often declared that their inspiration came from elsewhere in a similar manner. Mozart is perhaps a supreme example of this: we are told that he heard his compositions in their entirety but compressed in time; then he had to toil to transfer the sounds he knew were possible into a form that his audience would appreciate and that his musicians would understand. If Mozart's inspiration operated in the same way as the daemon of Socrates or Churchill's warning voice, it would seem that whole ideas are inserted into the human mind, rather than that voices are actually heard. The SUBCONSCIOUS then translates the message into a form that the conscious mind will understand.

This sort of inner voice is usually regarded as coming unbidden. On the other hand spiritualists consult their guides at will, and it is also a common technique in hypnotherapy and various forms of counselling and psychotherapy (such as psychosynthesis) to consult one's inner adviser, as Jung did in his ACTIVE IMAGINATION. Julian Jaynes has suggested that such voices originate in the right hemisphere of the brain.[90]

DEATH-BED VISIONS – See NEAR-DEATH EXPERIENCES.

DECLINE EFFECT In experiments with EXTRA-SENSORY PERCEPTION and PSYCHOKINESIS scoring often deteriorates, either because the subjects lose interest or because they try too hard. This is known as the 'decline effect'. Both boredom and tension have an adverse effect on PSI performance. The most conducive attitude is relaxed alertness.

DEJA-VU A déjà-vu experience, literally, 'already seen' (French), occurs when one has the feeling that something which one is ostensibly doing for the first time has happened before. Such unexpected feelings are most commonly reported as occurring on first visits to strange places, places which seem uncannily familiar, even to the extent that one seems to know what one is going to meet around the next corner. Other situations in which these feelings of apparent recognition can arise are funerals, marriages and job interviews. Because of the emotions involved in these particular situations, some psychologists have suggested that the combination of excitement and nervousness could stimulate an unconscious desire to find something familiar in the new experience. When vaguely similar memories are aroused these become distorted by the need for familiarity so that they make a more perfect match with the new situation, and one is no longer afraid of the new because it feels familiar. This defence mechanism theory may account for a few instances of déjà-vu, but it sounds very unrealistic as an explanation for most of them. People seldom start off by being really anxious before the onset of the déjà-vu experience, which far from inducing a sense of security can actually be rather unnerving.

An alternative hypothesis put forward by orthodox psychologists is that the two hemispheres of the brain may sometimes operate slightly out of synchronization, so that data from the external world is processed by one part of the cortex in advance of the other. By the time the slower hemisphere has responded to the sensory input, it has already received the information from the other hemisphere and the new data therefore seems familiar. Despite the modern interest in the bi-cameral structure of the brain this particular theory is extremely hypothetical. There is no reason why the two hemispheres might operate at different speeds, and if they really do, we are indeed fortunate that the lack of synchronization does not happen more often.

According to other psychological explanations one may remember certain features of the new experience that have been met before, certain emotional responses for example, and mistakenly generalize that the whole situation is a repetition of a past event. This was part of the explanation put forward by Pierre Janet, one of the first to describe and analyse déjà-vu experiences (hence our continued use of the French term). He also called the effect *fausse reconnaissance* ('false recognition'), suggesting that it represented an inability to respond appropriately to the pressures of the present, which could only be accommodated by enforcing on it a similarity with the past. In other words it was an escape mechanism for those who could not face reality.

Although these theories may account for a few pathological cases of déjà-vu, such as cases which are obsessional or which accompany epilepsy, they do not satisfy the average person who has had one or two such experiences. For example, the apparent memory often relates to what is about to happen as well as to what has just happened. The uncanny feeling that most people describe is reminiscent of the feelings that accompany INTUITION and HUNCHES. It most commonly occurs when one is tired, relaxed, or in a heightened state of sensitivity, situations which also seem to be particularly suited to TELEPATHY, ESP and other psychic phenomena.

There are at least three possible psychic explanations. The most popular among some people is that the place which seems so familiar has been visited in a previous lifetime, or that there are similar past-life connections with the person one is meeting. This may account for some cases, but it would be unwise to jump immediately to such a conclusion. It has been shown that in dreams we often anticipate elements of future experiences, particularly the mental and emotional states associated with them.[47] The déjà-vu feeling could be an unconscious memory of such a dream event. Some have suggested that one could even engage in ASTRAL TRAVEL during sleep, reconnoitring, as it were, places which one would eventually visit physically. The intuitive, precognitive faculties of the mind might also be involved: if one is about to see a place or meet a person that will leave a lasting impression on one's mind for whatever reason, one might have a kind of momentary premonition of that impression or of the future significance of the encounter, and this is interpreted by the conscious mind as a kind of memory. It is worth bearing in mind that such 'memories' are always recognized as being unusual and not at all like normal memories. The déjà-vu experience is often described as being dream-like, which suggests that an altered state of CONSCIOUSNESS typical of clairvoyant impressions and many ESP phenomena may be involved.

DELPHIC ORACLE – See ORACLES.

DELTA BRAIN WAVES – See BRAIN WAVES.

DEMON The term demon is commonly applied to non-human spirit entities which have malevolent intentions. This polarized interpretation is not to be confused with the Greek DAEMON or daimon from which the word is originally derived. Socrates made a point of emphasizing that he was not directed by his daemon: he was still master of his own actions. Demons characteristically try to gain control of human beings. For example, the victims of POSSESSION appear to be possessed by a non-human entity which claims to be a devil. Certain hauntings also seem to have a non-human origin. Both these could be understood as demonic. Some people would want to include POLTERGEISTS under the catch-all term of demons, but poltergeists — contrary to what might be suggested by their popular image — seldom show ill-will, their violence being remarkable in the absence of injury to people and even property.

A recurrent source of worry to some of those who contact DISCARNATE spirits through a MEDIUM is the question of how to recognize whether the entity is good or bad. In the days of witch trials the smell of wet animal fur often accompanied phenomena which were felt to be genuinely evil. We no longer seem to have a nose for these things to such a degree. The simplest test is to ascertain whether the entity is seeking to control the humans it addresses. A demon only serves those it wishes to control: it does not empower individuals in their search for spiritual truth and their endeavours for greater awareness and integration with their HIGHER SELF.

Many spirit communications refer to a hierarchy of spirit beings — GUIDES, GUARDIANS and MASTERS, sometimes known collectively as the White Brotherhood, whose task it is to encourage human souls to evolve spiritually. But humans are also tempted by the entities which belong to the 'Dark Brotherhood'. Those who are not ready to 'move forward into the higher ground of spiritual achievement' will succumb to the temptations of these 'dark forces', which act as necessary testing agents, according to 'Hilarion' as channelled by a Canadian businessman, Maurice Cooke. One should not, however, exaggerate the power of these demonic entities. Control by them is never wholly forced; they tempt, but, as we see in the story of Doctor Faustus, domination must be invited and agreed to — hence the importance of the signature in all such stories of pacts with the Devil. 'They can only influence those who allow them the necessary access, and they would not waste their energy on souls who remain firm in the truth.'[32]

DERVISHES The dervishes are a SUFI sect whose rituals involve hypnotic chanting and rhythmic dancing. Their name comes from the Persian word for 'poor' ('darvish'), used in the same sense as 'poor in spirit' in the Bible, rather than as 'beggars'.

The famous 'whirling dervishes' are members of the Mevlevi

order, founded by the Persian mystical poet, Jalal al-D n Rumi, in Anatolia in the thirteenth century. The whirling moti , symbolic of the rotation of the universe, is intended to induc a state of ECSTASY which facilitates direct communion with Go Once the dance has begun the dancer's left foot should not leave he ground, and the gyrating dance, following an incessant rhythm, causes the exhausted dervish to fall into a trance. This altered state of CONSCIOUSNESS can bring about anaesthesia (during which hot coals are sometimes handled and the flesh pierced with knives), heightened perceptions, telepathic ability, and the power of healing. As in YOGA, all these faculties are incidental to the main purpose, which remains union with God.

DETACHMENT Detachment is one of the prime aims of YOGA, Vedanta and Buddhism. Possessiveness and craving are seen as the root cause of all pain and suffering and the reason why we continue to return to the earth time and time again. Detachment means not simply giving up something one wants, but giving up the desire for it. According to this doctrine a longing for paradise throughout one's life is no way to achieve spiritual salvation; only through detachment may we eventually attain MOKSHA, liberation from the wheel of death and rebirth.

DETERMINISM – See PREDESTINATION.

DEVA In Hindu and Buddhist teachings a deva is a divine being, a god, a devi being a goddess, and a devata a demi-god. The word 'deva' means literally 'being of light', and in English they are sometimes called the Shining Ones. (The Egyptian BOOK OF THE DEAD also mentions 'the Shining Ones' when referring to the realm of the spirit.)

In the West the word 'deva' is also used to denote a spiritual being or ELEMENTAL which has a particular responsibility in nature. At Findhorn in Scotland, where a small spiritual community achieved exceptional growth in the fruit and vegetables they tended, Dorothy Maclean met and communicated with nature spirits such as a Pea Deva, a Spinach Deva and a Tomato Deva. She learned that the landscape and the elements too had their spiritual guardians.[83]

DEVACHAN Literally the devachan (Sanskrit and Tibetan) is a place of light. It is where the 'Shining Ones' dwell, the spiritual or mental plane of being which is experienced between death and rebirth. The Egyptian BOOK OF THE DEAD also describes how the soul joins the 'Shining Ones' after death. The devachan is higher than the astral plane, or Kamaloka, where the kamadevas exist and where the recently deceased can be found. Having discarded the last desires of the personality in Kamaloka, in Devachan the ATMAN or SOUL establishes direct contact with Atman, that part of itself which never incarnates, sometimes called the HIGHER SELF. There the soul rediscovers all its past lives and becomes conscious of all it has learned through experience, so that guided by Atman (the transpersonal spirit) it can decide what experiences are still needed for its spiritual development. Eventually it gravitates back to the physical world for its next incarnation. Some occultists refer to devachan as the mental, rather than the spiritual plane.

DEW According to YOGA teaching there is a hole, called the Hole of BRAHMAN, in the top of the skull at the point where the crown chakra rests. Through this hole drips a dew from the 'Ocean of Nectar', the infinite CONSCIOUSNESS of Brahman, which cleanses and energizes the CHAKRAS, particularly the brow (ajna) centre, as it slowly trickles down. YOGIS sometimes try to stop this dew from trickling away altogether by curling the tongue back against the roof of the mouth.

In the West this dew is known by its Latin name, 'ros'. It enters the body via the PITUITARY GLAND (associated by some occultists with the crown and others with the brow centre) and trickles down into the nose and mouth where it also gives rise to phlegm (Latin: *pituita* 'phlegm').

This image of dew trickling down from the realm of spirit into the head has been known to arise spontaneously to people while they meditate, even though they have had no previous familiarity with the concept and are initially quite bewildered as to what it might mean.

DHARANA This Sanskrit word is usually translated as 'concentration' or 'holding' and constitutes one of the first stages of MEDITATION as practised in raja YOGA and Buddhism. The mind is focused on one particular object or idea to the exclusion of all else. As meditation progresses, the period of dharana is followed by DHYANA, in which thought processes are further reduced.

DHARMA Part of the doctrine of REINCARNATION is the notion that in each lifetime an individual has a particular task or mission to accomplish, through which the soul can best develop. This duty or obligation is known in Sanskrit as 'dharma'. A large part of this task may be accepting the conditions of one's life, accepting one's dharma, with neither resignation nor a sense of frustration, but with cheerfulness and courage. The word also refers to this right way of living in accordance with one's lot, right conduct. The Dharma Sutras are Hindu and Buddhist manuals of ethics. Other meanings of dharma (also dhamma in Buddhism) are 'truth', 'justice' and 'doctrine'.

DHYANA In raja YOGA, MEDITATION involves stemming the flow of thoughts in the mind, not only to the extent that one concentrates on one thing without distraction (DHARANA), but so that thought eventually stops altogether and one is simply aware of the essence of what one is concentrating on. This stage is known as 'dhyana' (Sanskrit). It is the equivalent of *ch'an* in Chinese and ZEN in Japanese, both words having 'dhyana' as their root. Dhyana is usually translated as 'contemplation' or 'reflection', and is characterized by a trance-like mental state divested of a sense of EGO. 'Dhyana consists essentially in a unification or an outpouring of the mind on the object held in view. If the object be a mental or a physical thing, you reach the stage of dhyana. If it be an abstract or a spiritual thing you ultimately attain the final stage, which is SAMADHI.'[26]

DIMENSIONS We see three-dimensional space around us in the physical world. The magus Daskalos regards the psychic world as four-dimensional: to our familiar three dimensions is added a fourth which enables an individual to move from one place to another instantaneously. In the next dimension beyond that, the noetic world, the laws of time are also transcended, allowing one to be anywhere at any time.[122]

Investigating the various rates at which a pendulum rotates for different substances, Tom Lethbridge believed that he had evidence for a plane of existence like a fourth dimension.[112] The things we see around us exist somehow in that dimension too. People who engage in ASTRAL TRAVEL regard what they perceive of their environment as being in this other dimension on the ASTRAL PLANE.[133] Everything has a much more vivid appearance astrally, shining with their own inner light rather than with reflected light as in our physical dimension.

A plane is a section of a three-dimensional body. If a three-dimensional object passed through a two-dimensional world it would naturally appear two-dimensional, and if time were added its apparent two-dimensional form might change inexplicably as seen by two-dimensional creatures. Similarly, if beings existing in another dimension passed through our space-time they might appear and disappear miraculously, simply because we are not aware of the extra dimension. (See also FOURTH DIMENSION.)

P.D. Ouspensky used analogies like this to expound his view that there are six dimensions. 'Six-dimensional space is reality, the world as it is.'[140] Ouspensky argued that we already appreciate the physical world as four-dimensional, time being the fourth dimension, but time is also a limiting factor. 'Three-dimensionality is a function of our sense. Time is the boundary of our senses. ... Every six-dimensional body becomes for us a three-dimensional body existing in time, and the properties of the fifth and the sixth dimension remain for us imperceptible.' In the fifth dimension, eternity, all time past and future becomes perceptible. We then see the 'shape' of the fourth dimension, time, instead of seeing it simply as a straight line as we do now. The fifth dimension, ETERNITY, is the dimension in which time has its existence, the Eternal Now, the state of BRAHMA. The sixth dimension is the dimension in which eternity exists, 'the line of the actualization of other possibilities which were contained in the preceding moment but were not actualized in time.'[140] This is very similar to the views on time and probabilities channelled through Jane Roberts by the entity known as SETH.[166]

In 1921 a Polish physicist, Theodor Kaluza, proposed another dimension of space for electromagnetism, making five-dimensional space-time, but this was never proved. Nowadays, however, mathematicians and physicists often talk of extra dimensions, hyperspace and parallel universes. (See also IMPLICATE ORDER.)

DIRECT VOICE/DIRECT VOICE MEDIUM Direct voice phenomena are not to be confused with CLAIRAUDIENCE. The latter is essentially a private event — an individual hears utterances that are not audible to others, as when Joan of Arc heard her voices. Some clairvoyants are actually clairaudient and hear voices telling them what to say while giving a sitter a READING, but the sitter hears nothing. However, in a circle with a direct voice medium, all the sitters hear a disembodied voice coming from a particular part of the room, perhaps through a cone-shaped 'trumpet'. This phenomenon is also an example of what is known as exteriorization.

The direct voice phenomenon has usually been classified as a form of physical mediumship, because the voices produced are believed to have objective reality. The traditional spiritualist view went so far as to suggest that vocal cords actually materialized, which seems absurdly simplistic. If vocal cords were needed for the effect to be produced, then so was a full set of vocal equipment including larynx, pharynx, mouth and nasal cavity. But if auric field energy can condense into matter, why should it not also produce sound waves directly without any materialization?

Sir William Barrett (1845–1925), one of the founders of the Society for Psychical Research, was convinced of the ability of an American direct voice medium, Mrs Etta Wriedt from Detroit. She was able to carry on a conversation with one sitter while another voice was heard in the trumpet held by another sitter.[130]

Another American direct voice medium was George Valiantine, whose circles a language expert, Dr Whymant, was invited to attend, with the express purpose of questioning the many foreign voices which manifested. What resulted was an amazing exchange between the academic and a voice claiming to be Confucius, in which the pronunciation of Mandarin Chinese twenty-four centuries ago was discussed. (*British Journal for Psychical Research*, March 1928.)

In Britain in the 1940s Louisa Ashdown was a medium who carried on chatting to her guests while voices of deceased individuals were heard coming from another part of the room. The DISCARNATE entities were either identifiable by one of the sitters or conversant with events which were familiar to them. In the case of another physical medium, Helen Duncan, figures actually materialized and spoke.

It is unfortunate that some of the leading direct voice mediums were so often accused of fraud (as were George Valiantine and Helen Duncan). The scarcity of examples of direct voice phenomena since the arrival of easily operated recording facilities makes it tempting to suspect that perhaps not all the voices reported in the past had as much objective reality as was claimed for them. But even if some form of fusing of minds is involved, whether by group HYPNOSIS or in a mass HALLUCINATION or in some as yet undefined co-operative mental feat whereby another level of reality is glimpsed, the existing evidence is still suggestive of psychic faculties unexplained by science and worthy of study. The subject also has a long lineage: 'a voice from heaven' was heard when John the Baptist baptised Jesus. (Matthew 3, 17; Mark 1, 11; Luke 3, 22.) (See also RAUDIVE VOICES.)

DIRECT WRITING Probably the most famous case of writing coming directly from a spirit entity (in contrast to AUTOMATIC WRITING, when a medium writes while apparently controlled by a spirit) is the biblical account of the judgment written on the wall on the eve of Belshazzar's assassination: '*Mene, Mene, Tekel, Upharsin*' (Daniel 5, 25).

In the early days of spiritualism in the nineteenth century it was common for a slate and chalk to be brought into SEANCES so that communicating spirits could write their messages. However, the slate was invariably out of sight when the message was heard being scratched on it, usually on the underside of the table, or concealed by another slate, and it is generally thought that most examples of 'slate-writing' were fraudulent.

More creditable examples of direct writing are recorded in one of the early works on the subject, *Psychography* by Stainton Moses, the medium and ex-curate (1839–92) who wrote under the pseudonym 'M.A. Oxon'. He was a prolific automatic writer himself, and once while writing automatically he was told to let go of the pen, which continued to write without any physical means of guidance or support. His analysis suggests a great variety of conditions in which psychics can produce direct writing. 'In some it is apparently increased by fasting and seclusion. In others its flow is greater when the vital strength has been stimulated by a hearty meal. Some psychics are independent of external aid from a circle. Others obtain phenomena more readily when surrounded by a more or less numerous body of sympathetic friends.'[131]

Other examples of direct writing (and drawing) have been associated with POLTERGEISTS and uninvited communications. Matthew Manning was to become a full-time healer, but while still a schoolboy he was surrounded by various poltergeist effects. One wall in his family home became covered with signatures of people who had lived in the seventeenth and eighteenth centuries.[118,120] The drawings of faces which appeared on the floors of a house in Spain have never been satisfactorily explained.[117] And the messages received both on paper and on computer in Dodleston, England, appear to have come from a man living on the site in the sixteenth century, yet communicating from his own time.[208]

DISCARNATE When a MEDIUM produces a communication while in trance or receives a mental impression of a message for someone present, the common perception is that the agent supplying the information is a discarnate entity. The implication is that this is a deceased individual, one who has previously incarnated, although not all mediums consider that this is definitely the case. Eileen Garrett for example, believed that 'the entities are formed from spiritual and emotional needs of the person involved' and regarded her own CONTROLS as parts of her own psyche. The term 'discarnate' is not usually applied to spirits who never incarnate.

DISEMBODIED A disembodied spirit is one that is separated from the body, and is usually understood as being one that no longer has a physical body, i.e. a DISCARNATE spirit.

DISPLACEMENT EFFECT In ESP experiments intended to test for TELEPATHY it has been found that subjects guessing cards turned up by the 'transmitter' sometimes start identifying instead the *next* card to be turned up. This has meant that the parallel lists of target cards and guesses have to be scrutinized to see if there is any displacement which could be accounted for by this. Obviously the experiment then tests PRECOGNITION rather than telepathy. Sometimes the displacement can be in the opposite direction, suggesting a time-lag in the ESP.

The phenomenon was first noticed by the British researcher W. Whateley Carington in 1939. Instead of the familiar ZENER CARDS 'transmitted' at a rate of several a minute, he used original drawings as targets at a rate of one a day. Every day for ten days he would randomly choose an object which he or his wife would then draw. In the evening the sketch was pinned to a bookcase in a locked room where it would remain until next morning, and every night subjects tried to draw that day's target picture. When an independent adjudicator tried to match both sets of drawings, Carington noticed that subjects tended to draw the target object not only on the target night, but also one or two days before and after the target night. ESP seemed to be operating in the past and the future.

Realizing the implication that ESP was not necessarily simultaneous, Carington brought his results to the attention of another researcher, S.G. Soal of London University, who had tried unsuccessfully to repeat J.B. Rhine's experiments with Zener cards. Urged to take another look at his records, Soal discovered that the results achieved by two subjects, Gloria Stewart and Basil Shackleton, were much more encouraging if one took into account the possibility of a displacement effect. Shackleton was recalled for further tests, and his performance showed that he often consistently missed the present target card guessing the next card instead. In other tests where the agent 'transmitted' at a faster rate, Shackleton guessed correctly *two* cards ahead.[181]

Russell Targ and Keith Harary have referred to displacement as 'a type of psychic noise'. They consider that the common problem in PSI experiments, 'that a viewer may accurately describe a picture that is in a pool of possible targets', comes about because the pictures are placed as it were 'in a psychic bubble', and even though they may be very different 'they become psychically associated'. 'So a viewer who tries to describe the designated target picture may have difficulty distinguishing that picture from the others in the pool. He may describe details of more than one picture, or give an excellent description of one that was not chosen as that session's target.'[193] The Stanford Research Institute consider that they overcame some of the drawbacks of displacement in their REMOTE VIEWING experiments by using actual geographical locations rather than pictures.

(This use of the word 'displacement' in parapsychology is not to be confused with displacement activities, the psychological term for excessive, stereotyped, habitual or repetitive behaviour adopted under stress.)

DISSOCIATION Psychologists since Freud have used the term dissociation (sometimes modified to *hysterical dissociation*) to refer to states of mind in which the usual sense of ego-awareness is lost, when one is so to speak 'beside oneself'. It has been applied particularly to TRANCE states, XENOGLOSSY, somnambulism, post-hypnotic suggestion, amnesia and the phenomenon of MULTIPLE PERSONALITY. As is usual in psychiatry, dissociation is regarded as a pathological condition.

Psychical research, however, whilst using the term to apply to the same basic states, accepts a broader definition which allows for a more positive attitude to some of them. The underlying condition is a mental state of abstraction from the outer world, typical of states of consciousness ranging from light reverie to deep sleep or trance (hypnotic and mediumistic). Some researchers prefer to use the term in a much less absolute sense, allowing for degrees of dissociation: consciousness is never entirely lost but the mind has a split focus, as for example when a MEDIUM carries on a normal conversation whilst continuing to produce a stream of AUTOMATIC WRITING. This type of dissociation among mediums is obviously self-induced. To achieve it involves eliminating distractions and adopting a state of mind that is both relaxed and concentrated.

This is the state of mind that many clairvoyants have described as being a prerequisite for the operation and practical application of all their psychic faculties.

DISTANT HEALING – See ABSENT HEALING.

DISTANT VIEWING – See REMOTE VIEWING.

DIVINERS – See DOWSING.

DJINN Spirits in Islamic mythology, (singular *djinni* or 'genie'), whose bodies are made of smokeless fire. (The bodies of the angels are composed of light.) They were created two thousand years before Adam in a hierarchy of five levels and live, reproduce and die as other forms of life. There are good and evil djinnis. Some live in particular places, and ghouls are a form of djinni that inhabit graveyards. INCUBI and SUCCUBI are also forms of djinni.

DOORKEEPER In spiritualism the spirit GUIDE who stays with an individual throughout earthly life is sometimes called the doorkeeper. Each person has only one doorkeeper. Other guides may come and go during a person's life, having special responsibilities to help in particular ways, but the doorkeeper is said never to change, assuming the role of GUARDIAN ANGEL before birth and continuing till death. This permanent guide is a kind of linkman between the individual and the spirit world, standing on the threshold between this world and the next, hence the term doorkeeper. The doorkeeper also controls the comings and goings of other guides, as the leader of the team, so to speak. Some people prefer to regard the door-keeper's role as being fulfilled by the individual's own HIGHER SELF, which the personality finds it too difficult to recognize except in the guise of another separate entity. Whether this guide is a separate entity or a projected identity, when reliable clairvoyants and SENSITIVES identify him or her, they are remarkably consistent.

DOPPELGANGER – See DOUBLE.

DOUBLE – Emilie Sagée was a teacher in a girl's school in Riga (Latvia). In 1845 she was dismissed from her nineteenth teaching post, not because of any professional failing, but because her pupils often saw two Emilies at the front of the class. Emilie herself was usually quite unaware of her double, which would behave totally independently, wandering about the school grounds and causing confusion to all who saw her, whilst the 'real' Emilie was teaching her class. This was a case of BILOCATION.

A doppelgänger of this kind is sometimes called an astral double, not because the astral BODY detaches itself from the physical body and visits the new location (although this is a common misunderstanding), but because the driving force behind the appearance of the double uses energy from the astral body. In Emilie's case conscious awareness stayed with the physical body and there was no recollection later of what the astral double had 'experienced'. So the astral double could not have been the full embodiment of her astral self with all its emotional baggage; rather it must have been the projection of a copy. The reasons why the copy was projected, however, may well have been emotional and probably were. This double is also sometimes referred to as the ETHERIC DOUBLE, but this is misleading, since the etheric and the physical are never separated. It is also worth remembering that neither astral nor etheric bodies need clothes, in which doubles are always seen, and this should suggest that psychic projection is involved, rather than an actual separation of one 'body' from the others.

Although Emilie Sagée's double was apparently projected unconsciously, people can decide to project an image of themselves into a place they are concentrating on, particularly if there is a strong emotional motive. A powerful longing to be in a particular place may result in such an APPARITION. Strindberg describes such an incident in his autobiography *Legends*. He was seriously ill in Paris once and wished he were with his wife's family in Germany. As he felt this longing he glimpsed his mother-in-law playing the piano. Later he received a rather concerned letter from his mother-in-law: she had actually seen him standing near her while she was playing the piano. The fact that Strindberg was ill at the time has persuaded some people to assume that this was an OUT-OF-THE-BODY EXPERIENCE (OBE), similar to a NEAR-DEATH EXPERIENCE (NDE). But the fact that Strindberg was seen (complete with clothes and other accoutrements) suggests that psychic projection was involved. Doubles of this kind are sometimes referred to as APPARITIONS of the living.

Another famous case was that of Mr and Mrs Wilmot, reported in the *Census of Hallucinations*.[179] In 1863 Mr Wilmot was returning home to Bridgeport, Connecticut, when the vessel he was travelling on, *The City of Limerick*, ran into a fierce storm. For over a week the storm raged and Mr Wilmot got little sleep. The morning after the storm abated Mr Wilmot's cabin-mate greeted him with a strange remark: 'You are a lucky fellow to have a lady come to visit you like that.' He went on to describe a scene which corresponded exactly with what Wilmot had thought he had dreamed, namely that his wife had visited his cabin in her nightdress, hesitated at the door on realizing that another man was in the room, then approached, bent down and kissed her husband. When Wilmot arrived home his wife asked if he had received her visit. Hearing about the storm she had lain awake worrying and had visualized herself crossing the ocean, finding the ship and enacting the scene witnessed by both Wilmot and his cabin-mate.

From these three cases it appears that the extent to which conscious awareness is projected with the double may be proportional to the amount of deliberate will behind the act of projection. Emilie Sagée's doubles were beyond her conscious control and she was not aware of their location; Strindberg wished and caught a glimpse of where his double appeared; Mrs Wilmot made a deliberate effort and remembered everything that her double saw and did.

In cases where one sees one's own double, or more commonly where one sees one's own body from the point of view of a double, we usually speak of an OUT-OF-THE-BODY EXPERIENCE. Although OBEs may be regarded as including cases where the double is seen, the majority are private experiences. Their frequency compared with instances of bilocation visible to others, suggests that the psychic projection of a visible double is more difficult, perhaps requiring more energy, than a simple projection of one's awareness.

Another kind of double is not covered by the idea of projection at all. Here PRECOGNITION or even TIME-SLIPS seem to be operating. Goethe once saw his own double riding towards him along a road in Alsace. He was with his fiancée at the time. The figure he saw was wearing a grey and gold suit. Eight years later he was on his way to visit the same woman and passing the same spot when he realized that he was now wearing the clothes he had seen in his earlier 'vision'.

DOWSING When the Israelites needed water in the desert, Moses was told by God to take his rod and 'smite the rock, and there shall water come out of it' (Exodus 17, 6.). Despite the over-simplified description, this could well be the earliest recorded instance we have of water-divining, dowsing for water. The art of dowsing is also called rhabdomancy. The dowser commonly uses a divining-rod, which is probably the origin of a magician's wand. Although the divining rod can be a simple straight stick, the most common method of dowsing for water is with a cleft stick: one holds the top two ends of a Y-shaped twig, and the other end dips up or down when one passes the spot where water can be found.

Almost anything can be searched for by this method, and almost any material can be used for a divining rod, although dowsers will usually have their favourite. The most frequent woods are peach, willow, hazel and witch-hazel. Bare hands have also been effective, giving rise to the name 'hand-trembler' for a dowser. Nowadays bent metal coathangers are particularly common; sometimes two pieces of wire are bent at right angles and slotted into the plastic casing of two old ballpoint pens, one held in each hand with the uncovered metal projecting away from the body. A PENDULUM can also be used as a dowsing instrument. Like the divining rod, the pendulum can be made of virtually any material. Sometimes it has a hollow cavity in which a sample of the material the dowser is searching for (known as the 'witness') can be inserted. The pendulum is particularly useful when map-dowsing without actually visiting the site in question.

One of the first to mention dowsing in unmistakable terms was a fifteenth-century alchemist, Basil Valentine. The physicist Robert Boyle (1627–91) was the first to describe the divining rod in England. He cites the use of a forked hazel twig to detect the presence of metallic ores in the ground.

Dowsing is one of the few unexplained phenomena which more and more orthodox scientists find they have to take seriously. Alfred Wegener was not taken seriously when he originally put forward his theory of continental drift; he also traced geological fault lines by dowsing with a pendulum. Now both his theory and his method are accepted. All major pipeline companies in the USA employ at least one dowser, and in the Vietnam war dowsers were used to find Vietcong tunnels.

Despite the proven usefulness of dowsing, no one really knows how it works. Dr Zaboj V. Harvalik investigated the phenomenon in the 1960s. He was a physics teacher at the University of Missouri and scientific adviser to the US army. He believed that dowsing, in which he had been interested in Czechoslavakia, was basically electrical. He discovered that everyone he tested was able to detect an underground electric current of at least twenty milliamps. Lower currents were detected by fewer people, but some could detect to even half a milliamp. Drinking a few glasses of water beforehand seemed to improve a dowser's ability, as did a small amount of whisky. Testing a German dowser, Wilhelm de Boer, he concluded that it was his adrenal glands that actually detected water, but he found that a piece of aluminium foil placed in the centre of the dowser's forehead completely inhibited his dowsing ability. (It is interesting to note that this is the site of the 'third eye' of clairvoyants, the external site of the brow CHAKRA of the SUBTLE BODY.)

Bearing in mind that brain activity is also electrical, Harvalik tried to sense the approach of people he could not see by using his dowsing rod. He found that he could and his ability was increased if the person approaching was thinking excitedly. This may suggest that the same basic principles could account for both dowsing and TELEPATHY, and that 'radiations' are not involved at all.

Other observations also suggest that dowsing is related to psychic faculties. Like ESP its effect is inhibited by hostile or sceptical observers, it works better when the dowser is not concentrating hard (the so-called 'DECLINE EFFECT'), and it can be affected by HYPNOSIS.

It is generally conceded that dowsing must be a mental effect. It is clear that it cannot be a purely physical effect because of the map-dowsing phenomenon, (unless the map is somehow imprinted with the same radiations as the territory which it represents — which would fit snugly with some ideas of SYMPATHETIC MAGIC but utterly confound modern science). So most investigators agree that the movements of the rod or pendulum are caused by the muscles of the hands, which are controlled unconsciously when the information being sought is registered by the mind. Holding a rod or pendulum enables the SUBCONSCIOUS to transform information that is hidden from conscious awareness into external events, which the conscious mind can then take cognizance of. In other words, the hand movement is a way of bringing unconscious perceptions to conscious awareness.

So according to this view it is the dowser who actually causes the rod or pendulum to move. In the same situation the same rod will move in different ways in different hands. A dowser can decide what kind of movement the rod will make to give the required information.

Although this view neatly dispenses with the need for radiations to explain the dowsing phenomenon, doubts still remain. It is difficult to banish the idea of radiations altogether. Dowsers can detect the extent of the AURA around the body, and some have traced the lines of force known as ley lines — two examples where radiations are thought to be involved. (See also RADIESTHESIA.)

DREAMS The average person starts dreaming after about an hour of non-dreaming sleep and then dreams once every ninety minutes for a period lasting from ten to thirty minutes. So in an average seven to eight hour night's sleep we have three to five dreaming periods, which gives the average adult a thousand dreams a year.

The dream phase was first recognized by rapid eye movements (REM sleep), but there are other physiological changes: the brain becomes more active, the pulse becomes less regular, blood pressure changes, and breathing can become shallower and quicker. One widely held belief is that dreaming is essential for the development and continued efficiency of the brain, whilst dreamless sleep is necessary for physical growth and well-being. DRUGS which reduce the amount of dreaming (alcohol, amphetamines and barbiturates) also affect mood and behaviour, and can result in HALLUCINATIONS. Contrary to what one might expect, anxiety and tension also reduce the amount of dreaming sleep.

Dreams are still not understood by modern science. One of the first physiological theories was outlined in the eighteenth century by Thomas Hobbes, who claimed that dreams were physical in origin: people dreamed when they were suffering from indigestion. Since then there have been many other theories, usually involving the needs of the brain and reflecting current understanding of its physiology. These theories are subject to fashion and often reflect the main preoccupations of the day. For example, the theorist will point out that the body gets colder when it sleeps, and will suggest that dreams might be the result of the brain 'warming up' ready for action when we wake — a theory which seems to owe more to the behaviour of the internal combustion engine than human physiology.

According to the *rubbish theory* the brain needs time to sort out the data gathered during the day; the data is sifted during dreams, rather like clearing up the paperwork in an office, and what is not worth storing is discarded. Another theory suggests that with so much new data coming in during the day fresh connections are needed in the brain, and these are made during dreams. These theories are clearly a reflection of the way bureaucracies deal with records.

Nowadays the brain is often likened to a computer. According to the *computer theory* dreaming enables the brain to assimilate new information, filing it away accessibly. An alternative view suggests that when we are asleep the 'computer' is switched off and starts functioning purely at random. This is sometimes called the *materialist theory*: dreams are the result of stray impulses taking the line of least resistance in the brain, and their content is fortuitous and lacking in significance.

This last theory has been modified by psychologists, who distinguish between the sleeping conscious mind and the UNCONSCIOUS, which they claim never sleeps. They consider the unconscious able to dramatize or dress up its preoccupations whilst the conscious mind sleeps, giving the materialist theory quite an unmaterialistic aspect. So Freud interpreted dreams mainly in terms of repressed ideas in the unconscious, particularly sexual frustrations, and Jung believed that dreams revealed the psyche.

Recognition of the fact that the body is virtually paralysed during REM dreaming sleep has given rise to the *genetic rehearsal theory*. Michel Jouvet carried out experiments on cats in which the part of the brain that kept the body paralysed during sleep was damaged, so that paralysis during sleep would not occur. As a result the cats acted out all the basic actions — fighting, feeding, etc. — while they were 'dreaming'. This is thought to explain the scenes we experience in dreams — the equivalent actions for humans being less basic and physical because we are social animals, so the situations we rehearse are usually social situations. However, the theory does not explain why we need to 'rehearse' in the first place.

In all these orthodox theories the higher brain, responsible for all thought process, is supposedly out of action or at least out of control. This means that the dreams are being created by the lower brain, but the lower brain is only concerned with essential bodily functions, the autonomic system. Ordinary dreams do tend to be irrational, governed by an association of ideas rather than any inherent logic; but dreams can include analytical thinking, particularly those known as *lucid dreams*. None of the orthodox theories adequately explains this phenomenon.

In *lucid dreams* the dreamer is aware of dreaming and can decide whether to continue the dream or bring it to an end; the dream is manipulated by the dreamer. The common dream experience of flying is typical of lucid dreams, and we seem to be able to train ourselves to 'fly' to specific places and bring back information. This is also known as ASTRAL TRAVEL, since the occult view is that the astral body disengages from the physical body during sleep. TELEPATHY and ESP have also been reported as a result of this kind of dream.

In recent years lucid dreams have been studied by psychologists and have increasingly been linked in their research with OUT-OF-THE-BODY EXPERIENCES, which most psychologists regard simply as lucid dreams. This has come about partly as a result of some psychologists' own experiences of OBEs, both deliberate and spontaneous, (e.g. Susan Blackmore, Celia Green), and partly because lucid dreams are usually much clearer than ordinary dreams and OBEs are renowned for the vibrant clarity with which the 'traveller' sees the environment. However, this identification may be spurious. The unusual clarity of a dream experience is in itself not sufficient reason to classify it as a lucid dream. Some people who periodically have premonitive dreams claim that these too are exceptionally clear — this is how they are initially recognized as premonitive, but they are beyond the dreamer's control.

Researchers such as Celia Green and Peter Fenwick claim that we can train ourselves to dream lucidly. But as with most OBEs, lucid dreams tend to start spontaneously. Only during the dream itself do knowledge and control come into play, as they do in OBEs — when the sudden idea of visiting someone down the road actually takes one there. But there is at least one major difference: in the OBE one has no control over what is actually going on when one 'arrives' at the desired place, whilst in the lucid dream we seem to be able to script other people's parts in the scene too.

The neurologist, Peter Fenwick, has experimented with lucid dreamers by asking them to do specific things in their dreams. When told to draw a large triangle on a board, the instruments recorded the dreamer's actual eye movement following movement of the dream hand. Psychiatrists have set people problems to solve in this type of dream. Subjects are given a task, such as deducing the next letter in a series immediately before going to sleep (O — T — T — F — F — ? — ?), to see whether they can wake up with the answer. They often realize that they have the answer during the dream (in this case S — S, for they are initial letters of the numbers one, two three, etc.), sometimes apparently waking themselves up at precisely that moment. Another simple question of this kind asked of sleepers by the American psychiatrist, Morton Schatzman, was, 'What one-syllable English word has no rhyme?'.

There are some famous instances of creative people coming up with ideas in dreams. Kekulé visualized the molecular structure of benzene in a day-dream after puzzling over the problem for weeks. This type of problem-solving seems to be related to intuition. Coleridge composed the poem 'Kubla Khan' in an opium-induced dream. Science has little to say on this aspect of dreams, yet it is a preoccupation that has been with humanity since the beginning of recorded history.

The ancient Egyptians and Greeks had their own way of exploiting the ability to solve problems during lucid dreams. They consulted the gods by sleeping in special rooms in temples or other sacred places in order to receive divine guidance in their dreams, possibly aided by special herbs. At Epidaurus, Asklepius the god of healing might appear in such an 'incubation dream', and on waking the dreamer's ills would be cured.

Compared with people of today, the ancient Greeks showed just as wide a variety of credulity and scepticism with regard to the significance of dreams. Plato described Socrates as writing poetry in obedience to an instruction received in a dream while awaiting execution, and the politician Demosthenes claimed to receive instructions from the gods during dreams. But dream interpretation also included the notion of wish-fulfilment, such as Plato's explanation of men's incestuous dreams of their mothers (long foreshadowing Freud), and these dreams were regarded as less significant.

Information acquired in dreams has often been regarded as having religious significance. The appearance of the ARCHANGEL Gabriel to Mohammed, which took place while he was asleep in a cave on Mount Hira, and which led to the writing of the Koran, could be described as a vision as much as a dream. In the first two chapters of St Matthew's gospel four dreams are reported, in which there was a warning or again the appearance of an ANGEL in the manner of a vision. Both dreams and visions can be revelatory experiences.

The revelation was of a more mundane kind in the case of the Chaffin Will. In 1921 a North Carolina farmer, James A. Chaffin died. His will drawn up in 1905 left everything to one of his four sons, leaving the other three and a widow unprovided for. In 1925, one of the other three sons dreamed that his father appeared at his bedside. The first time this happened, the father did not communicate, but later he appeared again and told his son to find his will in his old overcoat pocket. On searching the pockets the son found not a will but a piece of paper, bearing the message 'Read the 27th chapter of Genesis in my daddies's [sic] old Bible.' Between the pages at the appropriate place in his grandfather's Bible another will was found. This will was eventually probated and the case was successfully brought to court to enact the apparent wishes of James Chaffin.

It was the appearance in a dream of a dead friend that first brought D.D. Home's mediumistic abilities to his notice. As a boy he dreamed of his best friend who told him that he had died. The following day he received news that the friend had in fact died in the night.

Truly revelatory dreams are comparatively rare. But prophetic dreams of a more trivial nature are quite common, as J.W. Dunne proved.[47] Most people have an odd example of such a dream, which the sceptics put down to coincidence, but Dunne showed that by careful monitoring of one's dreams one can see that the predictive elements in them are far too frequent to be merely coincidental. He also came to the conclusion that it is not the actual future event so much as one's subjective perception of it, the future state of mind, which is brought to awareness in a precognitive dream. This can account for variation in the degree of objective accuracy of such PRECOGNITION.

The degree of certainty of a prophetic dream also depends on the level of awareness from which the insight is obtained. (See PROPHECY.) It is unlikely that actual future events are ever seen in dreams. What we can be made aware of are probabilities which have not yet been actualized. This enables the individual to take evasive action if the probability foreshadowed in the dream had a tragic outcome. Dreams in which you see yourself involved in a rail accident are popularly regarded as prophetic if you subsequently change your travel arrangements and then read of the train you did not take crashing. Yet the prophecy was wrong: you were not involved in the accident at all. This is a clear indication that most so-called prophetic dreams do not reveal the future: rather they draw attention to probabilities and still give relatively free rein to the individual.

In the instance of a dream about a life-threatening situation it is common for the dreamer to feel intense fear and panic. The degree of emotion involved suggests the activity of the astral (emotional) body, which operates on a level of awareness only slightly higher than normal. This is again in keeping with the idea that what we see are probabilities. If a tragic scene were witnessed in a dream without any emotion but with calm detachment, such awareness would be more characteristic of the so-called mental body, which has a much higher level of CONSCIOUSNESS, and the scene would be more likely to be an actual future event viewed from a higher perspective.

According to occult belief the astral and mental BODIES detach themselves from the physical and etheric during sleep. This can be understood as a change of gear, rather than of separate 'envelopes' unwrapping and detaching themselves in the manner of Russian babushka dolls. In waking life the soul's experience is mediated almost totally by what is perceived by the physical senses; during sleep perception is also possible in the astral and mental modes. Whatever is perceived in this way is usually lost to conscious awareness, although at the moment of waking, during the time when we switch back into the normal physical mode of perception, some of the experiences are transferred to the memory of the conscious personality. This transference often involves distortion, since perception on other levels of awareness can be represented only imperfectly in terms of physical reality. The idea that this transference actually takes place while we are waking up gains credence when we consider how much ESP has been reported as occurring in a HYPNOPOMPIC state. If we accept that similar phenomena also occur while falling asleep (HYPNAGOGIC images), then at those moments perhaps we manage to keep the channels to the conscious mind open while switching gear into that other mode of consciousness which prevails during dreams.

DROP-IN COMMUNICATORS MEDIUMS sometimes bring through messages from apparently deceased individuals of whom neither they nor their sitters have any knowledge at all. These unexpected visitors are sometimes called 'drop-in communicators'. For some reason drop-in communications seem to be much more common in home circles than with professional mediums. Often they come from individuals who seem lost in a sort of limbo (See RESCUE CIRCLE), sometimes the communicators just seem to want a chat, and on rare occasions they want to get in touch with a particular person who is still alive. If the information given by drop-in communicators about their lives can subsequently be verified, this might be taken as good evidence of survival. Supporters of this view can cite many examples of such cases, whilst their detractors have a stock list of objections and alternative explanations.

The most common explanations which apparently dispense with the need for survival are CRYPTOMNESIA and the SUPER-ESP HYPOTHESIS: either the medium is recalling long-forgotten material which had been stored in the memory unconsciously, or the information is being accessed by ESP. This super-ESP hypothesis can be neither proved nor disproved, and is used by some to explain any phenomen where the alternative theory involves DISCARNATE entities. In the case of drop-in communicators it means that the medium has virtually unlimited telepathic links with a variety of minds and paranormal access to other examples of stored information, such that a picture of the so-called communicator can be constructed and a dramatization of his or her presumed current mental state can be performed. To many this suggests a feat which stretches one's credulity even more than a belief in survival, and there remains the question of the medium's motivation in putting on such a performance. Furthermore, if such a faculty is as available to mediums as the anti-survivalists suggest, the implication seems to be that those in home circles have greater expertise in 'super-ESP' than the professionals, who seldom mediate drop-in communications. On the other hand the super-ESP hypothesis might be an irrelevance. For those who accept drop-in communicators at face value, their infrequency with professional mediums is simply a reflection of the fact that professional mediums focus their attention more successfully on the specific needs of their sitters, whilst home circles are to a certain extent open to all comers.

Geraldine Cummins was an extremely self-critical medium who was constantly on the look-out for instances where cryptesthesia (her preferred term for cryptomnesia) or TELEPATHY would provide plausible explanations. She always considered the possibility of material given in a SITTING being picked up by telepathy, which she regarded as a fusing of the minds of the medium and the sitter, and then dramatized. She even professed to prefer this explanation, 'For such is human vanity, I should prefer to think that my own mind had created without premeditation, without knowledge, a character that was wholly alive to a very clever, astute Prime Minister.'[39]

In March 1945 Geraldine Cummins was giving a sitting to her close friend and associate E. Beatrice Gibbes, who was hoping to obtain a message from her sister-in-law. Instead they received a message from 'a stranger intruding at a sitting', who had no connection with either of them. Her name was Marguerite Le Hand. 'She says she worked for a long time with an important public man — knew him well. She gives the name Frank. She says she wants to talk to David about Frank ... she has something important to say about Frank.' The way in which all Marguerite Le Hand's messages were relayed through the medium's CONTROL, Astor, is a reflection of the communicator's extremely cautious approach to making the communication. She always tended to stand back and seemed to want to give as little away as possible. After the sitting the medium seemed to remember that David Gray had been mentioned. He was the US Ambassador to Eire and had had a few sittings with

Geraldine Cummins in Dublin in 1943. A few days later at another sitting they asked for further information about Marguerite Le Hand. The control, Astor, gave more details about his previous exchange with her, saying among other things that 'She seems to have had a confidential post with Frank' and that Frank was 'the most important businessman in his country'.

In April 1945, two days after the death of President F.D. Roosevelt, Marguerite Le Hand again communicated for a second time through Astor, explaining why she had wanted to speak to David Gray: 'She wanted to warn him that Frank was coming over.' When Miss Gibbes wrote to Mr Gray he was able to confirm some of the details Astor had given about Miss Le Hand and set about verifying others such as the time and place of her death. Further Le Hand communications were made in May and June, and David Gray eventually attended a sitting with Geraldine Cummins in which he received messages which he accepted as being from Roosevelt himself. In November 1947 further communications from F.D.R. were addressed to a sitter whom Geraldine Cummins had been led to believe was a clergyman, but was in fact Mackenzie King, the Prime Minister of Canada, and he too accepted the messages and the Le Hand material as being entirely consistent with all he knew of the characters involved.

As well as the facts ultimately being verified one hundred per cent, a task which entailed consulting many different sources, one is struck by the consistency of character which the communicators demonstrated and which was further described by Astor. Miss Le Hand's professional position had depended on extreme discretion and her initial approach was coloured by the same caution. It was unusual for a communicator not to communicate in the first person, yet all of Miss Le Hand's messages were relayed through the medium's control, Astor. But perhaps more convincing than all the veridical information and consistency of character, all of which just might be explainable by some grand super-ESP hypothesis, is the fact that the medium should initially pick on someone as obscure and unknown as a confidential secretary who had died three years previously, about whom she knew nothing and of whom few people had ever heard. Geraldine Cummins believed that the initial motivation to communicate must have come from Marguerite Le Hand herself and that the Le Hand and F.D.R. material is evidence of 'continued characteristic mental activity on the part of deceased persons'. 'This series of communications,' she concluded, 'presents what may be regarded as first-class evidence of survival.'[39]

DRUGS Drugs have always been a means of attaining an altered state of consciousness. It is said that they have this effect by weakening the close-fitting alignment between the astral body and the physical, resulting in a tendency for OBEs. The orthodox medical view is that substances such as LSD, hashish, ether, chloroform and alcohol have a chemical effect on the brain which induces particular types of hallucination.

SHAMANS all over the world have used naturally occurring drugs, particularly mushrooms with hallucinogenic properties. In Siberia they used the fly agaric, 'magic mushroom', which some have identified with *soma*, the drink of the Vedic gods. The modern habit of smoking tobacco had its origins among native American tribes, who used it as a means of relaxing and withdrawing their attention from the world around them. They made other drugs from plants, such as cohoba, the peyote cactus, jimsonweed and morning glory as well as mushrooms, and used them to go into mediumistic trance and communicate with spirits.

In medieval Europe witches used a narcotic produced from the root of the purple flowered *mandragora* or mandrake. The drug supposedly had magical powers, especially as a love-potion, and the plant was also worn as a protection against disease. It is mentioned several times by Shakespeare (*Romeo and Juliet, Othello, Antony and Cleopatra*). Some see a resemblance in the mandrake's forked root to the human body without the head, and this may have contributed to the belief in its magical powers. It also led to the belief that uprooting the plant caused it to utter a scream which was so terrible that it could kill. This was no doubt an effective ploy to protect the interests of those who gathered the plant in medieval times, but they evidently ended up believing their own publicity and went to great lengths to protect themselves by gathering mandrakes by remote control, as it were, by tying a dog to the plant and leaving food for it just out of reach, so that the hungry animal would uproot the plant. The mandrake belongs to the potato family, as do thornapple (*datura*) and henbane (*hyoscyamus*) which also give rise to hallucinations, particularly of a sexual nature, and sensations of flying. This is the common explanation for the various experiences of witches at the witches' sabbath. (Henbane is also the poison administered to Hamlet's father.)

In 1800 Humphry Davy (1778–1829) discovered nitrous oxide, otherwise known as laughing gas. When he sniffed it he experienced a sense of exhileration: 'I existed in a world of newly connected and newly modified ideas. I theorized. I imagined. I made discoveries.' Roget (author of the *Thesaurus*) also tried it and declared 'My ideas succeeded one another with extreme rapidity, thoughts rushed like a torrent through my mind.'[207]

Nitrous oxide actually alters BRAIN WAVES. Although it can produce unconsciousness, in smaller doses it simply reduces inhibitions and makes one want to play like a child. A child's playfulness is characterized by the desire to experiment without passing judgment, which is also deemed to be of crucial importance to creative thinkers. Opium-induced dreams have been another source of creative inspiration: Coleridge composed the poem 'Kubla Khan' in this condition.

LSD also affects brain waves, but the resultant altered state of CONSCIOUSNESS is more characteristic of disorganised dreaming than of creative, playful inspiration. LSD induces hallucinations by overstimulating part of the brain. Familiar objects become extremely beautiful, the sense of time becomes distorted, and the senses intereact, so that music, for example, may produce visual experiences or bodily sensations.

There is sometimes a similarity between LSD-induced hallucinations and the clairvoyant perceptions of a MEDIUM: LSD subjects have reported meeting spirit entities and the astral bodies of the deceased. The difference is that the medium reports what is perceived to a sitter who can validate the information, whilst the LSD subject's experience is totally subjective, involving no other person, and cannot therefore be checked.

Some believe that research into the similarities between the altered states of consciousness of mediums and those brought about by LSD may indicate what happens in the brain. 'The LSD subject can, for example, suddenly enter a state similar to a mediumistic trance; his facial expression is strikingly transformed, his countenance and gestures appear alien, and his voice is dramatically changed. He can speak in a foreign language, write automatic text.'[71]

Mescalin, the most active chemical in the peyote cactus, has a similar effect to LSD. It was mescalin that Huxley took in his search for a beatific vision.[88] He noticed that whilst mundane objects were rendered extremely beautiful and vibrant, things that were normally seen as objects of beauty became dull. The mescalin-taker's response can switch inexplicably from uncontrollable laughter to extreme panic. In America peyote is still the most frequently administered drug in a religious context, and the religion Peyotism is a mixture of Christian theology and native American tradition.

Despite the frequently reported mystic visions and accompanying mystical feelings, drug-induced hallucinatory experiences are inherently different from the effects of MEDITATION. For one thing, whilst drugs lead to a distorted view of the world and the illusory perception of non-existent things, meditation results in a sharper perception of external reality. Also drugs can lead to 'bad trips' as well as good, suggesting an uncontrolled descent into the recesses of the unconscious where the Shadow, the darker side of the psyche, holds sway. This does not happen with meditation. Drugs seem as likely to access the lower reaches of the SUBCONSCIOUS MIND as the higher levels of the SUPERCONSCIOUS, whereas meditation is always directed towards the transcendant. This may be because meditation naturally requires discipline. Only when that discipline has also been applied when aiming for a drug-induced or drug-assisted experience, can one hope for a comparable positive result.

EARTH-BOUND Earth-bound spirits are SOULS that are unable to pass immediately to the 'higher' levels of existence after death. (See AFTERLIFE.) Too strong an attachment to material existence holds these souls back from progressing. It is a common assumption that earth-bound souls must be evil, but this is a misunderstanding. Selfish desires *can* hold a soul back, but it is just as likely that as Alice Bailey wrote 'great personal love for those left behind or the non-fulfilment of a recognized and urgent duty holds the good and beautiful in a somewhat similar condition.'[5] 'A mother, desperately longing to clasp her child once more to her breast, will frequent a place for some time after death.'[133] Moreover, at least a substantial proportion of HAUNTINGS are thought by many to be caused by earth-bound spirits who were almost invariably the victims rather than the agents of wrongdoing. Sylvan Muldoon and Hereward Carrington consider there are only four possible reasons why spirits can be earth-bound. They are conditions or functionings of the mind during the time leading up to death and continuing inappropriately beyond: desire, habit, dreams and insanity.

Severe cases of earth-bound spirits of the kind that give rise to

HAUNTINGS and POSSESSION can be dealt with by the ritual of EXORCISM. Less serious cases may be attracted to RESCUE CIRCLES, who take it upon themselves to point souls that are temporarily lost or disoriented in this way in the right direction.

ECSOMATIC – See OUT-OF-THE-BODY EXPERIENCES.

ECSTASY Although ecstasy is commonly understood as a physical sensation, in mystical terms it signifies the blissful state in which spiritual awareness, COSMIC CONSCIOUSNESS and visions replace the normal awareness of one's surroundings. The Greek origin of the word means 'standing apart' or 'being displaced'. The related Christian concept of rapture ('being seized') is a more sudden, violent form of ecstasy. Kabbalists went into trance and communicated with God through the ARCHANGELS while in this state. The equivalent in YOGA is the mystical consciousness of SAMADHI, the aim of MEDITATION. All these disciplines achieve ecstasy through quiet meditation and contemplation, but others such as the SUFI sect known as the DERVISHES use rhythmic chanting or dancing. Sufis also believe that in the experience of ecstasy the differences between Jew, Christian and Moslem disappeared.

The physical sensations associated with ecstasy are feelings of lightness, elevation or LEVITATION, and a vision of light. Illumination may be mental too. Time seems to stand still, and there is an intense feeling of calm and peace. In ecstasy one feels that one is in contact with a force beyond the self in a transpersonal realm. Christian mystics have equated ecstasy with a direct experience of the presence of God, following which 'mystic union' may occur.

Some believe that during this trance-like condition, labelled by orthodox psychology as a xenophrenic state, the body may actually die for a while (referred to in mystical writings as *mors osculi* – the death of the kiss) while the soul is transported to other realms. This accidental death could be momentary or permanent. Kabbalists believed that the major Old Testament patriarchs and prophets died in this way, and that this was the ultimate desire expressed in Solomon's Song of Songs.

A less mystical view of ecstasy has been put forward by Marghanita Laski (in *Ecstasy*), which is virtually identical to Maslow's concept of PEAK EXPERIENCES. The 'triggers' that can induce these ecstatic feelings include aesthetic experiences, natural scenery, sexual love, physical exercise and creative activity. This wider definition of ecstasy shows that one cannot automatically equate it with mystical illumination, although the two may overlap. Laski also notes that illumination can be a non-ecstatic experience, as may occur in the face of death or severe pain.[107]

ECTOPLASM When MATERIALIZATIONS occur in a SITTING with a PHYSICAL MEDIUM, the substance out of which they are formed is known as ectoplasm (Greek, literally 'exteriorized matter'). It has also gone under other names: *psychoplasm, ideoplasm* (mind stuff and thought stuff) and *teleplasm* when materialization is at a distance from the medium's body. The word 'ectoplasm' was first coined by Charles Richet (1850–1935), the French psychologist and psychical researcher. He believed it was formed in a way similar to the formation of mist out of water vapour with a drop in temperature. It was emitted slowly as a misty vapour from the pores and from the bodily orifices — mouth, ears, nipples, etc. — or as a more solid substance from the top of the head, the fingertips, solar plexus and chest. Richet described the process he witnessed in a French girl in Algeria, Marthe Béraud (also known as Eva C.): 'A kind of liquid, or pasty jelly, emerges from Marthe's mouth or breast which organizes itself by degrees, acquiring the shape of a face or a limb.'[161] Out of this substance solid parts of a body were formed, often slightly smaller than life-size, or two-dimensional representations resembling cardboard cut-outs.

To the touch ectoplasm has been reported as soft and elastic at first, like a spider's web, fine thread or elastic cord. Then after a few minutes it becomes more substantial and fibrous, but usually remains moist, cold, sticky and rubbery, only rarely being reported as dry and hard. Normally the ectoplasm returns to the medium's body or suddenly dissolves into thin air, but when samples have been retained with the medium's consent they have been found to contain salt and calcium phosphate and resemble animal tissue. When Harry Price investigated the medium Helen Duncan the ectoplasm he analysed appeared to be a mixture of wood-pulp and egg-white, which he claimed she had swallowed beforehand and regurgitated during the SEANCE. (Helen Duncan was later imprisoned for fraud.)

The frequency of fraud in the past may have contributed to the apparent reduction in cases of materializations in recent years and there has been little modern research into the phenomenon. Whatever ectoplasm is or is not, it need not be involved in all materializations. APPORTS seem to be dematerialized objects that are reconstituted. The emission of ectoplasm is also superfluous to the appearance of APPARITIONS, which occur without any medium being present. The logical conclusion could be that nothing is actually drawn from the medium at all. Yet when ectoplasm has been seen to retreat back to the medium's body, either because light has suddenly been shone on it or it has been seized by one of the curious sitters, the medium has invariably suffered pain and injury as a result, ranging from an open wound and haemorrhage to bruising and unconsciousness. This would be consistent with the theory that the medium's etheric body is involved, since damage to it must inevitably be externalized in the physical body. Another theory is that it is not ectoplasm itself that is drawn from the medium's body but a special kind of energy which allows ectoplasm to condense out of what would otherwise be insubstantial apparitions.

EGO Latin for 'I' ego often seems to be a most confusing word, used by different people in very different senses. These senses range from an idea of the self which belongs very much to the visible personality in the phenomenal world to a more esoteric, spiritual concept which is almost diametrically opposed to it.

In Freudian terms the ego is the rational self, that part of the personality which probably coincides most closely with the way we see ourselves, but influenced on the one hand by the instinctual id, and on the other by the internalized sense of duty, conscience, guilt, etc. preserved as the super-ego. The id, ego and super-ego constitute the whole psyche.

For Jung too the ego is the conscious self, that part of our psyche which has a continuing sense of personal identity; but it is subordinate to the SELF, which may be hidden from our awareness and which we gradually learn more of and bring to overt expression in the process of individuation; so the ego is also an expression of the Self.

In esoteric writings the word ego is used more in the sense that Jung used the word 'Self': the ego is the ruler of the psyche, it is the SOUL, the link between the body and the MONAD. According to the *Upanishads* the ego-body is the fifth of our BODIES (after the physical, etheric, astral and mental). Other occultists place the ego on the mental PLANE, just one level above the astral. Awareness of this ego is the most that can usually be achieved in MEDITATION. This is the level to which the soul eventually rises after death and prepares for its next incarnation, when the ego will take on a new body and a new personality.

Confusion sometimes arises when people use the word ego in its more popular psychological sense, signifying the egocentric aspects of the personality, even though they may be discussing esoteric teachings. When ego is used in this more limited sense, the term HIGHER SELF is sometimes used to denote the soul-level ego.

EGYPTIAN BOOK OF THE DEAD – See BOOK OF THE DEAD.

EGYPTIAN CONCEPTS By the second millennium BC the ancient Egyptians had developed a complex picture of the nature of humanity. According to this view an individual consisted of several entities. There was the natural, physical body (*khat*), with its life-force or KA, which also represented the personality and was regarded as a kind of DOUBLE, capable of an independent existence rather like the astral body; it could also dwell in a man's statue. The heart was the seat of the emotions and the intellect and was weighed in the Hall of Judgment after death, since it bore the imprint of the individual's character and the weight of all misdeeds. The soul-principle or psychic force was the BA which inhabited the ka and after death could also still visit the body. The ba was not visible, but the *khaibit*, the shadow or ghost, which was often associated with it, was. If we can equate the eternal ba with the soul, the *khu* represented the even more important eternal aspect of an individual, the spirit, although it was conceived not so much as a divine spark, as an intangible casing of light around the body, a spiritual body.

It is interesting to see to what extent this view coincides with later occult traditions. The ka is clearly related to both the etheric and the astral BODIES, although another less well understood life-force, *sekhem*, may have been closer to the modern concept of the etheric. Even the at first sight unfamiliar notion that the *ren* or name of an individual lived on as yet another independent entity in heaven may simply be a different way of describing the eternal impression our actions make on the AKASHA.

According to Egyptian cosmology the universe was created not out of chaos or pre-existing matter but out of nothing; the Creator-God was Ptah in northern Egypt and Khnum in the south. As well as creating the universe he created all the other gods. In the second century AD GNOSTICISM drew on Egyptian mythology, using old gods and symbols in new Christian rituals. Osiris became identified with Christ, Isis with Mary, and Hathor with Sophia.

EIDETIC IMAGERY/EIDETIC VISION The tendency to 'see' what the mind retains in memory as if it were 'out-there', as a form of HALLUCINATION, is known as eidetic imagery. After witnessing a bad motorway accident and helping the injured, people have been known to see injured passengers while continuing their journey home. The same term can be applied to the ability of some people to visualize an object or a scene in great detail, focusing on any part of it as if it were actually present before their eyes. Nicola Tesla maintained that he first built his inventions in his head and saw them working. This mental faculty seems to be common among creative people, another form of it being Mozart's ability to hear a whole composition in his head in a fraction of the time it would take to play.

This ability to visualize in minute detail could be involved in experiences that have been called TIME-SLIPS, when someone sees a building that no longer exists — or in some cases never did. But where eidetic vision of an actual past scene occurs, some form of ESP (RETROCOGNITION) would also have to be involved. There is clearly a connection between eidetic vision and hallucination. Eidetic vision can also be prompted by HYPNOSIS, so that hypotized subjects 'see' what they are instructed to see, which points to the conclusion that part of the mind (Thomas Jay Hudson's SUBJECTIVE MIND) can overrule the senses and dictate what is perceived.

EIDOLON A ghost may be thought of as the spirit of a deceased person, or as an astral shell or image of the body left on the astral PLANE when the SOUL which projected it has already passed beyond that level of existence. An eidolon is a ghost in this second sense. Most esoteric teachings state that the astral BODY dies only when the soul is finally separated from it at the extinction of that particular personality, although some say that the astral shell may survive longer, without the soul, until all the emotional energy which went into its creation has been used up. The view that a ghost or shade could have a separate existence from the immortal soul was part of many ancient belief systems, e.g. the Egyptian concept of *khaibit* and the Roman *umbra*.

ELECTRONIC VOICE PHENOMENA — See RAUDIVE VOICES.

ELEMENTALS The term 'elemental' is used in several senses. In one common meaning it is used to refer to the non-human nature spirits and DEVAS which nurture animal life and vegetation and are associated with the elements. There are six main groups: gnomes (spirits of the earth), salamanders (spirits of fire), sylphs (spirits of the air), undines (spirits of water and rivers), fauns or satyrs (spirits of animal life), and dryads (spirits of vegetation). Some of these groups include several kinds of spirit. For example fairies, brownies, elves and pixies are all considered to be sylphs, as are the classical oreades, Diana's mountain nymphs. Undines include the mermaids and mermen of Northern Europe and in classical terminology can also be subdivided into the oceanides and nereides of the sea and the naiades (nayads) of fresh water. There were also various kinds of gnomes − trolls, kobolds and dwergers, all feared by miners, who regarded them as responsible for accidents in mines. Elementals were often used as a way of explaining the inexplicable. Salamanders, the fire-spirits, were seen as Will o' the Wisp or Jack o' Lantern, the flames that appeared over marshland when marsh gas caught fire.

In another sense, occultists sometimes refer to 'elemental essence', 'psychic matter' or 'noetic matter', a substance on other levels of reality out of which our thoughts and desires, reinforced by the will, mould 'elementals'. (A THOUGHT-FORM or elemental in this sense is also sometimes called an 'elementary'.) An individual who harbours strong desires or broods on negative emotions creates an elemental which can be regarded as a living entity, capable of doing the bidding of its creator, conscious or unconscious, provided it has been invested with sufficient energy to survive long enough.

In certain cases elementals (in this second sense) may have been invested with so much energy initially that they achieve a certain degree of independence of their creator, as TULPAS can. They may then return to torment their creator in the form of HAUNTINGS or POSSESSION.

POLTERGEISTS are also sometimes referred to as elementals. This is fairly consistent with the occult view above, since most researchers into poltergeist phenomena regard them as being the result of repressed anger, fear or guilt, strong emotions which are externalized as violent bursts of energy.

Although elementals of this type are generally regarded in a negative light, they can be put to good use. American Indian medicine-men used to hold influence over dangerous animals by means of elementals of their own making. They created an elemental by visualizing for example a 'good' golden snake, which would always be with them and which would enter any physical snake they came across and render it tame and harmless.[17]

Elementals are normally invisible but they are perceptible to the trained clairvoyant. It has also been suggested that when certain

PHYSICAL MEDIUMS achieve MATERIALIZATIONS, it is not some departed spirit that appears to the sitters but a thought-form of the elemental (or elementary) kind, produced spontaneously and unconsciously by the medium and rendered visible to others present.

In another sense elementals are also regarded by some occultists as agencies of KARMA. An emotional thought-form which an individual created against others in a previous life will one day attach itself to the etheric body of its creator, who must then absorb it and transmute it through suffering in accordance with the suffering caused previously to others.

ELONGATION While going into TRANCE an individual may feel as if the body is expanding. This can be explained as the effect of loosening the normally rigidly-held links between the physical and the SUBTLE BODIES, and often one might feel that one has actually left the body. However, sometimes a MEDIUM in trance is seen by others to change, the most common change being an elongation of the body. When this happened to the Victorian medium, D.D. Home, he was measured and seen to have grown by as much as eleven inches. There are other physical changes that can affect a medium, in particular the face, which can take on the likeness of a communicating entity, a phenomenon known as TRANSFIGURATION.

EMANATIONS Emanations from a human being's various BODIES create the AURA, which is visible to SENSITIVES. Detection of the emanations from the etheric body enable the PSYCHIC to diagnose a person's state of physical health, whilst those from the astral body reveal emotional and psychological conditions. Sensitivity to these lower vibrations in the aura is fairly common among clairvoyants and people with psychic ability. Fewer psychics are sensitive enough to perceive the aspects of the aura which emanate from the mental body, the frequency at which awareness of the SOUL's memory (and past lives) may be experienced. Misunderstanding what is perceived at the astral level as originating at the mental level can lead to misinformation being given by an inexperienced sensitive. In such cases what the clairvoyant says may simply confirm a sitter's hopes and fears instead of providing insight into soul-purpose.

Many belief systems throughout the world include the notion that everyting in the UNIVERSE emits emanations. PSYCHOMETRY is thought to work on the principle that those emanations can be detected and interpreted by a psychometrist. The Melanesian word

MANA has been adopted to refer to this power emanating from objects. It includes the human L-FIELD and its counterpart in the inanimate world, both of which it is claimed have been shown to exist through KIRLIAN PHOTOGRAPHY.

Another use of the word 'emanations' refers to the agencies of creation in NEO-PLATONIST thought. The world consists of emanations from the First Cause, God the Ultimate, who is transcendent and stands behind the created universe. Such emanations were sometimes called *Aeons*. In Alice Bailey these emanations are the seven RAYS: 'all people are units of consciousness breathed forth on one of the seven emanations from God.'[5]

EMPATH An empath is someone who can tune in to another person's feelings, experiencing them as intensely as if they were their own. SENSITIVES can become aware of another person's emotional state by viewing the AURA, in particular that part of it originating from the astral body. This is perceived primarily through the heart CHAKRA, although understanding of the condition will be achieved by bringing higher centres into play, especially the brow chakra. Empathy without understanding is of limited value.

ENLIGHTENMENT The aim of YOGA is enlightenment, a state of CONSCIOUSNESS in which one passes beyond the present world to absolute peace. In Zen Buddhism this experience is known as SATORI. It is the means of attaining NIRVANA, extinction of the SELF and liberation (MOKSHA) from the WHEEL OF REBIRTH.

ENNOIA Menander, a Samaritan GNOSTIC in first-century Antioch, held that the UNIVERSE was created by Supreme Thought or Ennoia, acting through ANGELS or Aeons. He also taught that Christ was an Aeon who entered the body of Jesus at his baptism. It was the Aeon's departure from the body of Jesus on the cross which resulted in the cry of despair (the last words).

EN-SOF In KABBALISM God as Absolute Being, the Infinite, is known as En-Sof (Hebrew, 'No thing'). This aspect of the Divinity is similar to BRAHMAN in Hindu mysticism, although En-Sof is essentially transcendent, standing behind the phenomenal world, whilst Brahman is both transcendent and immanent.

ENTITY Entities that communicate through MEDIUMS or CHANNELS usually describe themselves as deceased personalities. Although non-human spirit entities are regarded as playing a key role in the cosmos, generally speaking they do not choose to communicate through mediums. Some mediums, such as Eileen Garrett and Geraldine Cummins, are content to accept that the entities that regularly communicate through them (their CONTROLS) may be sub-personalities of their own, rather than separate beings. In this respect the use of the word 'entity' does not necessarily imply separateness; it refers rather to a personality which is recognizable as such. In cases of MULTIPLE PERSONALITY new 'entities' with different identities may arise from within an individual in the manner of sub-personalities. If they are believed to come from outside the phenomenon is known as POSSESSION.

The word 'entity' has been used in a slightly different sense in the writings channelled from an entity calling itself Michael. Here it refers to what many call a GROUP-SOUL. The individual soul is referred to as a 'fragment' and anything between one thousand and one thousand two hundred fragments eventually reunite to form the entity of which they are a part.[216]

EPIPHENOMENALISM An epiphenomenon is an additional phenomenon, a by-product or a symptom. Epiphenomenalism is a theory of the relationship between the brain and the mind, first developed by Thomas Huxley (1825–95). He suggested that CONSCIOUSNESS was a by-product of nervous processes and that what we consider to be mental processes are merely 'epiphenomena' accompanying physical activity in the brain. The theory exists in several forms.

On the one hand epiphenomenalism is defined as 'the doctrine that consciousness is merely a by-product of physiological processes and that it has no power to affect them' (*Collins English Dictionary*). This is the orthodox scientific view of the mind/body dichotomy: the MIND is simply an aspect of brain activity, a secondary aspect of physical changes taking place in the brain. Although consciousness is different from the physical activity of the brain, it is nevertheless generated by that activity, and so the mind has no independent existence, no powers of causality or will. This is the *materialist* account of the mind. In its most extreme form, as subscribed to by behaviourists, this is known as the *peripheralist* view: the possession of mind is nothing more than a disposition towards certain patterns of behaviour. The less extreme (but equally materialist) *centralist* view, also known as the *identity* theory, is that all mental processes can be identified with physical processes in the central nervous system.

Most orthodox scientists subscribe to one of these versions of epi-phenomenalism, maintaining that the mind does not exist in its own right. It was in such terms that the British philosopher Gilbert Ryle (1900−76) denied the existence of mind, saying it was a 'category mistake' and he coined the famous 'ghost in the machine' metaphor to characterize the imaginary agent of consciousness.[172] Orthodox scientists regard the mind not as a separate entity, but as an epiphenomenon of the brain. They hold that the brain 'gives rise to' the mind, which is simply an abstract quality of the organic brain. Because they regard the brain and the mind as essentially one, they are sometimes called monists.

However, another definition of epiphenomenalism states that 'mental events, and especially consciousness, occur during physical brain activity *but are not caused by physical activity*. They are supposed, rather, to run in parallel but to be autonomous' (my italics). (Richard L. Gregory in *The Oxford Companion to the Mind*.)[70] The autonomy of the mind is denied by all other versions of epiphen-omenalism. This 'parallelism' is a more dualist interpretation, although it does not go so far as the absolute dualism of Descartes, who believed that the mind was completely separate from the robot-like brain, which it could control via the PINEAL GLAND. Whether they believe that the mind is an extension of brain activity or that it is autonomous and runs in parallel to the brain, all epiphenomenalists deny the ability of the mind to affect brain activity, or to initiate and control physical actions.

According to a more extreme kind of dualism brain and mind are regarded as separate and they interact with each other to create our experience. During the 1970s neurologists became increasingly dissatisfied with the ephiphenomenalist theories of mind/brain parallelism and mind/brain identity. More scientists came to suspect that mind and brain were different in kind and could interact. They started to reverse the bottom-up approach of the behaviourists, who claimed that physical states held causal control over mental activity, in favour of a new *mentalist* view, 'in which primacy is given to emergent top-down control, exerted by the higher, more evolved forces in nature over the less evolved. In the brain this means a downward control of the mental over the neuronal.'[70] (R.W. Sperry in Gregory (ed.): *The Oxford Companion to the Mind*.)

There has always been a thread of mentalist thinking (especially in Britain) which is at variance with epiphenomenalist theories: Charles Sherrington (1857−1952) and John Eccles (1903−) regarded the brain as the tool of the mind, the *detector* whereby the inner life of the soul is apprised of external experience. On the other hand, the Russian psychologist, A.R. Luria (1902–77), dismissed both mentalism and epiphenomenalism. 'It is implausible to think of the brain as a "generator of mind".' However, among orthodox psychologists and neurologists epiphenomenalism still seems to hold sway.

ESOTERICISM Many religious beliefs contain a core element of mysticism. This is usually poorly understood by the majority of the followers of a particular religion. The outer (exoteric) form of religious observance is generally so over-simplified and ossified that special training is necessary for those few who wish eventually to understand the inner (esoteric) truth that lies hidden (occult) within. In the words of C.J. Jung, 'All esoteric teachings are seeking to grasp that which is unfolding in the psyche without which it is impossible to have any insight.'

Some maintain that esoteric Christianity was the result of the influence of Greek MYSTERY SCHOOLS on early Christian teaching. According to this view, the essence of Jesus's message is a very simple idea: you don't need the Old Testament prophets any more; you can be your own prophet. When Jesus said 'Abide in me and I in you' there was no implication that he was referring only to his disciples; this was the message for all. But quite early on there grew up the notion that certain knowledge (*gnosis*) was suitable only for highly developed souls, initiates, and not for the ordinary believer. Origen, the third century Egyptian theologian, was one who drew this distinction most blatantly, speaking of the 'popular, irrational faith' of 'somatic Christianity' on the one hand and gnosis which led to 'spiritual Christianity' on the other.

But it is easy to see how dangerous some of the statements of esoteric religion might be to people who are not ready for them. To be told bluntly 'You are God' would be misunderstood by the average person and could lead to problems of psychological inflation. Esoteric training aims to awaken our spiritual awareness naturally (or rather reawaken it, since it is an awareness that we all once had before we 'fell' into matter) through self-discipline, inner work and outer action. To insist on two or three rigid grades of humanity as certain GNOSTICS did, is a fatal distortion of esotericism, just as misguided as the habit of fundamentalist sects which proclaim their own rightness while denying all others the validity of their Ways. An over-protective attitude on the part of initiates is a dangerous thing: esoteric teachings are reserved for those who seek them, but they should not be withheld arbitrarily.

Many of Jesus's parables have been given esoteric interpretations which it is suggested Jesus himself used to enlighten his inner circle of disciples. For example, the parable of the Prodigal Son (Luke 15, 11–32) is interpreted as representing humanity's descent into the world, our forgetfulness of the divine spark within and the subsequent rejoicing when we return to the Father. This descent of the soul into flesh and its eventual return is also symbolized in the *Song of the Pearl* in the apocryphal Acts of Thomas.

ESP – See EXTRA-SENSORY PERCEPTION.

ESSENES The Essenes had a philosophy similar to the PYTHA-GOREANS, although whether they believed in REINCARNATION is disputed. They always wore white, followed strict rituals with many ablutions, and had a complex system of initiations. They were vegetarian, made no animal sacrifices, had few if any personal possessions and did not engage in trade. They lived in Palestine at the time of Jesus and their activities were documented by Philo and Josephus. A similar sect existed in Egypt at the same time, the Therapeutae, although these were stricter, adhering to a reclusive life devoted to MEDITATION and fasting.

ETERNITY In common parlance 'eternity' means a period of time that seems to go on for ever: 'It lasted an eternity,' we say. But this is '*an* eternity'. Eternity itself is different entirely. It is not simply an unending extension of time, it is outside time altogether. Thomas Aquinas recognized this distinction when he wrote that God is eternal while hell is unending. Eternity is the counterpart in the noumenal world of time in the phenomenal world. Time is the shadow that eternity casts on the wall of Plato's cave. Plato himself described time as 'the moving image of eternity'. Poets see time as an ever-rolling stream, but mystics see it as part of MAYA. Absolute reality is eternity, where, as St John says, 'There shall be Time no longer' (Revelation 10, 6).

In moments of ECSTASY and PEAK EXPERIENCES people some-times have a sense of timelessness. This temporary 'escape' from the limiting conditions of time suggest that some kind of eternity or 'eternal now' exists and is accessible to us in special states of CONSCIOUSNESS. It then becomes conceivable that time could be an aspect of the way our conscious awareness organizes experience:

time is a function of consciousness. Raising or changing our consciousness in some way may then allow time to fall away and blend in with the rest of three-dimensional space. P.D. Ouspensky hypothesized six DIMENSIONS in all: he regarded time as the fourth dimension, eternity or the 'perpetual now' as the fifth, and a sixth dimension of 'the actualization of other possibilities which were contained in the preceding moment but were not actualized in "time".' Each dimension represents infinity to the dimension below it since it is impossible to measure it in terms of lower dimensions.[140]

If time is simply a creation of the mind in matter, can we expect to experience eternity as soon as we leave this world? The fact is that even now we do not experience time, the fourth dimension, in the way that we experience the other three. We can walk around a three-dimensional object and view it from all sides, but we are bound by time to move continuously in a straight line. 'We are one-dimensional beings in relation to time' (Ouspensky). Even the appreciation of the fourth dimension (time) that we do have develops slowly for each of us as we get older. So when we are no longer bound by matter and the senses, we may suddenly get an overview of four dimensions which is new to us and which we will have to learn our way around, just as a baby has to learn to cope with our three-dimensional world. This overview might explain how DISCARNATE communicators can 'see' a certain 'distance' into the future. But appreciation of the actual nature of the fifth dimension, eternity, in which souls presumably exist between lifetimes, must come as slowly and as partially as our own appreciation of time. Only by entering the sixth dimension will we fully comprehend the fifth dimension, eternity, and that can only come when the SOUL ultimately leaves the 'endless' cycle of rebirth. (See WHEEL OF REBIRTH.) This eternal cycle is depicted graphically in one of the most universal symbols for eternity, Ouroboros, the SERPENT biting its own tail. 'My beginning is my end.'

ETHER Hindu and Buddhist teachings speak of AKASHA (Sanskrit, 'space') as a universal medium. This concept was also used in the West when scientists such as the Dutch physicist Huygens tried to explain light as vibrations in the 'aether' by analogy with sound waves in air. Although the existence of the ether was hypothesized by many scientists such as the physicist and psychical researcher Sir Oliver Lodge (1851–1940), the generally accepted conclusion is that it does not physically exist at all in the way that they surmised.

However, in his presidential address to the Society for Psychical Research in 1939, the philosopher H.H. Price (1899—1984) postulated a different conception of the ether, one which Raynor Johnson later took up. 'I postulate a psychic aether or "substance" which partakes of some of the qualities of matter (such as localization in space and retention of form), and which is yet capable of sustaining thought-images and emotions: something, in short, which is a bridge between matter and mind.' This ether is 'a medium which provides a bridge between the material and the mental, which is plastic and influenced by matter on the one hand and modified by mind on the other to be a conveyor of thought-images.' This was Raynor Johnson's way of explaining many extra-sensory faculties such as PSYCHOMETRY and TELEPATHY as well as phenomena such as HAUNTINGS.[92]

More recent researchers see no need for such a MEDIUM, considering that it betrays too strong an attachment to superfluous and inappropriate spatial concepts. After all, the mind does not exist in space, so why should its functioning in what are commonly called psychic phenomena require a medium with spatial characteristics? To some people experiments in which one subject projects a mental image on a wall or screen which another subject then 'reads' suggest that the image is localized. Belief in the ability of non-spatial minds to communicate directly with each other, without the need for thoughts to be 'transferred' across space, does not necessarily conflict with the idea that THOUGHT-FORMS might be created in a spatial medium. In such a notion the ether is basically a substratum of the astral plane, and some occultists have called it the astral sphere. P.D. Ouspensky wrote that, 'The "astral sphere" of the occultists which permeates our space is an attempt to find a place for phenomena which do not fit into our space. ... The "astral sphere" from an ordinary point of view may be defined as the *subjective world*, projected outside us and taken for the *objective world*.'[140]

Going back to the Hindu origins of the concept of the ether, as it was adopted by western Theosophists in the nineteenth century and before it was corrupted by the pseudo-scientific materialist interpretation of spiritualists, we can recognize it as a useful philosophical concept. It represents the whole of the space-time continuum, the whole of the phenomenal universe of which we are aware. P.D. Ouspensky suggested that to beings living in a two-dimensional world, the third dimension would be non-existent, or if it were surmised it would be called the ether. According to this line of thought the ether represents the boundary between our universe of space-time and eternity, the fifth dimension in Ouspensky's system. (See DIMENSIONS.) From a viewpoint in eternity one can see everything that has ever happened in the phenomenal world and everything that ever will happen. The events are impressed on the outer surface of this ether, visible from eternity, in the same way that the surface of a two-dimensional figure is visible from a third dimension at right angles to it. Hence the AKASHIC RECORD.

ETHERIC BODY – See BODIES.

ETHERIC DOUBLE If by 'double' we mean an apparently separate copy or image of an individual, the use of 'etheric' is misleading. (See DOUBLE.) The etheric BODY is the energy-field which surrounds the physical body and sustains it as a living organism, being separated from it only at death.

EURHYTHMY An art devised by Rudolf Steiner, eurhythmy sought to allow people to express themselves in the manner of poetry with their whole being. According to certain principles, all poetic feeling which would formerly have been expressed in speech was translated into movements of the body. 'The new art of Eurhythmy seeks to give direct expression, from out of the individual performer, to the rhythm which pervades the human organism and Nature.' This is not to be confused with the Dalcroze Eurhythmics.

EVOLUTION Occult belief asserts that man has not descended from the ape, but that the ape has degenerated from man.

Human evolution is developing mentally and spiritually. If we consider the religious attitudes and preoccupations of past civilizations we see a progression. The ancient culture of India developed a complex system of metaphysical philosophy by exploring the high spiritual planes. The Indians were true mystics. The next great civilization was that of the Egyptians, whose mysteries were more concerned with the astral plane and developed in their initiates the ability to experience astral consciousness and leave the physical body. The Egyptians were not so much mystics as occultists. The Greek civilization which followed was much more concerned with the aesthetic aspects of the physical plane. Although Platonic philosophy attached supreme importance to the notion of ideal forms in the realm of ideas, our knowledge of these was obtained by building on our experience of actual physical reality, however flawed. Finally, modern Western civilization has become totally absorbed in the physical plane, preoccupied with the 'conquest of matter'.

This downward trend from higher levels to the lowest may seem depressing, the Fall writ large and spread over millennia, so to speak. But if we consider the knowledge that Western civilization has acquired over the last few centuries we can also see the reverse trend. Humanity began with very speculative ideas about the external world and about the human organism. Physics, chemistry and biology were developed until the workings of matter and the human body are understood today as never before. Meanwhile the scientific discipline of psychology has gone some way towards improving our understanding of the human personality. Might not the etheric BODY also be subject to scientific scrutiny in the near future? Occultists have long believed so.

The trend now is towards tempering the reductionist techniques of detached science with a feeling for the harmony of the whole, which can so easily be destroyed by many human activities. In penetrating deeper and deeper into the mysteries of matter, human understanding is not necessarily getting further away from the higher spiritual PLANES, although the danger of losing sight of the higher levels is that much greater.

Teilhard de Chardin believed that the evolutionary process on earth was now in the realm of CONSCIOUSNESS rather than in biological life. 'Since man's arrival the evolutionary pressure seems to have dropped in all the non-human branches of the tree of life. And now that man has become an adult and has opened up for himself the field of mental and social transformations, bodies no longer change appreciably; they no longer need to in the human branch; or if they still change it will be only under our industrious control.'[196]

In Hindu teachings everything evolves from the densest matter, through various forms of life, from one kingdom to another, until it reaches spiritual purity. 'The various stages of existence ... are inanimate things, fish, birds, animals, men, holy men, gods, and liberated spirits; each in succession a thousand times superior to that which precedes it; and through these stages the beings ... are destined to proceed, until final emancipation is obtained' (*Vishnu Purana*). Teilhard de Chardin's synthesis of evolutionary theory and Christianity is reminiscent of these ideas. He considered everything as evolving towards the OMEGA POINT or God-Omega in which all would eventually rest when the phenomenal world came to an end.

EXOMATIC/EXOMATOSIS – See OUT-OF-THE-BODY EXPERI-
ENCES.

EXORCISM People are sometimes apparently possessed by demons
or by DISCARNATE human spirits; places are sometimes haunted or
affected by a POLTERGEIST. Exorcism is the process by which the
person or place is freed from the offending influence. It may involve
prayer and ritual; it may take the form of gentle persuasion or
strenuous command.

POSSESSION and exorcism are both part of Christian and Moslem
belief. Jesus 'cast out unclean spirits'. Paul and Silas were imprisoned
in Macedonia because they cast out a spirit which had enabled the
employers of the possessed girl to make a large profit from the
spirit's predictions. This particular exorcism is sometimes taken as
grounds for condemning MEDIUMS and CHANNELS because the
'spirit of divination' was not obviously evil and in fact exhorted
everyone to listen to Paul and Silas, following them for several days
shouting that 'These men are the servants of the most high God,
which shew unto us the way of salvation' (Acts 16, 16–17).

In both the Anglican and the Roman Catholic Church there are
a few priests who specialize in exorcism. The desired effect may be
achieved by one simple command from someone such as St Paul: 'I
command thee in the name of Jesus Christ to come out of her.'
Exorcists of lesser authority may take much longer. In 1974 the
exorcism of thirteen-year-old Karen Kingston in North Carolina
took three whole days, during which time she underwent profound
physical changes and even levitated. Thirteen demons were expelled.

Whilst the phenomena we call possession and exorcism undoubtedly exist, there is less certainty concerning whether and in
what proportion of cases discarnate spirits are involved. A large
body of opinion holds that the so-called possessing entity is a
repressed or unacceptable part of the individual's own personality.
It is a fact that an important part of the process of exorcism seems
to be naming the possessing entity. This was also part of Jesus's
technique as an exorcist: 'And Jesus asked him, What is thy name?
And he answered, My name is Legion: for we are many.' This
naming achieves two things: first it gives an identity to a complex
of actions which the possessed person could not accept as their
own, and then it enables that behaviour and whatever feelings and
motivations are associated with it to be banished for good, whilst
the person is absolved of all responsibility. It has been noticed that
most cases of possession and MULTIPLE PERSONALITY are in people

who have suffered some terrible trauma, often as a child. Karen Kingston, for example, had seen her mother kill her father when she was seven. Ever since she had been withdrawn and 'mentally retarded' and her physical condition deteriorated inexplicably. But through the crisis brought on by her condition and the exorcism she was cured.

Even though exorcism works, there are dangers involved. In 1975 an Anglican priest exorcised a man in Barnsley, Yorkshire, and within a few hours the man had murdered his wife in a most brutal way. Was he really possessed, or had the priest's ritual simply convinced him that there was a devil in him rather than that it has been driven out? As Eliphas Lévi, the French occultist said, 'He who affirms the devil, creates the devil.' This may be the technique involved in exorcism.

Even if a large proportion of cases of possession are actually multiple personality, some of the details which come out during exorcism still strongly suggest that discarnate spirits are sometimes involved. One girl was apparently possessed by her two sisters who had been smothered at birth because the parents could not face the prospect of bringing up triplets. In this case possession was initially by invitation, and for many people it is a much easier explanation to accept than the alternative theory, that the parents' subsequent feelings of guilt were somehow transferred to the surviving child who had never been told of the crime.

Exorcism of haunted places is also considered to be very evidential of the idea that discarnate spirits are involved, because no individual living person can be seen as the root cause. It was to such a discontented discarnate spirit that SPIRITUALISM owed its beginnings in the 1840s. Poltergeist phenomena have often been associated with young people with excess psychic energy, but they have also sometimes been exorcised by persuading the offending spirits that they are dead and must 'move on'.

EXPERSONATION While in a dissociated state, such as a trance or having an OUT-OF-THE-BODY EXPERIENCE, an individual consciousness may temporarily enter the body of another. This form of 'possession' is known as expersonation to distinguish it from POSSESSION by a DISCARNATE entity. Tibetan mystics sometimes used a form of expersonation to transfer knowledge from master to pupil or to guide the actions of a ruler. Alice Bailey considered that she was OVERSHADOWED in this way by 'The Tibetan' when producing many of her occult writings.

EXTRA-SENSORY PERCEPTION/ESP The term 'extra-sensory perception', usually abbreviated to ESP, was first coined by J.B. Rhine in 1934. It is defined by G.N.M. Tyrrell as 'A term of very general scope used to cover all cases in which knowledge of things or events is acquired by a person, in whatever manner, without the use of the ordinary channels of sense-perception, of logical inference or of memory.'[203]

Certain mental, psychological and physiological conditions have been found to be favourable and perhaps necessary for the successful operation of ESP. Many psychics, Eileen Garrett for example, believe that a certain kind of attention is necessary for ESP. In some ways this type of attention is similar to blankness of the mind; it is like thinking about nothing at all — passive alertness. Celia Green has also tried to define this mental state, noting that it is not easily described in current psychological vocabulary: it is a state of detachment, something like expectancy.

In ESP experiments scores often fall to chance when subjects are told that they are doing well. On the other hand, fear of failing can cause stress, which is also counter-productive. Boredom is also deleterious.

According to J.B. Rhine, 'alertness is favourable, drowsiness unfavourable'. Caffeine administered when a subject (Hubert Pearce) was tiring and scoring badly improved his performance. The same happened in PK (PSYCHOKINESIS) tests. But it is impossible to say whether this improvement was due to the physiological effect of the caffeine or the psychological effect of suggestion. Could the same effect have been achieved by a placebo?

Objective proof of ESP will always be difficult if not impossible to find because ESP events are subjective phenomena. Emotional involvement, human need or desire — very subjective attitudes — seem to be the best catalyst for ESP to occur, and these are so often totally absent in a laboratory. A century ago Thomas J. Hudson recognized this and suggested that it was our SUBJECTIVE MIND that received telepathic impressions subliminally. The information was then conveyed to our 'objective mind', the only part of our mind of which we had conscious awareness, and which had no knowledge of how the information had been acquired. ESP can also operate more effectively under HYPNOSIS, which is another way of gaining access to the subjective mind. (See COMMUNITY OF SENSATION.)

The French philosopher and psychologist Henri Bergson (1859–1941) regarded the brain as a filter which processed information coming into the mind. Extra-sensory information could only be received by the mind when the brain was somehow disengaged, as in dreams, hypnosis, trance states, or when thinking about nothing.

Most modern researchers seem to postulate a PSI faculty that operates in a physical way which science has not yet discovered. 'Psi-events are sensory, not extra-sensory,' maintains the materialistic Jenny Randles.[155] The alternative, minority view is that minds can operate independently of what we regard as normal timespace, by-passing the brain. Randles misrepresents people who hold this mentalist view by attacking an unnamed lunatic fringe: 'If psi is a real force, it is open to us all. This is not the ground for mystical acolytes or cult-ridden misfits.' Yet the 'occultists' Randles is apparently attacking here have always maintained that ESP is a universal faculty, but like all faculties, not everyone is equally good at it or at an equal stage of development in it. This remains the case whether one believes that the faculty is still evolving in humanity, or whether it is one that has atrophied through lack of use.

The super-powers have long recognized that effective, controlled ESP could give an advantage in intelligence work, giving rise to research into 'ESPionage'. For this reason two ESP researchers Russell Targ and H.E. Puthoff were funded in their work at Stanford University by the US Pentagon. Targ eventually left and with Keith (Blue) Harary set up 'Delphi Associates'. They funded their research into REMOTE VIEWING by using their psi ability to speculate on the stock market.

For further categories of ESP, see CLAIRVOYANCE, CLAIRAUDIENCE, DOWSING, PSI, PSYCHOKINESIS, PSYCHOMETRY, REMOTE VIEWING, SENSITIVES, SUPER-ESP HYPOTHESIS, TELEPATHY. See also RESEARCH.

EXTRA-TERRESTRIAL ENCOUNTERS – See UFOS.

FACULTY X Colin Wilson has coined the term 'Faculty X' to denote the mental power which enables us to loosen the hold which our present surroundings have on our attention and to become aware of other places, other times, other realities. As well as coming into play in such phenomena as TIME-SLIPS, PRECOGNITION, PSYCHOMETRY and practically all PSYCHIC faculties, it is also involved in PEAK EXPERIENCES. Wilson suggests that the change of gear or focus, the switching over or even switching off which seems to mark the onset of many of these experiences coincides with the shifting of CONSCIOUSNESS away from the left hemisphere of the BRAIN to the right. 'Left-brain consciousness is not "normal" consciousness but a rather specialized and abnormal form developed as a tool for controlling the world.' But the result is that 'the left brain has deprived us of a whole dimension of meaning. If by "normal" we mean something that tells us the truth, then Faculty X is far more normal than our everyday awareness and the reality seen by mystics is the most normal of all.'[214] Faculty X also marks a level of consciousness (Level 7 in Wilson's grading) which precedes mystic experience.

FAKIR A fakir (Arabic, 'poor') was originally a Moslem ascetic who gave up family-life to live as a beggar. The name is applied in particular to certain SUFIS whose devotional exercises develop in them psychic powers. Hindu YOGIS who develop similar powers are also sometimes called fakirs, but these fakirs are often compared unfavourably with yogis. They are renowned for feats of endurance such as self-mutilation apparently without pain or standing on the same spot for years on end. These are intended as ways of tearing themselves away from normal awareness and raising their CONSCIOUSNESS, but some fakirs seem to have made the means into an end in itself. Sufis might inflict wounds on themselves while in ECSTASY, but immunity to pain is not the purpose of the exercise. The psychic powers which are developed by Sufis and yogis are incidental and should not be sought by the true yogi, nor particularly valued, and certainly not displayed for money. Yogis are always warned to beware of being distracted by them.

Fakirs seem to be adept at HYPNOSIS, of themselves (when piercing their flesh without causing any wound) as well as of others. To achieve the Indian rope trick, in which a rope is thrown up into the air where it hangs while a boy climbs up it and disappears, the fakir probably uses a combination of TELEPATHY and will-power to make the spectators see what he wants them to see. It is a form of mass hypnosis. The fakir also makes use of the hypnotic effect of his reed-pipe to render the deadly cobra comparatively inactive as it 'dances' or remains with head raised while the music plays.

FALSE ARRIVAL The phenomenon of false arrival refers to an APPARITION which appears before the arrival of the actual person, who is presumably concentrating so hard on the destination that a DOUBLE is projected there, or a thought is transmitted telepathically to those waiting so that they experience a group HALLUCINATION.

FAR MEMORY Far memory is the ability apparently demonstrated by some people to remember past lives. Some famous examples of far memory have been used as the basis for novels: Arthur Guirdham's *The Island* was set in ancient Greece; Janet Taylor Caldwell's *The Romance of Atlantis* was originally written when the author was twelve years old. Miss A.L. Stewart recalled an INCARNATION as James IV of Scotland, recorded in *The Falcon*. Probably the most famous of all far memory authors was Joan Grant (1907–89)[66]: some of her novels like *Winged Pharaoh* and *Eyes of Horus* were set in ancient Egypt, *Return to Elysium* was set in classical Greece and *Life as Carola* was set in Renaissance Italy. Christine Hartley expressed surprise that these people could apparently remember lives in such detail: she herself recalled only moments of intense emotion.[82]

It is not only imaginative authors who have recalled past lives. Thoreau (*Letters and Journals*) claimed to have lived in Judaea at the time of Christ without ever hearing of such a person and to remember a life as a shepherd in Assyria where he knew Nathaniel Hawthorne. One of the earliest philosophers to discuss REINCARNATION, Pythagoras, recalled having died after being wounded by Menelaus at the siege of Troy.

If reincarnation is a fact, why do we not automatically remember our previous lives? Are death and birth so traumatic that our memories are wiped out? How then do some people acquire the ability to remember other lives either in trance, in dreams, or in meditation, and where do the memories reside?

There is considerable evidence from people who have almost died that something very peculiar happens to the memory at the moment of death; people have reported seeing their whole life pass before them in a flash.

In the Far East, the most frequent cases where a past life is spontaneously remembered involve young children. The past life is usually one that ended not long before the birth of the child who recalls it, and as the child grows older and establishes a new individuality the past life understandably fades. A counter-theory to explain such occurrences states that such children are extremely sensitive in the same way that MEDIUMS are and that they pick up the psychic vibrations or 'husk' of a personality that has recently died. This PSYCHIC factor, so the theory goes, eventually dies or breaks up into its constituent parts in the same way that the physical body does, but it survives long enough for mediums and SENSITIVES to pick up the memories and personality traits contained within it.

Past lives may also be remembered under HYPNOSIS (in REGRESSION), although this has been dismissed by psychologists since a hypnotized subject is notoriously open to suggestion from the hypnotist, even telepathically, and can also be extremely inventive and creative.

Sometimes people talk of 'soul-memories'. This suggests that if we are to recall past lives accurately we should reach a level of consciousness appropriate to the soul, i.e. beyond the astral. The astral is associated with our desires and emotions, the mental is not so contaminated. The difficulty is how to know when we are meditating whether we are operating at an astral or a mental level. (see PLANES.)

The same difficulty is reflected when other terminology is used. When considering the UNCONSCIOUS MIND many people distinguish between the SUBCONSCIOUS and the SUPERCONSCIOUS. (see Figs on pages 327 and 333) Both can be the repository of past-life memories, but whereas the superconscious is transpersonal, cosmic, divine, infallible, the subconscious contains much that is personal, created by the individual. Via the subconscious we are also in touch with others and can access creations of their minds. So the same question arises: how do we know whether an apparent past-life memory comes from the superconscious (or the AKASHIC RECORD, which in this instance amounts to the same thing) and is therefore true, or from the subconscious, in which case it could be a fabrication?

Ideally one should be able to train oneself to recognize the level at which one is perceiving information, just as clairvoyants should recognize when they are 'reading the aura' of the sitter and simply reflecting the sitter's state, confirming their hopes and fears perceived at an astral level, or giving higher guidance perceived at the SOUL-level. Far more people are curious about their past lives than are able to recognize these levels of awareness in themselves. Consequently we can subconsciously invent for ourselves lifetimes which seem valid.

A useful exercise is to judge whether a past-life appears to have

KARMIC validity. We recall in a dream a life as an invalid, totally dependent on someone whose attitude in our present incarnation we find rather over-protective. It seems to fit. We think we now 'understand' this over-protective attitude and accept it more easily, even lovingly, with gratitude. The interesting point is that the apparent past-life recall has been beneficial. If the experience of such a past-life recall can in itself have such an effect, does it matter whether the memory was true or not?

It is often suggested that certain otherwise inexplicable phobias might have their origins in past lives. A baby with an intense fear of fire (which normally arouses curiosity and delight until the more cautious response is learned) might have ended a previous incarnation by being burned to death. Just as psychotherapy can cure certain conditions by exposing to conscious awareness an earlier traumatic experience which had been repressed, so REGRESSION to trauma in a previous life can sometimes be similarly liberating.

FENG SHUI The Chinese have long recognized that landscape and environment have an effect on the human organism. The earth and mankind are both part of one energy system, pulsing with life which is fuelled by CH'I, the energizing principle linking spirit and matter. The flow of *ch'i* in the earth affects and is affected by two forces, *feng* (wind) and *shui* (water). When these flow harmoniously in a beautiful landscape, the earth breathes harmoniously too, and *ch'i* — like the Hindu PRANA, the breath of the earth — invigorates all the life in that area. *Feng shui* is the name given to the art of recognizing landscapes that are harmonious in this way, if necessary modifying landscapes to make them more harmonious, and knowing where and in what orientation particular buildings should be sited. In *feng shui* the principles of YIN and YANG are applied to the land: gently undulating ground is yin, female, and rocky hills and cliffs are yang, masculine. The ideal proportions in which the two occur are 2:3 and the most propitious position in such a landscape is where the two currents meet.

Although it is expressed in unscientific terms this may represent an overall pattern which is only just receiving the attention of modern scientists. Since the 1950s scientists in Europe, America and Asia have noticed a correlation between solar activity and certain health conditions, particularly coronary artery disease and other blood disorders. An increased incidence of heart failure, for example, coincides with peaks of solar activity. The link is to be found in the earth's geomagnetic field, which is affected by solar activity, and changes in the geomagnetic field also register as changes in the weather — wind and water, *feng shui*.

We are immersed in the earth's radiations and it would indeed be surprising if they did not affect us somehow. Psychiatric disturbances have been seen to increase according to the intensity of the geomagnetic field. Naturally occurring radioactivity is increasingly thought to be linked with the occurrence of cancer, a fact which Baron von Pohl recognized in the 1930s with the help of a dowsing rod. The suggestion is that we carry around with us our own electro-magnetic field, which has been variously known as the BIOPLASMA body (by Russian scientists), the LIFE-FIELD, the energy body or the etheric body, and when this is affected by the earth's electromagnetic field the effects are manifested in the body.

FINGERTIP VISION — See PAROPTIC VISION.

FIRE-WALKING This phenomenon can serve different purposes. As an ordeal it may be a means of ascertaining the innocence or guilt of an accused person, the assumption being that the gods will protect an innocent person walking over the red-hot coals. More commonly fire-walking is a religious ceremony, either as part of a seasonal festival or as part of an initiation ceremony. People handle or walk on red-hot coals while in a state of religious ecstasy, and their immunity is a sign both of their devotion and of the approval of their gods or of the spirits of their ancestors. The practice was studied in Burma, Fiji, Tahiti, and particularly among the Kahunas of Hawaii by Max Freedom Long.[114] Preparations usually begin with much chanting and dancing, which — so the theory goes — could lead to temporary anaesthesia, in the same way that DERVISHES, FAKIRS and YOGIS are sometimes immune to pain. However, TRANCE, ECSTASY or HYPNOSIS do not explain how material as well as human skin escapes being scorched when touched by red-hot coals. Long believed that 'genuine magic' must be involved. Spiritualist MEDIUMS have also demonstrated similar feats. D.D. Home both handled red-hot coals and laid them on a handkerchief which remained unscorched.

FLYING SAUCERS — See UFOS.

FORMATIVE CAUSATION Arthur Koestler considered the hypothesis of formative causation to be 'immensely challenging and stimulating'. It was put forward by the biologist Rupert Sheldrake in 1981 in a book described by the journal *Nature* as an 'infuriating tract' and 'the best candidate for burning there has been for many years', such was its effect on the biological establishment.

Orthodox biology sees life, growth and regeneration as controlled by genetic programmes in the chemistry of DNA. Yet these mechanistic principles of causation cannot account for the fact that identical cells in different parts of an embryo develop in completely different ways according to the organ they are destined to be part of. In contrast Sheldrake proposes a process of formative causation, whereby the form and growth of an organism and any part of it are conditioned by an undetectable field — a non-physical, non-energetic MORPHOGENETIC FIELD. The field somehow stores the information about the final form and then guides the growth and development of the embryo so as to achieve it. 'The hypothesis of formative causation proposes that morphogenetic fields play a causal role in the development and maintenance of the forms of systems at all levels of complexity.'[178] There is no energy in the field, but it affects the organism by a process which Sheldrake calls morphic resonance — the organism follows the pattern already laid down in the field by resonating with it.

The resonance works both ways, forms affecting the field as well as the field affecting forms: 'the forms of previous systems influence the morphogenesis of subsequent similar systems.'[178] So once nature has grown a particular organism, other organisms can be guided to develop in the same way. By this token, nature is apparently a creature of habit.

Morphic resonance applies not only to nature but to any system that can grow and develop, from the growth of crystals and the effects of drugs to the processes of learning and memory. It is not always easy to produce crystals from a new chemical compound for the first time. There are also several forms that the crystals could take. Yet Sheldrake claims to have noticed that once new crystals have been produced somewhere, they are easier to produce again and they are more likely to take the form that they have taken before. (Since there is no energy in the morphogenetic field, its affect is not attenuated by distance.) Sheldrake maintains that morphic resonance can also account for the HUNDREDTH MONKEY effect: once something has been learned, others will find it easier to learn — as if information is acquired by the COLLECTIVE UNCONSCIOUS.

Like most scientists the British physicist Paul Davies does not accept Sheldrake's hypothesis. But he has noted that ideas such as these 'illustrate the persistence of the impression among scientists and laymen alike that the universe has been organized in a way that is hard to explain mechanistically, and that in spite of the tremendous advances in fundamental science there is still a strong temptation to fall back on some higher principle.'[41]

FOURTH DIMENSION Spiritualists have sometimes suggested that the existence of a fourth dimension in space explains the phenomenon of TELEPORTATION and APPORTS. If a two-dimensional plane is folded over in the third dimension, two positions on it can be brought together: so folding the plane enables a point on it to jump a considerable distance. Similarly, the theory goes, objects can jump from one position to another in three-dimensional space by crossing in the fourth dimension. The same basic idea has often been used in science-fiction.

Three-dimensional geometry has also been extended hypothetically into four dimensions. We can take four one-dimensional lines and arrange them in two-dimensional space to form a square; we can take six two-dimensional squares and arrange them in three-dimensional space to form a cube; by analogy, we should be able to take eight cubes and arrange them in four-dimensional space to form a *tesseract*, a hypothetical solid sometimes called a 'hypercube'. Any one side of a square touches two of the other sides, each of which touches the fourth situated opposite the first. And in a cube any one face touches four of the other faces, each of which touches the sixth, situated opposite the first. In the same way any one cube in a tesseract would touch six other cubes, and each of them would touch the eighth situated opposite the first in four-dimensional terms. The mathematics is fun, but the spatial geometry is science fiction.

A more serious contender for the fourth dimension is time. Again the theory can best be understood by starting with the idea of two-dimensional figures. To perceive a two-dimensional figure completely, we need to be in a three-dimensional world in order to stand away from it and see it as a whole. (Two-dimensional figures in a two-dimensional world would see each other simply as one-dimensional, i.e. straight lines.) Similarly, to perceive a three-dimensional object as a whole we need to be in a four-dimensional world: we need *time* to walk around an object in order fully to comprehend it. Without time three-dimensional objects would see each other as two-dimensional. So time is the fourth dimension.

One of the problems with this line of argument is that the last step depends on the fact that our favoured mode of perception uses light, which travels in straight lines. If light moved in curved lines we could see all sides of a three-dimensional object instantaneously, without the need for an additional fourth dimension. But the analogy is useful in that it demonstrate how DIMENSIONS can be built up in a way one can picture in one's mind. And the theory of relativity conceives of physical reality as a four-dimensional space-time continuum in any case.

By following the same line of thought as above, we see that to view four-dimensional creatures in their entirety one's viewpoint would need to be in the fifth dimension — ETERNITY. (This demonstrates the error in regarding eternity as simply an endless extension of time. It is different in kind.)

FREEMASONRY Little is known of the true origins and early development of Freemasonry, much of its history having been constructed retrospectively. It probably grew out of the medieval guild of English masons as a religious fraternity which made itself responsible for social duties such as burying their dead and insuring the widowed against poverty as well as guarding the secrets of their craft. Then the brotherhood started also concerning itself with the religious and moral education of its members. There has always been a certain puritan ethic in freemasonry and the masonic image of God as the Divine Architect fits in reasonably well with Protestantism, so following the Reformation Freemasonry co-existed comfortably with the church in Protestant countries but tended to be antagonistic to organized Christianity in Catholic countries. The ritualistic elements derived from mystery religion — initiations and symbolic endurance tests (some of which we see represented in Mozart's *Magic Flute*) — also satisfied a need for mystery which the Protestant church no longer satisfied. In this respect as an ESOTERIC organisation Freemasonry bore the same relation to the English church as ROSICRUCIANISM did to the German Protestant church. Some of the basic aims of Freemasons, to strive for moral betterment, work for the welfare of others and bring about a universal league of mankind, are common to the teachings of many other groups which arose later, such as the THEOSOPHISTS. Freemasonry is basically a male preserve although a form of it exists called Co-Masonry which admits both sexes.

FREE-WILL Materialistic science has great difficulty in accounting for free-will and creativity. Behaviourists deny mental events
altogether; everything boils down to chance and habit. Others
suggest that in creativity there is an underlying chaotic process
which causes certain mental states to be amplified, so that they are
experienced as thoughts, and we may have the impression that in
thinking and acting on some of these thoughts we are exercising
free will. Free will seems to be an epiphenomenon resulting from
chance and chaos.

Mechanistic determinism is tempered somewhat in the new mentalist theory of consciousness which arose in the 1970s. This theory
allows for the choice of action to be determined at higher levels by
conscious mental events, involving personal wishes, feelings and
values. But a non-material self having control over the body is still
denied.

The concepts of choice and responsibility form the basis of all
religions. In the PERENNIAL PHILOSOPHY which is at the heart
of all religions all souls were originally created perfect, one with
God. In order to be true companions of God they were also granted
free-will, the right to choose. Different traditions vary in the extent
to which they believe that human SOULS were involved in creating
their worlds of experience and experimenting with them, but there
is a general consensus that something went wrong: we were enticed
by material life and by exercising our choice we 'fell' into matter
and actually became trapped in it. But as souls we still have free-
will, and we can choose (some would say that ultimately we all will
choose) to return to God.

Religious difficulties with free-will usually centre on the question
of God's omniscience and predestination: if God knew what the
consequences would be of granting mankind free-will, the argument
goes, everything is happening in accordance with God's will and is
predestined. But the basic premise of God's omniscience needs
questioning. In Genesis we are told that God 'repented' of having
created mankind; in other words He did not know what would
happen. As Edgar Cayce said, 'Having given free-will, then —
though being omnipotent and omnipresent — it is only when the
soul that is a portion of God chooses, that God knows the end
thereof.' In other words, God's omniscience is not complete since
it is dependent on mankind's free-will. Nothing is therefore predestined. In modern terminology we would say that we are in an
unfolding universe and that it is an open system. And the keys
to this open system are not chance and chaos but free-will and
creativity.

G

GAIA At a conference in Princeton in 1969 James Lovelock first used the name Gaia (the Greek earth goddess) to denote the single organism comprised by the biosphere, atmosphere and lithosphere of the planet Earth. This way of thinking of the planet as a holistic self-regulating system was in sharp contrast to and a reaction against the prevailing view of 'spaceship earth', which Lovelock has described as 'the depressing picture of our planet as a demented spaceship, for ever travelling, driverless and purposeless.'[116]

According to Lovelock's theory, all living creatures are interconnected and behave in such a way that they contrive to maintain environmental circumstances appropriate for the continuance of all life. For example, salts are constantly deposited into the world's seas by the rivers that flow into them, yet these salts remain at a constant concentration of three per cent. This regulation is essential, for if the level of salinity were to double, few sea creatures would survive.

Some have seen this as tantamount to saying that the earth has a mind which governs its action, although Lovelock has never claimed this. Scientists have warned against seeing any teleological characteristic in the earth's behaviour. 'One must resist the temptation to suppose that biological processes were guided by final causes in a specific way,' writes the physicist, Paul Davies. He is obviously impressed by the evidence, but draws no particular conclusions from it other than that is how the earth behaves. 'The apparently stable conditions on the surface of our planet serve to illustrate the general point that complex systems have an unusual ability to organize themselves into stable patterns of activity.'[41]

GANZFELD An absence of sensory stimuli seems to encourage paranormal experiences. John Lilly noticed this and developed sensory deprivation tanks in an attempt to induce mystic experiences. Charles Honorton at the Maimonides Division of Parapsychology and Psychophysics carried out experiments in TELEPATHY, CLAIRVOYANCE and PRECOGNITION, in which he surrounded his subjects with a similar 'Ganzfeld' effect – literally 'whole field' –

of constant uniform low 'white' noise through headphones and darkness with cotton wool and halved billiard balls over the eyes. This technique was particularly successful in cases of REMOTE VIEWING. Honorton concluded that ESP effects were heightened by Ganzfeld conditions.[16]

GEHENNA In Jewish tradition Gehenna is the equivalent of HELL, a place of burning and torment for the dead. The name is derived from a valley outside Jerusalem, Ge Hinnom, where the city's rubbish was burned.

GENETIC MEMORY Biologists do not believe that memories can be transmitted from one generation to another genetically. Nevertheless some people prefer to think that memories transmitted in this way might be responsible for cases of so-called FAR MEMORY. This is a relatively implausible theory, since incidents recalled 'genetically', if remembered as happening to oneself, could only be remembered by a descendant if the ancestor became a parent *after* the event.

GENIUS In the ancient classical world a genius (Latin) or DAEMON (Greek) was a kind of GUARDIAN ANGEL or spirit GUIDE whose task it was to protect and prompt the person entrusted to its care. It was originally also a spirit of male fertility in a family and the continuing spiritual power of the ancestors.

GHOSTS In England surveys have shown that one in six people say they 'believe in' ghosts and about one in fifteen say they have seen a ghost. This is taken to mean that they think they have seen the spirit of a dead person, although some people may interpret the apparition in other ways — as a 'recording' in the environment, or as a telepathic message from a living person, for example.

How does one prove that a ghost of a dead person has been seen? If the APPARITION is seen and identified by someone who is unaware that the person is dead, it could be claimed that the deceased actually appeared to that person. It is interesting that these CRISIS APPARITIONS are often so life-like that they are mistaken for real people, and are not what is commonly understood as 'ghost-like' at all, but some researchers suggest that the life-like appearance of these ghosts is consistent with the idea that they are in fact HALLUCINATIONS.

Complications arise when much more than the deceased individual is seen, which perhaps suggests that the ghost is not actually there as an objective entity. For example, Johann Hofer was seen driving his car through the village of Val d'Adige at a time when he was actually being crushed in a collapsing tunnel over twenty kilometres away.[117] There is a widely held view among researchers (such as Edmund Gurney and R.H. Thouless) that apparitions of this kind are telepathic messages from the person seen, but this still means that the person's consciousness has survived at least for some time after the death of the body.

An alternative view is that crisis apparitions are the result of paranormal perception, plain ESP. If we ascribe intentionality to the 'ghost' this also accounts for apparitions of the living, when people apparently project their doubles to appear to other people. In *Apparitions* Celia Green and Charles McCreery estimate that a third of the cases reported to them were apparitions of living people.[68]

Most people who do see a ghost are utterly convinced of its objective reality at some level of existence, regardless of their previous views on the subject, and as a consequence they generally come to accept the likelihood of personal survival after death. Some accounts are also strikingly suggestive of survival to people who did not participate in the event. A child claimed that she was visited at night regularly by two unknown grandparents. Later she recognized these strangers in a photograph: they were in fact her mother's grandparents who had died before her birth. The sceptics explain this as TELEPATHY: the mother knew that her parents had looked forward to having great-grandchildren and it had been a great disappointment to all concerned that they had not lived long enough to see them. She had therefore communicated this wish telepathically to her daughter, who had consequently 'seen' her great-grandparents while in a relaxed and receptive state of mind in bed in the form that her mother remembered them. Scientists always claim that they choose the most economical explanation, yet to many people this telepathically communicated wish-fulfilment by proxy seems much more unwieldy than a straightforward survival and visitation by the grandparents themselves.

GHOUL T.C. Lethbridge used the term 'ghoul' to refer to APPARITIONS that are associated with particular places and which, he claimed, seem to be imprinted on the electrical field of water in the area.[110] The word comes from the Arabic for a kind of demon which ate stolen corpses.

GLOSSOLALIA Glossolalia, often referred to as 'speaking in tongues', is a particular form of XENOGLOSSY in which the person in TRANCE speaks a language which is not simply foreign to the speaker when in a normal state of CONSCIOUSNESS, but is also completely unknown and possibly unintelligible to the listeners. Glossolalia occurs most typically when mystics achieve a state of ECSTASY and their unintelligible devotional utterances are filled with emotion, and in this sense it is associated with Pentecostal churches.

When the apostles first gave evidence of the gift of tongues on the Day of Pentecost (Acts 2), all those listening understood what was said as being in their own language. This suggests xenoglossy rather than glossolalia. But if several speakers of different languages understood one apostle as if he were preaching in their own language, this would suggest glossolalia in a situation where some different form of communication was used, by raising the consciousness of everyone in the audience or perhaps communicating telepathically. St Paul referred to both speaking in tongues and the interpretation of tongues as gifts of the Spirit (1 Corinthians 12, 10), implying that there are other 'spirit' languages which can carry meaning.

Jane Roberts, the American channeller of communications from 'SETH', also spoke an unknown language she called Sumari. At first she heard this language while in an altered state of awareness and certain 'words' were so persistent that she started to repeat them. Later she spoke at length in the language and also sang in it. 'Seth' translated some Sumari terms into English and described the language as 'an expression of the consciousness at a different focus' and 'a bridge between two different kinds of consciousness'.[166] Our normal language so conditions our perceptions that we experience the world in terms of our language, and using a new language enables us to escape the restrictions of our CONSENSUS REALITY and appreciate new experiences more directly: 'The [Sumari] language will effectively block the automatic translation of inner experience into stereotypes.' 'Seth' also said that the speakers of Sumari 'could be compared to a psychic family, a guild of consciousness who worked together through the centuries, ... a brotherhood.'[165]

As well as speaking foreign languages in trance, people have been known to hear a hallucinatory voice speaking an unknown language and repeat it for an interpreter to translate. This has also happened under the influence of DRUGS. Dr Jean Houston, an American psychologist, administered a dose of LSD to a patient, who proceeded to describe a scene in which he had a conversation with Socrates. The patient could not understand classical Greek, but what he repeated was perfectly intelligible to Dr Houston, who could. The two theories which 'explain' this phenomenon are CRYPTOMNESIA and TELEPATHY. In this particular case the more likely explanation is telepathy, although of a very individual kind. The patient's SUBCONSCIOUS MIND seems to have access to the psychologist's subconscious, drawing on their shared knowledge to create new communication.

GNOSTICISM Gnosis means knowledge (Greek), as distinct from faith (*pistis*). Gnosticism is a mystery religion in which recognition of revealed knowledge leads to the liberation of the soul. Some of the main features of Gnosticism were inherited from Zoroastrianism and baptizing sects such as the Essenes, i.e. before Christianity. It was also influenced by Indian and Greek thought (Orphism and Platonism), by Judaism and Christianity. The Cathars with their roots in Manichaeism were the last stronghold of Gnostic belief in Europe in the thirteenth century. The Mandaeans or Christians of St John, are a Gnostic sect still in existence south of Baghdad. (*Manda* means the same as *gnosis*.)

In common with other mystery schools the Gnostics regarded every human being as housing a divine spark trapped in matter. Adam Kadmon, the man of light, was the symbol adopted from the KABBALAH. He was the first man, mirror of the macrocosm, but in the process of incarnation he is deceived by the Demiurge (who created this lowest, material level of reality) into forgetting his true heritage. The flesh produced forgetfulness of the soul's origins. It was the Gnostics' fervent hope that they would one day be liberated and united with the true God in the PLEROMA (i.e. not the Demiurge), but the journey was hazardous and could take many lifetimes — most Gnostic systems included a belief in REINCARNATION.

There was a certain élitism in the Gnostic doctrine. All humanity were divided into three types: the great mass of people were *hylic*, 'fleshly'; next up the hierarchy were the *psychic* or *credenti*, partially enlightened people or believers, which was usually taken to mean that they were nominally Christian; finally there were the *pneumatic* or *perfecti*, the fully enlightened, the Gnostic, who had been apprised of the secret revelations of Christ and his disciples.

Gnostics were 'knowers', and Gnosticism appealed more to the intellectual than to the masses, placing knowledge above faith.

This was one of the paramount factors which made St Paul campaign so vociferously against it. 'O Timothy, keep the securities of the faith intact; avoid the profane jargon and contradictions of what is falsely called *Knowledge*' (i.e. Gnosis) he writes at the end of the First Epistle to Timothy. Simon Magus was the earliest known leader of a Gnostic movement, described in Paul's account of the 'magician's' encounter with the apostles in Acts 8, 9–24.

Different Gnostics had different conceptions of God the Creator and applied a variety of names to such an entity. For Menander of Antioch the Primary Power of the Universe was unknowable and the world was made of ENNOIA, Supreme Thought. For Basilides of Alexandria the Supreme Being was called ABRAXAS. For many Gnostics the Creator was a Demiurge, inferior to the true God, an anti-god, usually identified with the Old Testament Yahweh. Consequently Lucifer (= 'light-bearer') could be regarded as the bringer of ENLIGHTENMENT in encouraging Adam and Eve to eat of the Tree of Knowledge, an act which was to be equated not with the Fall, but with the first step on the path to Gnosis and liberation from matter. The actual Liberator was often seen as Christ. He was generally regarded as the son of the true God, but like the more recent THEOSOPHISTS most Gnostic sects believed that Christ was a purely spiritual being who temporarily inhabited the body of Jesus.

People often associate the Gnostics with the so-called dualist heresy – regarding the world of matter as wholly evil, as the Cathars did – but this doctrine was neither originally part of Gnosis nor peculiar to it. It continued to affect mainstream Christianity from time to time by inspiring a rejection of the world of matter: for example, St Augustine of Hippo originally espoused MANICHAEISM.

GOD/GODHEAD – See BRAHMAN, EN-SOF, LOGOS, OVERSOUL, PLEROMA.

GROUP SOUL Human beings are individual souls. The spiritual life-force which inhabits animals is generally regarded as being common to all of a particular species, so that when an animal dies, its spiritual energy returns to the 'pool'. In this sense animals are sometimes said to have group souls.

The term is also used for humans. A group of individuals may reincarnate at particular times together, rather like so-called soul-mates, but to call such a group of souls a group soul is really a misuse of the term. A group soul is rather a spiritual being which gives birth to individual souls. These souls incarnate repeatedly, the HIGHER SELF being the link between each successive life and the soul itself. Each soul stands in a similar relationship to the group soul, as the incarnations do to the soul. In the same way that these lives are experiences of the soul, from which the soul learns, so the souls are also experiences of the group soul. Eventually, when the souls have progressed sufficiently so that they no longer need to incarnate, they can unite fully with the group soul which gave birth to them and the group soul can continue to evolve towards the Godhead.

GUARDIAN ANGEL A spirit entity or GUIDE who stays with you throughout your life on earth is often referred to as a 'guardian angel'. This is one of the areas where traditional Christianity and SPIRITUALISM appear to meet, although there are major differences between the two concepts. For one thing orthodox religion generally plays down the role of ANGELS, regarding a person's direct relationship with God as far more important than any relationship with an intermediary, whereas for spiritualists their dealings with their guides are very significant.

An even more basic difference concerns the status of the guardian angels. Generally speaking angels are regarded as being a higher level of creation than humanity; they are spirit beings who did not 'fall' into matter in the way that humanity did. Most occult teachings agree that there is a separate spiritual species which can be called angels. For this reason most spiritualists prefer the term DOORKEEPER or main guide to describe the role of the guardian angel, and this doorkeeper, like all spirit guides, is understood to be a human spirit, someone who has lived on earth. The Christian view, on the other hand, is that guardian angels are truly angelic, that angels are angels and human souls are human souls and the one cannot fulfil the role of the other. To this spiritualists may counter that the Christian view on angelic, non-human intermediaries between us and God is not entirely consistent: if one can pray to the saints, who are human souls, to intercede on one's behalf, why should other human souls not be placed in the position of guardian angels?

In the Bible angels appear to people in dreams and visions and even as materializations. These are usually considered to be messengers of God, although those who warn of danger in a dream could well be regarded as guardian angels. Jesus referred to guardian angels simply as angels in Matthew 18, 10: 'Take heed that ye despise not one of these little ones; for I say unto you, that in heaven their angels do always behold the face of my Father which is in heaven.' These sound almost like recording angels, but they are concerned with recording not the sins of their charges but the injustices inflicted on them.

If we do have our guardian angels, what do they need to guard us against? Why do we need protection? To some people the implication seems to be that we need guardian angels because we are somehow under attack. Others believe that few of us are ever under attack anyway, and if we are in God's light that is protection enough. But just in case we start to stray from the path, it is said, our guardian angels are there to lead us back to it. So the guardian angel also represents the voice of conscience. In this respect both Christianity and spiritualism probably come close to agreement, and there are obvious links too with other traditions such as that of the DAEMON as experienced by Socrates.

GUARDIANS OF THE THRESHOLD In mystical and occult terminology the guardians of the threshold are the beings or guides encountered on the inner planes by the aspirant working for spiritual development. The First Guardian of the Threshold, sometimes called the Lesser Guardian, has been compared to Jung's concept of the Shadow and represents everything in the personality which resists the individual's spiritual progress. It is the product of our past, a THOUGHT-FORM which we ourselves have created and which we must come to terms with before we can progress further. (Such an encounter is described in Bulwer Lytton's *Zanoni*.) Meeting with the Second, Greater or Higher Guardian, which embodies all our past KARMA accumulated over many lifetimes, is a more mystical experience, by which the soul eventually recognizes the limitations of the flesh and is freed from the world of the senses. The individual thus reaches a level of soul-consciousness not experienced before.

Although it is an occult concept the First Guardian of the Threshold does seem to have a parallel in modern Jungian psychology, in that one must deal with one's Shadow before one can recognize oneself as a complete, unfragmented person. The meeting with the Second Guardian is the logical equivalent on a spiritual PLANE and is equally necessary if one is to realize oneself as a SOUL.

GUIDE To some people they are spirit guides, to others they are inner guides, but whether they are regarded as external and separate or part of an individual's total psyche, the guides' purpose, their effect and the ways in which an individual can make contact with them are remarkably similar. In many respects only the terminology is different.

Through MEDITATION, GUIDED IMAGERY, day-dreaming and ACTIVE IMAGINATION, depending on one's school of thought, one can get in touch with figures of wisdom which seem both archetypal and personal. At the psychological end of the spectrum they are simply subpersonalities; they represent qualities that have been suppressed, probably through our feelings of worthlessness, so that all our positive strength and natural wisdom is embodied in part of our psyche which has become split off. Midway between the purely psychological approach and the spiritual view is the idea that guides are archetypal figures in the COLLECTIVE UNCONSCIOUS, a much deeper level than the personal SUBCONSCIOUS. Jung's view seemed to be a mixture of these two. He attributed *psychic objectivity* to his guide Philemon, who both fulfilled the role of Jung's mentor, since no one could perform that duty in the external world, and also embodied something of the guru-figure, the wise old man, that Jung himself was destined to become. The process of entering into dialogue with such guides, as described for example by Edwin C. Steinbrecher in *The Inner Guide Meditation*, shows how we can access our own inner wisdom directly instead of becoming dependent on external figures by projecting it on to analysts, teachers, priests and gurus.[182]

The occult view, the view held by most mediums, put forward in most spiritualist teachings, and supported for example by the Edgar Cayce writings and other channelled communications, is that our guides are separate spirit entities, human spirits who have lived before and whose task it is now to help us as individuals to follow our own spiritual path. It is usually assumed that they are more experienced souls than the ones they guide, although this may sometimes simply be the effect of having immediate access to their own soul-level, which we as incarnate souls have difficulty in reaching. It should also be remembered that our guides are probably working with us as part of their own spiritual progress, so that the co-operative venture benefits both parties. It is often suggested that we have had previous incarnations contemporaneously with those of our guides, that we are linked karmically, and that in future the roles may be reversed. For example, someone who is a HEALER now may have had a previous incarnation as a doctor whose partner in that lifetime is now their healing guide. When a person has more than one guide it is generally assumed that each one has a particular area of responsibility, such as healing or teaching. These guides may come and go, some staying with an individual long-term and others for relatively short periods. Only one guide, the DOORKEEPER or GUARDIAN ANGEL, remains the same throughout a person's life.

Sometimes people wonder whether their spirit guides might actually be other personalities that they themselves have had in previous lifetimes. The question then arises, why should a personality we had several lifetimes ago be in a position to advise us now? That would presumably mean that we had dropped back instead of progressing spiritually. On the other hand, some suggest that our HIGHER SELF could assume the guise of one of our past incarnations when making contact with our present level of CONSCIOUSNESS. After all, many spirit guides have said that it matters little what we call them and how we see them: their names and personalities are for our convenience only, since we find it easier to deal with them in those terms. Amending this view slightly we could regard a guide as both the product and the channel of communication between the conscious self and the Higher Self.

The psychological and spiritual views on guides are not necessarily incompatible. If our psyche contains elements which we interpret as guides, that does not preclude the possibility that we are also helped by spirit entities who appear to us in a similar guise. Mediums often say they can 'see' our guides, psychic artists may even draw them, and the descriptions generally coincide. Is this evidence for the spirit hypothesis? If we accept that mediums may use TELEPATHY, and that we are able to create THOUGHT-FORMS unconsciously, which clairvoyants can then perceive, then the answer is: 'No, the evidence from mediums does not require that spirit guides have an independent existence.' When, however, different mediums identify the spirit guide of a baby and their descriptions agree, then there is some justification for giving credence to such a guide as a separate independent entity.

GUIDED IMAGERY The technique of prompting the imagination so as to experience both archetypal and personal symbols rising from the UNCONSCIOUS goes under various names: guided imagery, guided fantasy, directed day-dream[43] (Robert Desoille's "*rêve éveillé dirigé*"), initiated symbol projection (Hanscarl Leuner), or even led MEDITATION and inner guide meditation (Edwin C. Steinbrecher).[182]

The procedure usually begins with relaxation, regular breathing and the sinking into a passive meditative state. A prompter then narrates the outline of, for example, a walk up a mountain, supplying varying degrees of detail but always leaving the greater part of it to be evoked by the day-dreamer who is in 'an intermediate hypnoidal state which shades between wakefulness and sleep'.[43] The purpose of the process is usually therapeutic, whether by evoking universal healing symbols or transforming personal symbols of conditioning or both, so the prompter who guides the imagery is often a therapist. Alternatively the outline can be read before starting the meditation by those working on their own.

In psychosynthesis the technique can be used to consult one's own inner wisdom in the form of a 'wise old being' at the top of a mountain.[3] There is a story that the first time one man was led through this imagery he misheard the counsellor and met a 'wise old bean' at the top of his mountain, but he still received a very worthwhile answer to his question. Other systems seem to ascribe varying degrees of reality to the entities one meets on the 'inner planes'. Whatever the true status of such inner guides they do seem to be more effective the more an individual regards them as entities with whom one can dialogue, as Jung did with Philemon, for example. Jung's ACTIVE IMAGINATION is different only inasmuch as his process was freer, not conditioned or guided by the promptings of another person and not directed at all other than self-directed inward.

Tarot cards can also be used as the stimulus for experiencing the inner world of symbol and archetype. Instead of following a brief description for the guided imagery one studies the design of a particular card and enters it to meet and perhaps converse with the figures depicted.

Another form of imagery, usually called 'visualization', is used to stimulate the body's natural self-healing powers. The patient imagines the body's defences attacking invading viruses, for example white blood cells become knights in shining white armour, or miniature spacemen are seen vapourizing cancerous cells.

GURU A guru is a spiritual teacher, one who guides the seeker in the disciplines of YOGA. A guru is usually expected to be an enlightened YOGI already, but there is also the view that the only way to progress further up the ladder is by raising others who are behind on to the rung which is just below us. In this sense we are all both learning and teaching.

There are many self-styled gurus nowadays. This is an aberration. It has often been suggested that 'no true MASTER imparts spiritual truths for money; no true Master appears in public as a leader or teacher or New Messiah: therefore, any man who advertises himself or allows others to advertise him as such cannot be a Master.'[176]

It is also worth remembering that no guru should ever teach others unless they come voluntarily as seekers. 'To attempt to lead those who as yet do not seek, is both a presumption and a folly, but to guide the few who seek, hoping that others may follow in their wake if they be so inclined, is the benevolent deed of the true altruist.'[176]

It is interesting that simultaneous with the upsurge in self-styled gurus today there is a noticeable movement towards disciplines which aim for less dependence on external figures of authority and more reliance on one's own inner teachers.

HADES For the ancient Greeks and Romans Hades was the Underworld where human spirits, the shades, wandered aimlessly after death. In common with many cultures at that time, only a few heroes who were specially chosen by the gods were granted eternal life with them (in Olympus), although another favoured group had a pleasant existence in Elysium, the Elysian Fields.

HALLUCINATIONS A hallucination is the perception of something which has no objective reality, a subjective experience, usually visual, in which the percipient initially accepts the 'imaginary' neural stimulus as coming from something real in the external world.

Hallucinations are recognized by the medical profession as symptoms of psychosis and other mental illness, but the majority of people who have hallucinatory experiences, seeing visions or APPARITIONS, are probably not mentally ill. Surveys in Britain and America suggest that between a tenth and a quarter of the population believe that they have at some time sensed the presence of another person who was not physically present. About one third of visual apparitions are seen by more than one person.

There is a difference between an illusion and a hallucination. An illusion occurs when we see something and make a mistake when identifying it by trying to match it with something in the bank of past perceptions stored in our memory. For example, the first time someone sees astraturf from a distance, they will probably mistake it for real grass, particularly if they have never heard of it either. This is an illusion. Something real is perceived, but the sensory data is misinterpreted. In a hallucination there is no external stimulus to provoke the sensory response. Instead, some internal stimulus causes the mind to evoke brain responses *as if* something real were being perceived. For this reason hallucinations look real. A hallucination of a person looks solid, like a real person, not semi-transparent in the manner of Hollywood ghosts.

Hallucinations can be induced by DRUGS and other food substances. In 1951 many people in a French village started seeing weird visions as a result of eating bread made from grain that was infected with the ergot fungus (*Claviceps purpurea*).

Hallucinations can also be induced by sensory deprivation. It has been suggested that the restrictions of sensory data received by the brain when driving on a monotonous motorway can have the same effect, and people cite the number of UFO sightings reported in such circumstances as evidence of this. Another type of apparition has often been reported by mountaineers, explorers and lone sea-voyagers: men trekking across the snow and ice of the Arctic or Antarctic have found themselves talking to an additional member of their team who was not actually there. It has been suggested that this is the same phenomenon as the imaginary playmates that many children have, although the circumstances are so different as to make this seem rather unlikely. However, the mental state in which such explorers find themselves, constantly alert but with very little variety of sensory data being received by the brain, may be similar to the state which many clairvoyants and researchers into the paranormal say is conducive to experiencing psi-events.

The round-the-world yachtsman, Sir Francis Chichester, is one of many who have reported seeing flying saucers (UFOs) while at sea. One hears far less about phantom ships these days, almost as if they have been superseded by UFOs. Some researchers have cited this change in emphasis in the events currently reported as evidence that such phantoms are hallucinations: the mind makes the vision fit the preconceived images already in the memory bank.

Dr Morton Schatzman treated a woman called Ruth who suffered from frightening hallucinations of her father. It was clear that she was not seeing a ghost, because her father was still alive. Neither was he interested in projecting himself 'astrally' to her. So there was no doubt that Ruth was suffering from hallucinations and she recognized as much. The psychiatrist's treatment was to train her to create the hallucinations at will, such that she was also able to 'switch them off'. Neurological tests revealed that when a hallucinated figure was positioned in front of a television screen in Ruth's visual field (in this case a hallucination of her eight-year-old daughter sitting on her lap), the brain no longer registered any visual impulses from the 'concealed' screen image. This has interesting implications for the status of the MIND as a controller of the brain, rather than as an EPIPHENOMENON of it.[174]

Many APPARITIONS are most commonly interpreted as being hallucinations. When Edmund Gurney collected the cases described in *Phantasms of the Living* he came to the conclusion that they were usually hallucinations created by the percipient's unconscious as a response to information picked up by telepathy from the mind of the person 'seen'.[76] Most modern researchers such as Celia Green and Charles McCreery seem to share this view.[68] In the words of Jenny Randles, 'All psi-events are just sensory translations of an emotional message picked up and decoded in the mind.'[155] The moot point lies in the word 'all'. Just because the 'Gurney hypothesis' neatly explains many cases of ASTRAL PROJECTION and CRISIS APPARITIONS as hallucinations instigated by TELEPATHY (with the mind of a living person), there is no need to conclude that all apparitions, GHOSTS and HAUNTINGS are hallucinatory.

HALO Saints and other holy figures are often portrayed with a disc of light encircling the head. This halo or nimbus (Latin: 'cloud, radiance') represents different forms of spiritual power, wisdom, holiness, etc. in Hinduism, Buddhism, Mithraism and (since the fourth century) Christianity. It probably originated as a pictorial representation of the AURA or part of it. Since the aura envelops the whole body there is reason to think that the halo might represent the emanations from a particular CHAKRA, the most likely being the crown centre.

HAUNTING Hauntings are associated with particular places. They are typically APPARITIONS which pass through walls and through which the percipients may pass their hands. There may be noises (especially footsteps), and objects may move. Sometimes there is simply a strong sense of not being alone, perhaps accompanied by a feeling of coldness, or a sense of being choked, and these 'presences' can also have a frightening effect on ANIMALS. Only rarely are haunting apparitions heard to speak, and they behave more often in a repetitive, zombie-like manner than in an interactive way with those who see them. All these phenomena have been reported in the same terms for at least the last four hundred years, and hauntings were described by St Augustine and by the ancient Egyptians.

According to the standard spirit theory, hauntings are usually associated with earth-bound spirits of the dead. After death they find themselves on the lowest level of the astral PLANE, perhaps not even realizing that they are dead, and attachment to the earth plane, emotions such as sorrow, a feeling of loss, or a desire for revenge, prevent the soul from tearing free and progressing. With this in mind it is not surprising that so many hauntings are associated with violent death.

If we have a shocking experience we sometimes tend to dream about it repeatedly. Some believe that in these dreams we actually re-enact the event astrally. A similar phenomenon occurs when a place is haunted by the 'ghost' of someone who suffered a violent death. The victim re-enacts the event or part of it in the astral body as if in a dream.

Sometimes a 'low spirit' may have little will of its own and it may become the vehicle for the emotions of the living. The KAHUNAS believe that everyone has a low spirit of this kind, which after death may be put to malevolent use by a living magician. When the MEDIUM Eileen Garrett investigated a haunting in the 1930s, (the Ash Manor ghost in Sussex), her spirit control, Uvani, said that the family living in the haunted house were actually responsible for holding the spirit back and using its capacity to haunt as a means of continuing their own protracted emotional battles with each other. (In the case of Ash Manor Eileen Garrett allowed the haunting spirit to speak through her to explain his reasons for his attachment to the place. He gave a long account of his life in medieval England, but it proved impossible to substantiate any of his claims by historical research.)

One particular characteristic of hauntings makes the spirit theory less satisfactory as a valid explanation of all − some would say of any − hauntings, and that is their persistence. Sometimes hauntings have been successfully exorcized, and this gives added weight to the view that in those cases an EARTH-BOUND spirit was responsible, but sometimes a haunting is more persistent and continues for decades, even centuries. Are we to understand that the spirit has been static, incapable of progressing for all that time? Or is there another possible cause for hauntings?

F.W.H. Myers developed a theory that some people have the ability to loosen and detach some of their spiritual energy or to project it elsewhere.[76,135] This energy was then able to modify space and create an image of the person, along with any other objects which formed the person's self-image at that particular time. These images Myers described as *psychorrhagic* — 'soul breaking loose' and could explain apparitions of the living, ASTRAL PROJECTIONS, and DOUBLES, and if they were imbued with enough energy to persist they could explain apparitions of the dead too — ghosts and hauntings. (The advantage of this theory over the telepathic HALLUCINATION theory of Edmund Gurney and many current researchers is that it allows for more than one person to see the apparition and share the experience without invoking any hypothetical notion of collective hallucination.)

These psychorrhagic images are more than just mental constructs; they are etheric forms, although it is not the person's ETHERIC BODY that is seen. H.H. Price regarded the ETHER as a 'bridge between mind and matter' and when 'charged' in the way put forward by Myers because of an emotionally intense experience, another mind could interact with it, using a certain amount of its own psychic energy and thus perceive the haunting image. So according to Price, 'Haunting is a kind of deferred TELEPATHY resulting in a post-dated phantasm.' One might expect places where there had been numerous emotional experiences — law-courts, hospitals, etc. — to be more prone to such hauntings, whereas in fact the most common sites for hauntings tend to be relatively lonely spots. This, Price suggested, was because a heavy saturation of such images meant that no single one could be perceived clearly, like the confusion of fingerprints on a glass that had been held by many people.

The dubious status of the ether among more orthodox researchers has led to alternative versions of the same basic 'playback' or 'tape-recording' theory. Tom Lethbridge noticed that hauntings were often associated with underground water and were usually only visible from certain positions. He suggested that the emotional psychic energy which caused such an apparition could be imprinted on the electromagnetic field of an area which was retained by the water.[110] Don Robins has considered the possibility of a similar imprinting on the internal lattice-structure of stone, particularly with reference to stone circles.[167,168]

There have been cases where houses have been haunted by so-called doppelgängers or astral projections of the living. In one such case a woman often dreamt of a house which she decided was her ideal home. She searched for it among the properties for sale and eventually found it. She was surprised at the low price being asked, and the agent admitted that it was because the house was supposedly haunted. But the agent reassured her that she had no need to worry: from the owner's descriptions he had recognized the 'ghost' and the prospective purchaser as one and the same.

HEALERS/HEALING Healing is described in various ways depending on the method used by the healer and the means by which the patient is thought to be healed. A *faith healer* is usually a member of a particular religion, often an evangelical Christian preacher, and the crucial requirement is the faith of both healer and patient in the power of God to heal. Spiritualist faith healers are often called *spirit healers*, a term with slightly different implications. Most spirit healers consider it to be of little importance whether or not the patient 'believes in healing'. They claim to be channels for healing energies, and DISCARNATE entities might also be involved in the process, helping in particular with diagnosis and in what has become known as PSYCHIC SURGERY. Those who describe themselves as *psychic healers* have different beliefs again, often regarding it as their own energy which is used in the healing process. Some also believe that the healer may be adversely affected by the patient's condition, and certain semi-ritualistic actions are practised in order to reduce this risk. Despite all these differences between the various systems of healing, many healers nowadays prefer to be known simply as healers.

Early Greeks such as Hippocrates (fourth century BC) believed that certain people were imbued with a special power, *dunamis*, which gave them the ability to heal by touch. This continued into Roman times in the Middle East, and in the New Testament Jesus is reported as recognizing when a woman touched the hem of his garment in order to be healed: 'Jesus, immediately knowing that virtue (Greek: *dunamis*) had gone out of him said, Who touched me?' (Mark 5, 30.) There was already a tradition of using relics in this way: in Old Testament times people were healed by touching the prophet's staff (II Kings 4, 18–37), and a dead man was restored to life by contact with the bones of Elisha (II Kings 13, 21).

The Church initially allowed the laying on of hands by priests when praying that the sick be cured by the Holy Spirit, as the apostles had done. But this practice was soon outlawed, lest it be thought that the priests themselves were the agents of healing and to allow the prosecution of other such healers for witchcraft. In some parts of the non-Catholic Church the laying on of hands has made something of a come-back in recent times, with the healers being regarded as channels for God's healing power. The seventeenth century Irish healer Valentine Greatrakes became famous in England as well as Ireland for healing by touching or stroking his patients. Later Mesmer's animal magnetism (MESMERISM) seemed to apply a similar technique until it was discovered the crucial factor was hypnotism.

It is easy to see how hysterical illnesses could be cured by SUGGESTION. A patient may genuinely want to escape from the habit of a certain condition, but not until someone inspiring confidence to the degree that Greatrakes did will they have the conviction required to succumb to the healer's suggestion. Since psychosomatic illnesses originate in the mind, it is relatively easy to accept that the mind succumbing to suggestion or HYPNOSIS could effect a cure. One problem is that no one can agree on what proportion of sickness is psychosomatic. Since it has been proved that the effectiveness of the body's immune system can be reduced by depression and enhanced by positive mental states, it seems likely that there is a psychosomatic element of varying degrees in most if not all illnesses, although some obviously have more external causes than others. Yet if weals and burns can appear on a hypnotized subject's skin when touched by an imaginary piece of hot metal, is the reverse process by which such wounds can be healed under hypnosis any more remarkable?

In 1950 a sixteen-year-old boy was admitted to hospital in East Grinstead suffering from a rare disease which affected his skin: the whole of his body was covered with black warts and the horny skin of his hands was as hard as his fingernails. Dr Albert Mason, the anaesthetist attending the boy's skin transplant operation (which was a failure) decided to try hypnosis. He hypnotized the boy and told him in TRANCE that the warts on his left arm would disappear. After a few days they did, falling off and revealing perfectly normal skin. At first the anaesthetist was not aware of the momentous nature of this cure, but when he told the surgeon in charge of the case, his attention was drawn to the exact nature of the incurable 'fish-skin' disease — ichthyosiform erythrodermia. His subsequent attempt to clear the boy's right arm of warts by hypnosis was 95 per cent successful. He went on to treat the boy's legs and feet in the same way, resulting in a 50 per cent cure.[150]

The obvious conclusion is that once a seed of doubt has been sown in the hypnotist's mind, the effect is reduced. In fact none of Dr Mason's attempts to treat other sufferers from this complaint by hypnosis were successful. Doubt on the part of the subject seems to have the same inhibiting effect: when the original patient returned for further hypnotic treatment three years after his first cure, it proved impossible to hypnotize him at all.

This sheds light on the question, to what extent healing depends on the faith of the patient. In cases where a cure is effected through a visit to a holy shrine such as Lourdes, or with the aid of relics — as when the sick were healed by contact with clothes that had been St Paul's (Acts 19, 12) — it would seem that faith might be paramount and all that is required. On at least one occasion Jesus actually said, 'Thy faith hath made thee whole.' But Dr Mason's experience suggests that the conviction or perhaps rather the trusting open-mindedness of the healer is more important than the patient's faith in a cure, if results are to be achieved.

It may be that the faith of the patient is crucial, but that different people may require varying degrees of support for that faith from the healer. We should also bear in mind that this faith and its healing power are UNCONSCIOUS and that the healer's strongest influence is probably also at an unconscious level. As patients wanting to be healed, we may consciously profess to have greater trust than we actually have, or on the other hand we may give exaggerated voice to our doubts. Somehow the healer has to maximize our unconscious faith.

It has been shown that there are clear links between TELEPATHY and hypnosis: telepathy operates more easily under hypnosis, and hypnosis can be induced telepathically. This suggests a means by which distant or ABSENT HEALING might operate. By telepathy the healer communicates to the patient the desire to be healed, and the patient then uses the body's own healing powers to effect a cure. But sometimes an earlier intention to send out healing may be just as effective: Lawrence LeShan's absent healing team once forgot to 'transmit' to a particular patient who was nevertheless cured.[108]

By the process of VISUALIZATION the healing power of the mind can be activated without the aid of a healer, although a therapist or counsellor of some kind still usually offers invaluable support. It has been shown that white blood cells (our defence against disease) increase when a patient experiences positive emotions. A famous example is Norman Cousins, who believes he cured himself by laughter.[33] The reverse is evidenced in psychosomatic illnesses which are so often linked with depression, and which are no less real simply because we judge that they start in the mind.

It is intriguing to ask whether all illnesses might actually start in the mind. Perhaps even epidemics are facilitated by suggestion. Do we sometimes deliberately (at an unconscious level) lay ourselves open to certain infections? If so, there is reason to suggest that recognizing the fact and understanding why we did so is perhaps more important than actually being cured. Otherwise we may simply follow the same cycle of illness again and again. Some people would say that this is the most important part of the true healer's role, for it may be a disservice to provide the patient with a quick cure without the inner understanding of why the condition arose in the first place.

This is not to say that we inflict illnesses on ourselves unnecessarily, nor that all illnesses are the result of our present way of thinking and behaving. Some may be karmic (see KARMA), in which case the healer would need to be of a spiritual level (a) to be aware of the soul's karmic needs, and (b) to offer the individual guidance in appreciating and accepting those needs. This is indeed a far cry from the level of awareness shown by the majority of healers, who offer comfort only on a physical and emotional level.

A healer's stage of development in this sense is sometimes described in terms of the CHAKRAS, depending in particular on which ones are activated. Physical healing is understood as being channelled through the solar plexus, and the emotional sympathy and understanding which usually accompanies the healing is naturally from the heart centre. An ability to diagnose may be equated with the creative and inspirational function of the throat centre, and understanding on a more intuitive, spiritual level arises with the activation of the brow centre (the opening of the THIRD EYE).

HEART CENTRE – See CHAKRAS.

HEAVEN Heaven was originally the abode of the gods (Olympus in the classical world) or of God and his ANGELS. In Old Testament times the average person, however devout, did not have access to heaven after death. The few who were destined to dwell there, such as Enoch and Elijah, were carried off bodily at the end of their earthly lives.

A more universally accessible heavenly state after death is referred to in the New Testament: Jesus tells of a beggar, Lazarus, who died and was 'carried by the angels into Abraham's bosom' (Luke 16), and later, on the cross, he says that the robber crucified with him will walk with him 'in PARADISE'. It is worth noting that this state is prior to any judgment and general resurrection. The Koran refers to Paradise as the ultimate destiny of the righteous.

The notion of a comfortable existence after death is sometimes described as SUMMERLAND by spiritualists. Messages received through MEDIUMS from the recently deceased suggest that whatever an individual's circumstances and preoccupations in the body, they are enhanced in the AFTERLIFE: we apparently live comfortable lives on the other side, much improved in quality, but not very different in kind from the life we know on earth. The general occult view is that this pleasant existence is of our own creation. Just as our focus while in the physical body is on the physical world, so when released from the physical body our focus changes to the astral world. In this state we surround ourselves with THOUGHT-FORMS in keeping with our astral state. The astral BODY is also known as the desire body, and our existence on the astral plane after death is ruled by our desires and emotional attachments. In this way we can form our own HELL too. Not until we have released ourselves from these needs will we progress to the next plane of existence, where we may eventually decide on our next incarnation.

When considering the different levels of existence or PLANES of being which are described in occult teachings it is worth remembering that the Bible often refers to heavens as well as heaven, and Paul refers to being 'caught up to the third heaven'. (2 Corinthians 12, 2). The first heaven may be regarded as Paradise, like the Spiritualists' Summerland; the second heaven is the level at which one remains between lives, surveying the most recent life and determining the conditions for the next; the third heaven would then be a higher spiritual level, at which the soul is aware of all its earthly incarnations and can fully appreciate all that it has learned from the experience, the point mid-way between the dense physical and pure spirit, the causal or higher mental plane which may rarely be touched in moments of ENLIGHTENMENT.

HELL Just as the Greeks had their Hades, the Hebrews their Sheol, and the Mesopotamians their Kurnugia or 'land of no return', the Babylonians their Aralu, 'the region of darkness, the road whence the wayfarer never returns, the house whose inhabitants see no light', and the Hindus their Naraka, 'situated beneath the earth and beneath the waters', hell has been a prominent feature of Christianity.

Augustine was the religious thinker who perhaps more than any other sought to prove that the damned suffered physically in ever-lasting fire. In literature hell has taken other forms. For Milton it was subject to extreme seasonal changes and could also be a frozen continent, but for the damned there was the possibility of hope – their punishment was not necessarily eternal. For Dante the torture was exaggerated further: the bodies of the damned could be destroyed and from the ashes grow again. For Sartre, hell was other people, being confined with them to continue indefinitely the futile arguments and unresolvable conflicts.

SPIRITUALISTS tend to skate over the question of hell, but the standard occult view is that we create it ourselves. It resembles the Sartrean hell more than any other, but it is conditioned by our expectations while on earth: if being tormented by devils is what you expect, that might be what you experience, but it would be your own projection. The hell that we create is a direct result of our earthly preoccupations. It might be closer to the traditional idea of purgatory, with the important difference that it is not imposed from outside: the individual soul is responsible for its own state immediately after death. Hell and purgatory are our own astral creations, and sooner or later we grow out of them.

The soul's realization that the immediate AFTERLIFE is its own astral creation has an interesting effect. The image of Tantalus in Hades suggests that we continue to create the shadow forms of what we desire – even our bodies are *shades*, but we can no longer actually enjoy them, as we perhaps did in the PARADISE we first created. Yet the soul still craves the things it enjoyed while in the flesh. So also the unhappy ghosts in the Tibetan Pretaloka continue to long for what they can never enjoy. This too is hell. But it does not last forever. Sooner or later a decision is taken, perhaps at some sort of JUDGMENT, and the choice is made to return to another earthly life. In very few instances will this judgment point lead to liberation from the wheel of rebirth on the one hand, or ultimate damnation – if ever – on the other.

This is in complete contrast to the terminal view of hell and damnation as propounded by most Christian sects, whose concept of hell was influenced strongly by the exaggeratedly lurid pictures painted by the medieval Church, but it is close to some of the teachings of early Christianity. For example, Origen (185–254), believed in ultimate salvation for all: all souls would incarnate again and again until they learned, progressed and were finally saved.

The common element in most pictures of hell is that they are in the underworld. Even when hell-fire is considered, it is the fire of volcanoes and the molten fire at the core of the earth, rather than the light-giving fire of the sun or the fire of the Holy Spirit. As Rodney Collin points out, there is something about hell that reminds us of the mineral kingdom. 'All descriptions of hell combine these three ideas in one way or another – the idea of a subterranean mineral or volcanic realm, the idea of darkness, and the idea that time there is immensely long, everlasting, endless, in comparison with human measurements of time.'[31] This is where 'petrified souls' are 'melted down'; hell is 'a cosmic melting-pot'. 'The purpose of hell, then, would be to restore faulty psychic products to their original state of sound raw material, which in due course could be used again, that is, re-absorbed into growing forms.' Collin cites a passage from the Hindu *Vishnu Purana* which shows the EVOLUTION of forms from one kingdom to another, all the way from inanimate things to liberated spirits. So a descent into hell, even into the ultimate, apparently permanent state of utter abandonment and destruction, is not eternal suffering nor annihilation, but simply the reverse of spiritual evolution, and spiritual evolution is ultimately the route that the whole of creation will follow.

HERMETICISM The basic tenet of Hermetic doctrine is the unity of all things. God is all, and God is within, giving life to our flesh and inspiring all we do. The famous injunction 'as above, so below' comes from *The Emerald Tablet of Hermes*, a Hermetic text whose origins go at least as far back as the eighth century and are probably earlier. The eighteen surviving books of the *Corpus Hermeticum* dating from the first centuries AD represent the oldest collection of Hermetic scriptures. They were the sacred texts of a relatively small sect who venerated the Egyptian god Thoth, and they brought together the wisdom of Greece and Asia as well as Egypt. Thoth was the ibis-headed god, lawgiver, divider of time and counter of the stars, a most important role on which the annual flooding of the Nile and prosperity of Egypt depended. He was identified with Hermes, the Greek deity concerned with wisdom and learning.

The sacred texts were regarded by some classical mystics as

having been inspired, perhaps even actually written, by Hermes — hence the name *Corpus Hermeticum*, by which the teachings are still known. This Hermes is sometimes called 'Hermes Trismegistos' — Thrice Greatest, and historians have speculated that there may have been three different historical figures who contributed to the final composite character. Plato referred to the first Egyptian Hermes also by the name Theut. He was identified with the earthly agent of the divine Creator and the one who named every creature. The Roman poet Ovid regarded him as the inventor of speech. Historically the first Hermes was probably a pharaoh, who was also the author of many writings on magic, and he is referred to in the Egyptian BOOK OF THE DEAD as a wise physician and magician.

One of the most important of the *Corpus Hermeticum* texts is the *Poimandres* or *Pymander* (Shepherd of Men), which describes in allegorical language how the spiritual MONAD within each of us first descended into matter, fell in love with nature and was consequently trapped in space and time. We are urged to repent: 'rid yourselves of darkness and grasp light; forsake corruption and partake of immortality'. Self-discipline and a certain asceticism are required of the initiate, who is then told to meditate in silence. 'Then only will you see the vision, when you cannot speak of it, for the knowledge of it is deep silence, and suppression of all the senses.' This is described as a vision of light: 'This alone, the knowledge of God, is man's salvation; this is the ascent to Olympus; by this alone can a soul become good.' And there is a consequent rebirth of the initiate: 'I am not now the man I was; I have been born again in spirit.' Those who experience this rebirth have a new sense of identity with the whole of creation and with God himself. 'We must not be afraid to affirm that a man on earth is a mortal god, and that a god in heaven is an immortal man.'

HIGHER SELF The Higher Self is our spiritual self, beyond the personality. It can be equated with what Paul Brunton called the OVERSELF, but should be distinguished from the Freudian super-ego, which is simply a socialized version of the SELF. Freud regarded the super-ego as being the voice of conscience because of the internalized rules that we learn from adults while we are children. The Higher Self is the voice of conscience because it exists beyond reason, being transcendental and noumenal, representing faith and higher reason. It is also the creative impulse, attracting us to higher aspirations. It is the 'God within', the SOUL.

In the *Upanishads* an individual is likened to two birds sitting in a tree, one constantly fluttering around — our temporary conscious EGO, the other motionless, watching — the eternal ATMAN. Roberto Assagioli drew a similar picture of the Higher Self (which he also sometimes referred to simply as the Self). 'This Self is above, and unaffected by, the flow of the mindstream or by bodily conditions; and the personal conscious self should be considered merely as its reflection, its "projection" in the field of the personality.'[3] Assagioli believed that the Higher Self was a scientific reality because 'it is proven by direct experience; it is one of the primary experiences which are evidences of themselves ... and therefore have full scientific value, in the broader sense.'[80] Conscious awareness of the Higher Self is possible in mystical experiences: 'The experience of the Self has a quality of perfect peace, serenity, calm, stillness, purity and in it there is a paradoxical blending of individuality and universality' (Assagioli).[3] Through self-knowledge we learn to strengthen the links between the conscious self and the Higher Self, bringing the personality more in line with the soul. This was the Work of the alchemists, for whom the Higher Self was symbolized by the PHILOSOPHER'S STONE.

HUNA RELIGION — See KAHUNAS.

HUNCH
A hunch is a flash of insight or intuition which cannot be explained logically, but why is it so called? Stan Gooch maintains that it is associated with 'hunchback', because it is (he claims) controlled by the cerebellum, which is at the back of the BRAIN like the deformed back of a hunchback. He also notes that the cerebellum is bigger in women than men, which he suggests explains why women are more intuitive than men.[62,63]

HUNDREDTH MONKEY PHENOMENON
In 1952 wild colonies of monkeys were being studied on the Japanese island of Koshima. The researchers started leaving provisions for the animals so that they could observe their behaviour at close quarters and among the food provided were raw sweet potatoes. The monkeys liked this new delicacy, although the fact that the sweet potatoes were covered with sand and grit was a slight handicap. Or so it seemed until a bright eighteen-month-old female called Imo came along. She discovered that she could carry the fruit to the beach and wash the sand off in the sea. The salty sea-water might also have added something to the taste. Soon her playmates started imitating her, and then some of the adults started copying their offspring. The

role-reversal of the young being an example for the old rather than learning from them was duly reported in the scientific journals (*Primates* **6**, 1965).

Then something more surprising apparently happened. The gradual increase in the number of monkeys washing their sweet potatoes in the sea changed dramatically so that virtually all the monkeys adopted the practice as if a critical number had been reached which caused the habit to sweep through the rest of the population. Furthermore, monkeys on other islands suddenly started to follow the example of Imo's colony, with which they had had no reported physical contact whatsoever.

In calling this the Hundredth Monkey Phenomenon the figure of one hundred has been chosen arbitrarily to represent any critical number, which once reached appears to induce a sudden change in a much larger population. Lyall Watson believes that the phenomenon explains the sudden blossoming of innovation in tools in the Mousterian culture after at least a million years of static tool design in the Lower Palaeolithic period.[206] Rupert Sheldrake believes that biological evolution works on similar lines, by a process he calls FORMATIVE CAUSATION.

HYPERACUITY The way we use our senses appears to change according to our expectations. Certain tribes in Africa and South America can point out the position of Venus during daylight. A few hundred years ago sailors used Venus to navigate by whenever it was above the horizon regardless of the time of day. Today most people would only be able to see the planet by excluding the surrounding daylight somehow — looking through a narrow tube, for example. Our inability to see Venus in bright daylight is partly a matter of habit, and partly because we no longer expect to see it. Lack of expectation can even result in invisibility: when Captain Cook's ship approached a South Pacific island for the first time, it was simply not seen by the inhabitants, who had never seen such a vessel before.

So with a little practice we could see much more detail than we usually see, especially if we needed to see such detail. J. Milne Bramwell, who wrote the first major English study of hypnotism in 1903, discovered that under HYPNOSIS the ability to see in finer detail is increased enormously.[18] A person can be hypnotized and shown several blank pieces of paper. Told that each apparently identical piece of paper bears a different picture, the subject will be able to identify each one correctly even when they have been shuffled. The brain can therefore recognize minute differences in the paper, small marks, creases, irregularities, the position of the watermark, which in 'normal consciousness' would go unnoticed.

In his research into hypnosis Pierre Janet (1859—1947) discovered that hypnotized subjects could distinguish between one piece of blank card and another. In his experiment he told a subject to hallucinate a picture on a blank card, which was then shuffled in amongst a set of other identical blank cards. When asked to do so the subject was able to pick out the card which 'showed' the imaginary picture. The reason is that whilst the suggestion was being made by the hypnotist, the subject's attention was fixed on the card to such an acute degree that every grain and blemish in the card was noticed and memorized. This is not simply a theory: when questioned under hypnosis some of these subjects have actually described the differences they see and use as cues to discriminate between apparently identical blank surfaces.

Eugène Marais called this talent 'hypnotic HYPERAESTHESIA. He believed that we are innately more sensitive to sensory stimuli than we suppose, and that we have developed our intellect at the expense of our more natural sensory ability. Under hypnosis, however, we are able to free ourselves from the inhibitions which rationalization has placed on our senses. In 1922 Marais showed how a hypnotized subject could distinguish easily between twenty apparently identical snail shells, or determine who had handled certain objects by the sense of smell alone. He devised similar experiments to show that humans also have an amazing sense of direction. To some this suggests that the homing instinct and sense of direction of animals, although not yet fully 'explained', is a natural facility, which in humans becomes somehow suppressed or dormant by our other more conscious learning.[121]

HYPERAESTHESIA A heightened sensitivity to sensory stimuli is known as hyperaesthesia or HYPERACUITY. This term is also sometimes used for anomalous sensory phenomena, such as the 'fingertip vision' of Rosa Kuleschova. This phenomenon was described by Cesare Lombroso (1836—1909) as 'transposition of the senses', and he cited cases of seeing through the skin of the ear and nose, and smelling through the chin and heel.[113]

HYPERPNEA BREATHING extra deeply, or taking rapid breaths, is known as hyperpnea (Greek: 'to much breath'). By reducing the amount of carbon-dioxide in the blood and allowing more oxygen to get to the brain it can cause slight anaesthesia and induce trance-like conditions.

HYPNAGOGIC In the transitional state of CONSCIOUSNESS while falling asleep people often hear voices and see visions. These 'hypnagogic' images (Greek: 'leading to sleep') seem to intrude into awareness uninvited, just as one is about to fall asleep. Music may also be heard, and this may be inspirational: Wagner's Overture to *Das Rheingold* was supposedly so inspired.[157]

The hypnagogic state is regarded by some as the gateway into the paranormal and as conducive to ESP and PRECOGNITION. Experimenters have used the method of getting subjects to fall into a hypnagogic state (by, for example, covering their eyes with halves of billiard balls — the GANZFELD technique) in order to induce TELEPATHY. Thomas Jay Hudson considered the moments just before falling asleep and just after waking up ('hypnopompic') as the best times for experiments in sending out healing vibrations. This is when the 'objective mind', always inclined to scepticism, has the least blocking influence on the SUBJECTIVE MIND.

Andreas Mavromatis proved to his own satisfaction that telepathy is facilitated if either sender or receiver is in a hypnagogic state. First he noticed that if he began to doze while his students were practising PSYCHOMETRY, he started to see, rather than simply envisage, the scenes they described. Then, while still in this self-induced hypnagogic state, he deliberately altered the scene he saw, with the result that the student's description changed in accordance with his new version.

Rudolf Steiner said that the best time to contact spirits of the dead was just before falling asleep and just after waking up.

HYPNOGOGIC — See HYPNAGOGIC.

HYPNOPOMPIC The sounds and visions that arise during the transitional state between sleeping and waking consciousness are called hypnopompic images (Greek: sent or escorted by sleep). The hypnopompic state is similar to the HYPNAGOGIC state that occurs just before one falls asleep, and seems to be similarly conducive to paranormal perception. A common test is to decide in advance that immediately on waking one will automatically ask oneself the time and know the answer without looking at the clock. The results are often amazingly accurate. In the same way while in this hypnopompic state one can often identify instantaneously the origin of letters heard dropping through the letterbox. Other private ESP experiments can be tried to predict events that will happen that day.

HYPNOSIS/HYPNOTISM The Marquis de Puységur learned the technique of 'animal magnetism' from Franz Mesmer in the 1780s. During his treatment of a certain Victor Race for inflammation of the lungs, he was surprised to discover a new condition which he called 'magnetic sleep', in which his patient was extremely suggestible and would carry out instructions unquestioningly. He recognized this as a different state of awareness and believed that everybody operates as a double system, one part governed by the normal waking 'I', the other by something which is more pliable, more open to external influences.

The Abbé de Faria (1755–1819) was one of the first investigators to contradict the supposed physical cause of mesmerism in the form of a magnetic fluid and maintain that the phenomenon was the result of some change in the subject.[52]

In the nineteenth century this state was studied in Britain, in particular by William Gregory, a professor of chemistry at Edinburgh, who recognized its similarity with sleepwalking and called it 'artificial somnambulism'. Another Scot, James Braid (1795–1860), practising as a surgeon in Manchester, maintained that the state depended on the subject's nervous condition. He discovered that he was able to conduct surgical operations on patients who were under hypnotic anaesthesia. Because of the link with the nervous system Braid initially called the process *neurypnotism*, and later changed it to *hypnotism*.

The basic characteristics of the hypnotic condition were now well known: loss of personal consciousness, with the possibility of a new identity and new memory, and enhanced suggestibility with apparent insensibility to pain. In the 1880s one of the leading investigators into hypnosis was Jean-Martin Charcot at the Hospital of the Salpêtrière in Paris. He believed that the hypnotic state was an artificially induced neurosis, and even if it could be used therapeutically to cure certain symptoms (often only temporarily), it was essentially (a) a pathological condition, similar to HYSTERIA, and (b) a peculiar state of the nervous system which was recognizable by definite physical signs. At the same time a rival school of thought grew up in Nancy, around the work of an unassuming provincial doctor, A.A. Liébault (1823–1903), a supporter of Bernheim's notion of SUGGESTION, (H. Bernheim (1837–1919): *De la Suggestion*).[8] They regarded hypnosis as a normal psychological phenomenon to which virtually everyone was susceptible. Their understanding of hypnosis as a mental effect, rather than a physiological one, came to be known as the 'animist' position. But the theory of suggestion was very simplistic, and as F.W.H. Myers said, 'If Bernheim's theories, in their extreme form, were true, there would by this time have been no sufferers left to heal.'[135]

Despite two hundred years of research hypnosis is still largely a mystery to science. No single aspect of behaviour has been found to be peculiar to hypnosis. There is consequently no sure way of ascertaining whether someone is actually under hypnosis or not, other than by simply asking them. Its evolutionary purpose is also a mystery. There may be a clue in the fact that some animals seem to be hypnotized by the repetitive movements of their prospective mate prior to the act of mating. The methods by which human beings can be put into hypnotic trance also usually involve visual or auditory repetition — words repeated monotonously to induce a state of relaxation, and a reduced variety of visual stimuli with a bright object swinging to and fro, filling the subject's whole visual field, much as a peacock's fanned tail might to the entranced peahen.

Following in the steps of Mesmer, subsequent practitioners used hypnosis as a HEALING technique to cure skin complaints, inflammations, warts, and the like. Conversely, if hypnotized subjects are told that they are to be touched with a red-hot needle, blisters appear at the appropriate spot on the skin when lightly brushed with a feather. In recent years more dramatic physical changes have been effected by means of hypnosis, including increased bust measurement in women.

Hypnosis and ESP have been shown to be closely linked. When considering ESP under hypnosis one must be careful that in a particular experiment ESP is actually involved and not simply HYPERACUITY. In one of Charcot's favourite experiments hypnotized subjects hallucinated a picture on a blank card and were subsequently able to pick out that card from many other identical cards, but they accomplished this by recognizing minute blemishes on the plain surface of the card (hyperacuity) and not by ESP, and they themselves explained this while under hypnosis.

However, ESP has often been clearly demonstrated under hypnosis. In the 1840s Alexis Didier played cards while blindfold under hypnosis, and he could identify not only the cards in other people's hands but also those placed face down on the table (which could not be explained by mere telepathy).[44] His ESP abilities under hypnosis included PSYCHOMETRY (which he performed for Alexandre Dumas) and REMOTE VIEWING, reporting scenes and events in distant places ('travelling clairvoyance' as it was then called). These skills have been demonstrated in many hypnotized subjects since then. For example, under hypnosis and with eyes closed people have been known to read a newspaper held by another person on the other side of the room.

The links between hypnosis and TELEPATHY are even more striking. In 1885 a Dr Gibert in Le Havre actually induced hypnosis in a patient called Leonie simply by thinking of her. They were at opposite ends of the town at the time. On other occasions she was aware that the doctor was trying to hypnotize her at a distance, but she refused to co-operate. These incidents were witnessed by the French psychologist Pierre Janet and the English researcher Frederic Myers.[135] A few years later Dr Paul Joire caused hypnotized subjects to follow his telepathic instructions: they obeyed his mental commands. In the 1920s a Russian scientist, L.L. Vasiliev, carried out similar experiments in what he called 'distant influence'.[204] It seems that telepathy is facilitated by hypnosis. This could have serious implications for REGRESSION.

In the 1880s Professor Carpenter of Boston took up experiments in hypnosis and liked to show that it could enhance the powers of the mind. Under hypnosis a subject would be introduced to the spirit of a famous thinker, such as Socrates, and encouraged to carry on a philosophical conversation with him. The subject would report back to the hypnotist what the great thinker said and the ideas and arguments put forward would always seem to be of a far higher level than the subject himself was thought to be intellectually capable of. The experiment was repeated with many different stand-in philosophers (including an erudite talking pig), and the ideas expounded in the conversations revealed what Carpenter described as 'a wonderful system of spiritual philosophy'. Carpenter himself was a total sceptic regarding 'spirits', which was why he so deliberately invoked the imagination of the hypnotized subjects to conjure up the these philosophers. Neither was he at all sympathetic to the 'spiritual philosophy' which his subjects expounded, so they could certainly not have been voicing his ideas picked up by telepathy. Imagination backed up by CRYPTOMNESIA would be the current orthodox explanation.

There are two fairly obvious conclusions from these experiments. First, it may be by this mechanism that MEDIUMS channel in trance, if we equate TRANCE with self-hypnosis. Thomas Jay Hudson thought this. As a Christian he firmly believed that the SOUL survives death, but he was equally convinced that SPIRITUALISM has nothing to say on this matter. He believed that all 'spirits' contacted by mediums were creations of 'the subjective mind'. However, if we accept this explanation of 'spirits', we must also admit that somewhere in the recesses of the human mind there is a firm belief in a consistent spiritual philosophy of which most of us are consciously unaware.

HYPOMETABOLIC ALERTNESS An altered state of CONSCIOUSNESS can be achieved by deep relaxation and MEDITATION, or it can be induced by inhaling nitrous oxide (laughing gas). In such a state, perception of external reality is enhanced. One does not usually hallucinate in this state. It inspires a feeling akin to what St Paul called 'the peace that passeth all understanding', what Buddhists call SATORI, and YOGIS SAMADHI or MOKSHA — in other words 'true awareness', ENLIGHTENMENT.

Hypometabolic alertness is the biological term for the physiological state, whether achieved by ingesting or inhaling a chemical such as nitrous oxide or by practising meditation. It is generally accepted by adepts of all schools, however, that enlightenment cannot be artificially induced by DRUGS, but can only be achieved by the strict discipline of meditation.

HYSTERIA The condition known as hysteria has meant different things to different people, with effects ranging from emotional hyperactivity at one extreme to paralysis at the other. It originally referred to the state in which women were susceptible to frenzied emotional outbursts (from Greek *hystera*, 'womb'). Even when Freud adapted the term to 'conversion hysteria', he had difficulty convincing the medical world that it could afflict men as well as women. He used the term to denote the process by which repressed sexual desires were converted into physical symptoms such as paralysis in an attempt to dispel the unconscious anxiety. 'Hysterical patients,' said Freud, 'suffer mainly from reminiscences.' Other psychologists used the term 'hysteria' to refer to a wider range of symptoms characteristic of DISSOCIATION — suggestibility, amnesia, TRANCES and MULTIPLE PERSONALITY.

It is partly in this last sense that Lyall Watson used it when he wrote, 'Christianity owes its establishment as a formal religion to an outbreak of mass hysteria amongst its first disciples at

Pentecost.'[207] The disciples were demonstrating XENOGLOSSY (speaking in tongues) and possibly TRANCE, whilst the listeners were perhaps more susceptible to suggestion and became caught up in the mood of the crowd, causing the psychology of crowd behaviour to take over from the more usual individual response. Watson has postulated a kind of group mind which influences behaviour in this way, and for which he has coined the word SAMA.

The use of the term 'mass hysteria' is fairly common in everyday speech nowadays. It is used as an apparent explanation for the irrational behaviour of ordinary people. In the Middle Ages panic would occasionally spread through a country as people convinced themselves that they had been poisoned, or they would infect each other with a compulsive desire to dance ceaselessly. (It was one such occasion which gave rise to the Tarantella.) Some of these instances may have been sparked off by the consumption of 'bad bread', made from grain infected with the ergot fungus, but it is unlikely that such external chemical agencies were ever the sole cause. Even in modern times mass hysteria has often been held to be responsible if not for the outbreak at least to some extent for the prolonged incidence of otherwise inexplicable illnesses, ranging from gastric complaints that imitate food poisoning to the modern 'sick building syndrome'.

I CHING Pronounced 'Yee Jing', The Chinese *Book of Change* has been used in divination for millennia and is possibly the oldest book in the world. It has been amplified and refined over the centuries, but the first legendary figure to be associated with its authorship was Fu Hsi, a ruler of China around 3000 BC, to whom the discovery of the eight trigrams was attributed. Legend has it that he first discovered the trigrams — three-line symbols — in the markings on the shell of a tortoise as it emerged from the Yellow River, where he was meditating. These groups of YIN and YANG lines represent the various forms of interaction between the two complementary forces which lie at the root of all change in the UNIVERSE. Nature is ruled by duality, positive and negative (or receptive), heaven and earth, yang and yin. With two lines one can represent four seasons, and with three lines one can represent the eight elemental forces which govern conditions on earth and in the cosmos: Heaven, Lake, Fire, Thunder, Wind, Water, Mountain, and Earth. The earliest version of the *I Ching* incorporating these eight trigrams was used as a manual to ascertain the prospects for hunting, fishing and farming.

Then King Wen, founder of the Chou dynasty (1150 BC), saw a vision on the wall of his prison cell while imprisoned by the tyrant Emperor Chou Hsin. The vision was of the sixty-four hexagrams, formed by combining any two of the trigrams.

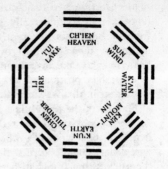

The eight trigrams, which form the basis of the sixty-four hexagrams of the I *Ching (This arrangement is attributed to Fu Hsi. Each trigram is built up from the centre outwards.)*

In the commentaries he wrote on these sixty-four hexagrams, his concerns were with their social and political significance, and his judgments showed how the world of human civilization was influenced by the elemental forces of nature. His son, Wu, having led a rebellion against Chou Hsin, in which he rescued his father from prison and put him on the throne, continued the work on the *I Ching* by writing commentaries on each individual line in every hexagram — the Commentaries of the Duke of Chou (*c.* 1122 BC). Later supplements continued to be written, most notably the *Ten Wings*, attributed to Confucius (551–479 BC) but probably written by another.

The basic premise at the root of the *I Ching* is that cosmic order and human nature are one. Divination by drawing yarrow stalks or randomly throwing coins is a means of stopping time to see the changes that are in progress at this precise moment, so that one can align oneself with them, going with one's TAO instead of fighting vainly against it, and discovering one's SELF in the process. Consulting the *I Ching* captures the moment not only as one of the sixty-four hexagrams but also by indicating which (if any) yin or yang lines are so heavily yin or yang that they are on the verge of becoming their opposite and thus transform the whole hexagram. It is the commentaries on these 'changing lines' that usually constitute the most significant part of the oracle's answer to the querent's question.

Once one has chosen the method of determining whether a line is yin or yang (usually by ascribing the numbers two and three to heads and tails or vice versa), consulting the *I Ching* is one of the most straightforward, objective and least 'psychic' of all forms of divination, requiring no special sensitivity or aptitude for clairvoyance. Interpretation of the Chinese symbols and the references to rulers and 'the superior man' may prove difficult, but there are many modern versions which are more accessible to the modern Western reader.

IDEODYNAMICS When a person makes barely perceptible movements (dynamics) in sympathy with some idea that has been expressed, an expert observer of ideodynamics can recognize the tell-tale signals of involuntary body-language and proceed to tell the individual a wealth of detail about their thoughts, personality and life. This is the method consciously employed by many a fairground fortune-teller, and sceptics claim that as an unconscious technique it also explains away the CLAIRVOYANCE practised by honest SENSITIVES. Even though it is almost impossible for a sitter not to provide the clairvoyant with indications of the degree of accuracy of what is being said, most reputable clairvoyants have at least one story of a sitter who insisted on having the clairvoyant facing the wall or who sat silent and impassive throughout the sitting, only to congratulate the clairvoyant finally on the accuracy of the reading.

IDEOPLASTICITY When representations of faces or parts of the body materialize in a physical circle, it is suggested that energy from the MEDIUM'S AURA is used. Because the aura consists of radiations rather than matter, the transformation of that energy into objective ECTOPLASM or psychoplasm has been described as ideoplasticity, (= 'idea' + 'form').

IDIOPHANY Since the word HALLUCINATION is so closely associated with mental illness, Ian Stevenson (*American Journal of Psychiatry* Dec, 1983) tentatively coined the term *idiophany* (literally 'private' + 'appear'), to denote 'idiosyncratic perception', or an apparently hallucinatory experience which is not shared by others and which has no pathological cause.

ILLUMINATI One group known as the Illuminati were the followers of Emmanuel Swedenborg (1688–1772), the Swedish scientist, philosopher and mystic. He was approaching his fiftieth birthday when he had a vision in which he was told to teach his interpretation of the Bible. Following this experience he practised AUTOMATIC WRITING, describing himself as 'only the secretary', and had further visions which were precognitive or in which he experienced the ASTRAL WORLD.

Another group also called Illuminati were members of a materialist sect with symbolism borrowed from Freemasons. The sect was founded in 1776 in Ingolstadt, Bavaria, by another seer and visionary, Adam Weishaupt (1748—1830). Their aim was to propagate a religion based on enlightened reason which was open to direct influence by Divine Reason and not dependent on church or state. They regarded themselves as the creative minority in what was to become a new democratic world order.

IMAGERY — See EIDETIC IMAGERY, GUIDED IMAGERY, LED MEDITATION.

IMAGINATION Whenever someone starts trying to develop their psychic faculties — CLAIRVOYANCE, for example — one of the most common reactions is the temptation to dismiss one's first impressions as imagination. This is understandable because the channel of INTUITION, the means by which the conscious mind becomes aware of psychic impressions, appears to be the same channel through which the creative imagination brings images to conscious attention: both intuition and imagination present ideas to us as if spontaneously, without any conscious process of reasoning on our part. Some have equated this to the functioning of the right hemisphere of the BRAIN, in contrast to the logical mode characteristic of the left hemisphere.

Some methods of MEDITATION start by exercising the imagination by disciplining the mind and developing the ability to visualize deliberately in great detail. The meditative process then continues by allowing the images thus evoked to change of their own accord and generate further images. If one is meditating with the purpose of receiving clairvoyant impressions, the spontaneously arising images will then fulfil this purpose and should be interpreted accordingly. Dismissing them as imagination simply blocks the process. Yet insisting that they have nothing to do with imagination is also misleading, since developing the imagination does help this form of clairvoyance. Perhaps one should rather accept the pointlessness of trying to separate imagination from psychic awareness, and recognize that the imagination can be put to effective use as a psychic tool as well as a source of creativity.

Another way in which the imagination is used as a channel between the conscious rational mind and other levels of awareness was described by one of Dion Fortune's 'communicators' in answer to the recurrent question concerning the objective reality of discarnate masters. 'What we are you cannot realize and it is a waste of time to try to do so, but you can imagine us on the astral plane and we can contact you through your imagination, and although your mental picture is not real or actual, the results of it are real and actual.' [54] In other words, the form such entities take is governed by our imagination, just as the way we perceive the physical world is governed by our senses. What matters about our mental picture of the external world is that it enables us to deal with it, rather than whether it is a true representation of its objective reality — which is unprovable. Likewise, what matters about our appreciation of other levels of reality, mediated by the imagination, is not whether the picture is accurate, but whether it is effective.

The poet and mystic William Blake (1757—1827) believed that the world of the imagination was in some ways more real than the material world in the same way that the spiritual realm is more real. (See PLATONISM.) 'This world of Imagination is the world of Eternity; it is the divine bosom into which we shall all go after the death of the vegetated body. The world of Imagination is infinite and eternal. ... There exist in that eternal world the permanent realities of everything that we see reflected in this vegetable glass of nature' (*Descriptive Catalogue*). It is not surprising therefore that the imagination can be a gateway to the eternal world of spirit.

IMPLICATE ORDER The physicist, David Bohm, has suggested that what we consider to be the material universe is the explicit manifestation or unfolding of a more fundamental order, an implicate order of reality. The implicate order is not a transcendent level of reality; on the contrary, it underlies what we regard as reality. 'This implicate order implies a reality immensely beyond what we call matter. Matter itself is merely a ripple in this background.' This is why quantum theory has failed to 'explain' basic reality. The ambiguity of quantum particles — in experiments one can ascertain the momentum or the position of an electron but never both — seemed to be a reflection of the ambiguous nature of mental phenomena, and many physicists started to suggest that consciousness was somehow involved at this level of matter. Science was in a paradoxical situation: biologists were maintaining that MIND was reducible to the mechanism of the BRAIN which was explainable by chemistry and physics, whilst physicists started to say that consciousness lay at the root of physical reality. 'Pure idealism would reduce matter to an aspect of mind. ... Pure materialism attempts to reduce mind to an aspect of matter. ... My view does not attempt to reduce one to the other any more than one would reduce form to content. ... They're interwoven. They're correlative categories of reality, always woven together just as form and content are woven together.'[13]

In Bohm's view everything from an electron to a living organism has an information field around it (analogous to Sheldrake's MORPHOGENETIC FIELD) in multi-dimensional space. In the implicate order everything is interconnected because of the undivided wholeness of reality. It is like a hologram, in which the whole can be seen in any part of it. Normal consciousness focuses on the explicate order but in other modes of consciousness we may attune to the implicate order and the result is paranormal perception.

INCARNATION – See REINCARNATION.

INCUBUS Originally an incubus was any demon that disturbed one's sleep by invading the mind or materializing in some horrifying form. Then it came to be restricted to a particular kind of demonic materialization which appeared to women and had intercourse with them, the complementary phenomenon for men being the SUCCUBUS. Both St Augustine and St Thomas Aquinas believed in the reality of such DEMONS. Modern psychology classifies these entities as figments of the imagination, delusions or hallucinations evoked in all probability as a response to repressed desires. The writer Stan Gooch has gone further than most in speculating about their origin and in experiencing the effect of the succubus at first hand.

INDIVIDUALITY The individuality is an individual's essence, the essential self as distinct from the personality. In some esoteric and occult writings it is equivalent to the HIGHER SELF, as opposed to the Lower Self. It is sometimes referred to as the MONAD.

INITIATION To anthropologists initiations mark an individual's entry into the tribe or passage from one stage of life to another. Initiations are equally widespread throughout the world in a religious context, marking a person's spiritual maturity.

Initiations are always turning points. In Christianity baptism is an initiation, and Paul saw baptism as death to the old life and rebirth in Christ. SUFI initiations refer to three deaths. Interestingly, the 'rebirth' following initiations like these was often on the third day. The many legends of journeys to the underworld in classical mysteries represented initiations. It is believed by some that the initiate had to lie as if dead in a shallow oblong pit found in some Mithraic temples. It has also been suggested that Egyptian initiates left their physical body while lying in the stone sarcophagus.

Considerable training was necessary before most initiations. The Jewish historian, Josephus, records that a two-year period of instruction preceded initiation into the ESSENE sect. The GURU who teaches the Hindu seeker also conducts the initiation and gives the initiate a MANTRA.

Some initiations, such as in Mithraism, included ordeals, real or symbolic. Nowadays we sometimes regard certain experiences in life as being initiations, in that by going through them and dealing with them we speed up our spiritual progress. In this sense Dion Fortune has described initiation as 'condensed evolution'.[54]

INSPIRATION Some occultists use the words 'inspiration' and 'INTUITION' interchangeably, but if a distinction needs to be made 'intuition' refers to the realization and recognition of an idea which arises in the mind in a flash as if from nowhere, and 'inspiration' is usually a longer process of transmitting a sequence of ideas which seem to come from somewhere else, as if another mind were linking somehow with our own.

Many mystics have declared that the teachings they convey were divine revelations. St Teresa and Jacob Boehme are among the many who profess not to have known what they were writing while putting their mystical works on paper.

Socrates in the fifth century BC is one of the earliest figures to declare that the best of what he did was at the instigation of another force, his DAEMON. In Plato's *Ion*, Socrates is made to describe the process by which poets are inspired 'possessed as it were by a spirit not their own, and in a state of divine insanity'.

This conviction that the words or music with which one is inspired seems to come from a source external to the poet or musician has continued throughout history. William Blake maintained that all credit for his writings was due to his 'celestial friends'; he often wrote 'from immediate dictation, without pre-

171

meditation and even against my will'. Rabindranath Tagore (1861–1941) described one of his books as being written by a 'disembodied being ... using my pen and mind. There is an unseen hand that drives the spirit on, like a submerged propeller.'

INTUITION Intuition is a sudden knowing, independent of any logical thought process and often even at first sight contrary to logic. On a mundane level we may call this a HUNCH or SIXTH SENSE, but great thinkers also operate intuitively. Scientists have often received some of their best ideas by intuition – 'not by painstaking research but as it were by the grace of God, and as a sudden flash of truth' (Karl Friedrich Gauss (1777–1855), the German mathematician). The philosopher Karl Popper (1902–85) said, 'There is no such thing as a logical method of having new ideas, or a logical reconstruction of this process. Every great discovery contains an irrational element or a creative intuition.'[153] It was because of this little understood intuitive faculty that Koestler said of the brain: 'Evolution has wildly overshot the mark.'[105]

Isaac Newton became intuitively aware of many ideas which he was unable to prove. Orthodox psychology maintains that such discoveries are the result of ideas arising from the individual's UNCONSCIOUS, but does not tell us why the proof for Newton's ideas on the roots of equations, for example, had to wait two centuries to well up in another mathematician's mind.

The German chemist, Kekulé von Stradonitz, had been trying to prove that the chemical properties of chemicals were determined by the structure of their atoms. He worked out the structure of several carbon compounds but was having great difficulty with benzene. Then one day he was sitting on a bus when in a flash of inspiration he saw the atoms spinning before him in a ring, rather like a snake eating its own tail.

Mendeleyev made a set of sixty-three cards on which he wrote the chemical and physical properties of each of the known elements. He recognized that there was order somewhere in this array of elements and spent every spare moment he had trying to find that order. On 1 March 1869 he had spent hours arranging the cards in one pattern after another, vainly searching for the elusive order underlying the elements, and he fell asleep. On waking up he knew the answer and immediately placed the cards in order of atomic weight in eight vertical columns leaving spaces occasionally where the characteristics in the horizontal columns did not coincide. This arrangement has stood the test of time to such an extent that it is still used today when another forty-four elements have been inserted into Mendeleyev's table.

Psychologists suggest that in such cases as these the scientists had been thinking for so long on the problems that preoccupied them, that the unconscious mind started working on them independently of the conscious mind. This seems more likely for mundane problems (e.g. remembering a name or solving a crossword clue) than in creative thought. Here the element of concentration is probably important. Devoting one's attention to one particular object for a considerable time can lead to a lack of awareness of other sensory stimuli, and this can easily give way to a state of reverie, a slightly altered state of consciousness, in which information can be perceived in a different way — paranormally. It seems clear that Kekulé was in a state of relaxed almost trance-like attentiveness which is akin to the state of meditation and which many psychics describe as being essential for clairvoyance. This state is also experienced on waking, when HYPNOPOMPIC impressions may provide us with the answer to a problem after 'sleeping on it', as Mendeleyev's experience shows.

Perhaps we can train ourselves to find answers this way. It may explain how the Japanese manage to learn how to sex one-day-old chickens. The method is never explained. Chicken-sexers are taught simply by having an expert say 'Yes' or 'No' as they practise. Thinking about it is actually discouraged as applying reason seems to block the intuitive capacity. The semi-hypnotic effect of repeatedly picking up and putting down a chick, attentive awareness but excluding distractions, concentration without thinking, all this satisfies the criteria to enter a slightly altered state in which intuition works. It is even claimed that fertile and infertile eggs can be identified in the same way.

In esoteric terms intuitive awareness is on the soul-level. This is 'higher' than either mental awareness or astral perception. Rudolf Steiner described intuition as the highest of the three faculties by which human beings can become aware of the supersensible worlds, the other two being imagination and inspiration. 'The "I" of a man, which comes to life in the soul, draws into itself messages from above, from the spirit-world, through intuitions, just as through sensations it draws in messages from the physical world. And in so doing it fashions the spirit-world into the individualized life of its own soul, even as it does the physical world by means of the senses.'[183] The brow CHAKRA which is associated with the PINEAL GLAND is sometimes regarded as the organ of intuition. Inspiration, on the other hand, is received via the throat CHAKRA.

JINX Jinxes are not commonly considered to be a paranormal phenomenon and few books on the paranormal even mention them. Yet the concept is one which — if mere coincidence is not to be invoked as an explanation — seems to involve non-material forces. The word 'jinx' is used in two ways. In one meaning it applies to objects and places that bring bad luck and is the equivalent of a CURSE. In the second use, which has a similar meaning but perhaps a different explanation, it applies more directly to people.

Some people are unable to wear wristwatches because of the frequency with which they go wrong. Others seem to have more than their fair share of problems with electrical equipment. These conditions may stay with a person throughout life or they may be only temporary, but something physical definitely seems to be happening without an obvious physical cause. They could be regarded as mild but more persistent cases of the POLTERGEIST phenomenon.

A possible clue to what is actually going on is the incidence of this kind of jinx with electrical equipment. In the now famous case of the Rosenheim poltergeist it was discovered that the presence of a young woman was having a disruptive effect on the electric and telephone circuits in her office building. Somehow her own 'electric charge' was interfering with the normal operation of telephones, lighting and electrical gadgetry in the office.

There have been many studies which have shown that the human body has an electromagnetic field around it. This has been variously described as a LIFE-FIELD or a body or BIOPLASMA and seems to be the scientific equivalent of the energy body or ETHERIC BODY. KIRLIAN PHOTOGRAPHY and the investigations of Harold Saxton Burr have shown that our inner state, both physiologically and psychologically, is reflected in our energy field. It is generally accepted that a large proportion of poltergeists are associated with young people around puberty, in whom one might not be surprised to find a highly charged and easily unbalanced energy field. The less violent phenomenon of jinxes could be a similar effect on a smaller scale, originating in a slight imbalance in the life-field or etheric body, or even just an unfortunate coincidence between the predominant frequencies in the life-field and the ones to which gadgets are most susceptible. The mechanism is not yet understood but there are certainly pointers.

The effect might even be magnified by a habitual mistrust of gadgetry. It has been suggested that the human energy field is instrumental in PSYCHOKINESIS, an idea supported by some Kirlian photographs of Uri Geller's hands while attempting to produce a PK effect. The belief that one has this 'jinx' and the expectation that the machine will fail to work properly could actually induce the electro-magnetic interference. We are familiar with the impossibility of obeying an injunction against thinking about something ('Think of anything except an elephant'), and apprehensive expectation works in the same way: fearing that we might do something actually encourages us to do it, and so the jinx effect is induced.

JUDGMENT Ancient Egypt and India seem to have been the first cultures to introduce the idea of judgment into the fate of the dead. In the BOOK OF THE DEAD there are vivid descriptions of judgment before Osiris before whom the heart of the deceased is weighed in a balance against a feather, representing Maat, the principle of morality. Ammit, the crocodile-jawed devourer of the dead, was ready to receive those who failed this test.

In Zoroastrian belief the soul of the deceased comes to a point called the Bridge of Chinvat. With the help of conscience the righteous soul passes safely, but the wicked become terrified by the proximity of the abyss and fall headlong into hell.

Some writings make it clear that judgment is not immediate on the soul's arrival in the next world but follows a period in which various other fears or longings are experienced. *The Tibetan Book of the Dead* gives detailed descriptions of the visions of gods and demons which may visit the soul at this time, but adds, 'Fear not. Be not terrified. Be not awed. Recognize them to be the embodiment of thine own intellect.' In other words the apparent PARADISE, HELL or purgatory in which we first arrive after death has no objective reality: we create it ourselves.

Nevertheless *The Tibetan Book of the Dead* also speaks of an actual hell following judgment, and 'falling therein, thou wilt have to endure unbearable misery, whence there is no certain time of getting out'. So what form does the judgment take? *The Tibetan Book of the Dead* also describes the soul's existence in the desire body, its ability to pass instantaneously to whatever place it wishes, its 'power of miraculous action'. However, 'These various powers of illusion and of shape-shifting desire not, desire not.' W^l en the soul realizes that it is creating its own reality, does it self indulgently continue to do so, or does it move on to other things?

In *The Tibetan Book of the Dead* there is a vivid description of a judgment scene presided over by Yama-Raja, the flaming Lord of Death. This is followed by a now familiar reminder: 'Apart from one's own hallucinations, in reality there are no such things existing outside oneself as Lord of Death, or god, or demon, or the Bull-headed Spirit of Death. Act so as to recognize this.' Again, judgment is carried out by the various sides of one's own nature; judgment proceeds by the operation of natural laws within oneself. This is implied in the choice of presiding judge: he is always an example of divinity incarnate, a god made man or a man made god — Christ, Ahura Mazda, Osiris.

Most judgment scenes contain a common element of being weighed, the operator of the scales being, for example, St Michael, Rashnu (Zoroastrian), the dog-headed Anubis (Egyptian), or the monkey-headed Shinje (Tibetan). The hope when being weighed is that one's soul will be shown to be lighter, so that it may rise. If it is heavy it will fall, and hell is always represented as being below, in the underworld. But there are three possible outcomes to this judgment: liberation, damnation or rebirth. In the Egyptian judgment picture of the heart being weighed against the feather, the man's spirit flies overhead in the shape of a man-headed hawk, waiting for the outcome. Also present are the goddesses of birth. Why should they be there, if not to guide the soul to its next incarnation? Indeed, there is also a shapeless form bearing a human face, the embryo of the next incarnation waiting to receive the KARMIC inheritance as decreed by the judgment, which will shape its life to come.

In Christianity, the parable of the talents (Luke 19, 11) can be understood as an allegory on judgment and the extent to which one makes full use of one's life. This fits in with the general pattern of beliefs under consideration, but the idea of one day on which all are judged, the *Last Judgment*, is peculiar to Christianity and Islam.

KA In ancient Egyptian religion the ka was a spiritual double, rather like an ASTRAL BODY, which was fashioned by the god Khnum on a potter's wheel at the same time as the physical body. The two were born united and were separated only at death, after which in certain circumstances the ka could reanimate the body.

The term ka also referred to the creative and preserving power of life, rather like the ETHERIC BODY which sustains the physical body. Plants and animals had ka which gave sustenance to the human ka when used as food during life, and even inanimate objects were thought to have their own ka. It is similar to the concept of PRANA in India and CH'I in China. The symbol which represented the ka was a pair of upraised, outstretched arms, as if receiving vital energy from the gods.

Even after death the ka still resided in the tomb with the body, where a special area was reserved for it, and offerings of food and drink left in the tomb were in fact for the ka. Further offerings were often left on an altar in front of a false door carved or painted on the wall of a sealed tomb; the ka was thought to be able to pass through this and partake of the food. Rather than actually eating this food, it has been suggested that the ka was thought to subsist on the subtle emanations of its smell. If insufficient food was provided in this way, it was feared that the ka might wander abroad (as a ghost) in search of sustenance. The ka could also reside in statues.

The basic difference between the ka and the BA was that the ka was a 'material' SOUL, including intellectual faculties, whereas the ba was spirit, although the Egyptians' use and understanding of both terms varied over time.

KABBALAH/KABBALISM Jewish teachings are of three kinds according to their degree of ESOTERICISM. There is the Law, particularly as formulated in the Pentateuch, which should be learned by all Jews; there is the Talmud, which is studied by priests and rabbis; and third there is the Kabbalah, the secret knowledge which is imparted only to initiates, a kind of Jewish mysticism. The

Kabbalah is an unwritten tradition; its teachings have only been partially committed to paper and much of that in relatively recent times (compared with the age of the tradition). The word 'Kabbalah' or 'Qabalah' (there are various spellings) means tradition, or something that is received.

The essence of Kabbalist teachings is contained in the concise *Sefer Yetzirah* (*The Book of Formation*, or *The Book of Creation*), written in Hebrew in the first century when the tradition was already long established. The work is attributed to a rabbi, Akiba ben Joseph, who was originally a shepherd. He founded a Kabbalistic school which reputedly had 24,000 followers by the time of his martyrdom at the hands of the Romans in AD 138.

The period of Kabbalism's greatest development was in medieval times, and the Provencal-Spanish school of Isaac the Blind and Moses de Leon in the twelfth and thirteenth centuries had a most lasting effect on the teachings. Probably the greatest book on Kabbalism is the *Zohar* or *Sefer-ha-Zohar* (*Book of Splendour* or *Book of Lights*), written in Aramaic by the rabbi Moses ben Leon of Guadalajara, leader of the School of Guadalajara in Spain, in about 1290.

God is described in the *Zohar* as EN SOF ('No-Thing'), the endless, the infinite and the all. God projected from himself ten rays of light, the SEPHIROTH (perhaps 'sapphire rays') which made the divine perceptible and comprehensible. The last of these is the Shechinah, the presence of God in people and places.

Originally there was perfect unity between God and the world, but the harmony between En Sof and the Shechinah was broken when evil appeared and in the resulting disorder the Shechinah was exiled. The aim of existence now is to restore that unity between God and the individual and between God and the community. This will be achieved with the coming of the Messiah. The *Zohar* also teaches that the key to unity with the divine is love: 'Love unites the highest and lowest stages and lifts everything to the stage where all must be one.'

Elements of Kabbalism seem to have been drawn from three main sources. The contrast between the unchanging reality of God and the mutability of the physical world is NEO-PLATONIST. The dualism of good and evil is probably Persian in origin. And the Kabbalists have, of course, always used their own existing holy scriptures, every letter of which was absolutely unalterable.

They believed that the language of the Old Testament contained coded secrets, hidden from the casual reader. By assigning a number to each letter of the Hebrew alphabet, and each accent mark, they devised a system of esoteric interpretation known as *gematria*. The numbers corresponding to the letters in a word or phrase were added up and compared with the totals of other words and phrases. In this way it could be shown that words and phrases with the same totals had similar significance or had a special relationship. For example, the holiest name of God, the tetragammaton (= 'four letters'), totals twenty-four, which is both the number of hours in the day and a number associated with many elements of creation and the natural world. While the art of gematria exploited the correspondences between letters and numbers, the special relationships between words and sentences could also be shown by applying the rules of *notarikon*: certain words could be elaborated on by recognizing that they were acronyms formed by the initial letters of each word in a particular sentence.

Kabbalism contains a complete system of symbolism, angelology, demonology and magic. It includes a complex cosmology, teaches the nature of humanity's origins in and relationship with God, and considers the doctrine of REINCARNATION. It has been repudiated by many Jewish thinkers, and it has also been a means for others of conversion to Christianity. On the other hand, there have also been many Christian students of the Kabbalah, particularly in the Middle Ages and in later occult schools of thought. The Kabbalist TREE OF LIFE has also been incorporated into many modern discussions of the TAROT and astrology.

KAHUNAS The Kahunas (literally 'keepers of the secret') are the magician priests of the Huna religion in Hawai. They were first brought to the attention of the West by Max Freedom Long who went to Hawai as a schoolteacher in 1917. He subsequently wrote several books on their belief system, focusing in particular on their 'miraculous' feats, such as FIRE-WALKING. [114,115]

According to the Huna religion, an individual has three souls: a low self in the solar plexus, comparable to Freud's unconscious; a middle self, normal consciousness; and a high self, above everyday CONSCIOUSNESS, capable of CLAIRVOYANCE and similar to what Myers called 'the SUBLIMINAL MIND'. Every living thing can be linked, regardless of distance, by mysterious threads called *aka*, via which the high self can know all about another's well-being. The life-force which imbues the whole UNIVERSE from the mineral kingdom to human beings and which carries the information along the *aka* is MANA. The lowest form of *mana* is the energy of the low self, incorporating the physical body, the emotions and that part of the mind that deals with memory. A higher frequency of *mana* supports mental reasoning (the conscious soul), and the third and highest form of *mana* is the life-force on the soul-level, by which clairvoyance, materialization and dematerialization are achieved.

KARMA (Originally pronounced more like 'kurma', with full pronunciation of the 'r') karma is the natural cosmic law of cause and effect. It is the Sanskrit word for 'action'. We 'make karma', good and bad, by our thoughts, words and deeds and our life in general. Karma is then our store of merits and demerits. This then determines our character and circumstances in a subsequent incarnation, so we are also the passive recipients of karma: the active karma of past existence has produced the passive karma of this life. Rudolf Steiner said, 'In each life the human spirit appears as a repetition of itself with the fruits of its former experiences in previous lives.' 'The human spirit has to incarnate over and over again; and its law consists in its bringing over the fruits of the former lives into the following ones.'[183]

Karma is like any other 'law of nature'; it is the way the universe works. It is not, like human laws, a law of retribution. It is a mistake to think of good karma as a reward or bad karma as a punishment. All our THOUGHTS, emotions and actions eventually return to us. This is simply the natural way by which we grow in understanding. Judgment is not involved. Neither can karmic debt be paid off in the strict sense simply by the (self-sacrificing) death of a martyr. Martyrs advance their own evolution more rapidly by paying off so much of their own karmic debt all at once. Obviously they do help humanity by their example, which is an inspiration to others who may be inspired to evolve spiritually themselves. Their way is in the long run the only way – the way of love, and forgetting of ego.

Karma YOGA is one of the most down-to-earth forms of yoga: it is a means of attaining union with God through right action, through doing one's duty willingly and indeed joyfully, by doing one's work to the best of one's ability, without attachment and regardless of the nature of the work, which is unimportant. When performing one's work one should feel no sense of obligation and no desire for reward; there is simply a desire to be of service. Only by recognizing the mutual interdependence of all life and acting accordingly can one progress spiritually.

KILNER SCREEN Through a Kilner screen, it is claimed, people can see some of the denser aspects of the human AURA. It is named after its inventor, Walter J. Kilner (1847–1920) of St Thomas's Hospital, London. In *The Human Atmosphere* he claimed that ninety-five per cent of those who had looked at people through the screen (under his supervision) had seen the mist which enveloped the body, 'the prototype of the nimbus or halo'.[102] The screen consisted of two layers of glass containing a diluted solution of a dye, usually dicyanin or carmine. As with KIRLIAN PHOTOGRAPHY, sceptics claim that there is nothing mysterious about this visual effect and that it does not indicate the presence of an auric field.

KIRLIAN PHOTOGRAPHY In 1967 a group of Russian scientists published the results of their investigations into what they called BIOPLASMA, the energy which surrounds and permeates a living organism. In the next few years the world heard that a method of electro-photography had been developed to photograph the part of this energy which formed a kind of aura. Today people have Kirlian photographs of their hands interpreted by New Age palmists. But we find ourselves in the unusual position where orthodox science in the West dismisses a phenomenon which Russian science has seen fit to research very seriously.

When Kirlian photographs are taken in America and Western Europe today, the apparatus is almost always a simplification of what Semyon Kirlian and his wife Valentina originally used in the 1930s. Nowadays the object to be studied is placed directly on to the film, which is actually on the negative electrode. Passing a high voltage current between two electrodes naturally produces a corona discharge, a glow around the electrodes caused by the excited electrons, and electromagnetic activity inevitably affects the molecules in photographic emulsion. It is not surprising that any object photographed in this way appears to have an AURA, and because of this orthodox scientists have tended to dismiss the phenomenon as of no significance.

Originally, however, the Kirlians did not place their film between the electrodes, where as they knew it could be directly affected by the electric current. They placed the film at a distance from the electrodes and used lenses in the normal way to gather and focus the light from the corona discharge. Since any discharge of this kind includes electrons of the surrounding gases in the atmosphere, it was decided that these should be eliminated. The Kirlians modified their apparatus by enclosing the electrodes and object to be photographed in an artificial atmosphere of a known composition, so that they could filter out those light frequencies produced by the surrounding air and photograph the effect produced by the object alone. Various other precautions were taken when photographing hands, for example, to discount the effect of skin moisture and pressure.

The Moscow Institute of Normal Physiology has used Kirlian photography as a diagnostic tool, detecting tumours as effectively as X-rays, and incidentally dispensing with the need to inflict such potentially harmful radiation on the body. Temporary states such as tiredness or the effect of alcohol are also detectable. Changes in the aura of a healer's fingertips before, during and after giving healing have suggested that the healing process may involve a transfer of energy from one so-called bioplasmic body to another. Interestingly, when two people each place a finger on the same film their coronas usually withdraw from each other, although those of a husband and wife may merge. Other photographs of fingertips show the effects of listening to music, or of being in a state of meditation. Kirlian photographs of a leaf, first when freshly picked and then ten and twenty hours later, show that the aura changes as the life drains out of the leaf, supporting the idea that it really is a LIFE-FIELD, or energy body.

KOAN A koan is an apparently nonsensical statement, an impossible question or a riddle to which there is no logical answer. It is used in certain forms of ZEN Buddhism to baffle the intellect and thus still the over-active mind. It keeps the mind occupied, but the thinking is to no useful purpose from a common-sense point of view. The mind struggles to find a solution to the problem but sooner or later has to abandon the project. Realization that the usual Yes-or-No, subject-object, cause-and-effect view of life is not the only reality opens the mind to the possibility of a new dimension, and the Zen pupil catches a glimpse of this in a flash of ENLIGHTENMENT. In modern terms we might describe this as escaping from the tyranny of the left hemisphere of the BRAIN, and logical function which seems to rule so much of our thinking.

Some of the best-known examples of koans are, 'What is the sound of one hand clapping?' 'What was your face like before you were born?' 'If all things return to the one, where does the one return to?'

KORAN Like many religious sects that have arisen in the last two thousand years (Christian Science, the Mormon Church, etc.) Islam was based on the inspired writings 'channelled' by one person. The Koran was revealed or dictated to Mohammed (570—632) by the ARCHANGEL Gabriel, while he was meditating in a cave on Mount Hira. Mohammed belonged to the Quraishi tribe, to whom was entrusted the care of the holy Kabah. The black meteoric stone housed in the Kabah was already the centre of a cult before Islam took it over.

KUNDALINI Kundalini is a Sanskrit word meaning 'coiled' and refers to the image of a coiled sleeping serpent at the base of the spine, the location of the base CHAKRA. As the chakra pulsates (symbolized by the breathing of the sleeping serpent), it feeds and stimulates the other chakras. By special techniques involving breathing exercises, sexual discipline, concentration and chanting of mantras certain YOGIS and ADEPTS train themselves in the 'arousal of the kundalini'. Energy then erupts and ascends through all the centres, as if the serpent were waking, uncoiling and standing erect and upright. The trembling sensation up the spine from one centre to the next is accompanied by experiences of brilliant cascading colours and strange sounds, until the kundalini subsides and the serpent curls up again to sleep. Successive arousals of the kundalini reach higher centres, although very few adepts succeed in taking the kundalini to the highest (crown) chakra. As the energy passes through one centre after the other, each one is activated, giving the individual heightened perception and increased powers. If the adept is not fully prepared for this, it can result in a feeling of intense heat (the energy is associated with the element of fire) and can cause psychic damage. It is often said that the premature opening of chakras can lead to mental illness, and many occultists warn of the dangers of arousing the kundalini. Despite these dangers the awakening of the kundalini has been regarded by many teachers as essential for spiritual progress, (e.g. Ramakrishna, 1836—86).

In contrast to the usual occult view, Gurdjieff believed that the whole kundalini exercise was a dangerous waste of time, resulting at best in illusory powers and false understanding. 'Above all, Kundalini is not anything desirable or useful for man's development. In reality Kundalini is the power of imagination, the power of fantasy, which takes the place of a real function.' This formed part of Gurdjieff's insistence that we are all asleep. 'Kundalini is a force put into men in order to keep them in their present state. ... Kundalini is a force that keeps them in a hypnotic state.'[141]

LED MEDITATION Sometimes people meditate as a group. Someone acting as the leader of the group starts by describing the relaxation process and continues by outlining the situation which each person visualizes, in the manner of GUIDED IMAGERY. This may lead the meditators to a state where they are ready to meet their inner GUIDES, receive higher wisdom or find the answer to a question that is concerning them at the moment.

LEFT-HAND PATH All systems of MAGIC are intended to help the seeker to be in harmony with the cosmos and to empower the practitioner in the use of natural energies for the general good. Black Magic is the use of magic for selfish ends, to achieve power over others, and to choose the left-hand path is to decide to study occultism and practise magic in this way.

LEMURIA According to occult tradition, Lemuria is the continent and civilization which preceded ATLANTIS.

Madame Blavatsky described the origins of the human race in *The Secret Doctrine*.[12] The first two 'root races' were purely spiritual and bodiless, but the third race felt a longing for physical earthly existence and descended into the material plane — the so-called Fall. This race lived about eighteen million years ago on the continent of Lemuria, situated in the Pacific Ocean. Modern Australia and Easter Island are supposedly fragments of the original Lemuria, which was eventually destroyed in a cataclysm and sank into the ocean.

According to Rudolf Steiner Lemuria was where the Indian ocean is now, extending 'approximately from Ceylon to Madagascar. What is today southern Asia and parts of Africa also belonged to it,' although he adds that in reading the AKASHIC RECORD 'it must be emphasized that nowhere is a dogmatic character to be claimed for these communications.'[184] The Lemurians had no memory and no language, but communicated telepathically. They also 'understood plants and animals in their inner action and life.' They were intuitively aware of divine wisdom, and 'They experienced a communion with the beings which built the world itself.' They acted instinctively, building without any understanding of engineering, simply by using their imagination. When memory started to develop, first among the women by virtue of their more highly developed imagination, the idea of good and evil arose, initially as a response to remembering what would be useful tomorrow and what should be avoided. By imagination and an act of will Lemurian men could also increase their physical strength as necessary. Bodies were still much more malleable at that time: 'This body still changed form whenever the inner life changed. ... The physical human body in fact received a fairly unchanging form only with the development of the faculty of reason.'

Most people regard this as essentially an allegorical account of a mythical Golden Age. A few might prefer to think of it as a future potential or alternative among the probable universes which our consciousness could conceivably create, or even as a possible foreshadowing of human evolution.

LEVITATION F.W.H. Myers described levitation as 'A raising of objects from the ground by supposed supernormal means: especially of living persons; asserted in the case of St Joseph of Copertino, and many other saints; of D.D. Home, and of Stainton Moses.'[135]

Spiritual ECSTASY seems to have induced bodily levitation in a few individuals devoted to the religious life. Saint Teresa of Avila (1515–82), as well as describing her experiences, was seen struggling to hold herself down; Philip Neri (1515–95) (who also experienced BILOCATION) was also seen resisting being swept off his feet into the air; and there were over a hundred eyewitness accounts of the flights of the Franciscan friar, Joseph of Copertino in the seventeenth century. It is clear that all these were unwilling participants in the act of levitation and the authorities were greatly embarrassed by the phenomena, particularly in the case of Joseph since it happened so frequently, and there was always the possible wrath of the Inquisition to contend with. Nothing at all was to be gained by fabricating such stories and there was potentially a great deal to lose. A later Italian ecstatic was Gemma Galgani (1878–1903); as well as levitating she manifested STIGMATA and experienced the presence of devils.

It is thought that Joseph of Copertino may have been mentally retarded; he was certainly not very intelligent. It is conceivable that in acquiring familiarity with the CONSENSUS REALITY we learn intellectually that such feats are impossible and that this

185

creates a mental block to their occurrence which the more simple-minded can more easily overcome.

In the nineteeth century levitation became a pre-occupation of spiritualists. In 1866 a rather fat young lady, Agnes Nichols, later to become Mrs Guppy, floated up into the air at a SEANCE attended by Alfred Russel Wallace, friend and colleague of Charles Darwin. She could also produce APPORTS and is even reported as having become an apport herself in 1871.

The most famous levitator of all at this time was Daniel Dunglas Home. Sir William Crookes witnessed Home's levitation and saw him rise 'with a continuous gliding movement and remain about six inches off the ground for several seconds, when he slowly descended.' 'On another occasion ... he rose eighteen inches off the ground, and I passed my hands under his feet, round him, and over his head when he was in the air.' On other occasions the chair Home was sitting in would also rise up in the air with him in it. (*Journal of the S.P.R. Vol VI*, 1894.)

Another MEDIUM famous for occasional levitations was Eusapia Palladino. In November and December 1908 Everard Fielding, W.W. Baggally and Hereward Carrington of the Society for Psychical Research went to Italy and investigated Eusapia in a Naples hotel. They concluded that success was affected more by psychological than physical conditions: domestic problems or an irritable frame of mind had a bad effect on results, and much more so than physical health. Relaxation and alertness were shown to be beneficial; conflict and anxiety were detrimental. Confidence was usually beneficial, but if belief in the subject's abilities was mentioned, it set up the need for the medium to prove herself, and as so much was at stake − a reputation to defend, for example − this could have a bad effect on results.

It is interesting to note that all these conclusions are remarkably similar to the effects of similar psychological conditions in ESP experiments as reported by J.B. Rhine and others.

L-FIELD/LIFE FIELD In the 1930s Harold Burr, an American professor of anatomy, separated the cells of a salamander embryo and mixed them up by placing them in an alkaline solution. He discovered that if this amorphous mixture of cells was then placed in a slightly acid solution they would re-form into an embryo. This, he said, was because of the life-field which all living things possess. It was the equivalent of the ETHERIC BODY in occult literature, and Harold Burr realized that it could be registered electrically.

Working with the philosopher F.S.C. Northrop of Yale University, Burr discovered that every living organism produces a weak electric field, measured in millivolts, extending around it. This L-field (life-field) remains relatively stable but is also subject to transient changes. For example, the L-field around trees was seen to vary slightly according to changes in light, moisture, storm activity, sunspots, the phases of the moon and the seasons. Disease also causes fluctuations in voltage and Burr was able to diagnose cancers of the uterus in women even before they were aware of them. Burr discovered that seeds that were to grow into healthy plants had L-fields that were noticeably different from seeds that produced stunted plants. Even an unfertilized salamander egg already had an L-field.

Burr and Northrop published their first paper on *The electrodynamic theory of life* in 1935 (*Quarterly Review of Biology*), but it was not until 1972 that the work received wide attention with the publication of Burr's *Blueprint for Immortality*. Burr believed that the L-field actually shaped the organism that apparently produced it. 'When we meet a friend we have not seen for six months, there is not one molecule in his face which was there when we last saw him. But, thanks to his controlling life-field, the new molecules have fallen into the old, familiar pattern and we recognize his face.'[24] Orthodox biologists with a modern understanding of genetics see no need for Burr's L-field, although Rupert Sheldrake has postulated his own version of the idea as the MORPHOGENETIC FIELD.

Russian researchers have made similar experiments on what they call BIOPLASMA or the bioplasmic body.

LOGOS In Greek logos can mean 'word', 'speech' or 'thought' in one sense, and as a mathematical term 'ratio' or 'balance'. For the philosopher Heraclitus the Logos represented a universal principle of stability in a changing world. The Stoic philosophers adapted this as the Divine Reason behind the UNIVERSE. The Hellenic concept was incorporated into early Christian ideas as the power and wisdom of the Word of God. John's gospel opens with the words 'In the beginning was the Logos,' and the Christian Logos became identified with Christ.

In esoteric traditions the Logos is God the Creator. Some teachings speak of a hierarchy of Logoi — a universal Logos, a solar Logos, and a planetary Logos. In mystical terms the divine Logos is usually regarded as a masculine creative energy, the feminine counterpart being wisdom, Sophia. The Gnostics looked forward to the eventual union of Logos and Sophia, which would mark the end of the Aeon, the apocatastasis, when all things would be restored to their primal state of unity.

LOWER SELF – See PERSONALITY.

LUCID DREAM A dream experience in which you know that you are dreaming, and which you can choose to end or not as you wish, is called a lucid dream. (See DREAMS.)

LUMINOUS BODY – See SUBTLE BODY.

MAAT Maat the ancient Egyptian goddess of wisdom and truth, was the embodiment of law, justice and order which formed the foundation of the whole of existence. Other gods depended on her for their sustenance, and she was often depicted giving life to a pharaoh by holding the *ankh* to his nostrils. Her symbol was the ostrich feather, against which the human heart would be weighed after death in the Hall of JUDGMENT.

It is interesting that even in the Egyptian pantheon, with its complex subdivision of divine responsibilities, order and justice should be so intimately linked with the basic laws of existence.

The Ankh

MAGIC Aleister Crowley defined magic as 'the science and art of causing change to occur in conformity with the will'. This suggests a very materialistic view. The religious view would be that the human will should be aligned with divine will, so that change occurs within the individual as much as in the external world. This distinction demonstrates the two forms of magic: the way of dedication and service of the world and the way of personal power and self-aggrandizement; the right-hand path and the left-hand path; White Magic and Black Magic; THEURGY and thaumaturgy.

'Thaumaturgy, or low magic . . . is the production of wonders by the use of little known powers of the mind,' writes Gareth Knight.

'Theurgy, or high magic, is the raising of CONSCIOUSNESS to the appreciation of the powers and forces behind the external world in a pious intention of developing spiritual awareness and subsequently helping to bring to birth the divine plan of a restored earth.'[103]

Magic was long associated with evil in Western societies, probably as a result of biblical references. In the Bible magic is usually mentioned only when the prophets or apostles were in competition with rival magicians, as when Aaron's rod turned into a snake which devoured the snakes produced by Pharaoh's priests. Similarly Elijah competed with the priests of Baal by successfully calling down fire to consume his sacrificial offering. All these 'false' prophets, servants of 'false' gods, were mediators between the people and their divinities in the manner of SHAMANS, as were the Hebrew prophets. In the New Testament Simon Magus was a MAGICIAN whose powers rivalled those of the apostles and who wanted them to sell him their secrets.

MAGICIAN/MAGUS The 'wise men from the East' who were recorded by St Matthew as being present at the Nativity of Jesus were traditionally regarded as 'Magi'. There is little difference in meaning between a magus and a magician, although the one is historically the forerunner of the other, and St Matthew's magi were regarded as Persian priests, Zoroastrian or Mazdian. At the time priests were still very different from ordinary men, well versed in the laws of the universe (hence 'wise' men), and able to play a special role as intermediaries between God and humanity.

The magician has been called a modern Western equivalent of the SHAMAN, a 'shaman-in-civilization'. 'Both stand as mediators of an inner impulse to the outer world: the shaman as a public figure, the centre of his tribe's relationship to the gods; the magician as a private figure, working often in obscurity, but continuing to mediate cosmic forces to his fellow men.'[124] The magician uses ritual, visualization and a complex symbology to align himself fully with the universe.

In working with the secret laws of the cosmos, the magician does not seek power so much as understanding. One who becomes preoccupied with establishing control over the natural world, including his fellow men, for self-aggrandizement is said to have chosen the left-hand path, practising the 'black arts' as a sorcerer or 'black magician'. One such was Simon Magus, who bewitched people in Samaria and offered the disciples of Christ money for the powers of the Holy Spirit (Acts 8). (Elsewhere he is reported to have entered into competition with Peter in Rome, levitating and flying out through a window before crashing to the ground and receiving fatal injuries. Nero, whose court magician Simon was at the time, immediately imprisoned Peter.) The true magician works in harmony with the laws of the universe without exercising personal power; no one must be harmed by his actions and natural balance must always be maintained.

Some magicians such as Roger Bacon in the thirteenth century were proto-scientists, investigating nature experimentally as well as learning the corpus of knowledge handed down by tradition. His magical device called the 'Brazen Head', which was reputed to answer any question put to it, could just as easily have been a primitive computer. In medieval times a magician was often also an alchemist, seeking to transform himself as well as to learn the secrets of the material and spiritual world.

Elizabeth I's astrologer, Dr John Dee, was probably the most influential magician of his time. He also communed with the spirit world through the medium he discovered, Owen Glyndwr.

MAGNETISM/ANIMAL MAGNETISM – See MESMERISM.

MAGUS – See MAGICIAN.

MAHATMA In a general sense the Hindu word mahatma simply means a 'great soul'. It is a title conferred on great moral leaders such as Gandhi. Used more precisely it can mean an ADEPT, one who through self-denial and self-development has acquired a high degree of knowledge and the ability to control spiritual and material forces. With this knowledge and power comes the responsibility of leading the rest of humanity in its spiritual evolution. In the *Bhagavad Gita* the Teacher says that 'Having come to be the Mahatmas do not again obtain birth.'

MAITREYA When Buddha, i.e. Gautama (*c* 563–483 BC), achieved Buddhahood, he had the choice of leaving this world and entering NIRVANA or remaining here to teach others. He chose to teach. Such a BUDDHA appears at intervals in world history and at the time when he became Buddha, the next Buddha was a BODHISATTVA. This 'coming Buddha' was called Maitreya and is identified by some as the Christ.

MANA People of the South Pacific islands believe that an impersonal spiritual power, a vital force, permeates everything. This *mana* is totally neutral, neither good nor evil, and void of intelligence, but it can carry the ideas and impressions of human beings and can be used by them and by spirits to perform all kinds of tasks generally regarded as magic.

If we compare this life energy to electricity, the wires along which it travels are the invisible substance of the body known as *aka*, which can be drawn out like the threads of a spider's web, enabling minds to pick up information in the manner of TELEPATHY, PSYCHOMETRY and CLAIRVOYANCE.

The notion of such a subtle energy or 'fluid' is not peculiar to Melanesia where the word *mana* originates. It is similar to the Hindu PRANA, which permeates the whole universe, like the ETHER of THEOSOPHY.

MANAS In Buddhism, Hinduism and THEOSOPHY an individual possesses an intelligence higher than that which is mediated by the five senses. This intelligence is known as manas. In Buddhism it is a sixth sense which allows total perception of an object, almost to the point of identification with it. In Hinduism and Theosophy it is the 'lower mind' − the faculty of reason, as distinct from the 'higher mind', BUDDHI. Despite this distinction, manas is regarded in some theosophical writings as the cosmic intelligence of the MONAD, the individuality which continues from one incarnation to the next. As such it is understood as one of the seven BODIES or vehicles of human consciousness, bearing the substance of the mental PLANE.

MANDALA A *mandala* (a Sanskrit word meaning 'circle') is a symbolic diagram set in a circle representing existence, universal wholeness and perfection, humanity's unity with the cosmos. Used in Hindu ritual a mandala serves as an invocation to the deity. It also forms the ground plan of a Hindu Temple with gates or doors to the four cardinal points. In view of their symbolic significance mandalas are often used in MEDITATION and Buddhist temples in Tibet have walls covered in such mandalas.

Jung believed the mandala to be an archetypal image of the psyche, SELF or SOUL. 'During those years, between 1918 and 1920, I began to understand that the goal of psychic development is the self. .... I knew that in finding the mandala as an ultimate expression of the self, I had attained what was for me the ultimate.'[97]

Mandala painted by C.G. Jung   *A Buddhist mandala from Tibet (19th Century)*

For a period Jung even started each day by drawing a new mandala, later studying the series as an expression of his process of 'individuation'. He often stressed the significance of the mandala's common pattern of four corners or a cross inside a circle. In Jung's analysis the EGO is represented by the number three, which also symbolizes the process of growth, the constant recurrence of change and conflict represented by the sequence − thesis, antithesis, synthesis. But the real self is static and whole, represented by the number four, (harking back to the Pythagorean idea that the soul was a square).

People have sometimes found that during meditation they have seen images which seem profoundly significant but whose significance they cannot explain. When they later draw pictures of these images they are almost invariably in the form of a mandala, despite the fact that the individuals have usually had no previous exposure to such designs. This gives added weight to Jung's theory that the mandala is the true symbolic expression of the experience of being an individual and can represent the soul's feeling of total completeness, unity with nature, unity with humanity, unity with God.

MANES (1) Manes is another form of the name Mani, the founder of MANICHAEISM.

(2) According to ancient Roman belief the *manes* were spirits of the dead. They were of three kinds: those that haunted the living,

those that were confined to HADES, and the rare few who were admitted to Olympus as gods (such as Hercules).

MANICHAEISM In the third century Mani tried to found a new world religion in his native Persia, combining existing Zoroastrianism with certain GNOSTIC principles including a belief in REINCARNATION. It was essentially dualistic, expounding the pre-existence of good and evil long before the cosmos came into being. The material world was created out of the powers of evil and was the embodiment of the powers of darkness, with only a small spark of light left imprisoned within it. The human body was also formed by the powers of darkness. Jesus was seen as the personification of all light imprisoned in matter. According to Mani, it was Jesus, the Messenger of Light, who persuaded Adam and Eve to eat of the Tree of Knowledge. Mani also maintained that Christ was identical with Mithras and that he himself was the Comforter (Paraclete) that Christ had promised to send.

In common with many Gnostic sects, Manichaeism divided humanity into three groups according to their spiritual development: there were the Elect, who lived an ascetic life and after death entered the Paradise of Light; the Soldiers or Hearers formed the general mass of believers, who would have to return again and again to this life until they were ready to join the Elect; the third group, the sinners, were confined to hell after death. As a youth, St Augustine of Hippo was a follower of Mani and his later writings still show traces of Mani's influence.

MANIPURA – Sanskrit for solar plexus centre. See CHAKRAS.

MANTRA In Hinduism, Buddhism and Sikhism a sacred formula or rhythmically chanted prayer is known as a *mantra*. The Sanskrit word means literally 'speech' or 'instrument of thought' (from *man* meaning to think). A mantra may consist of only one word, or even one syllable (such as *Om*), the essential quality being obtained by repetition and intense concentration, so that the mind is filled with the idea of the devotional image, usually a deity, and a feeling of spiritual union ensues. Prob- ably the best known mantra is the Buddhist *Om*

The syllable 'Om'

Mane padme hum meaning 'Hail jewel in the lotus, Amen.' The so-called 'Jesus prayer' – 'Lord Jesus Christ, Son of God, have mercy on me' – could also be regarded as a mantra, particularly as used by certain monastic orders such as the Hesychasts. The Catholic rosary and Muslim prayer beads serve a similar purpose.

Indian gurus give their pupils individual secret mantras for their private MEDITATION. These should not be disclosed to others. This tradition has been continued by those who practise and teach TRANSCENDENTAL MEDITATION (TM). However, in transcendental meditation the mantra is not repeated endlessly, nor chanted, either verbally or mentally. 'The mantra is not so much an object for the attention to be focused on as a vehicle on which the attention rests and which leads it down to the subtler levels of thinking. This is brought about by the passive rather than active nature of the technique, the meaninglessness of the chosen sound, and the greater charm of the finer levels which allow the attention to be spontaneously drawn within.'[171] The resultant mental state is often described as one of restful alertness.

Although TM mantras are not repeated, the sounds used are still crucially important. 'The sounds used in meditation are ones which resonate with the nervous system in a soothing harmonious manner.'[171] Occultists also believe that the vibrations produced by chanting a mantra can affect the SUBTLE BODIES. The effect of mantras on people's daily lives has certainly been felt in one surprising way. There are two types of mantras: 'recluse' mantras for monks and anchorites who have withdrawn from worldly affairs, and 'householder' mantras for people who wish to remain active in the world. Peter Russell reports that when people engaged in normal activities have mistakenly learned a recluse mantra, they have found that their lives have deteriorated, due to an apparent lack of desire to engage in their normal everyday activities.

The common lay explanation for the effect of mantras is that as well as enabling the meditator to exclude all other thoughts from the mind, they induce a mild state of self-hypnosis. This has been denied by practitioners who have been attached to electroencephalograms to record their brain waves during meditation. As in all forms of meditation, the BRAIN registers increased alphawave activity, particularly around eight cycles per second, which is indicative of unfocused, relaxed attention and not at all typical of HYPNOSIS.

MANU In Hinduism and THEOSOPHY, each age or race of humanity is governed by its own manu, who guides its evolution. In the cosmic hierarchy, the manus are spiritual beings, sometimes called MASTERS, who are one grade below the planetary LOGOS responsible for the creation of our UNIVERSE.

MASTER According to Hindu and Theosophist occultism, there are three great masters guiding different aspects of humanity's development: the Manu (concerned with evolution of the human race, physically, mentally and psychologically), the World-Teacher (concerned with religions) and the Mahachohan (also called the 'Lord of Civilization', concerned with cultural progress and the rise and fall of nations and civilizations). The World-Teacher deals mostly with the Love-Wisdom aspects of life, and the Mahachohan with the MIND.

These Masters, despite their exalted status and world-wide responsibilities, are believed by some still to occupy human bodies on earth, such as D.K. (Djwhal Khul) who resided in Tibet while inspiring Alice Bailey to write so many books. But others, including statements purporting to come from other masters, have denied this. The soul supposedly now acting as World-Teacher appeared formerly as Krishna and as Christ. (Many occultists believe that Jesus was not himself the Christ but was overshadowed by him during the last three years of his ministry. Jesus was at that time an Initiate and reached Masterhood in his next incarnation.)

Together the Masters form the so-called Great White Brotherhood. Others in the hierarchy have other responsibilities. For example, one who was St Paul in a past incarnation is primarily concerned with the development of psychic faculties in certain types of people.

According to some 'inner-plane' communications, Masters are 'Human beings like yourselves, but older. They are not Gods, nor ANGELS, nor ELEMENTALS, but are those individuals who have achieved and completed the same task as you have set yourselves.' 'The Masters as you picture them are all "imagination". Note well that I did not say that the Masters *were* imagination ... (they are contacted) through your imagination, and although your mental picture is not real or actual, the *results* of it are real and actual.'[54]

It has often been said that 'no true Master imparts spiritual truths for money; no true Master appears in public as a leader or teacher or New Messiah: therefore, any man who advertizes himself or allows others to advertize him as such cannot be a Master.'[176] An exception to this rule occurs once every 2000 years or so, when a world-teacher makes himself known.

MATERIALIZATION In one sense materialization is the phenomenon whereby APPORTS appear as if from nowhere, whether in the presence of a MEDIUM or GURU such as Sai Baba, or as part of

POLTERGEIST phenomena when for example stones might appear in mid-air and descend on a house. In a wider sense the use of the term includes the appearance of human forms and is usually understood as occurring during a sitting with a physical medium. One of the most renowned materializations recorded in the Bible was at Belshazzar's feast when there 'came forth the fingers of a man's hand', which wrote God's concise judgment of the King on the wall. This could equally be described as an APPARITION, although using the word materialization gives the apparition more substance, suggesting tangibility and the potential to affect the environment in which it appears rather than simply to be perceived.

The materialization of hands and faces, and even torsos and whole bodies, has been reported in relatively modern times, often in tangible form. In one case in the 1870s a surgeon, James M. Gully, even felt the pulse of one such materialized figure to compare it with that of the medium, Florence Cook. (He testified that they were not the same.) Materializations of this particular figure, Florence Cook's regular spirit contact, Katie King, were also photographed on several occasions by the scientist, Sir William Crookes, (President of the Royal Society and inventor of the cathode ray tube). Many people, including rival mediums such as the notorious Mrs Guppy, had claimed that Katie was Florence Cook in disguise, but the photographs were taken under test conditions with the medium bound hand and foot and the knots sealed with the signet ring of one of the sitters. The Polish medium Franek Kluski caused materializations of hands to appear in molten wax which then set so that plaster casts could be made of the impressions.

There was a spate of spirit photographs in the last quarter of the nineteenth century. Photography was relatively new and it was very easy to fake ghostly apparitions by double exposure or the addition of another negative in the printing process. It is perhaps no coincidence that so-called spirit images often resemble existing photographs of the person when alive so closely as to be virtually identical in expression, pose and angle of view. For many the concoction of such collages must have been a quite innocent pastime, although their artifice wreaked havoc on the increasing number of spirit photographs which the photographers themselves believed to be genuine. Public attacks caused many respectable investigators such as Crookes to abandon their research.

Nevertheless materializations, although not common, continued to occur and photographs continued to be taken. As a preliminary to the faces and figures mediums produced formless blobs of

ECTOPLASM, and these too were photographed. Although the development from the emergence of ectoplasm to a full materialization progresses slowly, it is characteristic of materialized forms to disappear quite quickly. If a shock causes the medium to come out of trance suddenly, the force with which the ectoplasm returns to the medium's body is said to be extremely dangerous and can cause physical injury.

In recent times, physical mediums have become more of a rarity, and when materializations have been reported the process seems to be that of an apport forming out of nothing rather than of ectoplasm emerging from the medium's body and gradually assuming a particular shape. These may be two different processes. Some have regarded materializations by mediums as objectified THOUGHT-FORMS, their short existence being determined by the power behind the thought or the medium's ability to hold that thought in mind. Tibetan mystics create TULPAS in the same way.

MAYA The Sanskrit word *maya* is usually translated as 'illusion', but this can be misleading. To describe the physical world as maya, does not mean that it is not real. The concept of maya does not deny the everyday reality of this world; it simply means that absolute Reality is so much more real that everyday reality seems like mere fabrication. Maya is the surface reality, material nature. It also stands for the divine power which forms Nature (*prakriti*). (The word 'measure' is derived from the same root as 'maya'.) As the product of divine creative power, Nature and the material world cannot by denied, but there is always a danger that appearances blind us to the divine within everything. Only in this respect might maya be regarded as evil and 'illusory'.

MEDICINE-MAN – See SHAMAN.

MEDITATION Meditation is a mental activity. It involves bringing the constant succession of thoughts and impressions in the mind to a complete halt and concentrating on an image or idea of such simplicity that one achieves a different state of CONSCIOUSNESS. The focusing or concentration varies according to different meditative techniques. At one end of the spectrum one may hold in mind the idea of nothing and become totally passive (or perhaps rather receptive – with the mind as an 'empty vessel'); at the other, one may concentrate and actually speculate on a chosen theme, examining all the impressions and associations evoked by a particular idea while the mind is in the relaxed state.

In YOGA meditation is an essential aid to mental development, spiritual advancement and ENLIGHTENMENT. The practice follows four main stages:

1 attention — *pratyahara* (= withholding)
    clearing the mind to exclude distractions (both ideas and sense impressions) by an act of will
2 concentration — DHARANA (= holding)
    focus consciousness on one thing
3 contemplation — DHYANA
    thought divested of the EGO, as if in a TRANCE (= Chinese *ch'an*; Japanese ZEN)
4 transcendent state — SAMADHI (= conjoining)
    Mindless awareness, no brain activity. Also NIRVANA (= extinction — Buddhist); SATORI (= illumination — zen); fan'a (= annihilation — SUFI); mystical union (Western).

The fact that one can be both relaxed and mentally alert during meditation is reflected in certain physiological conditions which can be measured. Meditation is accompanied by slow *alpha* and *theta* waves in the BRAIN, a decrease in oxygen consumption and in the elimination of carbon dioxide, a reduction in heart rate, blood pressure and muscle tone, and an increase in finger temperature and skin resistance. These physiological changes are associated with the so-called alert hypometabolic condition which some psychologists regard as a fourth state of consciousness, (the other three being normal waking consciousness, sleep, and hypnotic trance). Medical opinion suggests that a regular dose of such physiological conditions seems to be beneficial, particularly in reducing tension. Because of this therapeutic effect, meditation and relaxation techniques are increasingly being practised in the middle of the day by city workers, from high-powered executives to general office staff, and meditation is even being taught in some primary schools.

'Relaxed alertness' is also the state which CLAIRVOYANTS say is conducive or even necessary for the reception of clairvoyant impressions. The meditative state seems to depend on reducing external impressions through the normal five senses to a minimum. Then other inner-world or inner-plane impressions may be perceived.

MEDIUM/MEDIUMSHIP A medium is so-called because he or she is said to be used by spirit entities as a means of communicating with those who consult the medium. The definition given by Frederic

Myers, together with his reservations, still seems apt: medium — 'a person through whom communication is deemed to be carried on between living men and spirits of the departed. As commonly used in spiritist literature, this word is liable to the objection that it assumes a particular theory for phenomena which admit of explanation in various ways. It is often better replaced by AUTOMATIST or SENSITIVE.'[135] Today, if one wants to avoid the 'spiritist' or spiritualist associations and implications of the word 'medium', one often refers to a 'psychic' in Myers's sense of a 'sensitive'. To call someone a psychic, or even a CLAIRVOYANT, makes no assumptions about the existence or otherwise of spirits working with that person, although many psychics and clairvoyants also call themselves mediums and would maintain that the information they give their sitters (those who consult them) does come from spirit entities. They may identify the suppliers of this information as their own spirit 'CONTROL' or GUIDE, or deceased members of the sitter's family, or spirit guides and helpers of the sitter.

The modern medium is a descendant of the SHAMAN, although the shaman's role was much wider in scope than the medium's now is. For example, as well as allowing spirit entities to enter his body, the shaman would also leave his body to visit other levels of reality and bring back messages from the gods. The latter role is seldom played in such terms by the modern medium. Although he or she may apparently leave the body while CHANNELLING, there is usually no memory of being anywhere else during the period of absence. In general the modern medium seems to be far more 'attached' to the body than the shaman was, many choosing to relay what they are told or shown (mentally) by DISCARNATE entities without inviting the entities temporarily to possess their bodies: they speak as themselves, regarding themselves as something like a telephone exchange with 'lines' to the spirit world of varying degrees of clarity. Mediums also have much in common with Old Testament prophets, except again that they appear to have become more earth-bound: whilst the prophets heard the voice of God, most mediums tend to hear the voices of the recently departed relatives of their sitters. Another crucial difference is that whereas the shaman and the prophet served the tribe, the medium of today merely satisfies the lesser wishes of the individual.

Mediums are sometimes described as *physical* or *mental* (although this does not preclude the possibility of some mediums being both). Physical mediumship denotes the ability to produce physical phenomena: RAPPINGS, LEVITATION, MATERIALIZATION and

DIRECT VOICE. Physical mediumship does not seem to have been so characteristic of shamans, although many miraculous acts of the prophets may fall into this category. Mental mediumship gives rise to the more usual type of communication from discarnate spirits, either by using the medium's sensitivity to receiving psychic impressions from the spirit world (clairvoyant mediumship) or by allowing the communicating entity to use the medium's vocal apparatus (channelling) or hand (AUTOMATIC WRITING).

Both physical and mental mediumship may involve TRANCE to a varying degree. When practising clairvoyance many mediums seem to be in a perfectly normal state of mind, although they may be in a slightly dissociated state, 'seeing' and 'hearing' discarnate spirits either purely internally or externally in the manner of an APPARITION. Further dissociation may result in the condition known as 'control', whereby the medium does not fall into a complete trance and yet claims not to be in control of what is being said. The 'control', the one who 'overshadows' the medium, is the spirit or guide who speaks through the medium using the medium's normal voice. If the medium falls into trance and speaks, the voice is usually recognizably different. The control may relay messages from different entities, or different entities may speak through the medium with different voices. Such a medium is often called a CHANNEL. From the physical point of view this phenomenon is not unlike cases of MULTIPLE PERSONALITY, except of course that multiple personality is regarded as a pathological condition over which the individual has no control, whereas a trance medium deliberately invites the other personalities to make use of the channel (or invites the UNCONSCIOUS MIND to create such personalities).

It is notoriously difficult to test the authenticity of spirit communications through a medium. Even if everything a medium says is true, a sceptical sitter can always maintain that the information was acquired telepathically. This can undoubtedly happen, as the researcher Dr Soal proved to his satisfaction. He was investigating Mrs Blanche Cooper, a popular trance medium, who relayed messages supposedly from Soal's dead brother. He was impressed, but to test the medium further he mentally invented a fictitious Scotsman, James Ferguson. Sure enough the medium relayed further messages from 'a new spirit guide' called James Ferguson. A similar case concerned Geraldine Cummins, who used automatic writing when receiving clairvoyant information. While under control she once wrote a description of an old castle and its inhabitants, and thinking it might be of interest to W.B. Yeats she showed it to him. It turned out to be the outline of a novel that he already had in mind. In this case the mind involved belonged to a friend who was not even present at the time, although the medium was obviously able to make the appropriate connection.

This, of course, does not prove that all 'spirit messages' delivered through mediums are the result of TELEPATHY. Very often a message will include a piece of information which is as yet unknown to the sitter. The sceptics who wish to dispense with the need for any spirit entities at the other end of the line then invoke the SUPER-ESP HYPOTHESIS, but to many this seems even more incredible than the alternative spirit hypothesis. In some cases it is simpler to accept that a deceased person had a particular desire to communicate a particular message of which no one else at all was aware. Such a case was demonstrated by Swedenborg in the eighteenth century (well before the spiritualist movement was established). He was consulted by a widow who felt sure that her late husband had already settled a bill that some unscrupulous traders had submitted to her as still unpaid. Swedenborg contacted the dead husband who confirmed that he had paid the bill and explained where the receipt could be found − in a bureau which the widow had already searched, in a secret compartment of whose existence she was completely unaware. The receipt was found exactly as Swedenborg indicated.

Even such a well-attested case may not satisfy those sceptics who attribute all the expertise to Swedenborg himself. It was the widow's initial doubt and plea for help which first made Swedenborg home in on the problem and solve it, perhaps by means of his own superlative clairvoyant faculty − the super-ESP theory. There have, however, been cases where the deceased has contacted an unsuspecting medium to draw the attention of surviving relatives to the existence of a neglected will.

MEGALITHS A chance discovery made by a zoologist investigating bats revealed that at certain times of day standing stones emit high frequency sounds often in a pulsating rhythm, imperceptible to the human ear and identifiable only with an ultrasonic detector (used also to study the sounds emitted by bats). In 1978 the Rollright stones near Oxford were investigated. The pulsating sounds occurred around dawn every day, but lasted for several hours on those mornings in spring and autumn at the time of the equinoxes. Circles of stones were also found to create areas of ultrasonic silence within the circle whilst outside it the background sound levels were normal. The circles somehow protect the interior from cosmic radiation too, so the shelter the stones provide extends above the circles to form domes of protection, which some have called 'Stone Age Faraday Cages'.[168]

MEMORY Under HYPNOSIS people can recall an incredible amount of detail about past experiences. In police investigations witnesses who have been hypnotized have successfully recalled the numbers on car registration plates which they had barely noticed consciously. This kind of unconscious or subliminal memory has been invoked to explain certain apparent cases of hypnotic REGRESSION, when subjects appear to recall past lives. The process by which we somehow recall information that we have perhaps read about and subsequently forgotten is known as CRYPTOMNESIA. This has been used by many to explain retrocognition and certain 'spirit' messages as well as FAR MEMORY.

Biologists usually maintain that the imperfect human memory has evolved because its imperfection makes it more effective. 'Memory must be defective to be effective.' It is the orthodox view that if we retained absolutely everything in our conscious memory we would be driven mad by the overloading, but there seems to be no scientific evidence for such a claim. Although often stated as a fact, it is only an opinion, and a subjective one at that. Being accustomed to holding a very limited amount in our conscious memory, we naturally react with confusion at the idea of being able to remember a hundred times more. But if a less limited conscious memory were the norm, who can say whether the notion of 'overloading' would be applicable or not?

MESMERISM Through an apparent misunderstanding of Newtonian physics, the Viennese physician Franz Anton Mesmer (1734—1815) postulated an all-pervading physical force or fluid to which the human nervous system was somehow attuned. This vital force, reminiscent of the PRANA of the Hindus and the MANA of the Melanesians, Mesmer called 'animal magnetism'. He believed that many illnesses were caused by an imbalance between the animal magnetism within the body and that in the environment, and that illnesses such as paralysis could be cured by stroking the body with a magnet or gold to restore the flow. His treatment apparently did effect such cures, although his rationalization of the process involved was in error. He had in fact accidentally discovered HYPNOTISM (1780).

On one occasion Mesmer instructed one of his assistants, the Marquis de Puységur, to 'magnetize' a lime tree and then to tie a young man to it and pass a magnet repeatedly over his head to facilitate the flow of the curative energy. However, the Marquis's hand movements and presumably reassuring voice sent his patient into a hypnotic TRANCE. When told to untie himself he did so without opening his eyes and amazed the Marquis by answering his as yet unspoken questions. On other occasions Puységur was able to give this hypnotic subject orders mentally – by TELEPATHY, directing him to answer another's questions in a particular way.

Mesmer's therapeutic claims for 'animal magnetism' were investigated in 1784 by a commission of enquiry, chaired by Benjamin Franklin when he was Ambassador to France. Their conclusion was that the cures effected by this method were 'a delusion and fantasy', a statement which was no more scientifically accurate than Mesmer's own theory. Fortunately, as far as we know, the many patients who had been cured did not suffer relapses into their former conditions as a result of this pronouncement.

METACHORIC EXPERIENCES This term has been used by Celia Green (of the Institute of Psychophysical Research in Oxford) to describe three kinds of hallucinatory experience: LUCID DREAMS, OBEs and APPARITIONS. In all these, she maintains, the mind constructs a hallucinatory environment which replaces the normal 'real' environment. Green contends that scientists have avoided study of these undeniable psychological phenomena because they remind us of the fact that the mind creates its own view of reality and of the possibility that our 'normal' perception of the external world might also be illusory. (See also SOLIPSISM.)

METAL BENDING – See PSYCHOKINESIS.

METEMPSYCHOSIS Metempsychosis was the doctrine of REINCARNATION as propounded by Pythagoras in the sixth century BC.

MIND Orthodox science regards the mind as a product of the BRAIN. The philosopher Gilbert Ryle (1900–76) denied the existence of mind, saying it is a 'category mistake' and coined the famous 'ghost in the machine' metaphor for the imaginary agent of consciousness.[172] The mathematician, John Taylor, has said, 'Materialism does not deny consciousness, but tries to explain it in physical terms.' He supports what he calls a 'relational theory' of mind. 'In this approach the mind is regarded as the set of relations among physical events such as firings of nerve cells. . . . The mind develops as the complex set of relations of a given brain activity with all past actions.'[195] This is known as EPIPHENOMENALISM.

The alternative, opposing view is that the brain, far from producing mind as an epiphenomenon, is itself the tool of the mind. Even if in evolutionary terms human CONSCIOUSNESS was the result of an increasingly powerful brain, that does not necessarily mean that consciousness, mind, is now dependent on the brain. At every stage in the evolution of life, new forms have modified or otherwise dominated the situation which gave rise to them. This applies within an organism just as much as to individual creatures. Now, the mind rules the brain.

A case which demonstrates this concerns a woman called Ruth, who suffered from frightening HALLUCINATIONS of her father. The psychiatrist who was treating her, Dr Morton Schatzman, trained her to create the hallucinations at will, so that she could also 'switch them off'. During the treatment the psychiatrist carried out some experiments to measure Ruth's brain response while she was hallucinating. One of the interesting results was that when Ruth's hallucination was made to stand in front of some lights, Ruth's brain did not react at all to those lights. The lights were not perceived because the hallucinated image was standing in front of them. But the hallucination was a product of Ruth's *mind*. The obvious conclusion is that the mind, far from being a mere product of the brain, actually dictates to the brain what it shall and shall not register. The mind can be made subservient to the will, and the brain is subservient to the mind.[174]

Many have commented on the fact that the impressions perceived by the brain through the senses are a minute fraction of the data actually emitted by the environment. The brain actually gives us very little information about the world around us and acts rather as a kind of sieve. The French philosopher and psychologist, Henri Bergson (1859–1941), suggested, 'Perhaps our senses are intended to keep things out, rather than to let them in.' We construct our view of the external world out of a very narrow spectrum of sensory impressions. Science tells us that heat is caused by molecules in motion, yet to our senses a hot object appears just as motionless as when it is cold. Science tells us that in terms of space every atom consists mainly of emptiness, yet our view of the world depends on things being solid. 'The mind is a marvellously powerful instrument, but it is no more capable of *grasping* reality than I can eat gravy with a fork. It was not made for that job. It seems astonishing that human beings have failed to recognize anything so obvious: *that when we try to grasp reality, we falsify it.*'[214]

In *The Law of Psychic Phenomena* (1893) Thomas Jay Hudson put forward the notion of two minds — the 'objective mind' which deals with everyday life and its practical external problems, and the SUBJECTIVE MIND which is more concerned with the inner life. This 'subjective mind' was far more powerful than the conscious will and could overrule the senses and reasoning of the objective mind, as demonstrated in HYPNOSIS. However, the one weapon which the objective mind could successfully wield against the subjective mind was scepticism — hence many a PSYCHIC's inability to demonstrate successfully for sceptical scientific investigators.[86]

MINDKIN The philosopher C.D. Broad (1887–1971) tried to explain spirit communication by postulating a psychic factor in the mind of an individual, which survives the individual's physical death, and which can be temporarily united with a medium.

'This psychic factor is not itself a mind, but it may carry modifications due to experiences which happened to John Jones while he was alive. And it may become temporarily united with the organism of an entranced medium. If so a temporary mind (a "mindkin", if I may use that expression) will be formed. Since this mindkin will contain the same psychic factor as the mind of John Jones it will not be surprising if it displays some traits characteristic of John Jones, and some memories of events in his earthly life.'[19]

A comparable more recent suggestion from the world of physics is the notion of solitons, 'persistent packets of energy that can float around and even pass through each other without much harm'.[195] If a boat stops suddenly the mass of water which was being pushed in front of it continues ploughing through the surrounding waters at the same speed for some considerable time. John Taylor has considered whether the human body could create an electromagnetic soliton which could survive for some time after the body's death. A similar form of electromagnetism is seen in the phenomenon of ball lightning. But after suggesting the possibility of such a model of the SOUL Taylor discounts it, since all but short-wave energy associated with matter would disperse very rapidly.

MINDON In his book *The Roots of Coincidence* Arthur Koestler (1905– 83) postulated the existence of particles of matter which carried telepathic messages from one mind to another.[104] By analogy with elementary particles such as the electron and proton, he coined the term 'mindon' for these particles. They remain hypothetical.

MIRACLES Miracles are commonly regarded as violations of the laws of nature, whether by divine intervention, supernatural or human agency. Most scientists regard such definitions as paradoxical, since the laws of nature are fixed and immutable, and hence those who think they have witnessed miraculous events have been deluded. Some, however, see miracles as 'timely reminders that science is far from complete'.[207]

One of the most famous miracle-workers of modern times has been Sai Baba (born 1926) who produces, among many other things, a constant supply of sacred ash, samples of which those who visit him take home with them to use as a general cure-all. Whatever the quantity contained in the phial or envelope, it invariably turns out to be inexhaustible.

One day in winter 1949 the entire staff of a religious institute in Olivenza, Spain, was fed on three cups of rice, which while being cooked expanded and multiplied for four hours to fill many other pots and the bellies of 150 people. As a result of this and the subsequent investigations, the Vatican sanctified the Blessed Juan Macias of Olivenza. Lyall Watson suggests that such 'miracles of abundance' are a result of exercising 'conscious social energy' which changes the chemical state of matter.[207]

MOKSHA The goal of a YOGI is *moksha*, translated as 'liberation', 'liberty' or 'freedom'. This is not to be understood as an escape, which would mean unconsciousness. The yogi aspires to the freedom or state of 'unaffectedness' of God, unaffected by troubles and the effects of worldly actions.

MONAD In THEOSOPHY the spirit or individuality which incarnates is known as the monad (meaning a unit, from Greek *monas*). It is sometimes referred to as the 'divine spark', since it has its origins in the LOGOS with its three aspects of Will, Wisdom and Activity. The monad likewise has three essential natures – the divine cosmic principle (Will) of the ATMAN, NIRVANA, (Wisdom) of the Buddhic body, and the individual cosmic intelligence (Activity) of the MANAS or higher mental (causal) body. As the monad descends through the Spiritual, Intuitional and Mental spheres these various aspects are brought into and out of focus. When it descends further it tends to forget its higher attributes: acquiring mind and a mental body on the lower mental PLANE, emotions and an astral body on the ASTRAL PLANE and a physical body on the material plane. These three lower BODIES constitute the personality in the same way that the higher bodies constitute the soul, ego or monad.

MORPHIC RESONANCE/MORPHOGENETIC FIELD In *A New Science of Life*, in which he proposed his hypothesis of 'formative causation', the biologist Rupert Sheldrake maintains that living organisms can learn and adapt through a process which he calls *morphic resonance*.[178] In sense this is nature's memory. If a rat learns a trick in one place, another rat in another place will learn the trick more easily, and the more rats that learn the trick, the more easily other rats will learn it.

The theory is an attempt to describe the mechanism of the HUNDREDTH MONKEY PHENOMENON. Monkeys on an island started to eat sweet potatoes that were left for them on the sandy beach. One young monkey discovered that rinsing them in the sea was an effective way to get rid of the sand and soon others copied. Then, on a neighbouring island with which the monkeys had no physical contact, observers suddenly noticed that the monkeys were also starting to wash their sweet potatoes in the sea before eating them.

Morphic resonance operates through the morphogenetic field which surrounds organisms and is of variable size. In some senses it is reminiscent of Mesmer's 'subtle fluid which pervades the universe, and associates all things in mutual intercourse and harmony' (through which his 'animal magnetism' operated). Inanimate matter is also subject to morphic resonance. The first time that crystals are produced from a new chemical compound the process is usually extremely laborious and there are several possible forms which the crystals could take. On subsequent occasions the crystalization procedure is increasingly likely to follow the path already taken. The 'laws of nature' begin to look more like habits, which evolve as the universe evolves.

Another precursor of the morphogenetic field on the fringe of science is the LIFE-FIELD put forward by Harold Saxton Burr in the 1930s. Burr, who was Professor of Anatomy at Yale University, believed that all living things, plants as well as animals, were surrounded by an electric field, a 'life-field', which virtually held the living organism in shape. According to Burr's theory, it is this life-field that enables our faces to remain recognizably the same, even though the molecules that make up a face are replaced at least every six months.

Another biologist, Sir Alister Hardy, held similar views: 'Might it not be possible for there to be in the animal kingdom as a whole ... a general subconscious sharing of form and behaviour pattern — a sort of psychic blueprint — shared between members of a species?'[78] This would work alongside natural selection as a parallel influence on the evolutionary process, a psychic stream channelling the flow of information in the gene pool.

The fact that these theories remain on the fringe of science does not mean that they are unscientific. Science has simply not yet been able to refute them. As another biologist says, 'We know a great deal about the parts of living things, but next to nothing about the process which assembles those components into a functional whole.'[207]

MORTAL SOUL The 'mortal soul' is another expression for the ASTRAL BODY, which is neither physical nor truly spiritual as the SOUL itself is. After the death of the physical body the astral body houses the immortal soul but eventually dies too. (See AFTERLIFE.)

MU According to readings given by Edgar Cayce, the Mu were a brown-skinned people who inhabited the continent of LEMURIA, situated in what is now the Pacific Ocean. Possible evidence of their civilization came to light in the 1960s, when an expedition in search of molluscs discovered 'strange carved rock columns' 6000 feet below sea-level fifty-five miles off the coast of Peru (Dr Robert J. Menzies in *Science News*, 9 April 1966).

Elsewhere the Mu are more commonly known as the Lemurians. Although Madame Blavatsky[12] describes Lemuria as extending over the Indian Ocean rather than the Pacific, she is in agreement with Cayce on the essential point that the Lemurians predated and indeed seeded the civilization of ATLANTIS. For Blavatsky the Lemurians were the Third Root Race, and the Atlanteans the Fourth. The contemporary world is inhabited by the Fifth Root Race.

Although the races succeed each other they also overlap. According to Cayce, the continent of Lemuria was destroyed in the second of the upheavals which affected Atlantis in about 28,000 BC. Atlantis itself was not destroyed until about 11,000 BC.

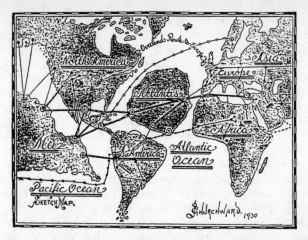

Map drawn by James Churchward showing his positioning of Mu and Atlantis

MULADHARA – Sanskrit for base centre. See CHAKRAS.

MULTIPLE PERSONALITY In fiction the classic case of multiple personality is *Dr Jekyll and Mr Hyde* (1886). The most famous factual account of this phenomenon is probably *The Three Faces of Eve* (1957).[199] Essentially the two cases seem to have similar starting points – a recognition by the individual at some level that the human personality is subject to conflicting urges. Dr Jekyll recognizes the 'animal nature' in himself, which he consciously (at first) tries to channel into a separate personality; Christine Sizemore (the real 'Eve'), the quiet, home-loving housewife – 'Eve White', suddenly and without conscious forethought changes into a seductive frequenter of nightclubs – 'Eve Black'. Even Jekyll's physical transformation, although obviously exaggerated in the novel, has its counterpart in reality, for Christine Sizemore's different sub-personalities were subject to different physical allergies: if she flipped over into a hypersensitive character, her skin reaction to whatever she was wearing would be immediate. While undergoing psychiatric treatment Christine Sizemore developed a third personality, Jane, who helped to unify the other two.

Dissociation of personality (the orthodox psychological term) is now regarded as a defence mechanism by the individual who is under some emotional strain: conflicting emotions are somehow split off and embodied in a new personality. It is interesting that the phenomenon became more common, or at least was more commonly described in terms of multiple personality, in the nineteenth century, when accepted norms of behaviour were still very strict, but when POSSESSION, the more likely diagnosis in the earlier less 'scientific' centuries, was no longer a favoured explanation. It has also been noted that many of the early cases of multiple personality were in young women who were being treated under HYPNOSIS by older men. The suggestion is that some of the more complicated creations of these patients were a deliberate, albeit unconscious attempt to provide the analyst with what was known to interest him. Pierre Janet was well aware of this danger. He tried to distinguish between the roles created under hypnosis through a desire to please the hypnotist and the genuinely repressed or thwarted desires often hidden since childhood.

Could this same unconscious desire to please explain why MEDIUMS in TRANCE 'bring through' the channelled personalities which are so in keeping with the expectations of those who sit with them? Could such 'spirit messages' also originate in the repressed desires of the medium? At first sight there may seem to be little in common between the eruption of a personality formed out of the previously repressed desires of a Mr Hyde and the spiritual pronouncements of a medium's 'CONTROL'. But very often mediumship has apparently been thrust upon an initially unwilling individual: the unconscious desire to recognize life's spiritual dimension could well have been repressed to such a degree that it too eventually takes over the individual's life in the same way that multiple personalities may do. This may well explain some cases of pseudo-mediumship, but it does not satisfactorily account for every aspect of either mediumship or even multiple personality.

Billy Milligan was arrested in Columbus in 1977 and charged with rape, but it would have been inappropriate and impractical to oblige just one of his twenty-four different personalities to stand trial. Our immediate reaction on hearing that these personalities emerged during his psychiatric treatment to assess his fitness for trial, by a psychiatrist who had reasonably successfully reconciled the sixteen personalities within the girl known as 'Sybil'[212], might be to assume conscious subterfuge on the patient's part in order to avoid trial, or again the unconscious desire to satisfy the psychiatrist. But no actor, however good, could have consciously invented and performed so many characters of both sexes so convincingly, even to the extent of showing distinct brain-wave patterns in different personalities. And how did the poorly educated Billy Milligan acquire his knowledge of Arabic and Serbo-Croat, both of which the respective personalities could speak fluently and read and write, or of physics and chemistry, which as another personality speaking with a British accent he discussed with professional expertise?[101]

Access to what would normally be inaccessible information, whether as a result of CRYPTOMNESIA, TELEPATHY or by more paranormal means, is a characteristic of several different but possibly related conditions: mediumistic trance, hypnotic trance, and multiple personality. In the case of multiple personality there seems to be a common procedure: the first 'other' personality to emerge is likely to be the antithesis of the overt conscious personality. Characteristically this other self knows all about the conscious ego, but not vice versa. When a third personality emerges, it is likely to know all about both the other personalities, but again neither of them is aware of the third, and the third is typically less egocentric, somehow above the emotional conflicts and prone to philosophize as well as to show how the disturbed conscious ego might be healed. There may be numerous other personalities in any individual case, but there seems to be a common pattern whereby after those personalities which embody emotional complexes there eventually comes one, or several, whose intention seems to be to heal. This healing aspect of the self may even provide its audience with anything at its disposal if there is a chance that this will result in the individual being treated in a way which will heal, restore balance, and make whole.

How these personalities acquire the knowledge of other languages, apparently adopting completely other minds, no orthodox psychiatrist can tell us. It seems inevitable that some group mind or COLLECTIVE CONSCIOUSNESS has to be invoked somehow. Perhaps the 'multiples' gain access to what has been called the AKASHIC RECORD. If so, it might seem strange that a pathological condition provides access to a store of knowledge and experience which to the vast majority of humanity remains inaccessible. But we should remember (a) that the intention of multiple personalities seems ultimately to heal the 'host' individual, and (b) that the conscious individual is not aware of the other personalities. In comparison with 'multiples' most human beings are relatively balanced individuals, but how is this balance maintained? Perhaps we all have recourse to the collective unconscious more often than we realize. Perhaps this is what keeps us whole. Our inability to recall what happens when we tap into the group mind does not necessarily mean that we never do it. Christine Sizemore was equally unable to remember anything of Eve Black's visits to nightclubs, or of Jane's advice to unify the first two conflicting personalities.

MUSIC It is quite common to talk in everyday terms about music of the head and music of the heart. This is a reflection of the ways in which in occult terms music can act on the etheric body, activating particular chakras or CENTRES such as the heart centre or the head centre to varying degrees. Sensitive people maintain that they can feel the effects of certain types of music on specific centres. Most western music can be divided into three basic types. A preponderance of heavy rhythm in music acts on the lower centres, the very physical effect of 'body-music'. The rich harmonies and chromatic melody of romantic music affects the heart and throat centres − the harmonies 'plucking at the heart strings' and the melody activating the creative throat centre, inviting the listener to join in. The purer harmonies and more regular melodies of the classical style can also affect the throat centre (since this is the origin of most music − to encourage participation), but this music acts primarily on the brow centre and through this can have a calming and curative effect on the whole body. The beneficial effect of this last kind of classical music on plant growth has been established experimentally, in sharp contrast to the deleterious effect of certain kinds of rock music.

Extremely sensitive people believe they can actually see the etheric body (in the form of the human AURA), and a few have similarly described the effects of music in visual terms: intricate constructions of light and colour build up over the space where music is being played (only to be shattered by the harsh sound of audience applause). The Theosophist, C.W. Leadbeater, described a variety of such atmospheric creations which were illustrated in *Thought-Forms*.[11]

Music has always held an important position in occult traditions. Sound, whether as word or tone, is created by air, and air, the breath of life, has always been the first evidence of the action of spirit in the created world. By intoning particular words (such as a MANTRA) or playing notes of a particular pitch, people of different cultures and religions have entered meditative states, invoking deities or achieving different states of CONSCIOUSNESS. In the Bible music was used as a preliminary for Elisha to hear the word of God and pass it on to his people, just as in SEANCES music has been used to encourage spirit communications to be channelled through a MEDIUM.

The source of many ideas about music in the occult tradition is PYTHAGORAS. He is reputed to have discovered the relationship between pitch and proportion: reducing a vibrating string by half produces the same note an octave higher and all the harmonic notes of a scale can be found by using strings vibrating in proportions of whole numbers between one and six. These relationships are also thought to have been one of the ways in which access was first gained to the secrets of numerology, the number of proportion being assigned some of the properties which the note thus produced seemed to have in relation to the tonic of the open string.

Rudolf Steiner believed that individual notes of particular frequencies had inherent properties, related to other symbolical systems such as the seven planets. For example the note approximating to our F was associated with the feminine and the Earth-Mother. (Beethoven's *Pastoral Symphony* is, of course, in F major.) Many people find such theories ingenious but difficult to accept, particularly since our modern standard pitch is considerably sharper than when composers such as Beethoven were alive. But this could be regarded as one of the contributory factors in our loss of contact with this primal power of music. Our Western ears have also been affected by the system of tempering, whereby our octave is divided into twelve artificially equal semi-tones. Despite modern scepticism as to the special properties of particular musical notes, some twentieth century composers (such as Scriabin and Messiaen) have maintained that there is a link between musical pitch and visual colour, so perhaps the deeper archetypal associations are not so far-fetched.

Other musicians interested in the effects of music on the psyche and its power to change consciousness have suggested that each individual has a personal musical note with which he or she feels particularly comfortable − hearing that particular note played continuously would never irritate (unless one were somehow at war with oneself), and singing it would foster a feeling of well-being and inspire confidence to express oneself freely. No particular archetypal significance need be attached to this note, but it has been suggested that singing or chanting each successive note above it (in the relationship of *doh, ray, me, fah, soh*) whilst focusing on certain CENTRES in the body in ascending order can be used as a technique in meditation to raise consciousness.[188]

MYSTERY/MYSTERY RELIGIONS/MYSTERY SCHOOLS The word 'mystery' is connected with the the Greek verb *muein* meaning 'to close the lips or eyes' in the sense of one who has vowed to keep silent. An initiate into a secret doctrine was not allowed to reveal its secrets. The original Greek mysteries were a survival from pre-Greek Earth-Mother worship, and religious cults were built primarily around Demeter (earth goddess) and Dionysus (god of vegetation and wine), and around the descents into the underworld of Persephone and Orpheus.

When St Paul said, 'Behold, I tell you a mystery,' he was referring to a revelation of the word of God, and he used many notions typical of the mystery tradition − illuminated, fullness, perfect, and wisdom. He wrote, 'We speak wisdom among the perfect,' and 'We speak God's wisdom in a mystery.' (1 Corinthians 2, 6−7).

Mystery schools are often regarded as a diverse group of religious cults whose only common characteristic is that their doctrines and ceremonies were kept secret. However, they all represent the ESOTERIC aspect of their respective religious traditions, and they often have more in common with each other than with their parent religions, by which they have often been persecuted − hence in part their attachment to secrecy. The symbolism and the ceremonies may vary, as to a lesser degree do the myths and legends on which they are based, but at the heart of all mystery doctrines is the belief that through initiation and training a seeker can achieve spiritual awareness and salvation, the ultimate aim according to most schools being the SOUL's release from the need to incarnate and ultimate union with God (*enosis* as taught by Plotinus). Paul spoke of union with Christ in similar terms: 'this mystery among the Gentiles, which is Christ in you.' (Colossians 1, 27)

The idea that earthly life is 'the projection below of the order of things above' (from the Hermetic text *Kore Kosmu*), the idea that the divine is the source of all existence and all values, that the divine is present in mankind, that this divine spark constantly seeks reunion with God, and the methods of training for the realization of this − all these are remarkably similar in all mystery schools.

The mystery tradition can easily be traced back as far as the Greek mysteries (Eleusinian, Orphic, etc.) and Egyptian HERMETICISTS (followers of Hermes or Thoth) in the first centuries AD and further still to PYTHAGORAS, who was probably initiated in Egypt before founding his own mystery school in Crotona, Southern Italy, in the sixth century BC. A century later Plato, initially a follower of Pythagoras, was sometimes accused of having revealed secret doctrines during public debate. (See PLATONISM.)

In Persia there was Zoroaster, a sage and teacher as great as the composite figure of Hermes, and who may have lived around 1000 BC. Zoroastrianism taught of a saviour who would combat evil and bring the struggle to an end. Mithraism was born out of the Persian mysteries, and the story of Mithras has so much in common with the story of Jesus that it has been suggested that Mithraism was a clairvoyant prefiguring of Christianity. In the Jewish tradition there were the KABBALIST schools. The GNOSTICS took over many of the teachings of the Egyptian Hermeticists, just as Plotinus and the NEOPLATONISTS combined Greek and Christian ideas. Later came the ALCHEMISTS, the ROSICRUCIANS, the FREEMASONS, the Hermetic Order of the Golden Dawn, all still secret. Since THEOSOPHY and ANTHROPOSOPHY opened their doors to all seekers, the 'secretive' aspect of schools of occult doctrine is no longer a deliberate ploy of the schools themselves: it is the degree of motivation and the level of understanding of the potential seekers that determine the apparent 'exclusiveness' of today's esoteric groups. The path to knowledge is accessible today as never before, the only hindrance being the individual him/herself.

MYSTICAL EXPERIENCE Surveys carried out by the Religious Research Unit in Oxford suggest that 36 per cent of the population have had some kind of religious or mystical experience.[79] They seem to be much more frequent than has often been supposed, by Bucke for example, who considered what he referred to as moments of 'COSMIC CONSCIOUSNESS' to be more typical of the religious person or the artist.

Direct knowledge of God, the inspiration that comes to us in a flash, during prayer, meditation or fasting, is known in most religious traditions. It is called 'baraka' by the SUFIS, 'baruch' (a blessing) in the Jewish tradition. Some maintain that it can be brought about as a result of taking psychedelic DRUGS, but devotees of particular religions strenuously deny the validity of such methods. The common characteristics of such experiences are a loss of ego boundaries and a corresponding identification with the whole cosmos — cosmic consciousness; there is feeling of total freedom, a sense of being beyond space and time, free from fear, free from separateness, at one with everything; even the senses seem to be unified in total perception of abundant clarity. To this cosmic feeling might also be added the feeling of overwhelming love for the whole of creation and of being loved by the Creator.

The continued distinction between Creator and created is an important factor for some Christian mystics, although others (monists) hold that the union ('mystic marriage') can be complete, when the devoted seeker is 'rapt' (See RAPTURE). These two ways of regarding the relationship between the Creator and humanity are also present in different traditions of Hindu thought. It is probably the result of linguistic argument that the two approaches have so often seemed mutually incompatible. One can regard the divine as both within and above, our origin and our destination. Jung seems to have been such a mystic; he thought of God as 'a hidden, personal, and at the same time supra-personal secret'.[97]

MYSTICISM Most religions have elements of mysticism if not actual mystic sects. The most common characteristic is a desire to feel one with God and the development of MEDITATIVE techniques to achieve this. Jewish Hasidism teaches contemplation on the immanence of God in everything in order to experience divine unity. Muslim SUFIS seek direct communion with God, and the whirling DERVISHES seek union with God in their dances. Hesychasts like the monks of Mount Athos invoke a vision of God's Light by pursuing asceticism and quietism, using breathing exercises similar to YOGA and repeating the 'Jesus prayer' ('Lord Jesus Christ, Son of God, have mercy upon me'), in the manner of Eastern repeated chants.

NATURE SPIRITS – See ELEMENTALS.

NEAR-DEATH EXPERIENCE/NDE The expression 'near-death experience', often abbreviated to NDE, was first coined by the American psychiatrist, Raymond Moody, in his book *Life After Life*.[128] He had spent eleven years researching 150 cases and had been surprised to find that they generally followed a common pattern. Since then, the data on NDEs has increased enormously, thanks in part to the increasing numbers of people who go to hospital to die (rather than dying – or nearly dying – at home, when the experience they reported would stay in the family, preventing the common pattern from being perceived as such) and thanks also to the frequency with which modern medicine actually brings people back from the threshold of death.

Whatever the pain or stress of the physical situation, the onset of the NDE is usually marked by a sense of peace and well-being. This is soon followed by an awareness of apparent separation from the body. Typical subsequent stages are entering the darkness, seeing the light and finally entering the light. Often there is a tunnel-like sensation while moving towards the light, and one may be made aware that actually entering the light would mean abandoning the body forever. There is often a sense that there is a definite boundary at this point. There are several other common elements: there may be a presence, usually unknown but always benign; there may be a meeting with deceased relatives, who often tell the person that it is not yet time for their reunion; a rapid life review sometimes flashes across the mind; and there is often a reluctance to return to the body, followed by a definite decision to resume one's life.

The subsequent effects on those who experience NDEs also show great similarity. Not surprisingly there is no longer any fear of death, but there is also a much greater exuberance for life and a sense of fulfilment in life. This has led orthodox biologists to suggest that the mental mechanism which gives rise to what they regard as HALLUCINATIONS while in a state of crisis has evolved by natural selection, since its effects are clearly positive and life-enhancing. It is simply 'a powerful and purposeful hallucinatory fantasy fabricated by the subject's own SUBCONSCIOUS self'.[51] But what purpose does such a tendency to hallucinate have for the body itself so close to death? One consequence is that one no longer fears death, so our hunter-gatherer ancestors might have been more likely to be killed as a result of losing that fear. So could this facility for such a specific type of hallucination really have evolved through natural selection?

Other phenomena associated with NDEs and their subsequent effects are even more difficult for the materialistic sceptic to explain away. NDEers often report seeing scenes (of this world) which they could not have perceived normally (as in other OBE's) and such information can be checked and is invariably accurate. They may see what is going on around their bed or in the ambulance or in other parts of the hospital. One woman who had been blind for over fifty years actually reported seeing the colour of her doctor's suit and described medical instruments she had never seen in her life. NDEers can even register telepathically the thoughts of the people around them, often trying in vain to tell them not to worry because they feel fine. An aptitude for telepathic awareness may even be retained after an NDE, along with other enhanced PSYCHIC abilities such as increased ESP and even HEALING. The NDE itself also sometimes includes a glimpse of the future, usually in the form of a subjective experience rather than as an objective event.

Further effects of an NDE on a person's subsequent life can be extremely profound. As Raymond Moody says, 'In my twenty years of intense exposure to NDEers, I have yet to find one who hasn't had a very deep and positive transformation as a result of his experience.'[129] Despite an initial reluctance to return to the body, NDEers invariably resume their life with much greater exuberance than before. They seem to be more in control of their lives, ceasing to worry about what they now know to be unimportant. Their scale of values may be completely different from before, including a realization that it is often the 'little things' that count. There is a recognition that the only things that matter, the only things that we take with us when we die, are love and knowledge. The new awareness of knowledge often impels NDEers to surprise all their friends by taking up intellectual pursuits as never before. There is also a new sense of connectedness with all things, in the way taught by mystics. Life is more precious than before, but of course there is no longer any fear death.

Those who have had NDEs generally describe them as being nothing like a hallucination; hallucinations have a certain vagueness or dullness about them, whilst NDEs are always reported as being extremely lucid, as are the OBEs that often signal the onset of an NDE. As well as perceiving earthly scenes that can later be verified, NDEers also sometimes 'meet' acquaintances 'on the other side' who they did not realize were dead, only to learn later that they actually are.

Orthodox scientists have suggested that the 'tunnel-effect' is a direct result of the reduction of the supply of blood and oxygen getting to the brain, thus reducing the size and strength of the mental image of the external world that our minds produce. The brain is encouraged to produce such hallucinatory images because in resisting the surfeit of painful impressions received via the senses of a body on the threshold of death, it also rejects accurate sense impressions of the outside world. It has been noticed that a spontaneous reduction of external data often accompanies other psychic phenomena, from TELEPATHY and CRISIS APPARITIONS to UFO sightings. The mistake many materialists make is to assume that this association is necessarily causal and that the phenomena are a result of sense deprivation. One could just as easily argue that we register awareness of 'psychically acquired' information unconsciously first and then block off the otherwise constant flow of sense impressions in order to bring that information to conscious awareness.

Some relatively materialistic researchers do subscribe to this view of telepathy, but then go on to reject the notion that what NDE subjects perceive of a possible post-mortem existence might bear any relation to what would actually be experienced after death. The paranormally acquired information is a result of ESP, they say, but the rest is subjective fantasy. To describe the experience as subjective is a misleading oversimplification. What experience is not subjective? Occult teaching and some religious texts (such as the Tibetan BOOK OF THE DEAD) also teach that the first experiences after death in the *Kamaloca* or on the ASTRAL PLANE are indeed subjective in the sense that they are created or projected by the personality. Only in this way can the emotions be purged so that the individual eventually becomes more focused in the mental body in the AFTERLIFE. It is misleading to describe such experience as 'fantasy' since for the individual concerned it is both totally real and the only reality at that time, it has a specific purpose and must be lived through. So according to the occult view, what some people have experienced in NDEs is simply the first stage of this mode of being.

If the NDE were 'pure fantasy' in the sense that materialists mean, there would surely be far greater variety in the experiences reported. The sceptics have pointed to the 'life review' as being a reflection of the 'Day of JUDGMENT' as preached by certain religions, especially when the NDEer also reports an encounter with a Supreme Being. But these elements are not restricted to those who have had a religious upbringing: they occur to non-believers too. Dr Kenneth Ring discovered that both religion and race are insignificant factors in NDEs.[162] In view of the fearful expectations of purgatory and HELL propounded by some sects, one might expect a larger number of hallucinatory experiences — if such they were — to contain these features. In fact Moody found only 0.3 per cent of reported NDEs could be described as 'hellish'.[129]

There is also evidence that very young children have had NDEs containing the same basic elements, even before they have learned how to describe them in words. This tends to refute the 'mental defence mechanism' theory, since young children have no fear of death anyway. Interestingly they usually regard death as a place one can come back from. But in a few cases where NDEs have been surmised in infancy, a child has, for example, asked whether a grandparent will have to go through that tunnel to get to God. Older children who have had NDEs have also said that during the NDE they were aware of no longer being children but of being adult, a clear indication that without our bodies we are ageless.

The tunnel effect experienced near the beginning of most NDEs has been compared by Carl Sagan to an unconscious memory of passing down the birth canal. What he overlooks is that even if the eyes were able to see the experience the baby's face is pressed against the sides of the birth canal, so how could the baby's first experience be associated with anything visual at all, let alone the bright lights of the hospital delivery room? When does the child have a later similar experience with which to compare it and therefore establish a firm memory of it? Even if the NDE were a memory of birth, why would the overwhelming majority of them be so positive, when birth itself is so traumatic and not a pleasant experience at all if it could be remembered (which is a sound evolutionary reason for it not to be remembered)?

The fact that people generally adopt a much more positive attitude to life after an NDE gives the lie to the psychologists who liken the experience to psychosis, delusions, or other mental disorders, which invariably lead to depression and despair. In fact medical comparisons often seem more likely to contradict than support the orthodox materialist view that NDEs are just like many other hallucinations. When the brain is deprived of oxygen the result is usually delirium, which is usually a bad experience, so how can an NDE be simply a brain reaction? An increased supply of carbon dioxide to the brain is also known to induce hallucinations of light, but why should these be transformed into life reviews? 'The fear of death,' the materialists reply. But they also claim that it is the brain's production of endorphins which induces a sense of peace and tranquility and a reduction of pain and stress, so how can they have it both ways? The effects cannot be the result of drugs administered by the doctors, because as Moody reports, those 'who had fewer drugs had the most powerful experiences'.[129]

Whilst experiencing an NDE people have been seen to register absolutely flat electroencephalogram readings (EEGs), but in hallucinations the brain is usually very active, so how can NDEs be hallucinations? In cases where NDEers have seen their bodies being operated on or resuscitated, the orthodox medical view is that although rare such autoscopic hallucination is typically associated with migraine and epilepsy. But ascribing a medical label ignores the fact that what sufferers from migraine and epilepsy see is usually a semi-transparent, rather unreal image of themselves outside their own body, i.e. their viewpoint is the same as usual — in the physical body. In NDEs (and OBEs) the viewpoint is outside the physical body, which appears just as real and solid as usual.

There is no medical answer at all to the question why the OBE element of NDEs include such accurate extrasensory impressions. It has been suggested that perhaps we all know what happens in resuscitation procedures anyway. But this is not so. Dr Michael Sabom of Atlanta found that twenty-three out of twenty-five patients made wrong assumptions about what had happened during their resuscitation procedures, whilst all NDEers reported them accurately.

There remains also the vexed question of what possible evolutionary purpose there might be in dying comfortably, or no longer fearing death. It is also worth noting that the effects on the individual of the very few bad NDE experiences that have been reported (of scenes reminiscent of hell or purgatory) are just as positive and transforming as the more usual kind.

A Gallup poll reports that eight million adults in the USA have had an NDE, approximately one in twenty. Most of these subsequently regard the bodies they temporarily left as a house for their spirit. They adopt a much more spiritual attitude to life. 'People who undergo an NDE come out of it saying that religion concerns your ability to love — not doctrines and denominations.'[129]

Dr Michael Grosso, a New York philosopher, believes that there is a collective transformation of consciousness taking place in response to the threat of nuclear annihilation. He suggests that the incidence of NDEs has run in parallel with UFO phenomena, which really started in 1947, a few years after the first atom bomb explosion. At the same time there was a sudden increase in reports of Marian visions.

But do we need such external reasons to explain NDEs? Open discussion of them has increased, just as discussion of almost all private inner experiences has increased in recent times. That perhaps is an example of a 'collective transformation of consciousness'. NDEs are subjective experiences of a personal nature. One of the few objective factors is that many NDEers have been technically dead before being resuscitated, yet even that fact is afforded no importance by the orthodox scientist. The fact that when facing a situation which is generally not discussed throughout life, so many people have similar subjective experiences of that situation, ought to suggest to the empirical scientist that there must be something in what NDEers say.

NECROMANCY The term 'necromancy' is used in two senses which have tended to infect each other. The basic meaning (from Greek *nekros* + *manteia*: 'corpse' + 'soothsaying') refers to the practice of conjuring up spirits of the dead, particularly for purposes of divination and prophecy. A second meaning is SORCERY or 'black magic' (from a medieval Latin corruption of *niger*: black). Consequently people tend to use the word 'necromancy' either when referring pejoratively to mediumistic practices, or to mean communicating with spirits for evil ends such as to gain power over others.

NEO-PLATONISM The Neo-Platonists constructed a coherent system of esoteric knowledge drawing on the philosophy of Plato and Aristotle, the religion of early Christianity, and the symbolism and magic of Mesopotamian and Egyptian teachings. They were particularly active in Alexandria and Rome in the third century. One of the leading exponents of Neo-Platonism was Plotinus (204−270), who was born in Egypt, studied with the MAGI in Mesopotamia, and taught from 244 onwards in Rome.

Plotinus taught that the UNIVERSE was one and everything in it interacted with each other. God was One, transcendent, the Absolute, and all else emanated from this First Cause. The stars were signs of events on earth but did not determine them; human beings still had free will. Plotinus was opposed to the GNOSTICS, accusing them of being too deterministic in their dogma in order to frighten people. One of the aims of Neo-Platonism was to free people from the conceptual limitations imposed on them by being confined in a physical body, and make them aware of spiritual reality. This realization or expansion of CONSCIOUSNESS was referred to as the encounter with Isis. According to Plotinus's view of the cosmos there were three levels of reality other than the material: the realm of the soul, the realm of reason (or spirit), and the realm of pure existence, absolute being, God.

Iamblichus (230−325), who founded a Syrian school of Neo-Platonism, made Plotinus's scheme of things more complicated by adding several intermediate levels of reality, even placing a higher 'Ultimate' beyond Plotinus's 'One'. He also introduced a magical

THEURGY, believing that divine powers or 'Intelligences' could enter the soul of the mystic and endow him with superhuman powers. He also taught that human beings had an immediate awareness of the gods and an innate knowledge of the 'Good', towards which they were naturally drawn.

The teachings of Iamblichus were inherited by the Byzantine philosopher, Proclus (412−485), who taught in Athens. He again emphasized the sympathy between all things and greatly simplified the complexity that Iamblichus had introduced. All proceeded from the One, below which were the unknowable 'Units of Henads'; then came the realm of Mind, subdivided into Being, Life and Thought, and then the realm of Soul. Since everything proceeded from the Divine, evil did not really exist. The imperishable spark of light within each individual enables direct perception of the Divine, but communion with the gods could also be achieved gradually by first contacting lesser spirits. Proclus called himself a HERMETIC philosopher and opposed Christianity, hoping that more people would turn to his ESOTERIC teachings. But Christianity was now in the ascendancy politically. The Emperor Constantine had adopted Christianity during his reign, being baptized on his death bed in 337. Theodosius imposed Christianity on the Empire in 391, forbidding all non-Christian forms of religion, and in 529 the Neo-Platonist school in Athens was closed by Justinian, forcing its members to flee eastwards.

Neo-Platonist ideas continued to infiltrate European religious thought periodically, most notably through the introduction of Aristotle (in Arabic translation with commentaries) in the twelfth century, and with the patronage and interest in Hermetic texts of Cosimo de' Medici in Florence in the fifteenth century.

NIGHT OF GOD The goal of EVOLUTION is the total synthesis of a manifested UNIVERSE with the consciousness of its Creator. When this is achieved, phenomenal existence ceases. This is known in Hindu Vedanta as the Night of God or *pralaya*. The manifested universe also withdraws after each phase of evolution, in a period known as the 'Night of the Ages', 'Old Night' or 'Lesser Chaos', during which the Creator's consciousness is modified by contemplation of evolution so far achieved.

NIRVANA The literal meaning of nirvana is 'extinguishing': when the flames of desire are blown out, one achieves absolute peace. Nirvana is the state of endless calm in which purified souls dwell when they have escaped the round of REINCARNATION and TRANSMIGRATION, free from the world of space and time, free from all craving, free from the senses, free from illusion. It is the goal towards which all Jains, Hindus and Buddhists ultimately aspire, although in the case of Buddhism the soul does not exist as an individual entity. Nirvana can be achieved in this life and the Buddha lived in it after his ENLIGHTENMENT.

There is no personal survival in Nirvana, since release from the round of births and deaths is attained by becoming perfectly enlightened, becoming BRAHMAN, a state in which 'becoming' ceases. It is easy to see how this has been interpreted in the West as extinction, although the extinction of self and of desires does not mean total annihilation. It is the realization that the ego does not really exist.

Nirvana is comparable to the SUFI concept of dying-to-self known as *fana*, which the eleventh-century Persian mystic and poet, Ansari, described as 'the dissolution of everything except God'. In Christianity the closest concept is that of mystic union with God, also described by some MYSTICS as a spiritual marriage, although it is debatable to what extent the idea of the self is lost in such an experience and to what extent the union is permanent. The state of COSMIC CONSCIOUSNESS also comes close to what is understood by Nirvana.

NOOSPHERE The noosphere (from *nous*, Greek: 'mind') is Pierre Teilhard de Chardin's term for the network of thought which surrounds the globe and links all humanity. The earth's crust forms the lithosphere, and around this is the atmosphere; on the boundary of the lithosphere and in the atmosphere is the biosphere, the domain of organic life. It took millions of years for the biosphere to evolve; the noosphere is the latest stage of development in earth's EVOLUTION. Just as the biosphere changed the other existing spheres, so the noosphere is having an effect on all other spheres.

Teilhard de Chardin's concept of the evolving Earth

OBE – See OUT-OF-THE-BODY EXPERIENCE.

OCCAM'S RAZOR William of Occam (or Ockham) (*c.* 1285–1349) was an English philosopher who revived nominalism, the belief that general terms or 'universals' had no real existence, as against the Platonic view that such abstract entities or 'Forms' actually existed. For Plato and the realists there was such a thing as beauty, or an idea of blueness; for William of Occam and the nominalists there were simply beautiful things and blue objects and no separately existing sum total of any quality. It was William of Occam's basic principle that 'entities should not be multiplied unnecessarily'. When analysing a problem or developing a theory one should choose the hypothesis which makes the least number of assumptions. This principle of philosophical parsimony is known as Occam's razor.

Occam's razor is often invoked by scientists when explaining paranormal phenomena: HALLUCINATIONS may account for some APPARITIONS, therefore they account for all; we know that the placebo effect works, so it can also explain the phenomenon of HEALING; some MEDIUMS have been shown to be frauds therefore they all are. Occam's razor always favours the easiest solution. But these conclusions are basically conditioned by prejudice rather than philosophical argument, for where natural phenomena are concerned one can easily carry the principle of Occam's razor too far. The fact that stress can cause headache does not mean that all headaches are caused by stress.

OCCULTISM/OCCULT SCIENCE The occult (literally 'hidden') has acquired unfortunate associations in the popular mind, ranging from superstition and fraudulent MEDIUMS to black magic and devil worship. The reason for this seems to be the perpetual smear campaign against occultism waged by orthodox religion on the one hand and empirical materialist science on the other – and mud sticks. But this was not always so. Most occult ideas were originally part of the major religions until they became ossified, and they

225

still form part of mystical and esoteric religious sects. Similarly early scientists like Roger Bacon and Isaac Newton were equally interested in aspects of occult science.

Occultism is 'the synthesis of science, mysticism, philosophy, psychology and religion'.[176] 'It accepts all the genuinely proven assertions of science and merely rejects its unproven negations; it accepts the basic truths of all religions and again merely rejects their untenable dogmas and superstitions.' And science too has its dogmas, to which the sceptic adheres unthinkingly. As Colin Wilson says, 'Scepticism is only another name for a certain lazy-minded dogmatism.'[214]

'It shows cosmic life to be other than that mechanical "order of things" which the materialist postulates, and it shows personal life as the "adventure magnificent" which does not merely begin with the cradle and end with the grave. Furthermore, it shows the *raison d'être* for all religions worthy of the name, for cults, movements, philosophies, arts and sciences, their evolution and various phases. It explains the apparently unexplainable without making impossible demands upon faith, advocating *reason* as the most reliable stepping-stone to knowledge.' (Cyril Scott.)[176] For occultists the key to understanding the UNIVERSE is the MIND.

Our modern inability to understand the mind and CONSCIOUSNESS is still an entry point to the subject for many people. 'Occultism is simply a recognition of man's "hidden powers" — that is, a recognition that everyday consciousness is merely the "partial mind". ... What attracted me about "occultism" was the same healthy element that lies at the heart of religion — that obsession with the mystery of human existence that created saints and mystics rather than "true believers".'[214] 'The goal of practical Occultism is an expansion of consciousness with its essential concomitant, unconditional *Happiness*.'[176]

Occultism is concerned with the moral, intellectual and spiritual EVOLUTION of humanity. This evolution means progressing from imperfection to higher states of physical and spiritual existence. In the progress of the individual this implies REINCARNATION. The occult view is that this evolution is directed by Higher Intelligences who have already reached the higher states. They operate from levels of reality that are perceptible only to the trained occultist. The normally perceptible world is only a small part of the whole which comprises inner and higher PLANES. The physical body does not generate consciousness but is just a garment of the immortal soul, and consciousness can exist independently of physical organisms. Other BODIES of rarified matter surround the physical body; these are perceptible to the trained occultist. The universe is an expression of energy, and all beings, embodied and disembodied, are store-houses and transformers of energy. The whole cosmos operates according to the law of KARMA. These are the basic tenets of occultism.

OD, ODIC FORCE The German chemist Baron Karl von Reichenbach (1788–1869), who among other things discovered creosote and paraffin, observed that certain sensitive people could feel a cool current near the north pole of a magnet, and in darkness they could see a bluish vapour or flame around it. From the south pole they reported a warm stream and an orange colour. Other substances such as rock crystal were said to emit other colours. He first noticed this sensitivity in people in pathological nervous conditions, but on further investigation he found that certain perfectly healthy people could perceive the same emissions.

Although the radiation which caused these emissions seemed to be associated with electromagnetism, Reichenbach wanted to distinguish it from electricity and magnetism, and he called it *od* after the Norse god, Odin. He tried to prove scientifically the existence of odic energy emanating from the human body, like an AURA, and he claimed to have found evidence that it was measurable. He believed that the odic force pervaded all nature, radiating from all objects and living things.

Reichenbach's ideas were later incorporated into Wilhelm Reich's concept of ORGONE. He can also be regarded a direct precursor of the twentieth century Russian scientist KIRLIAN and the notion of BIOPLASMA, and of Harold Saxton Burr's idea of a LIFE-FIELD. The only essential difference seems to be that these last two based their research on electromagnetism, whilst Reichenbach and Reich regarded their od and ORGONE as non-electromagnetic. Further back it made an appearance therapeutically as Mesmer's ANIMAL MAGNETISM, and more recently it has assumed the Chinese guise of QI GONG. The common link between all of these is the old idea of an energy body – an ETHERIC BODY.

It is interesting to note that Reichenbach's first subjects suffered from nervous conditions, which he believed made them more likely to be able to see the radiations. A lack of synchronization between the physical and etheric bodies has long been associated with nervous conditions (particularly epilepsy) and this could symptomatically lend greater sensitivity to external etheric radiations.

227

OMEGA POINT The French Jesuit priest, philosopher and palae-ontologist, Teilhard de Chardin (1881–1955), brought together science and religion in his synthesis of Christian belief and evolutionary theory. The Omega Point is both the goal of EVOLUTION, 'emerging from the rise of consciousness', and the dynamic principle which drives the evolutionary process, the 'Prime Mover ahead'. As God-Omega it is also transcendent. It explains 'the persistent march of things towards greater consciousness'. Evolution is now a process of convergence rather than of increasing complexity and diversification: 'When consciousness broke through the critical surface of hominization, it really passed from divergence to convergence.' 'Contrary to the appearances still admitted by physics, the Great Stability is not at the bottom in the infra-elementary sphere, but at the top in the ultra-synthetic sphere.' So Omega is both ultimate and actual. 'Omega is already in existence and operative at the very core of the thinking mass.'[196]

OPEN CHANNELLING Trance mediumship, in which communications purportedly coming from a spirit entity are voiced by a MEDIUM in TRANCE, is sometimes called CHANNELLING nowadays. Open channelling implies that the medium or channel is not in trance although under apparent CONTROL by the other 'DISCARNATE' personality. In trance mediumship the medium is not consciously aware of what is being said and has no recollection of it afterwards. In open channelling, however, the channel is able to 'listen in' during the communication, although full recollection afterwards may still be unlikely.

ORACLES An oracle was the ancient Greek equivalent of a modern PSYCHIC, CLAIRVOYANT, MEDIUM or CHANNEL. People could consult their chosen god by asking the priest or priestess at the appropriate oracular temple to reveal the god's message to them. This was often done by what we would now call TRANCE CHANNELLING, as in the case of the oracle of Apollo at Delphi, where the priestess spoke in trance. Other oracular methods were more indirect. In the oracle of Jupiter at Dodona divination was by the movements of oak trees and objects like drums and cauldrons hanging from them, or by the entrails of animals, interpreted by the priest. At the oracle of Hercules at Bura dice were used. At Epidaurus, Pergamum and Rome querents could sleep in the oracular temple of Aesculapius and would receive the answers to their questions in DREAMS.

The most famous oracle is probably the one at the shrine of Apollo at Delphi, the place which Jupiter designated as the central point of the earth, 'the navel of the earth'. An 'umbilicus' of white marble was later placed in the temple to show this. The Delphic oracle originally belonged to the earth goddess, Gaia – hence the symbolic earth-snake, Python, which was retained by the later cult of Apollo. The site began simply as a slab or lid covering a fissure in the ground as a protection against the noxious fumes rising from the bowels of the earth. Legend has it that these fumes were first discovered by a shepherd, curious at the strange behaviour of his flock. On breathing the fumes himself he fell into ECSTASY and spoke as if possessed or inspired. The tripod placed over the hole prevented the unsuspecting from being affected, but many came to experiment. One such was a girl who was eventually chosen to be the permanent mouthpiece of the oracle. She was known as Pythian or the Pythia; her inspiration came from Apollo, the slayer of the Python. Initially the Pythia had to be a virgin and she spoke only on one day of the year, the birthday of Apollo. This was later extended to the whole month and eventually to the whole year round, and the qualifying status was also amended: she had to be a woman of fifty. Whether as a virgin or as a mature woman, it is probable that she was generally of a naive and unsophisticated character. Socrates held that 'the prophetess at Delphi and the priestess at Dodona, when out of their senses have conferred great benefits on Hellas ... but when in their senses, few or none,' (Plato *Phaedrus*).

It was common for oracles to be sited near a cleft in the earth in volcanic areas, and in such cases the spirits of the dead were consulted in the same way that some people today might hope to receive advice from a deceased relative by having a sitting with a medium. Such mediumistic practices, sometimes known as NECROMANCY, are common to a wide variety of cultures throughout the world from SHAMANS to the lamas of Tibet (particularly the so-called red hats) and the girls known as *miko* who perform sacred dances at Shinto shrines and also communicate with the spirit world.

ORGONE In 1940 the Austrian-born American scientist, Wilhelm Reich (1897–1957), claimed to have discovered a non-electromagnetic force which was present everywhere throughout the universe. It was detectable as emanations around the body, like Reichenbach's ODIC FORCE, and like PRANA and MANA it was the universal force which sustained life. He believed that human beings could stimulate the production of this force by breathing exercises which converted red blood cells into orgone energy. He also claimed to be able to collect orgone in specially constructed accumulators made of wood or metal. Scoffed at by the academic establishment and mistrusted by the American authorities, Reich was arrested and died in prison.

OUIJA BOARD The ouija board is a device for obtaining messages and answers to questions from supposedly DISCARNATE sources. The operator(s) rests a hand or finger on the pointer or upturned glass which moves, apparently of its own volition, to each successive letter of the answer. 'Qui' and 'Ja' are respectively French and German for 'Yes'. The ouija board is so-called because as well as having every letter of the alphabet printed on it, there are also usually the words 'Yes' and 'No'. The pointer is sometimes an adaptation of the PLANCHETTE, with a peg replacing the pencil, which has sometimes led to references to the ouija board as a planchette, which is not strictly accurate.

Although the ouija board has been used by reputable MEDIUMS to bring through communications of undoubted worth, it would be a grave mistake to expect all messages obtained in this way to be of equal value. The most likely mechanism at work is unconscious control by the operator(s), and repressed sub-personalities of an unpleasant kind can be encouraged to express themselves in this way. TELEPATHY also sometimes seems to be involved, and it is possible that the people around the ouija board somehow form a group mind (like Lyall Watson's idea of SAMA) which answers the questions. Such a group consciousness may even be able to voice the memories and apparent responses of certain POLTERGEIST entities, such as the spirit of the murdered tinker, which made the Fox sisters into the mid-wives of SPIRITUALISM. Whatever the mechanism involved, this technique certainly seems to attract a large proportion of communications from relatively EARTH-BOUND spirits rather than material of a higher spiritual nature.

OUT-OF-THE-BODY EXPERIENCE/OBE ASTRAL PROJECTION and astral travel acquired a new designation in 1970 when Robert Crookall, the author of *The Mechanisms of Astral Projection* published *Out-of-the-Body Experiences*.[35,36] The phenomenon has gone under several other names: ESP projection, ecsomatic experiences (Celia Green), and separative experiences. Dropping the adjective 'astral' seemed to make the phenomenon more acceptable for psychological investigation by not drawing attention to the occult connection and the question of an astral body. But whether anything does separate from the physical body, or whether it is simply a mental experience of consciousness, still remains unanswered.

In a typical OBE the observer is aware of apparently observing the normal world, the actual environment around him, from a point of view which does not coincide with that of his physical body. In a hospital bed a patient might leave the body and see scenes that are not visible from his corner of the ward.

The observer sometimes sees a second body replicated at the point of observation. In such cases clothes too are replicated, suggesting that this version of the astral body is a mental construct. This has been reported by patients whilst under anaesthetic in the dentist's chair as well as during more serious surgical operations. Sometimes the observer feels like a balloon attached to the physical body by a string. But both duplicate body and the SILVER CORD are far from being universal factors in ecsomatic experiences. As well as feeling like a balloon, some subjects have reported being birds. It is, however, more common not to have any impression of a body at all at the point of observation.

One in ten people claim to have an OBE at some time in their lives. Most of these ten per cent have the experience only once and at a time of crisis, and only one or two per cent claim to be able to leave the body at will.

A five-year-old child underwent an operation to put a new valve in his heart. After the operation he complained that everyone had ignored his questions while the operation had been in progress, and he was able to give an accurate description of the valve as he had seen it from 'up by the ceiling'.

A blind man was in a coma. Some relatives who were passing through town unexpectedly visited him, but he did not respond. After several weeks he returned to consciousness and described a vivid dream he had had: he had *seen*, as if from 'a different plane', the scene around his bed when his unexpected visitors had come to see him. OBEs always involve vivid perceptions, even when these are inconsistent with the individual's actual physical condition.

One man found himself to be rising slowly out of his body while driving: he seemed to pass through the roof of his car and continue travelling with it. He seemed to be aware of everything around him, 'seeing' a full 360 degrees without turning his head.

A more controlled, more active projection of part of oneself beyond the body is sometimes achieved, as when Stuart Blue Harary in experiments at Duke University apparently succeeded in leaving his body to comfort a cat. Robert Monroe has been the most active popularizer of OBE in recent times. He reports instances when he has left his mark on friends he has visited astrally in the form of a bruise.[127] (For further consideration and examples of deliberate as opposed to involuntary OBEs see ASTRAL PROJECTION.)

Sense impressions change in crisis OBEs. There is no sensation of hot or cold, no sound, no feeling, but a vivid three-dimensional, 360 degree, full-colour view of the whole scene. This is consistent with the view that consciousness is with the astral body which has detached itself from the physical and the etheric (which is also called sensation body — hence no sensations).

Involuntary OBEs could have biological value in crisis situations. Those that report leaving the body in dangerous circumstances have often continued to drive a car, pilot a plane or free themselves from a fishing-net underwater while conscious awareness leaves the body and allows the individual to experience a state of peaceful detachment instead of the fear and panic which could have impaired physical performance of the life-saving actions.

Whether consciousness remains with the astral body in such cases is less clear, since the astral is the emotional body and one would not expect to escape the feelings of fear and panic by retreating to that level of awareness. But it seems even less likely that in such circumstances a higher plane of consciousness could be reached, however temporarily. There is a conceptual similarity between 'ecsomatic' (Greek: 'outside the body') and 'ecstatic' (Greek: 'standing outside'), but whereas one has to meditate long and hard to achieve ECSTASY, one is more usually pushed involuntarily into ecsomatic experiences. One thing they do have in common, however, is an all-pervasive sense of peace and calm.

OVERSELF The Overself is Paul Brunton's conception of the HIGHER SELF, our true SELF or SOUL. It is a Western equivalent of the Hindu Self (ATMAN). The overself is a point of contact between our own consciousness and the World-Mind, through which we can eventually realize that all souls are one Soul, the OVERSOUL.

OVERSHADOWING Not all mediums are TRANCE MEDIUMS, and even trance mediums do not always go into trance when consulted by clients. While giving a reading, many may start to talk semi-automatically, sometimes even assuming a slightly different physiognomy. This is an example of overshadowing, also sometimes called OPEN CHANNELLING. This gentle form of helpful possession or CONTROL by a DISCARNATE spirit or guide is mentioned in the KABBALISTIC *Zohar*.

OVERSOUL Emerson used the term Oversoul to refer to the Soul of the World, Anima Mundi. THEOSOPHY teaches that there is a fundamental identity of all souls with the Universal Oversoul. In the Universal Mind of God all souls eventually fuse as this one Soul, the Oversoul. In the *Bhagavad Gita* oversoul or *adhyatma* is the principle of SELF, by which we are made conscious of Self, but the theosophical concept of the Oversoul as the world of all souls is closer to BRAHMAN.

PA-KWA The Pa-kwa is the Chinese name for a circular symbol of the supreme integrity and indivisibility of duality in nature, the perfect balance and creative complementarity of YIN and YANG forces in all the universe. The word originally denotes a circle containing the eight trigrams which form the basis of the I CHING. It is also used to refer to the more common symbol of a circle divided into two halves by an s-shaped line separating the dark (*yin*) from the light (*yang*), each half containing a centrally positioned spot of the opposite colour. This symbol is also known as the *Ta ki*. In Japanese it is called the *tomoye*.

The symbolism of this sample design is very powerful. It can be regarded as the Cosmic Egg. In the beginning the UNIVERSE was a void, represented by an empty circle. Then the spirit of the great monad appeared and divided in two; as these two forces were in constant motion the dividing line is depicted as a curved S-shape. The dark and light shapes thus show that as darkness diminishes, light increases, and vice versa, seen graphically when the disc is rotated. In other words at the point where

The pa-kwa, or yin-yang symbol

the yin increases to its maximum, it gives rise to the yang and vice versa. Similarly the smaller circles show that each force contains in its centre the seed of the other. The two are held in tension, but not in antagonism. All is in a state of constant flux, the disc shape representing cyclic revolution and dynamism as well as totality.

Dividing the circle into four instead of two, with two S-shapes crossing at the centre, produces the *ogee* and shows the origin of the swastika (when the four curves are straightened as right-angled lines). As the swastika (Sanskrit), *gammadion* (Greek), *fylfot* (Anglo-Saxon), *wan* (Chinese) and *Manji* (Japanese), this has been used as a potent religious symbol all over the world. The significance of quaternity was noted particularly by Jung when he found that it formed an essential part of the MANDALA.

PANPSYCHISM Panpsychism is the belief that MIND pervades the UNIVERSE. Friedrich von Schelling (1775–1854) wrote, 'Mind sleeps in the stone, dreams in the plant, awakes in the animal, and becomes conscious in man.' It was a view whose origins were in Hindu thought. When Schelling put forward this part of his metaphysical philosophy it was supported by Gustav Fechner (1801–87), the physicist who is also regarded as the father of experimental psychology.

This idea that everything has a form of CONSCIOUSNESS, right down to the atom and even the electron, has been espoused and developed in the twentieth century by figures such as Teilhard de Chardin with his notion of EVOLUTION to the OMEGA POINT and by Freeman Dyson. 'I think our consciousness is not just a passive EPIPHENOMENON carried along by the chemical events in our brains, but is an active agent forcing the molecular complexes to make choices between one quantum state and another. In other words, mind is already inherent in every electron.'[49] The entity known as SETH, channelled by Jane Roberts, described matter as infused by consciousness in similar terms.[163,164,166]

PANTHEISM Pantheism is the doctrine that God and the universe are identical. The word was coined around 1700 but the doctrine is extremely old, being an important part of Hindu thought. In the *Bhagavad Gita* Krishna describes himself as the thread on which the pearls of the UNIVERSE are strung, the SELF existing in the heart of all creatures, and the beginning, middle and end of all things. The view that God is both immanent (as in Pantheism) and transcendent, in other words, that He is more than the sum total of the parts, is sometimes known as Panentheism.

PARABIOLOGY Another term for DOWSING or RADIESTHESIA, when the human body registers the presence of various substances underground. The use of this term rather than any other suggests that the speaker regards the act as a natural physiological process rather than one in which the mind is involved.

PARADISE The etymology of Paradise is a Persian word meaning 'garden' and in Jewish literature it refers to the primal state of innocence before the Fall. It then came to mean a state of blessedness or a place of blessedness, a concept which was carried over into Christianity and Islam. For these Paradise is usually seen as a glorified version of physical life, full of comfort, luxury and well-being. In this sense it is the first HEAVEN in which deceased souls find themselves shortly after death, a concept which can also be found in the account of the AFTERLIFE described in the Tibetan BOOK OF THE DEAD. In the *Upanishads*, Paradise is seen as a place of reward: 'Through his past works he shall return once more to birth, entering whatever form his heart is set on. When he has received full measure of reward in paradise for the works he did, from that world he returns again to the world of works.' Christianity and Islam also see Paradise as a place or state in which the soul receives its reward, but they tend to overlook the temporariness of this condition which is considered more fully by Eastern religions. Spiritualists have called this paradisical state of existence the SUMMERLAND.

PARAKINESIS The term parakinesis is not a common term and refers to the comparatively rare phenomenon when an object is moved by human physical agency which is apparently normal but which is actually inadequate to explain the movement. For example, there have been cases where a mother has saved her child from being crushed by a motor car by actually lifting the vehicle, a feat which would normally be quite beyond her physical capacity. This is not to be confused with PSYCHOKINESIS, in which there is no physical contact at all.

PARANORMAL Phenomena which do not fit into the currently accepted scientific view of cause and effect are generally described as paranormal. The use of the word does not suggest disbelief, but rather that the laws of nature which govern such phenomena have not yet been discovered. It is consequently a term frequently used by psychical researchers, who see their task as finding those laws.

The paranormal covers an enormous range of PSYCHIC faculties, 'supernatural' effects and anomalous events. The term is generally preferred over 'supernatural' and a distinction is made between the two, despite their similar etymologies. 'Supernatural' seems to imply that what is not yet fully understood must come from another dimension of reality in which natural laws no longer pertain, whereas researchers into the 'paranormal' are trying to find universal laws. Their area of study is sometimes referred to as para-science or the para-sciences, and that part which has to do specifically with the mind is generally called PARAPSYCHOLOGY.

PARAPSYCHOLOGY The word 'parapsychology' was originally coined in the 1930s by J.B. Rhine to refer to the academic study of psychic faculties, particularly ESP (another term invented by Rhine), TELEPATHY and PSYCHOKINESIS. Rhine founded *The Journal of Parapsychology* in 1937. Parapsychology includes all paranormal phenomena in which the mind is thought to be involved, including CLAIRVOYANCE, PRECOGNITION, REMOTE VIEWING, DOWSING, and HEALING. It is the successor to psychical research and covers much the same area, but avoids the spiritual and spiritualist associations which the 'psychical' had begun to acquire. In Eastern Europe the same field of study is called PSYCHOTRONICS. Areas such as POLTERGEISTS, POSSESSION and APPARITIONS are on the borderline of parapsychology as they are so difficult to investigate experimentally.

PARARCHAEOLOGY/PARA-ARCHAEOLOGY Pararchaeology is another term for PSYCHIC ARCHAEOLOGY, which includes DOWSING and PSYCHOMETRY when applied to archaeological sites and artefacts. This area of study could also include pronouncements or AUTOMATIC WRITINGS by 'spirit entities' through MEDIUMS when they refer to buried ruins and the like, as when a 'Brother William' assisted Bligh Bond in his excavations of Glastonbury.

PAROPTIC VISION/PARA-OPTIC VISION The ability to 'see' via any part of the body other than the eyes is known as para-optic or paroptic vision. A nineteenth-century Italian criminologist, Cesare Lombroso (1836–1909), investigated what he called 'transposition of the senses' and found people who were able to smell through the chin and heel as well as see through the skin of the ear and nose.[113] The most famous case of paroptic vision in recent years was Rosa Kuleshova who was able to distinguish colours and eventually read print through her fingertips. The Russian researchers investigating this faculty named it bio-introscopy (not to be confused with AUTOSCOPY).

Rosa Kuleshova, who was virtually blind, showed no signs of having any other PSYCHIC abilities, and the Russian investigators were at pains to suggest that this faculty was not PARANORMAL. She was also, however, subject to fits, a disposition which was universally associated with the suitability to be a SHAMAN and which has often been linked with imbalance or lack of synchronization between the physical and the etheric BODIES. The etheric body is also known as the sensation body and is said to be able to 'take over' certain sensory faculties when the physical organs fail to respond to the stimuli in the normal way. It is interesting to note that Rosa Kuleshova and the other blind people she trained reported that they actually *felt* colours: light blue was invariably described as 'smooth', whilst red was 'coarse and sticky'. This is in keeping with the notion that sensations can be experienced more generally by the etheric body, although it is not actual evidence for its existence.

An alternative theory is that paroptic vision is straightforward ESP or CLAIRVOYANCE, with the psychological support of a belief in the sensory ability of other parts of the body.

PATH, THE To be 'on the Path' is to be at a stage of mental development and understanding where one recognizes the importance of self-knowledge, working towards it and growing in spiritual awareness. Such a person glimpses something of the true quality and purpose of their life on earth and of the importance of service. THEOSOPHISTS distinguish between various stages of spiritual development by referring to different paths, such as the Path of Discipleship and the Path of Initiation; these are characterized by reference to the various centres or CHAKRAS which have been activated, another indication of the degree of spiritual awareness. This use of the term 'the Path' is not to be confused with 'the Way' or TAO.

PEAK EXPERIENCE Among mystics a peak experience, also referred to by some psychologists as 'a plateau experience', would be described as ECSTASY. But Abraham Maslow, who first coined the term 'peak experience', realized that one does not have to be a mystic to have a transcendental experience; one does not even have to be religious in the conventional sense. 'The term peak experiences

237

is a generalization for the best moments of life, for experiences of ecstasy, RAPTURE, bliss, of the greatest joy. I found that such experiences came from profound aesthetic experiences such as creative ecstasies, moments of mature love, perfect sexual experiences, parental love, experiences of natural childbirth, and many others.'[123]

Colin Wilson has described a peak experience as the sudden realization 'Aren't I lucky!' accompanied by a surge of joy, and 'completing the partial mind', as in Yeats's verse:

> Something drops from eyes long blind,
> He completes his partial mind,
> For an instant stands at ease,
> Laughs loud, his heart at peace. . . .

Or less poetically, 'the peak experience is simply the experience of grasping the world clearly and rationally'.[214] On a more mundane level, we have probably all noticed that allowing oneself to become tired and discouraged seems to increase accident-proneness, whilst conversely a feeling of relaxed optimism and of being 'fully alive' seems to put us in touch with an instinct for avoiding accidents.

Maslow has described one of the prime characteristics of the peak experience as 'total fascination with the matter in hand, getting lost in the present, detachment from time and place'. He also differentiates between two types of psychologically healthy people, two degrees of 'self-actualizing' people: they are the 'peakers' or 'transcenders' and the 'non-peakers' or 'merely healthy' people. 'The psychologically healthy self-actualizers adopt a way of life and a world view generated not only by the hierarchy of basic needs ..., but also by the need for the actualization of one's personal idiosyncratic potentialities. ... It refers to the fulfilment not only of one's specieshood, but also of one's own idiosyncratic potentialities. ... The other type (transcenders?) may be said to be much more often aware of the realm of Being ..., to be living at the level of Being, i.e. of ends, of intrinsic values, ... to have unitive CONSCIOUSNESS, ... and to have or to have had peak experiences with illuminations or insights or cognitions which changed their view of the world and of themselves.'[123]

PENDULUM A pendulum is often used as a means of DOWSING in place of a dowsing rod. This method of divination has gone under various names. Traditionally it was always called dowsing or even simply divining. The word *pallomancy* was coined by Tromp in 1949 for pendulum dowsing, as distinct from *rhabdomancy* (dowsing with a divining rod), but the term has not become current — most '-mancy' words now seem to have a very dated feeling.[202] RADIESTHESIA usually refers to the application of pendulum dowsing for medically diagnostic and therapeutic purposes.

T.C. Lethbridge was a keen investigator into pendulum dowsing. He believed that he had discovered a law of nature when he found that his pendulum would rotate for particular substances only when the thread was a particular length. Silver had a 'rate' of 22 inches, carbon 12, tin 28, grass 16. Other investigators would maintain that it was Lethbridge's own mind that decided on these convenient measurements (always an exact whole number of inches), particularly since they also applied to abstract concepts and emotions such as evolution, anger and sex.[111,112]

Many people have used a pendulum as a divination technique by asking simple questions and noting whether the pendulum rotates clockwise or anticlockwise in reply. Some people regard clockwise as 'Yes', others as 'No'. This apparent inconsistency does not reduce the effectiveness of the pendulum for those who use it. If one wants to start using a pendulum and is undecided and hesitant as to which swing or rotation should denote positive and negative responses, a simple method is to hold the pendulum over a piece of flex connected to some electrical equipment and ask whether the current is passing through the flex or not. Both answers can be verified by switching the current on or off and repeating the same question. An electric current seems to be the easiest thing for anyone to detect in this way.

Tom Graves recommends talking to one's pendulum as if it were a person. He also stresses the importance of not thinking, which some might describe as switching to a right-brain mode of consciousness. As well as the straightforward 'Yes' and 'No' answers, Graves also suggests the use of a 'neutral' answer, represented by a swing rather than a rotation, and of an 'idiot' answer, at right angles to the neutral swing, meaning not that the answer is 'yes-and-no', but that the question cannot possibly be answered by 'yes' or 'no'.[67]

Ideally the weight component of a pendulum is conical, with the point pointing down. It can be hollow, so that a sample of the material being sought can be inserted, as a so-called *witness*. This is also used in RADIESTHESIA as well as when dowsing for particular substances. Diagnosis can be performed by holding the pendulum over various parts of the body, but it can also be done without the patient being present, using a piece of hair or nail-clippings as the 'witness' and asking a series of Yes/No questions.

PERENNIAL PHILOSOPHY The title of Huxley's anthology of MYSTICAL writings and commentaries on them was originally coined by Leibniz — *philosophia perennis*. Huxley said this referred to 'the metaphysic that recognizes a divine Reality substantial to the world of things and lives and minds; the psychology that finds in the SOUL something similar to, or identical with, divine Reality; the ethic that places man's final end in the knowledge of the immanent and transcendent Ground of all being'.[87] The essential core of the perennial philosophy is present both in the spiritual beliefs of all primitive peoples and in the fully developed forms of all the major religions. It is their 'Highest Common Factor'.

As Ken Wilber says, 'It forms the ESOTERIC core of Hinduism, Buddhism, TAOISM, SUFISM, and Christian mysticism.' He has tried to sum up this 'metaphysic' in simpler terms: 'The essence of the perennial philosophy can be put simply: it is true that there is some sort of Infinite, some type of Absolute Godhead, but it cannot properly be conceived as a colossal Being, a great Daddy, or a Big Creator set apart from its creations, from things and events and human beings themselves. Rather, it is best conceived (metaphorically) as the ground or suchness or condition of all things and events. It is not a Big Thing set apart from finite things, but rather the reality of suchness or ground of all things.'[211]

PERISPIRIT Early spiritualists used to refer to the ASTRAL BODY as the perispirit: it is neither physical nor truly spiritual (as the SOUL is) and forms, as it were, a sheath around the spirit (Greek *peri* = around). As it houses the immortal soul but eventually dies itself, it is also called the MORTAL SOUL.

PERSONALITY In all spiritual traditions ranging from THEOSOPHY to the teachings of the KAHUNAS, the Personality, or lower self, is a conscious entity which withdraws from the body at death but continues in some form to live and function for a time as that personality (on the ASTRAL PLANE), still answering to the name it bore when in the flesh.

Theosophy distinguishes between three forms of consciousness: personality consciousness which expresses itself in the world of forms and appearances, egoic or soul consciousness which ultimately rules the personality and eventually gains fuller expression through it in the spiritually evolved individual, and the monadic consciousness of the divine spirit within. It is slightly confusing that each of these forms — personality, soul and spirit — covers more than one of the PLANES of being or consciousness and contains more than one 'vehicle' or BODY. The personality includes the physical body, the etheric or vital body, the astral or emotional body, and the lower mental body.

The personality can also be understood as the soul's projection into the world of matter. The personality's self-awareness rarely if ever reaches the depths of soul consciousness. 'The personality is continuously plunged into giving itself up to physical sensations or to the memories or anticipations of those sensations so that the experience of its own inward essence is continuously missed. ... It is too absorbed in the everchanging spectacle of the outside world to become a spectator of itself.'[21]

At death the physical and etheric bodies die and the personality continues to exist in the astral state. Initially its desires are the same as when it was in the body, and it creates its own world to live in until these are gradually burnt out. At this point it becomes conscious on the mental plane, the personality becoming merged with the soul. For most of us the soul's subsequent perception of the spirit is so dazzling that it induces a kind of sleep, during which a combination of memories of earthly life, unfulfilled desires and KARMIC influences call the individuality back into incarnation in a newly selected personality.

PEYOTISM Among native Indian people in the United States Christianity has fused with their own traditional religious belief system. Their ritual involves the sacramental consumption of peyote, the spineless cactus which contains the DRUG mescalin and is regarded as having the power to heal, to bring visions, revelation and awareness of the Divine, including the opportunity to talk directly to Jesus.

PHANTASM An APPARITION of a person which seems to have solidity, sometimes apparently illuminated by an inner light of its own, is known as a phantasm or phantom (from Greek *phantazein*: 'to cause to be seen'). There is essentially no difference between the two terms, although 'phantom' is more often applied to apparitions of the dead, and 'phantasm' to apparitions of the living, since the classic study by Gurney and Myers, *Phantasms of the Living*, even though Myers also spoke of 'phantasms of the dead' in *Human Personality*.[76,135]

Researchers have always wanted to find a single theory that will cover all phantasms, including CRISIS APPARITIONS, GHOSTS,

HAUNTINGS, FALSE ARRIVALS, ASTRAL PROJECTION, and BILOCATION. Myers came as close as anyone has to achieving this. He suggested that 'a point in space [can] be so modified by the presence of a spirit that it becomes perceptible to persons materially present near it. ... the invading spirit modified a certain portion of space, not materially nor optically, but in such a manner that specially susceptible persons may perceive it.'[135] This 'modified' point in space Myers called a phantasmogenetic centre.

The spirit causing the phantasmogenetic centre may do so involuntarily or deliberately, and when alive or dead. An involuntary haunting by the dead could be something like a dream for the deceased, and by the living too it may occur in the dream state or in waking life in people who are subject to 'psychorrhagic diathesis' — a tendency for the soul to break loose (as in FALSE ARRIVALS). Deliberate creation of a phantasmogenetic centre is also possible by both the living (in what is known as astral projection) and the dead. According to this theory the agent never actually projects a detached astral body, but simply modifies space in such a way that a self-image is evoked and seen, but the observers never actually see the agent, nor is what they see — the phantasm — the vehicle of the agent's consciousness, (even when the 'astral traveller' brings back information from the scene around the phantasmogenetic centre, as in OBEs). In other words, Myers was proposing a kind of space which could be impressed with THOUGHT-FORMS, similar to H.H. Price's conception of the ETHER. And in case this sounds too 'mental' it should be remembered that some of these thought-forms are powerful enough to be perceived in some way by ANIMALS. They are the effects of mental activities, but they are no longer purely mental once the apparition or phantasm has been created.

Modern RESEARCHERS have many scientific objections to Myers's theory. Basically there are too many unknowns, among them the nature of the phantasmogenetic modifications to space, the means by which the agent effects these modifications, the type of sensitivity by which the phantasms are perceived, not to mention the whole question of DISCARNATE intelligence. But the inability of science to come up with any more plausible explanation points to the need for a fundamental rethinking of the relationship between the creative mind and the world as we see it.

PHILOSOPHER'S STONE The popular conception of the Philosopher's Stone which the ALCHEMISTS spent their lives searching for is a substance which would act as a catalyst in the conversion of base metals into silver and gold. The equivalent effect on the human body, to restore it to youth, was achieved by the Elixir of Life, the Philosopher's Stone in a different guise. Both these were originally symbolic concepts for the means by which the individual might be reunited with the divine, restoring humanity's original purity and spiritual unity with God the Creator. All matter was thought to have been created out of a *prima materia*; discovering this substance anew represented a return to our own primal state.

Both the exoteric and esoteric aspects of the Philosopher's Stone are also reflected in its symbolic representation as a six-pointed star, also known as the hexagram (not to be confused with the hexagrams of the I CHING and the PA-KWA). The star consists of two superimposed triangles, representing fire and water, male and female, heaven and earth, and thus the unity of all, the reconciliation of opposites and the potentiality of spirit within created matter. (In Hinduism the same symbol represents the male and female energies of Shiva and Shakti.)

PHYSICAL MEDIUM/PHYSICAL CIRCLE The phenomena which may take place in a so-called 'physical' circle are: the TRANSFIGURATION of the medium's face; the manifestation of objects as APPORTS, which remain after the circle; the temporary MATERIALIZATION of forms such as faces and bodies or parts of bodies, made of ECTOPLASM, some of which may be seen or felt or both before they dematerialize; other unseen materializations which make their presence known by leaving impressions in wax or writing on paper or slates – the phenomenon of DIRECT WRITING; the production of voices without the agency of the medium's own voice-box – the phenomenon of DIRECT VOICE; the production of other sounds such as spirit RAPPING, which may be used as a Yes/No code for communication; the moving of objects such as the TABLE-LIFTING which became such a craze in the nineteenth century; the generation of odours. Other phenomena which come under the same classification but which do not necessarily occur in circles are thought photography, when a SENSITIVE projects an image onto an unexposed film, and electronic voice phenomena or RAUDIVE VOICES.

It has been noticed that physical mediums have tended to be larger and heavier than average, suggesting that whatever energy is used to generate these effects it is associated with the mass of the physical body. This lends support to the hypothesis that the etheric BODY is involved.

PINEAL GLAND The pineal gland is at the base of the brain and attached to the mid-brain. It is about the size of a grain of puffed rice. It responds to light and is regarded by biologists as an evolutionary relic of an eye, which still exists in certain lizards on the top of the head. Occultists believe that the pineal gland is also the seat of the THIRD EYE in humans, but its external projection is usually regarded as being in the middle of the forehead, much further forward than the gland itself.

Even though the pineal gland is not connected with sight it is still in a sense linked with light: it is responsible for the production of the hormone melatonin, a process which is dependent on daylight. Melatonin is associated with the regulation of biorhythms: for example, it stimulates the brain into producing serotonin which regulates our sleep pattern. Sleep is an altered state of consciousness and all mediumistic activities seem to involve other altered states of varying degrees. It is interesting therefore that the pineal gland has been found to be larger than normal in MEDIUMS; it is also more developed in women than in men, and larger in children than in adults. It is also said to be considerably larger in people from India than it is in the average European.[26]

Although it is associated with the third eye (the ajna CHAKRA or brow centre), many occultists consider it to be more intimately linked with the crown centre, the agency of spiritual feeling and spiritual clairvoyance. Madame Blavatsky says that the PITUITARY GLAND and the pineal gland 'are, respectively, the symbols on the physical plane of the metaphysical concepts called MANAS and BUDDHI (lower mind and higher mind).' This makes the pineal gland the organ that is associated with our highest spiritual function, a notion which has a very long history. The ancient Greeks re-

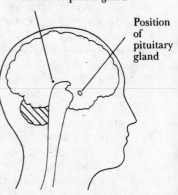

Position of pineal gland

Position of pituitary gland

Cross-section of the brain

garded the pineal gland as the seat of the SOUL as well as a regulator of thought. The philosopher Descartes (1596–1650) thought that it was the point of contact between mind and matter, linking the immaterial mind with the physical body.

PITUITARY GLAND The pituitary gland is located at the base of the brain, above the roof of the mouth and behind the bridge of the nose. It is about the size of a pea and has two lobes. It is the master gland of the body.

According to the occult view, the pituitary body receives the celestial dew, 'ros', from the cosmic ether or pneumosphere. This DEW then trickles down into the nose and mouth, incidentally producing phlegm (*pituita* Latin = 'phlegm'), but more importantly providing spiritual energy for the whole organism. This image has been known to arise spontaneously to people while in MEDITATION, even though they have no previous familiarity with the concept and are initially quite bewildered as regards its significance.

There remains some confusion among occultists concerning the exact pairing off of CHAKRAS and glands in the head. Because it is the controlling gland of the whole endocrine system some people link the pituitary gland to the Salasrara (crown chakra) but others have associated the crown centre with the PINEAL GLAND.

PK – See PSYCHOKINESIS.

PLANCHETTE A planchette (French: 'little board') is a construction sometimes used in AUTOMATIC WRITING. It consists of a triangular piece of wood on two wheels or castors with a pencil secured at one corner. Instead of holding a pencil in the normal way, which some mediums do when producing automatic writing, the hand can be rested on the planchette which then moves, causing the pencil to write.

A variation of the planchette, with a peg or pointer replacing the pencil, can be used with a OUIJA BOARD. Several people may then rest a finger on it while it moves from one letter to another.

PLANES Planes of being, planes of consciousness, worlds, cosmic ethers, levels of spiritual evolution – they go by various names, but virtually all esoteric schools are in general agreement as to their number and basic nature, as far as we in our present state can understand them. There are seven planes known in THEOSOPHY as Divine, Monadic, Spiritual, Intuitional, Mental (causal), Emotional (Astral) and Physical (Material). The first five also have Sanskrit names which are sometimes used by occultists: Adi, Anupadaka, Atmic, Buddhic, and Manasic. The so-called etheric does not constitute a separate plane but is a subtle level of the physical.

The highest plane that a human being has experienced is the spiritual or nirvanic plane, the plane of NIRVANA, the 'third heaven' of St Paul. Paul had 'visions and revelations of the Lord', in which he saw and heard Christ (whilst those around him did not). He said he was 'caught up to the third heaven' and heard unspeakable words. The highest that most can reach in mystical experiences is the intuitional plane.

The mental plane is sometimes called the Heaven-world, since this is where most souls remain between incarnations, provided they have a sufficiently developed mental BODY. This is the level at which mediums and sensitives practise true CLAIRVOYANCE, since it is from this vantage point that one can appreciate the whole of a life in its entirety.

There are different levels within each plane. For example, the astral plane is said to have seven sub-planes. After death each individual gravitates to that sub-plane appropriate to its astral body, depending on its 'coarseness'. Those with the coarsest astral bodies will stay in the lowest astral sub-plane, very close to the physical plane. These are the type of spirit sometimes referred to as 'earth-bound'.

As the astral plane is the lowest above the physical, it is beings on the astral plane with whom people sometimes manage to communicate through MEDIUMS. The higher the plane (or sub-plane), the more difficult it is for the 'spirits' themselves to communicate with us on earth. Those individuals who have developed their mental body more fully do not stay long on the astral level after death, which makes it less likely that they will be able to communicate through mediums except without a great deal of effort. From this it follows that the great bulk of communications from other planes are from lower rather than higher levels and are not very likely to come from particularly advanced souls.

Particular levels of spiritual beings have been associated with each of the planes:

Divine (Adi)	— God the Father, Shiva
Monadic (Anupadaka)	— Christ, Vishnu, ARCHANGELS
Spiritual (Atmic)	— ANGELS, Holy Spirit, BRAHMA
Intuitional (Buddhic)	— MASTERS
Mental (Manasic)	— Saints
Astral/Emotional	— Earth forces, ELEMENTALS
Physical and Etheric	— all material life

Some occultists have spoken of fewer than seven worlds, but this is not necessarily inconsistent with the scheme as described above. The modern MAGUS, Daskalos, says that we live simultaneously in three worlds: the material (physical), the psychic and the noetic. The psychic world is four-dimensional, allowing an individual to cover great distances in spaces in an instant. In the fifth dimension of the noetic world time too is transcended. This is not the whole story, however, for our physical, psychic and noetic bodies can die, but the soul is eternal.[122] This system clearly tallies with the three lowest planes, in which, as all occultists agree, we can be conscious while in the physical body.

PLANTS Cleve Backster proposed the existence of 'primary perception' in plants. In the 1960s he carried out experiments with plants and polygraphs, the 'lie-detectors' he had presumably gained experience of in his former work as an intelligence agent. He claimed that a plant could not only recognize the approach of a particular person who had been 'seen' to harm another plant but could also communicate its reactions of 'panic' to other plants.[4,201] It must be said that most biologists have dismissed Backster's findings as an aberration, and his experiments have not been successfully repeated.

Research is continuing, however, into Backster's claims that plants can somehow raise the alarm and warn other plants of the danger of attack. When there are signs of over-grazing, some plants produce chemicals such as tannin to deter the grazing animals from further destruction. It has also been noticed that plants which have not yet been attacked at all, but which are in the vicinity of those that are already being stripped of leaves or trodden down, can also increase their production of tannin as a pre-emptive defence mechanism. If there is no root contact between these plants, the only other 'mechanical' system to account for this would be some as yet undiscovered airborne pheromones, an idea which may disappoint those who would like to think that plants are linked to a plant-mind, but which is none the less the most likely explanation. Even so, such an explanation would confer on plants a degree of sensitivity which few in the past have acknowledged or even suspected.

PLATONISM Plato taught the immortality of the SOUL, following the PYTHAGOREANS in the doctrine of REINCARNATION and TRANSMIGRATION. Because the earth is such an imperfect place we should try to reach the realm of the gods as soon as possible, and to do that we have to become like God, in righteousness, holiness and wisdom.

In Platonic thought there is less emphasis on the Pythagorean doctrine that the soul is trapped in matter. Instead, everything in the material world is a pale reflection, a flawed copy, of an ideal form in the spiritual realm. It is this true, unchanging reality which can be perceived with the mind. 'You need eyes to perceive tables and cups, ... you need intelligence to perceive Tableness and Cupness.' In *The Republic* humanity is compared to prisoners in an underground cave, shackled with their backs towards the entrance, such that they see only the shadows cast by the outside world on the wall in front of them. The philosopher is the one who is released: at first he is dazzled by the brilliant light of day, but when his eyes have grown accustomed to the light, he recognizes the shadows on the cave wall for what they are. When he returns to tell the prisoners that they are living in a world of illusion, no one will believe him. This analogy is still the most telling demonstration of the illusory nature of what we confidently call reality — MAYA. In the words of William Blake (1757—1827), 'There exist in that eternal world the permanent realities of everything that we see reflected in this vegetable glass of nature' (*Descriptive Catalogue*).

PLAYBACK THEORY The so-called playback theory is a hypothesis used by some people to explain HAUNTINGS. A past event has somehow been imprinted on the physical environment in the manner of a tape-recording, and present-day witnesses see a re-enactment of the scene. The imprinting process is usually thought to require a great deal of emotional energy. It would be a similar process to that by which objects are also thought to be impressed with a record of their history which PSYCHOMETRISTS are able to detect.

A variation on the playback theory is that there is a kink in the flow of space-time so that the past events are glimpsed in a kind of TIME-SLIP. In both versions this is easier to accept as a plausible explanation of battle scenes than it is of individual APPARITIONS where an individual may to a limited extent interact with the percipient.

PLEROMA In GNOSTICISM the Supreme Divinity is known as the Pleroma (Greek: 'fullness'). This is 'the fullness of the Godhead', not the Demiurge who created the material world. The Pleroma consists of thirty spiritual beings known as aeons arranged in pairs, the first four pairs being Abyss and Silence, Mind and Truth,

Word and Life, and Man and Church. According to the Gnostic system of Valentinus (second century AD) the last and weakest of these thirty aeons was Sophia (Wisdom), who has an incestuous desire to know the Father of all and creates formless matter. In an attempt to resist the approaches of Sophia, Abyss and Mind produce the first Redeemer, Horus. In retaliation Sophia then produces Iadabaoth, Child of Chaos, the demiurge and creator-god of the Old Testament, Yahweh. He tries to imitate the perfection of the eternal Pleroma in the world of time and matter. But all of this creation is in need of redemption, so Mind produces two more aeons, the divine Saviour Jesus and the Holy Spirit. It is the task of the Saviour to redeem the souls of the Gnostics, marry Sophia and bring her back to the Pleroma, where the (feminine) souls of the Gnostics will also be united with (male) ANGELS.

PLEXUS A place in the body where many nerves and blood vessels merge and cross is known as a plexus (Latin = network). The same word is sometimes used as an alternative term for the CHAKRA or centre which corresponds to that part of the physical body. E.g. the SOLAR PLEXUS is the usual English equivalent of the chakra known as *manipura*.

PNEUMA *Pneuma* the Greek word for spirit, is not to be confused with psyche, SOUL, which is fed by and charged with spirit. As well as spirit, *pneuma* means breath, life, and energy. For the ancient Greeks the life-force was in the blood, stored in the liver and distributed around the body by the veins; but the psychic force was in the breath or pneuma, stored in the brain and distributed by the arteries. Pneuma was the fiery spirit which filled the universe, an all-pervasive divinity. It was also the individual spirit, like the Egyptian BA, with which the psyche (soul) would eventually be reunited, as described in the first-century Graeco-Egyptian alchemical text, *Komarios to Cleopatra*. The similar third-century GNOSTIC text by Zosimos of Panoplis, *The Visions of Zosimos*, describes the transformation of souls into pneuma and vice versa.

Just as the physical body breathes in air from the atmosphere, occultists believe that the ETHERIC BODY breathes in a vital force from the cosmic ether. This force goes under different names in different systems: PRANA (Sanskrit) in YOGA, *ruah* (Hebrew) in Judaism, *ruh* (Arabic) in Islam, CH'I (Chinese) in TAOISM.

PNEUMATIC According to the GNOSTICS there were three grades of human beings depending on the degree of their spiritual awareness. The great majority of humanity were *carnal* or *hylic*, beyond redemption. Those who lived by faith and good works were known as *psychics*: they would be redeemed but would not attain the PLEROMA. The chosen few were the *pneumatics* or *perfecti*, who were illuminated by the light of perfect knowledge (*gnosis*).

'Pneumatic man' has since been used to signify a spiritually aware individual, someone in whom the personality is in alignment with the SOUL, and the soul and spirit are unified. Jung referred to Pneumatic man as the individual of the future whose whole being would be infused by spirit: 'The *sarkikos* (carnal man) remains eternally under the law. The *pneumatikos* (spiritual man) alone is capable of being reborn into freedom.'

PNEUMATOCRACY By analogy with PNEUMATIC man and various other coinages using the Greek root *pneuma* (spirit), pneumatocracy has been defined as 'the rule of spirit in the soul aware person', (*kratos* = rule). In a pneumatocratic society everyone will be guided in their actions by their own HIGHER SELF, resulting in a flexible social structure with a natural hierarchy, based not on dominance but on spiritual awareness, sensitivity, creativity and self-expression. Everyone will recognize their responsibility not only for their own actions, but for life in general. 'Pneumatocracy can be seen as the individualization of democracy.'[154]

POLTERGEIST The word 'poltergeist' comes from German, meaning approximately boisterous or noisy spirit. Poltergeist phenomena are something akin to a HAUNTING with no visible 'GHOST', although whereas a haunting is associated with a particular place, a poltergeist is usually associated with a particular person. As well as noises being produced, objects may be thrown around or appear from nowhere, water may appear, marks and even writing may appear on walls and floors, and machinery may break down.

Poltergeist phenomena have also been described as 'RSPK incidents' (Recurrent Spontaneous Psychokinesis) by William G. Roll, Director of Research at the Psychical Research Foundation, Chapel Hill, North Carolina.

The noises are not hallucinatory, even though they have no identifiable physical cause: they register on electronic recording equipment. However, they show abnormal vibration patterns. Normal sounds produce a curve of increasing and decreasing vibration at the beginning and end of the sound curve; poltergeist noises begin and end abruptly, and the bangs do not cause objects in the vicinity to vibrate as normal loud noises do. There is a parallel here with the other common aspect of poltergeist activity — the movement of objects or their appearance as APPORTS: the onset of the movement or LEVITATION is never actually witnessed.

Poltergeist phenomena always seem to be a mixture of the violent and the gentle. Summoned by a tremendous crash, people have rushed into a room to find the contents of a china cabinet strewn around the room, yet as a general rule not one item is broken or even cracked. It is also noticeable that people are not injured by flying furniture, even when they are temporarily pinioned to the wall or floor by heavy sewing machines or pianos.

One case which received a great amount of publicity involved a spate of electrical faults in a lawyer's office in Rosenheim, Bavaria, in 1967. It was discovered that the activity centred around a nineteen-year-old girl called Annemarie. The reason seemed to be that she harboured a great deal of resentment against her employer, which she expressed unconsciously in this disruptive way, although how she actually did it remains a mystery to science. It is interesting to note that where a human agency has been identified in poltergeist activity, the person responsible has usually been female and under the age of twenty.

In 1979 Alan Gauld analysed 500 cases with the following results. In more than half of the cases investigated, the poltergeist activity was more active at night than during the day (58 per cent). Most cases involved telekinetic activity — objects were moved about (64 per cent), or doors and windows were opened (12 per cent), and in almost half the cases there was rapping (48 per cent). In only 24 per cent of the cases did the activity go on for longer than a year. In a few instances, 16 per cent, there was communication between the poltergeist and those affected by it, with direct responses apparently being provided to their questions.[59]

Aware of this opportunity to 'talk to' poltergeists, a Hungarian psychoanalyst, Nandor Fodor, working in America in the 1930s, decided to treat them psychoanalytically, as though they were disturbed personalities. He recognized that they were often associated with sexually-disturbed adolescents, and he concluded that they were the result of repressed fear or guilt, which in people with hysterical tendencies could be converted somehow into externalized energy. This response is not confined to emotionally pent-up children: an adult who feels rejected by her in-laws can convert the feelings of anxiety and frustration into an apparent haunting by the hated figure.

Guy Lyon Playfair agrees that disturbed adolescents can create the psychic energy used to cause objects to move, but he believes that the effect seldom materializes until some actual spirits come along and channel that 'football of energy' in a specific way. Sometimes these packets of energy explode in the air, leaving neat pools of water on the floor. These puddles are always perfectly round with no splashes round about; water discovered like this has obviously not been carelessly spilled.[149]

This theory resembles the belief of the Hunas. They believe that it is the low self of the dead that causes poltergeist activity. This is one of the three SOULS which are separated at death. The middle self becomes a mindless ghost attached to the places frequented in its past life, but the low self can be persuaded to cause mischief and even death on behalf of a practitioner of black magic. (See KAHUNAS.)

The fact that some poltergeists have been successfully exorcized supports the spirit theory. In these cases a MEDIUM ostensibly persuades the EARTH-BOUND spirits responsible for the disturbances that they are actually dead and should not be troubling the living.

Poltergeist phenomena may also be a sign, not simply of a disturbed adolescent, but of a psychically gifted individual, whose energies are not yet being channelled in a constructive way. While still at an English boarding school, Matthew Manning was the focus of a great deal of poltergeist activity, including the appearance on a wall in his home of dozens of seventeenth and eighteenth century signatures, which mediums would call DIRECT WRITING. The disturbances ceased when the boy started drawing 'automatically' in the style of such artists as Dürer and Beardsley.[118] His energies were eventually channelled even more constructively in his work as a HEALER.

It is obviously difficult to conceive of any single hypothesis that will account for all cases of poltergeist activity, but it is almost certain that some kind of psychic energy is being exercised — energy which the Hunas call MANA, which occultists equate with the ETHERIC BODY, which Russian researchers have called BIOPLASMA, and which may have been photographed in KIRLIAN PHOTOGRAPHY. A Kirlian photograph of Uri Geller's finger as he tried to exert PSYCHOKINETIC energy on a watch in an attempt to make it stop showed a flare of energy stretching out from the finger. Kirlian photographs have also shown what appears to be a stream of energy passing from healer to patient. If PK and healing can be associated in this way, it seems likely that poltergeist phenomena could enter the same equation.

POSSESSION Apparent possession by another entity may be voluntary or involuntary, with positive or negative effects. Involuntary possession is usually considered to be unpleasant, if not downright evil, but this is not always the case. The possessing entity may be a human personality or a non-human entity (usually 'evil' or demonic), and if human it may appear to be an actual deceased person, an unknown personality or even a known living person. It is difficult to imagine a single theory which would account for a phenomenon with so many variables.

Probably the most common popular interpretation of 'possession' is that it is involuntary and that the possessing entity is an evil spirit (non-human). Lyall Watson reports a case he witnessed in the Philippines. A child of about ten years old was apparently afflicted by a strange disease which had caused half of his body to age. His left leg was shorter than his right, his left foot was clawed, his left arm and the left side of his face were covered in running sores. The teeth on the left side of his mouth were widely spaced and protruded like fangs from his bloody withdrawn gums. He seldom spoke and when he did he produced deep grunts and growls which were in keeping with the monstrous appearance of the left of his body. Then he started talking a strange language which Watson recognized as Zulu. This is the clue to Watson's theory regarding what actually happens in many cases which have been misleadingly described as possession. He doubts whether the child would have spoken Zulu at all if he himself, the only one for miles around who had any knowledge of the language, had not been present. It is also worth noting that Watson was familiar with the language when he was about the same age as the child. The theory is that the child's UNCONSCIOUS tapped into some group mind fed by or composed of all the minds of those around him. The fact that it was the left side of the body that was affected points to the influence of the right hemisphere of the brain, which many have regarded as the instigator of many of our 'unconscious' actions.

It later turned out that the child's problems had started three years earlier when his mother had been mutilated and killed by a truck while they were walking together holding hands. The boy was eventually taken to an *aniteras*, the local female SHAMAN, who successfully carried out ritual EXORCISM, driving out the evil spirit or *busao* which possessed him. Within hours of the exorcism the boy was talking and walking normally, and within a week he was restored to complete health without a blemish on his skin. Only a disease with mental or psychic origin could have been cured so quickly.[207]

It is thought that most cases of apparent possession operate in the same way. The case of Karen Kingston in North Carolina in 1974, on which the film *The Exorcist* was based, also began with a child suffering a tragic shock: she saw her mother stab her father to death.[34,145] Her mental and psychological withdrawal was accompanied by her physical transformation into an ugly, deformed old woman, comparable to the condition of the Philippino boy. Her malevolent utterances were similarly drawn from the group mind of those around her. It seems to be the case that when a priest tries to exorcise a person who is possessed, he actually provides the disturbed person with the mental imagery appropriate to the DEMON that he is fighting against, as indeed do all those around. This type of possession is a culturally determined condition.

Naming the possessing entity is always a significant part of exorcism. In the case of Karen Kingston the 'demon' took the name of Williams. When the complex of symptoms assumes a name, that is the signal for the individual to assume control again. Naming the demon enables the sufferer to disown it and reject it. It is as if Karen and the Philippino boy felt so sullied by their experience that they could not help manifesting their self-loathing in this extreme way. Only by finally denying the human origins of such evil are those possessed in this way able to escape the condition. By naming the demon they deny that the cause of their suffering is within themselves, part of the human condition, and are able to cast it off.

In this respect the biblical account of an exorcism by Jesus is revealing 'He said unto him, "Come out of the man, thou unclean spirit." And he asked him, "What is thy name?" And he answered, saying, "My name is Legion: for we are many."' (Mark 5, 8–9.) The demon's name is interesting: it fits in neatly with the theory that the individual creates the possessing entity out of a complex of ideas and images drawn from a COLLECTIVE UNCONSCIOUS or group mind, from what Lyall Watson has called SAMA.

It has been claimed that this process, working at an unconscious level if not telepathically, might also explain why certain psychiatrists seem to have attracted patients with so many sub-personalities. Perhaps the patient taps the psychiatrist's store of memories and creates additional personalities out of the unconscious material. But the extent to which different sub-personalities are distinguishable from each other as well as from their 'host' is amazing. Sybil's fourteen personalities all had different brain patterns, which are supposedly as individual as fingerprints. Some of Billy Milligan's personalities spoke different languages (XENOGLOSSY), such as Arabic and Serbo-Croat, and were unintelligible to each other.[101] The ability to tap a common unconscious 'sama' nourished by the psychiatrist's own unconscious, would still not explain the origin of the patient's first invasive personalities, but the mystery surrounding these is gradually being dispelled. The generally accepted explanation of MULTIPLE PERSONALITY is that it is a coping mechanism: an alter-ego is created which has a practical purpose; it is a means of coping with an emotion or situation that the individual cannot handle.

It is tempting to conclude therefore that all possessing entities are creations of the unconscious, either the individual's unconscious alone (sub-personalities) or in co-operation with a group unconscious (pseudo-spirits), and that even so-called spirits are complexes of emotions in the group 'sama' rather than entities with will and individuality. But in some cases spirits and sub-personalities have both communicated through the same person and they have identified each other as such, and the spirits have revealed themselves as credible individualities. Should we believe what these entities say?

Ideally sub-personalities should be absorbed into the individual's total personality; possessing spirits, if such they are, should of course leave. In one case the psychotherapist Dr Ralph Allison was treating a woman who had successfully absorbed all but two sub-personalities.[2] These two then revealed that they were actually twin sisters who had been smothered at birth and that the patient was the only surviving child of triplets. The surviving baby had originally 'invited' the other two to share the new body with her, but now the therapist had to persuade them to leave. This version of events, unknown to the patient, was subsequently confirmed.

Cases of involuntary possession by DISCARNATE personalities are not necessarily evil, unpleasant, or even detrimental. The triplets were friendly even though ultimately they caused some distress. In 1907 Dr James Hyslop, president of the American Society for Psychical Research received a visit from Frederic Thompson, a goldsmith. He had recently been impelled to start drawing and painting, although he was completely untrained, and he noticed that the onset of this compulsion had coincided with the death of the landscape painter, Robert Swain Gifford. He then started to hear Gifford's voice and to see visions of landscapes. It later turned out that some of his sketches were identical to paintings that Gifford had been working on at the time of his death, and he drew recognizable scenes of places he had never seen, but of which Gifford had been particularly fond. So far the evidence could be explained by sceptics as an extreme case of CRYPTOMNESIA, but to add to all this, Hyslop was told by various MEDIUMS that they had received messages from an entity claiming to be Gifford, who maintained that he was in fact influencing Thompson.[169]

Possession may seem too strong a word for Thompson's case, since he always remained himself: he felt the urge to draw and complied, never allowing his own personality to be submerged under the influence of the 'invading' entity. A modern equivalent of this is Matthew Manning who produced at rapid 'automatic' speed instantly recognizable drawings in the style of artists such as Dürer, Leonardo and Beardsley. People like Thompson and Manning operated more like mediums than men possessed, but the process is obviously the same, the difference being simply one of degree.

Mediums more often practise voluntary possession and demonstrate the positive use of it. In Dahomey the god or possessing spirit is said to enter the head of his servant while in a state of trance, and in many other parts of Africa mediums are said to become the property of the spirit speaking through them and are referred to as the 'wife of God'. In all such cases the possession is voluntary and the possessing entity is invited. Involuntary possession is also present in cultures like these and is a much more unpleasant affair. A local deity called a bhagwan (not to be confused with the Hindu term of respect) can be so angered by the failure to sacrifice that he possesses the offender, who seems to go into a TRANCE, shaking and sweating and then being raised up in the air and dashed to the ground repeatedly.

There have also been cases suggestive of possession by the living. An American psychiatrist, Adam Crabtree, has treated many people who he has been forced to conclude were possessed. One was a university professor, Art, who was constantly troubled in his mind by the critical voice of his possessive and domineering mother, Veronica, who was still alive. During Art's treatment he spoke as Veronica to the psychiatrist, who eventually persuaded her to stop troubling her son. This could easily be explained away as Art's own internal problems which caused him to create a sub-personality in the form of his powerful mother, except that while Art was 'possessed', Veronica was herself withdrawn and drained of energy and developed a cancerous growth. As soon as Art's possession ceased, Veronica too was transformed into a healthy, active woman. The probably unconscious influence which she had exerted on her son was unhealthy for both of them.[34]

The American psychiatrist, Ralph Allison, would describe Veronica's possession of Art as an example of the third degree of possession on his scale of five. The first two are hardly possession at all, but they demonstrate a spectrum of increasing loss of independence. Level one is best described as obsession — compulsive neurotic behaviour, such as any serious addiction. Level two is the type of multiple personality which is seen as a coping mechanism — a form of psychological self-defence against some unbearable trauma, by which the main personality seeks to protect itself by creating new sub-personalities and eventually to heal itself by absorbing them. Level three is when someone is so tormented by another (living) person that their mind seems to be invaded by the mind of that other person. This sometimes coincides with deliberate attempts by the 'invader' to use magic rituals to put the evil eye on the sufferer. The level four type of possession is when a discarnate human spirit invades a person, causing them to behave in a totally alien way, such as continually walking to a particular place to search for the discarnate's family. Level five applies to possession by apparently non-human spirits, spirits that claim to be devils, perhaps invoked by *umbanda* practitioners (the Brazilian version of voodoo, described by David St Clair in *Drum and Candle*).[173] Cases of possession of types three, four and five have been effectively cured by exorcism.

Other investigators suggest three types of multiple personality disorder or possession. The first is when some trauma causes an individual's main personality to retreat and is similar to Allison's level three. The second is possession by EARTH-BOUND spirits, which accounts certainly for level four, and possibly for level five if we allow that human spirits may claim to be 'devils' or that the category 'earth-bound' can include non-human spirits too. A third type of possession is then confined to the uncontrolled emergence of an individual's past incarnations. Only the second of these categories is treatable by exorcism. In types one and three a cure is effected by merging the various personalities.

Another three classifications of possession have been suggested by the modern Greek Cypriot magician, Daskalos, (the pseudonym of Spyros Sathi).[122] He divides possession into three types depending on the possessing spirit: human spirits, demons, and elementals. All are powerless to invade unless there is already a rapport between them and the individual: a malevolent spirit can only possess someone in whom there is a resonance of malevolent vibrations. An ELEMENTAL is in fact created by the individual as a powerful THOUGHT-FORM, a strong desire or negative emotion, and it then, like the Tibetan notion of a TULPA, may develop a certain degree of independence and return to torment its creator.

The emphasis Daskalos places on prior rapport between possessor and possessed provides a link between the positive use of voluntary possession in the case of mediums, whether modern CHANNELS or ancient ORACLES, and the more negative states attracted by the apparently unwilling victims of 'demonic' possession. Intent seems crucial, whether conscious or unconscious.

PRANA According to Hindu belief the universe is suffused with a life force known as *prana*.

Many traditions hold the same basic view. The Polynesian MANA is similar, as is the *orenda* of the Iroquois and *baraka* in Islam. For the ancient Egyptians the universe was permeated by *sa*, originating in the semen of the god Ra, and special rites were enacted by which the pharaoh could receive extra strength from this divine essence by contact with the statue of the god. The linguistic relationship between the life-force and semen is noticeable in Chinese: *p'o* means both semen and the physical soul or etheric BODY, the vehicle of the life-force, although the energy itself is called CH'I.

There sometimes seem to be two forms of prana: the force which energizes the physical body, like CH'I or BIOPLASMA, and a more subtle psychic energy which infuses the part of an individual which survives the death of the body.

Pranayama ('breath-way') is one of the forms of YOGA which concentrate on the physical body, the others being *asana* (posture) and *pratyahara* (sense control). Pranayama and asana combined form what is known as *hatha* yoga. Pranayama uses BREATHING techniques, usually with special chants (MANTRAS) and ritual hand positions (*mudras*). Certain methods of rhythmical breathing are said to lead to increased lightness of the body, enabling the Tibetan marathon-walkers (the *lun-gom-pas*) to speed by as if walking on air. Achieving lightness at will is one of the *siddhis* (paranormal powers) claimed by yogis and finds its supreme form in LEVITATION.

PRECOGNITION F.W.H. Myers defined precognition neatly as 'a knowledge of impending events supernormally acquired'.[135] A fuller definition which tries to narrow the field by cutting out chance was provided by G.N.M. Tyrell: 'If knowledge is acquired of an event which has not happened, but which later happens as foretold; and if this knowledge could not have been obtained by logical inference from present facts, and could not result from an intention to fulfil the prediction, and is of too precise or detailed a character for its fulfilment to be attributed to chance, then the case is said to be one of precognition. Precognition thus means the *direct* perception of events which have not yet happened.'[203]

In J.W. Dunne's Oxford experiments into precognitive DREAMS participants dreamed just as much of the future as they did of the past, suggesting a different kind of memory that operates in both directions, or perhaps even in *all*, surveying probabilities in the past and future as well as what was and will be actualized. We are 'travelling fields' and what we call TIME is an illusion or 'hybrid' as Dunne calls it.[48] Dunne came to the conclusion that it is not the future event itself which we perceive but our personal reaction to it. It seems to be our emotional involvement with the event which determines what, how and indeed whether we perceive anything of it. Precognition in this sense is an awareness not so much of a future event as of our own future state of mind.

This idea has been substantiated by Targ and Puthoff in their experiments on REMOTE VIEWING. These experiments were designed to test TELEPATHY rather than precognition, but it turned out that the subjects receiving the telepathic messages were more successful if they themselves subsequently visited the sites which represented the transmission data and from which the 'transmitters' tried to send their telepathic message.

Many theories about precognitive dreams and HALLUCINATIONS involve ways in which information available to the UNCONSCIOUS MIND is brought to conscious awareness. What would happen if this information were not successfully brought to conscious awareness? Would we still perhaps amend our actions in the light of unconsciously recognized danger, for example? Statistics suggest that this is actually the case. William Cox studied the figures for railway passengers in America over a twenty-year period, comparing the numbers of passengers on trains which had accidents with the comparable figures for those trains in the month leading up to the accident. The result was that fewer passengers always travelled on the trains that crashed.[69] Needless to say, more sceptical investigators have contested Cox's conclusions, maintaining that he had not discounted the effect of all other variables, but proof of this kind is never likely to be one hundred per cent convincing. As with so many PSI phenomena we will only ever find evidence of tendencies.

Striking examples of possible precognition have appeared in fiction. *The Wreck of the Titan*, written in 1898 by an American novelist, Morgan Robertson, showed remarkable similarities with the actual *Titanic*, which similarly sank on its maiden voyage from Southampton to New York in 1912. It is known that the author wrote semi-automatically: when he was inspired he felt that he was being taken over by another writer, and at other times he was unable to write at all.[7] If one is unwilling to subscribe to the view that a DISCARNATE spirit was keen to write a novel based on a forthcoming event, one can hardly escape the possibility that in some altered state of CONSCIOUSNESS the author himself had access to the future.

The scope and certainty of precognition and prophecy increases as consciousness expands. As one moves up the scale of PLANES of consciousness, progressing to higher and higher levels of awareness, time moves faster, and the present moment encompasses a wider focus which includes more and more of what we would regard as the past and the future. As consciousness expands, so time contracts. On an earthly level we are aware of innumerable possibilities in the future. A mind on a slightly higher plane, the astral, say, will be aware of a smaller number of probabilities, although these will still be large enough to allow for a great deal of uncertainty (and the operation of free will). Higher still the probabilities will be reduced further because the MIND or SOUL is increasingly aware of which probabilities are actualized. Eventually the fully aware soul can be aware of the 'eternal now' in which all events, past and future, are eternally present.

On the question of how accurate predictions may be, one other consideration is the ability of the CLAIRVOYANT. Everyone creates THOUGHT-FORMS from their own hopes, desires and fears. A clairvoyant, seeing these, may mistake them for actual events in the future. A good clairvoyant should always be able to distinguish between such emanations from the individual and conditions that are true potentialities. People do not usually consult a clairvoyant simply to have their hopes and fears confirmed. The best clairvoyant will recognize what are the individual's hopes and fears and should be able to advise whether they are justified or not, mentioning perhaps how to make best use of the prevailing conditions and drawing attention to factors that the individual might have over-looked. (See PREDESTINATION.)

PREDESTINATION There are two recurrent questions concerning the predictions made by clairvoyants. First, when certain events are predicted accurately, does that mean that those events were predestined? And second, why do people who are known to be good clairvoyants sometimes make false predictions, i.e. predictions that do not come true?

Both questions can be answered in the same way: Free-will. Although there may be a preferred path for each of us to follow in this lifetime, we always have the choice whether to follow it or not and at what pace. Nor is there any guarantee that what the clairvoyant sees is such a preferred path, or that the sitter will follow it. The clairvoyant may see the most likely *probability*, perhaps based on our past and present circumstances rather than on any predestined path, but between the prediction being made and the predicted outcome, our own actions may make that outcome less likely. Free-will can always intervene. As Jenny Randles says, 'We never *view* the future, only a probability of that future constructed out of images from our past.'[155] Nothing is utterly predestined, except the fact that we will eventually settle our KARMIC debts, and even then the time factor is very fluid.

The more evolved a SOUL is, the more free-will it exercises, so it is more difficult for a clairvoyant to make accurate predictions for certain individuals than for others. The 'easy clients' are those for whom life itself seems to make all the decisions, external factors over which the individual has little control, (although they are determined, of course, by past karma).

As a theological concept predestination refers to the notion that every event has been preordained by God. This view was once standard in the monotheistic religions, among Jews who regarded Israel as the Chosen People, in Christianity from Augustine to Calvin, both of whom believed that individuals had no choice in the matter of their own salvation, and in Islam, according to which everything happens according to God's will. But it stems from a basic misunderstanding of the nature of time, the nature and means of spiritual evolution, and God's position outside time. From a position in ETERNITY God sees the whole of time simul-taneously, so every event may be perceived but not necessarily ordained. All that is ordained is that ultimately, however long it takes, every spark of divinity undergoing the process of incarnation will be reunited with its source, the Godhead. (See EVOLUTION.) A preferred path for an individual life may have been planned by that individual's HIGHER SELF while in the spirit realm between incarnations, when it can better appreciate what the soul needs for its own progress, but this is not what is usually meant by the theological use of the term 'predestination'.

Scientists such as Newton also believed that the universe was operating in a predetermined way, like clockwork, once God had set everything in motion. This view is sometimes called 'predeterminism'. (See also PREDESTINY.)

PREDESTINY Predestiny is usually no different from PREDESTINATION, a concept that finds no place in modern science. However, some modern scientists have recently started to suggest that the laws of the universe are such that life in general, and human life in particular, are almost bound to arise, the so-called ANTHROPIC PRINCIPLE. 'The belief that the universe has a predisposition to throw up certain forms and structures has become very fashionable among cosmologists,' writes Paul Davies. People who hold this view are called predestinists. As Paul Davies suggests, this form of predestiny is perhaps more appropriately referred to as a predisposition. 'Predestiny merely says that nature has a predisposition to progress along the general lines it has. It therefore leaves open the essential unknowability of the future, the possibility for real creativity and endless novelty. In particular it leaves room for human free will.'[41]

PREDICTION – See PRECOGNITION, PREMONITION.

PREMONITION A premonition, literally 'an advance warning', involves precognitive awareness of an event that one might wish to avoid. (See PRECOGNITION.) Most people have their own experience of a HUNCH that paid off, or an intuitive sense that something unfortunate was going to happen – a presentiment. A smaller number may have actual premonitions where they sense the nature and perhaps the details of the misfortune. Sometimes premonitions occur in DREAMS. Those who regularly have such dreams remark on the different nature of premonitive dream experiences from 'normal' dreams: the dreamer usually recognizes immediately both that it is a dream experience (a lucid dream) and that it is a premonition.

PRESENCES When a disturbing presence is experienced in a particular place with no obvious physical cause, the place is regarded as being HAUNTED. On the other hand, some places seem to be affected by a benevolent presence. Several people, including scientists, have felt such a presence at the Royal Institution, London. Dr Eric Laithwaite, Professor of Electrical Engineering at Imperial College, London, goes so far as to tentatively identify the presence as that of Michael Faraday, much of whose work was carried out at the Institution. He claims that when others mention having sensed the presence of the same figure, they invariably identify the same spot where he stands as well as the same reassuring feeling.

Is Michael Faraday still there? Or did he while living simply impress his feelings of goodwill on the place by means of some emotional energy that science has not yet identified? Could such an emotional charge in that lecture room be somehow reinforced by the energies of those who are sensitive to it, such that the charge is never fully drained?

Sometimes the phenomenon of a presence follows a pattern similar to that of a GHOST or APPARITION. Andrew Mackenzie describes a case in which a man sensed, but did not see, a woman sitting in a particular chair in the kitchen. He and his wife eventually came to the conclusion that it was a friend of his wife's, whom he had never met, and whose death neither of them knew of at the time of the impressions.[117]

The idea of presences includes the unseen companions often sensed by people in dangerous and exhausting situations, such as polar expeditions. But these companions are not necessarily of the same order as the presences to which the percipient ultimately ascribes a particular identity, someone who is now dead. Are these comforting figures DISCARNATE entities with an interest in the endeavours of the living, as in the case presumably of Michael Faraday? Or are they the result of a natural mental phenomenon whereby we project or somehow make ourselves more aware of parts of our own psyche when we need to recognize them?

A similar doubt arises when considering the invisible (imaginary?) playmates that many children talk about (when their stories are not discouraged by disbelieving adults).

Not everyone is equally sensitive to these presences and MEDIUMS are among the most sensitive in this respect. In particular places mediums sometimes tune into another dimension of reality where they seem to become aware of the spirit of that place. For example, while visiting the House of Commons Rosalind Heywood felt the presence of 'a profoundly wise and powerful Being who I felt was brooding over the Houses of Parliament. In that inner space he towered so high that the actual buildings seemed to be clustered about his feet.'[84] Others have called this the 'Angel' of the House of Commons. Such beings are generally referred to as presences, non-human spirits on a much higher plane than we generally have access to, whose task it is to guide the actions of those men and women whose minds are open to their influence. Such presences may be felt in buildings where there is intense mental or spiritual activity on the earth plane. Others of a different kind may be felt in nature. They are also called DEVAS and the realm where they live is the DEVACHAN.

PROOF When investigating PSI and the PARANORMAL, proof seems almost impossible to come by. Psychical RESEARCHERS and investigators into the paranormal have discovered that it is much easier to satisfy themselves of the reality of certain phenomena than it is to provide evidence that others will accept as proof. As Colin Wilson says, 'The paranormal has its own equivalent of the uncertainty principle.' Why is this?

Although it may sound facile simply to reply 'That's the way things are,' it is clear that if the matter were otherwise, life would be so completely different that our motives for doing anything might be questionable. The real business of life must be life and the way we live it. To be obsessed with communicating with the 'other world' would be just as counter-productive as living a totally materialistic life. The ambiguity of the evidence and the doubt it engenders are in fact essential if one is to live the right kind of life for the right reasons.

PROPHECY The term 'prophecy' is usually understood as being a divinely inspired form of PRECOGNITION which the prophet then shares with those concerned.

PROXY SITTING When someone consults a CLAIRVOYANT on behalf of another person, either for personal reasons or as part of psychical RESEARCH, the place of the sitter is taken by a proxy and the consultation is known as a proxy sitting. Investigators prefer this kind of 'blind' sitting to avoid the unconscious use by the clairvoyant of clues from IDEODYNAMICS such as body language. It may also rule out the use of TELEPATHY in cases where a MEDIUM 'brings through' a deceased relative of the absent sitter.

'The object of proxy sittings is to render untenable the hypothesis of telepathy from the living as an explanation of veridical communications.'[39] However, sceptics who deny the influence of spirit entities will in the event of a 'successful' proxy sitting invoke the SUPER-ESP HYPOTHESIS.

PSEUDOPODS Materializations of extra limbs protruding from a medium or manifesting at some distance from a medium are known as pseudopods (Greek: 'would-be limbs'). The French researchers, Richet and Geley, investigating a Polish medium, Franek Kluski, set up a complicated experiment in which the medium was required to materialize a hand in a bowl of paraffin wax, wait for the wax to set and then dematerialize the hand. The mould left in the wax could then be filled with plaster to produce a cast of the hand. The cast was in fact of a pair of clasped hands. As was usual with PHYSICAL MEDIUMS, Kluski operated only in complete darkness, so the scientific establishment (including Houdini at the time) had always claimed fraud.

In another instance a pseudopod was pricked with a knife by one of the sitters. When the medium cried out in pain, this was claimed as proof that the so-called pseudopod was actually the medium's own hand, but when the lights were turned on, no mark was to be found on the medium's hands. This does, however, suggest that the medium is linked at a very physical level to the materialization, if such it is. One is reminded of the theories that suggest that materializations use energy from the medium's ETHERIC body (hence among other things the physical injuries sustained when ECTOPLASM is withdrawn into the medium's body too suddenly). The etheric body is also traditionally known, perhaps not inappropriately, as the sensation body.

PSI We use psi-faculty, psi-factor and psi-function as alternative terms for 'ESP, paraperception, paracognition, etc. Psi is the name of the first letter of the word *psyche*, (Greek: 'soul'). It was first used to denote what was generally called the SIXTH SENSE in 1946 by Dr R.H. Thouless of Cambridge University.[200] Psi was intended as an umbrella term to cover PSYCHOKINESIS (PK) as well as all forms of EXTRA-SENSORY PERCEPTION (ESP) sometimes called General ESP. As J.B. Rhine wrote, 'ESP and PK are so closely related and so unified logically and experimentally that we can now think of both mind-matter interactions as one single fundamental two-way process.'[160]

Psi can be subdivided into eight main areas: CLAIRVOYANCE, CLAIRAUDIENCE, TELEPATHY, PRECOGNITION, RETROCOGNITION, PSYCHOMETRY, RADIESTHESIA (DOWSING), and PSYCHOKINESIS.

Although all these examples of psi are believed to operate on the same principles, the means by which energy or information is conveyed is still a mystery to science. The pioneer Russian parapsychologist, Leonid Vasiliev (1891–1966) of Moscow University, discovered that a Faraday cage, a radiation-proof cabin which excluded all electromagnetic emissions, did not hinder ESP.[138,204]

In all psi activities certain factors are often considered to be conducive to positive results while other factors seem to hinder success. Relaxed interest, enthusiasm, sympathy and a belief in what is being done, all seem beneficial, whilst concentration, anxiety, boredom, scepticism and prejudice are detrimental. The boredom effect or DECLINE EFFECT is also noticeable in that laboratory tests provide better results near the beginning and the end of experiments. Caffeine can temporarily increase accurate scoring in tests, but soporifics such as alcohol reduce it. Atmospheric conditions seem to have an effect, stormy weather coinciding with poor test results.

PSI-BLOCKING Psi-blocking is a slightly confusing term. It does not refer to the blocking of the psi-faculty by the presence or involvement of unsympathetic sceptics (psi-inhibitors), but to the disruption caused to recording equipment by the presence of the psi channel or practitioner. So often when a demonstration of ESP or PK has been recorded the equipment has broken down, as if because of some mysterious JINX. Sometimes the mere arrival of someone like Uri Geller or Matthew Manning has been enough to cause lights and cameras to fail. Arthur Koestler has likened psi phenomena to the ink-fish, which confuses predators by surrounding itself in a cloud of ink and escaping capture.

PSI-FIELD In 1956 Dr G.D. Wassermann postulated the existence of psi-fields around objects which could interact with other fields to produce psi-effects. In TELEPATHY a psi-field interacted with the so-called B-fields of both sender and receiver. Wassermann also proposed the idea of an M-field which accounted for morphogenesis, long before Rupert Sheldrake came up with his version of the MORPHOGENETIC FIELD in *A New Science of Life*.[178]

W.G. Roll hypothesized a similar psi-field of psychic force surrounding physical objects which he thought was responsible for ESP and PK phenomena. This 'region of space in which psi-phenomena are detectable' could receive impressions from both physical and mental events and could duplicate these impressions in other psi-fields. He believed that the field strength reduced with increased distance.

PSIONICS – See RADIONICS.

PSI-TRAILING There is much anecdotal evidence that domestic ANIMALS have followed their owners across huge distances, sometimes crossing sea as well as land, in order to be reunited with them. This is not the homing instinct, since the destination is completely new territory, identifiable only as the place where the familiar humans now are. In many such cases no sensory clues are available either. J.B. Rhine called this ability 'psi-trailing'.

PSYCHIC When Thomas Jay Hudson used the word 'psychic' in his book *The Law of Psychic Phenomena* (1893) he meant what we would mean by 'psychological' or even 'mental'. The book dealt particularly with HYPNOSIS and Hudson's notion of two MINDS.

Nowadays the word 'psychic' is not used in this mental sense of psychological; its meanings and uses have diverged in two directions. The modern 'psychological' meaning applies to the whole psyche, soul or SELF, most typically in Jungian psychology: a psychic event is something that happens in the psychological development or process of an individual. The modern 'mental' meaning, which is probably the more common use in everyday language, is more closely related to 'intuitive' or CLAIRVOYANT, and has to do with phenomena which seem to go against natural laws, as in PSYCHIC SURGERY, psychic HEALING and PSYCHIC ARCHAEOLOGY. People who are psychic in this way are often referred to as SENSITIVES. However, when someone says or does something which evokes the retort 'You must be psychic!' it is often a case of coincidence, SYNCHRONICITY or SERENDIPITY rather than psychic sensitivity.

PSYCHIC ARCHAEOLOGY Also known as pararchaeology, psychic archaeology covers any PARANORMAL method of gaining information while conducting archaeology, including DOWSING on site to ascertain the position and depth of buried ruins and artefacts, map dowsing for the same purpose, and PSYCHOMETRY to ascertain the history of archaeological artefacts. It might also include various mediumistic activities such as consulting the AKASHIC RECORD, AUTOMATIC WRITING and trance communications purportedly coming from the spirits of those who lived on the site in question.

One of the most famous cases of psychic archaeology was that of Bligh Bond. In 1908 he was appointed director of excavations for the ruined abbey at Glastonbury, and his subsequent success in organizing digging at exactly the right spot amazed his employers, the Church authorities. In 1918 Bond published *The Gate of Remembrance*, an account of the AUTOMATIC WRITINGS and plans of the abbey received (before his appointment) through his friend John Bartlett from an entity calling himself Guilielmus Monachus (William the Monk).[14] These had both guided his excavations and apparently been vindicated by them. While carrying out the excavations he had continued to consult a group of entities who called themselves the Company of Avalon. The Church was appalled. Within four years, not only was Bond dismissed and the excavation budget drastically cut, but many of the trenches were filled in and landmarks obliterated.

It has been suggested that Bond's record of events could have been composed retrospectively, but then his success in the excavations and his ability to put together such a detailed account of the history of Glastonbury, much of which had previously been deemed to be mere legend, would be even more remarkable. Then some people insist that spirit entities could not have been involved. But does this matter? Jeffrey Goodman, author of *Psychic Archaeology*, writes, 'It really makes little difference whether or not he really was communicating with deceased spirits or some element of Bartlett's or even his own mind which had clairvoyant access to the past.'[65] Goodman also notes 'a consistent humanness in the sittings' with the spirit entities betraying just the same obsessive desire to preserve Glastonbury's past that Bond had, but also having continual difficulty in expressing themselves (in Latin and medieval English) and often being misunderstood. One wonders why the unconscious would go to so much trouble if that were all that was involved. As is so often the case with such arguments, the SUPER-ESP HYPOTHESIS, a pseudo-scientific term for what was traditionally called reading the Akashic record, seems to involve a greater leap of the imagination than accepting the communications at face value.

Edgar Cayce was one who did read the Akashic record. When he was in trance it was not another personality that came through but a more enlightened part of Cayce's own psyche, perhaps his HIGHER SELF. When giving READINGS to individuals there was often incidental information given about the circumstances and environment around a SOUL's earlier incarnations. For example, when describing the early history of Egypt, Cayce stated that the people were Negroid rather than Caucasian, a contention which went against scientific opinion at the time. Subsequent studies of Egyptian skulls, however, have supported the view that pre-dynastic Egyptians were Negroid.

PSYCHIC ATTACK Just as our physical bodies can be bruised by a physical blow, so our astral bodies can be hurt by barbs directed at us on the astral level, and whatever appears on higher levels will eventually be manifested on the lower levels. The terminology may vary, but the phenomenon is known throughout history. In the sixteenth century Paracelsus claimed that he could injure another person through prayer.

The usual reasons for psychic attack are greed, revenge, fear of betrayal, lust, and a desire for power. As these are emotional impulses, an attack may be launched unintentionally and unconsciously by someone who could equally well be regarded as a victim of these malignant feelings. Consequently it would be misguided to respond to attack with a counter-attack.

One of the first signs that such an attack may be in progress appears in DREAMS, which may be accompanied by a sense of weight upon the chest, as if someone were kneeling on the sleeper. This feeling of oppression may then spread to the waking hours, causing an inexplicable sense of fear, leading in extreme cases to nervous exhaustion and even mental breakdown.

How does this happen? 'The essence of a psychic attack is to be found in the principles and operations of telepathic suggestion.' Initially the victim is the creator of the afflicting sense of fear, encouraged to evoke the feeling by TELEPATHY. Dion Fortune remarks that we are only open to such a telepathic instruction, a process she refers to as piercing the AURA, if we allow ourselves to be open. 'Until the aura is pierced, there can be no entrance to the SOUL, and the aura is always pierced from within by the response of fear or desire going out towards the attacking entity.' In other words it takes two to tango: the feelings we harbour against the attacker are the seed from which attack grows. 'If we can inhibit that instinctive emotional reaction, the edge of the aura will remain impenetrable, and will be as sure a defence against psychic invasion as the healthy and unbroken skin is a defence against bacterial infection.'[55] What occultists refer to as 'sealing the aura' would be pointless if not accompanied by the right inner attitude towards those who might become one's attackers.

The first question to ask oneself when entertaining the possibility that one is under attack psychically is not 'Who is doing this to me?' but 'Have I misread the symptoms? Are they in fact caused by some imbalance I have created in myself?' As Dion Fortune says, 'We have to distinguish very carefully between psychic experience and subjective HALLUCINATION; we have to be sure that the person who complains of a psychic assault is not hearing the reverberation of his own dissociated complexes.'[55]

PSYCHIC CORD – See ASTRAL CORD, SILVER CORD.

PSYCHIC DETECTIVES – See PSYCHOMETRY.

PSYCHIC DEVELOPMENT YOGIS always maintain that PSYCHIC faculties develop spontaneously while one is training oneself in the discipline of YOGA. They emphasize that these are a distraction and that one should attach no importance to them; to pursue the training simply to become proficient in psychic skills is a travesty and a sure sign that one's spiritual evolution has reached an impasse. Theosophists have continued to voice the same injunctions, which explains much of their antipathy to SPIRITUALISM despite some common philosophical ground. Nevertheless, throughout the history of occultism, training in psychic faculties and spiritual development seem to have continued in parallel, rather than at the expense of each other.

PSYCHIC HEALERS/PSYCHIC HEALING – See HEALING.

PSYCHIC IMPRINTS – See TELEPLASTY, PSEUDOPODS.

PSYCHIC PHOTOGRAPHY Although the term 'psychic photography' originally included the idea of SPIRIT PHOTOGRAPHY, it is more often restricted nowadays to the impressing of an image on an unexposed film without the aid of lens and camera. The Dutch psychic Peter Hurkos produced images on film simply by concentrating and focusing his attention on the lens of the camera. The distinction between the two possible interpretations of 'psychic photography' was first drawn by James Coates in *Photographing the Invisible* (1922), who called these other psychic photographs 'thoughtographs'.[28]

At about the same time a Japanese Professor of Physics had lost his job as a result of testing and supporting the claims of a MEDIUM whose thought impressions had been registered on unexposed photographic plates. Professor Fukurai moved to England where he continued to investigate 'thoughtography' with William Hope, who had also worked with Sir William Crookes as a spirit photographer.

In the mid-1960s Ted Serios was the subject of lengthy investigations at the University of Colorado. Under test conditions he produced over 400 images on film which had been loaded into a camera but not exposed or which was still in its original wrapping. He was able to create images of randomly selected target scenes. In addition he caused prints of almost total blackness or whiteness to be produced, irrespective of any exposures that had actually been made. Serios drank heavily during the test sessions and he also had a ritual of pointing an open-ended cylinder at the camera containing the film. As with other PARANORMAL faculties ranging from LEVITATION to STIGMATA, this may suggest that a relaxed, 'simple-minded' attitude of trust encourages the effect.

PSYCHIC PORTRAITS Some MEDIUMS are able to sense their sitters' GUIDES and deceased relatives so clearly that they can draw portraits of them. In such cases the guide's CONTROL is usually the spirit of an artist who guides the medium's efforts to create a true likeness of the person as they once were. It is interesting to note the extent to which the medium's other senses are involved when creating a psychic portrait: when attempting to draw the eyes of someone who had been blind one such medium found that her own eyes were suddenly very painful.[152]

PSYCHIC READINGS – See READINGS.

PSYCHIC(AL) RESEARCH – See RESEARCH.

PSYCHIC ROD – See PSEUDOPODS, ECTOPLASM.

PSYCHIC SURGERY Psychic surgeons are distinct from psychic HEALERS in that they apparently operate on the physical body.

The most famous psychic surgeons have come from Brazil. Arigó, the pseudonym (meaning 'simple one') of José Pedro de Freitas, claimed to have been taken over by a German surgeon who had been killed in the First World War. Since then, in 1958, until his death in a car crash in 1971, he preformed operations with any instruments that came to hand – kitchen knives, scissors, tweezers and the like. Witnesses said he would hold only one handle of the scissors yet the other would move as they cut through the flesh, which stopped bleeding after a prayer from Arigó and healed over as he pressed the edges of the wound together.

Edivaldo Silva, another Brazilian, uses no instruments other than his bare hands, which he plunges into people's bodies, rummaging around in their entrails. The patient feels a wet plop as the hands go in, followed by the sensation of profuse bleeding, but after the treatment the flesh is apparently intact.

Most psychic operations seem to be carried out in subdued light and there is generally much mystification. It seems likely that HYPNOSIS or at least suggestion is involved, and there is plenty of scope for deception. When tumours have purportedly been cut out, the remnants that have been preserved have proved to be animal tissue and not human. Nevertheless many people have been cured by these dubious means. The writer Guy Lyon Playfair underwent such operations at the hands of Edivaldo Silva and went on to investigate other psychic surgeons at the Brazilian Institute for Psycho-Biophysical Research (IBPP).[148,149]

PSYCHOGRAPH A psychograph is a rotating disc on which the fingers of a MEDIUM can rest while it moves to the appropriate letters of the alphabet on a OUIJA BOARD and spells out a message. It serves the same purpose as the modified PLANCHETTE. The device was suggested by entities communicating through a German medium, Baron Langsdorff, who held regular SEANCES for the Tsars Alexander II and Alexander III. (In 1880 he successfully predicted an explosion at a dinner where Alexander II was expected. The Tsar's life was saved by his deliberate late arrival, but he died a year later, killed by another bomb while his medium was away in Paris.)

PSYCHOGRAPHY – See AUTOMATIC WRITING.

PSYCHOKINESIS/PK Often abbreviated to PK, psychokinesis is defined by Thalbourne as 'the direct influence of mind on a physical system without the mediation of any known physical energy'.[198] In other words it is the power of mind over matter, the power to move objects by thought or will-power alone. It is also sometimes known as telekinesis ('movement at a distance'), and less commonly cryptokinesis ('hidden movement') and TELERGY ('action at a distance'). Although psychokinesis literally means 'mind movement' the term has been applied to all kinds of PARANORMAL action ranging from

POLTERGEIST phenomena to PSYCHIC PHOTOGRAPHY.

In the sixteenth century Paracelsus claimed that he could through prayer injure another person, and a century later Francis Bacon, the proto-scientist, proposed the idea that the movement of objects such as dice could be affected by the power of imagination.

In 1934 a gambler claimed that he too could influence the fall of the dice. His claims were investigated by Dr Joseph Banks Rhine at Duke University, who discovered after testing many subjects over eight years that when people were 'fresh' they could influence the dice, but after a while they seemed to get bored and gradually lost the faculty. This became known as the DECLINE EFFECT.

In the 1960s Russian scientists studied a Leningrad housewife, Nelya Mikhailova, who moved objects such as apples and wine glasses without touching them and even separated the yolk of an egg in a tank of water placed ten feet away. Others have claimed that PK can affect the rate of radioactive decay.

It has been noticed that groups of sitters are more likely to achieve psychokinetic results such as RAPPING or LEVITATION of tables once an appropriate sound or movement has been acknowledged by those present as caused by invisible forces. This allows each individual to escape any inhibitions and lend all their energies to the process, assuming that the effect is a result of conscious social channelling of mental energy.

Research into this area of PARAPSYCHOLOGY has suggested that the energy can be channelled unconsciously by certain individuals. In one series of experiments at St John's University, New York State, subjects were set boring tasks to perform while a random number generator ran in the next room. They were not told that they would only be relieved of their task when the generator produced a particular series of numbers. This could theoretically take two or three days, but certain people proved to be particularly adept at somehow contriving to be relieved within forty-five minutes. Scientists are hardly likely to accept that these people were 'born lucky', but the alternative still finds little favour with orthodox scientific belief: not only did they manage to influence the random number generator, causing it to produce the desired sequence of numbers sooner than the laws of probability predicted, but they did this unconsciously, having also unconsciously − and tele-pathically − learned what would be accepted as the signal for the end of their monotonous task. The individual steps of finding out that the number generator was the key to their predicament and then identifying precisely what numbers and in what order would obtain their release were not necessary. The process is understood to be 'goal-oriented' — as indeed are all learning processes.

When John Taylor, the London University Mathematics Professor, investigated metal-bending he complained that he was never able to observe the spoons or keys in the process of bending, a phenomenon he dubbed 'the shyness effect'.[194] He later decided that all such phenomena were not psychokinetic at all. He proposed several non-paranormal explanations. Either the metal-benders physically bent the metal, whether deliberately or unconsciously or a combination of the two — for example, rubbing the key without realizing the pressure they were building up, thus fooling themselves that the metal had bent of its own accord. Or there were instances where quite innocently one suddenly noticed a kink that was already there and mistakenly thought that it had just appeared. 'Spoon bending — like beauty,' Taylor declared, 'is in the eye of the believing beholder.'[195]

The biologist, Lyall Watson, has apparently not discounted the possibility that some metal-bending is psychokinetic and has suggested that the 'shyness effect' has something to do with our unwillingness to take conscious responsibility for such faculties in ourselves or to acknowledge that they actually exist in others. The effects are facilitated by group action, a group being more effective than an individual, and a disbelieving individual in the group can act as a block.

PK seems to be associated with *theta* BRAIN WAVES. Some investigators believe they have found medical correlations between certain physiological conditions and the tendency to cause mechanical or electrical failure in appliances. People suffering from Parkinson's disease seem to have troublesome watches more often than the average, suggesting that they are more prone to cause watches to stop or function erratically. When their nervous balance is restored by drugs, their problems with their wristwatches also cease. Epileptics have similar experiences, constantly being confounded by electric appliances that break down. On the other hand we all know people who seem to have a knack with machinery, as if their presence alone were enough to put right any slight mechanical fault.

The occult view of this phenomenon is that an individual's etheric BODY can affect the workings of devices in the vicinity of the physical body in a similar, albeit attenuated way to the manner in which it affects the physical body. It is flaws and imbalances in the etheric body which are the root cause of nervous conditions such as Parkinson's disease and epilepsy and such imbalances might also affect other delicate mechanisms, especially electrical devices.

PSYCHOMETRY A psychometrist is a SENSITIVE who is able to describe individuals or scenes associated with them by physical contact with objects that have belonged to those individuals. In a wider sense psychometry is the skill to 'read' the history of an object simply by holding it and 'tuning in'. What one actually 'tunes in' to, no one has been able to establish, but the most generally accepted theory is that every object carries its history preserved in an ETHERIC counterpart. Somehow psychometrists read these etheric images with their own etheric faculties. This may be related to the 'tape recording' and PLAYBACK THEORY of GHOSTS and HAUNTINGS, put forward by Oliver Lodge and supported by many since, according to which strong emotions can be imprinted on their surroundings or on objects.

Any etheric counterpart must also necessarily contain not only historical information but all the details of the nature of the thing itself. This is where psychometry had its beginnings. The term 'psychometry', meaning literally 'soul-measurement', was first coined by an American scientist, Joseph Rhodes Buchanan in 1842. Buchanan (1814–99), who was a Professor of Medicine in Covington, Kentucky, discovered that eighty per cent of his students could register the effects of drugs simply by holding them. When an emetic was handed to the subject he could only escape vomiting by a suspension of the experiment. The physical impact of this early demonstration of psychometry is a reminder that the etheric body is also traditionally known as the sensation body.[22]

Buchanan's experiments came to the notice of William Denton, a Professor of Geology in Boston. Working with meteorites and fossils he found that one in ten men and four in ten women were sensitive enough to detect something of the history of such objects, often giving vivid descriptions of scenes surrounding the objects.[42]

One particular kind of psychometry has also been called par-archaeology, intuitive archaeology or PSYCHIC ARCHAEOLOGY. Over a two-year period during the Second World War, Stefan Ossowiecki was presented with various objects from the Museum in Warsaw in a series of tests of his psychometric ability. Not only did he correctly identify the nature and age of these objects, but he was also able to give detailed descriptions of, say, life in a palaeolithic settlement, simply by holding a pointed piece of metal which he identified as part of a spear.

Ossowiecki's description of the process is interesting. 'I begin by stopping all reasoning, and I throw all my inner power into perception of spiritual sensation. I affirm that this condition is brought about by my unshakeable faith in the spiritual unity of all humanity. I then find myself in a new and special state in which I see and hear outside time and space. ... I seem to lose some energy, my temperature becomes febrile and the heartbeats unequal. ... As soon as I cease from reasoning, something like electricity flows through my extremities for a few seconds. ... then lucidity takes possession of me, pictures arise, usually of the past.'[65]

In 1953 the Dutch CLAIRVOYANT, Gerard Croiset, gave descriptions of cave-dwelling people and their religious ceremony working with a tiny bone fragment brought back from Lesotho. More recently George McMullen, a Canadian truck driver, has helped Norman Emerson, Professor of Archaeology at the University of Toronto, in his field excavations, not only giving vivid descriptions of the way of life of Iroquois Indians, but also marking out on the bare ground the limits of a long house, which was later excavated exactly where McMullen said it was.

In this last case psychometry and DOWSING seem to work hand in hand, and both have the advantage of being testable as they are predictive in nature. Tom Lethbridge, using a pendulum, believed that he could distinguish between a pebble that had been thrown by a human being and one that had lain on the beach tossed around simply by the elements. By setting his pendulum at the rates he had discovered for male and female he could further distinguish between a pebble thrown by a woman and one thrown by a man.[111,112]

Psychometry and HYPNOSIS have also often been associated. Just before the First World War a German doctor working in Mexico City, Dr Gustav Pagenstecher, was treating a Maria Reyes de Zierold for insomnia. Hypnosis proved to be more effective than drugs, but under hypnosis the patient identified so closely with the hypnotist that she reported experiencing the same sensations as him – a phenomenon known as COMMUNITY OF SENSATION. When given an object she identified with that too and was able to give a history of it, describing a fall through space or an underwater scene when holding a meteorite or a seashell. The details of such descriptions were investigated by the American Society for Psychical Research and their accuracy was authenticated even when they differed from what the researchers initially expected, a completely different account, thus ruling out TELEPATHY.

Many early experiments in psychometry would be managed very differently today. Some were discounted even by other contemporary researchers because hypnosis was involved. But since in many cases the original investigators themselves knew the origin and history of an object, telepathy could seldom be ruled out as the operating mechanism. 'Pure' psychometry can only be considered when no one knows the history of the object concerned but it can subsequently be confirmed, or when new information is provided which can later be verified. So psychometrists should be given objects by people who have no knowledge of their history, or even on some occasions objects whose history is as yet unknown but can be verified, so that telepathy cannot be invoked as an explanatory factor.

Psychometrists operate blindly in this respect when they try to help the police in criminal investigations. Robert Cracknell is a well-known psychic detective. Once in the late 1970s he gave the police information about a murder case which tallied so exactly with evidence they had not publicized that he himself became a prime suspect. He has since often assisted the London Metropolitan Police.

PSYCHON The psychologist Cyril Burt suggested that thought might be made up of sub-atomic particles which he called 'psychons'. Their status would appear to be similar to that of the ETHER and the 'bridge between the material and the mental' postulated by the philosopher H.H. Price.[92]

PSYCHOPLASM The word 'psychoplasm' was first coined by James Burns, although the alternative term ECTOPLASM gained greater currency. Burns preferred 'psychoplasm' because it emphasized the psychic or spiritual origin of the matter which was formed out of psychic emanations from the body. The AURA is made up of emanations on different levels or PLANES of being, commonly referred to as the various subtle BODIES. This aura is to a certain extent subject to the individual's will, such that it can be extended. Some MEDIUMS are also able to cause extensions of their aura to condense into a denser form − ectoplasm, or psychoplasm. In one sense the whole of the physical universe is a condensation into form of spiritual emanations. Burns wrote, 'Nature around us is a condensation into palpable forms of previously aerial and inscrutable forces. ... We are all materialized spirits. ... This fluid within man's body is called "psychoplasm" because it is so highly visualized that the soul can mould it into organic form.'

277

PSYCHOPOMP/PSYCHOPOMPUS Anubis was the jackal-headed god of the ancient Egyptians who guarded the dead and the mysteries of the realm of the gods. It was he who led initiates into that realm to learn the truth. As this 'soul-leader' Anubis is an example of a psychopomp. Hermes, Mercury and Merlin are among others who have assumed the same role. In certain forms of MEDITATION people are sometimes taken on journeys by their own inner plane GUIDES who might also be described as psychopomps.

PSYCHOTRONIC ENERGY/PSYCHOTRONICS In 1945 Robert Pavlita, a Czech scientist, postulated the existence of psychotronic energy as the psychic power behind such phenomena as PSYCHOKINESIS. He also constructed a psychotronic generator which he claimed could draw off and accumulate psychotronic energy in a way reminiscent of Reich's ORGONE accumulators. (See also BIOPLASMIC ENERGY.) In Eastern Europe PARAPSYCHOLOGY and the investigation of PSI phenomena has gone under the general heading of psychotronics, the preferred term since 'para' means 'beside', suggesting that such phenomena are outside the bounds of current scientific thought. The use of the term 'psychotronics' emphasizes the belief that psi phenomena fall within the purview of physical science.

PURGATORY The Roman Catholic concept of purgatory was defined by the Council of Trent in 1563 as a state after death for those whose sins were not grave enough for them to be condemned to HELL but who had a remaining debt of punishment to pay. This concept represented a step towards the understanding which had been prevalent in the East for millennia. The Tibetan BOOK OF THE DEAD taught of three successive after-death states, the second of which — kamaloca — involved visions which the soul created for itself, according to the desires, fears and emotions left over from its recent life. This was a kind of purgatory. Only when the individual's emotions were exhausted with the realization that all the visions were self-created, could the soul progress to the next stage where preparations would be made for the next incarnation.

PYTHAGOREAN SCHOOL Pythagoras (582–497 BC) was born at Samos in the Aegean. After excelling in the sports of the Olympic Games, he embarked on a period of extensive travel, studying the science and priestly disciplines of the cultures he visited from Egypt to Chaldea and possibly India. He finally established an ESOTERIC school at Crotona in Sicily.

Pythagoras taught the immortality of the soul and a belief in REINCARNATION and TRANSMIGRATION. His followers had to be strict vegetarians. Great respect was shown to animal life, and the reputed power Pythagoras had over animals suggests a possible knowledge of HYPNOSIS. As well as the study and practice of natural medicine, Pythagorean science developed a system of music and mathematics, founded on newly discovered mathematical relationships and proportions associated with pitch. The basic tenet of Pythagorean belief was that man reflected the whole universe within himself, a notion which supposedly came from Hermes Trismegistus and which after Pythagoras was taken up by Plato.

QI GONG (pronounced 'chee gung'). Acupuncture restores balance in the flow of CH'I by placing needles at particular points in the body. Another Chinese technique to restore this balance is by transmitting energy from one body to another but without physical contact. It is perhaps clearer in such cases that although a considerable amount of physical movement may be involved the Qi Gong practitioner is primarily treating the ETHERIC BODY.

RADIESTHESIA (Also 'radiothesie', now obsolete) Radiesthesia is the anglicized form of *radiesthésie*, a word coined by Bouly in 1927 for the process of divining or DOWSING, particularly with a PENDULUM. Use of the term implies a belief in the theory that dowsing operates through the dowser's sensitivity to certain radiations. The dowser is thought to register and react unconsciously to the impressions that these radiations evoke. The theory does not claim that the radiations themselves cause the movement in the dowsing instrument.

The various movements of the pendulum have specific meanings for the dowser: swinging to and fro is usually considered to have a neutral meaning; rotation clockwise and anti-clockwise are either positive and negative or vice versa. It is important to realize that there is no universal rule for this. People have to experiment for themselves to find out their own system of responses. This is the main evidence for the claim that the radiations cannot produce the effect without the agency of the dowser.

However, the pendulum can also be held over a map with the same results, which suggests that actual physical radiations are not involved. This has sometimes been called teleradiesthesia. Even on-site dowsers often do some preparatory map-dowsing first to save time. The success of map-dowsing tends to negate the theory of actual emanations from the physical objects or substances themselves in favour of a CLAIRVOYANT faculty.

Radiesthesia is also used in medical diagnosis. In Switzerland in the 1920s, having seen how a pendulum could be used to dowse the whereabouts of underground tunnels and streams, the Abbé Mermet started using the same method to detect irregularities in a person's bloodstream. He believed that the human body emits radiations to which his own body was sensitive and the pendulum registered that sensitivity. He was also able to operate at a distance from the patients being diagnosed, so long as he had something from the patient to concentrate on such as a photograph or a lock of hair.

Aspects of the theory behind radiesthesia were incorporated independently in the work of Albert Abrams's who developed RADIONICS, the science of the supposed radiations detected by radiesthesia. The first British Congress of Radionics and Radiesthesia was held in London in 1950.

RADIONICS/RADIONIC THERAPY Radionics is the science of the supposed radiations detected by DOWSERS either with a divining rod or a PENDULUM.

Albert Abrams was an American neurologist who discovered that tapping the body of a patient in particular places on the abdomen and noting whether the sound was hollow (healthy) or dull (unhealthy) gave an indication of the patient's complaint. More importantly the same procedure could be followed with a healthy subject holding a sample of tissue from a sick patient — the patient's symptomatic responses would be reproduced. The conclusion was that the diseased tissue was emitting measurable radiations. Abrams then constructed a simple variable resistance box and found that each sample of tissue when introduced into the circuit as a 'witness' (along with the abdomen of a healthy substitute) could have its effect cancelled out by a particular resistance. Furthermore the sample from the patient did not need to be diseased, in the sense that cancerous tissue is obviously diseased: a dried drop of blood was sufficient for Abrams to get results with his 'black box'. Unfortunately other people were not able to reproduce his results and Abrams died discredited by his profession in 1924.

Abrams's technique was simplified by Ruth Drown who replaced the actual abdomen of a healthy substitute in the circuit with a rubber diaphragm. She also claimed that the modified diagnostic apparatus could also be used to treat the still absent patient by radionic therapy or 'radio therapy', restoring the balance of energies in the patient's body. Drown consequently fell foul of the American authorities and was arrested in 1951, accused of fraud and imprisoned.

The Abrams-Drown apparatus was further developed by George de la Warr, a British engineer dedicated to capturing the more subtle emanations of nature. As another radionic practitioner Lavender Dower recalls, 'I can remember one happy afternoon spent in his garden capturing the sound pattern of a common daisy on a tape recorder'.[45] In 1960 he too was sued by a woman who claimed that using de la Warr's diagnostic instruments had caused her neurosis. Unlike earlier cases in America, in this 'Black Box Case' the defendant actually won.

The common misunderstanding that lies at the root of most legal or scientific assaults on radionics is that the apparatus is mistakenly regarded as a diagnostic or therapeutic machine rather than a mere instrument in the hands of a human being. As with RADIESTHESIA the human being is an integral part of the circuitry which produces the effect. The machine itself gives no answer and no treatment. But in that case it is tempting to wonder why so much cumbersome equipment has been added by radionics practitioners to the simple pendulum, 'witness' and diagram of the body originally used by the Abbé Mermet. It is hardly surprising that detractors have misinterpreted the significance of the machinery. Might it not be relatively superfluous? It seems likely that radiesthesia, radionics and PSYCHOMETRY are all aspects of the same process. One of the essential ingredients in the process is the operator's trust that it works, and the radionics equipment is there more to boost the practitioner's belief than physically to register the effects.

Malcolm Rae who developed and refined many more radionic instruments for diagnosing and healing believed that healing energy followed thought and that controlled breathing was a means of promoting the trasmission of thought. This is ABSENT HEALING pure and simple. Some people prefer to use the term psionics to get away from the notion that something like radio waves might be involved and show instead the use of the mind and the psi faculty. As Lavender Dower says, 'If we had learned to use the full potential of our minds, instruments would not be necessary.'[45] The question remains: Does the use of such instruments encourage dependency, when we might be doing more to develop the potential of our minds?

RAGNAROK In Norse mythology the last day, when the world and all life, including the gods, would be destroyed, was known as Ragnarok or the twilight of the gods. In Christianity the equivalent is JUDGMENT Day. In Hindu cosmology it comes at the end of a day in the life of BRAHMA. The element of fire plays a major part in all such scenarios. There is even an equivalent theoretical concept in science too now, the so-called Big Crunch, being the opposite of the Big Bang, in which the UNIVERSE having long since ceased to expand, collapses in on itself, incidentally also generating increasing amounts of heat, until it forms a contracting version of the initial fireball. There is speculation regarding whether the whole process might then start again. In the Hindu scheme of things, after the Night of Brahma another day will follow, some versions of Ragnarok admit the possibility of a new creation, and after the Christian Judgment Day existence continues either spiritually with God in heaven or in damnation in hell.

RAJA YOGA – See YOGA.

RAPPING/RAPS Some of the earliest spirit messages communicated through spiritualist MEDIUMS used the rapping technique. The Fox sisters, who sparked off the table-rapping craze which marked the birth of SPIRITUALISM in America in the nineteenth century, asked questions of their POLTERGEIST and used a code whereby the spirit spelt out its answers by giving the appropriate number of raps for each letter according to its position in the alphabet. From this seemingly tedious routine a great deal of information was communicated about the murder of a tinker whose body was buried in the cellar of the Foxes' house.

D.D. Home, one of the most successful physical mediums of all, used the same method. In Edinburgh in 1870 he held a SEANCE during which the name 'Pophy Sophy' was spelled out. This was the pet name of a child who had died of scarlet fever and whose aunt was present at the seance. The message continued, 'You were not to blame, and I am happy.' The aunt had reproached herself for not having adequately protected the child against the disease.[1]

Rapping sounds were also heard around the bed of D.D. Home when he was ill or asleep, as they were around the death bed of Margaret Fox. In the case of the medium Henry Slade, famous for PK effects and SLATE WRITING, raps on the walls and furniture around his bed were accompanied by movements of furniture when he was growing old. This suggests that the same uncontrolled energy which can cause poltergeist effects around children and young adolescents may produce similar phenomena when sick or aging mediums begin to lose their grip on their powers.

The force which causes raps may be the same force that causes clocks to stop, spoons to bend and knives to break. When under conscious control such effects are known as PSYCHOKINESIS, but they also occur spontaneously. It was the sudden inexplicable splitting of a walnut table-top and the breaking of a bread knife two weeks later that led Jung into a life-long interest in the PARANORMAL, starting off with his investigation of a young medium, on which he based his doctoral dissertation in 1902 ('On the Psychology and Pathology of So-Called Occult Phenomena').

In his autobiographical *Memories, Dreams and Reflections* Jung describes how while he was discussing his theory with Freud that such effects originated in the UNCONSCIOUS MIND, there was a sudden loud explosion from a bookcase. 'There!' he said, 'That is an example of the exteriorization phenomenon.' Freud disputed this vehemently. 'And to prove my point,' Jung continued, 'I now predict that in a moment there will be another.' And there was.[97] Jung believed that he himself caused the effect; he had felt increasing heat in the area of his diaphragm as he and Freud had argued. This is also the region (centring on the SOLAR PLEXUS) from where mediums feel energy being drawn off to produce physical effects.

RAPPORT Two people are said to be in 'symplastic' rapport when one, for example, tastes what the other is eating, as when hypnotized subjects apparently share the sensations of the hypnotist (first documented by the French physician, Dr E. Azam). The term extends to the situation where impressions made on an object are also felt by the human subject: when a hypnotized person is put in rapport with a wax doll and a hair is pulled out of it, the person cries out. TELEPATHY may explain the COMMUNITY OF SENSATION between subject and hypnotist, but seems less satisfactory as an explanation of such rapport between the subject and a doll. One theory is that ASTRAL PROJECTION is involved. This phenomenon is also invoked to explain why mediums sometimes bear the marks of 'injuries' inflicted on materializations.

RAPTURE Rapture, the ECSTATIC experience of being rapt (from the same root as 'raped'), is the feeling of willingly abandoning oneself totally to the Holy Spirit. The SOUL of men and women is commonly regarded as female and is described as the bridge of God in such experiences. This mystical union was the aim of much MYSTERY teaching, as well as of Christian mystics such as St Teresa, whose painful vision of an angel holding a golden spear vividly described the experience. (At the root of the word 'religion' is the idea of 'a bond', which binds God and humanity together.) It can be claimed that this mystical union on a more permanent basis was being invoked by Jesus's words 'Abide in me and I in you', and by Paul's injunction to 'walk in him, rooted and builded up in him'. (Colossians 2, 6.) In Eastern religions the equivalent experience would be NIRVANA.

RAUDIVE VOICES In 1959 Friedrich Jurgenson, a Swedish opera-singer, painter and film producer recorded bird songs in the country near his villa in Sweden. When he played back the recording he heard in addition to the birds a human voice speaking in Norwegian about nocturnal bird songs. At first he assumed that his equipment had somehow picked up a radio station, although it was an odd coincidence that the topic of the programme was so relevant to his present activity. But when he made further bird song recordings and played them back, other voices addressed him by name, giving personal information and claiming to be deceased relatives and friends.

In 1965 Jurgenson met Dr Konstantin Raudive (1909–74), a Latvian psychologist who had fled his native country at the time of the Soviet invasion in 1945. He had studied psychology in Switzerland (under Jung), Germany and England, and he now took up full-time research into the voice phenomena to which he gave his name. In 1969 the Swiss Association for Parapsychology awarded their first prize jointly to Konstantin Raudive and Alexander Schneider for their work on DIRECT VOICE messages recorded on tape.

Raudive assembled thousands of recordings by leaving a tape recorder running in an empty room under controlled conditions. When he returned he found that strange whispering voices had been recorded, even though no one had entered the room between his own exit and return.[156] There have been suggestions that the voices captured in this way use sound frequencies that are not normally audible to the human ear, but mediated by the recording instrument they are distorted sufficiently to fall within our aural range. Comparison can be made with time-lapse photography, whereby movement which is imperceptible to the observer present can be made obvious to the viewer of the film, showing for example the growth of plants and the gradual opening of flowers. Another theory suggests that impulses could be impressed on the tape by some psychokinetic force, similar to the way in which Peter Hurkos is believed to project images on to photographic emulsion simply by focusing his attention on a shuttered camera.

Detractors of the Raudive phenomenon maintain that its proponents are picking up radio transmissions or that they delude themselves by interpreting random sounds in a background of white noise as comprehensible words, just as we see images in the inkblots of Rorschach tests or in the red-hot coals of a fire. It is interesting to note that monolingual people usually receive messages given in one language, their own, whilst people who speak many languages (like Raudive himself) discern phrases in which languages are mixed up. This does suggest that the mind of the listener is involved somehow, although it may simply be as a catalyst rather than as an instigator of the phenomenon. The whispered speech is usually nearly double the normal speed, delivered rhythmically like a chant, with a great deal of rushing background noise.

A more recent electronic phenomenon has arisen with computers. Whole messages have been received from a sixteenth century Englishman calling himself Tomas Harden via a computer in a house on the site of the home of which he was eventually dispossessed. Unlike Raudive voices these communications became a two-way process, and they were accompanied by POLTERGEIST effects, including DIRECT WRITING. The whole case was more like a TIME-WARP than anything else, as the communicator seemed to be living his life from day-to-day during the period in which his messages were received. Commentators apparently from the future also communicated through the computer in an attempt to explain what was happening.[208]

RAYS According to the teachings of Alice Bailey (inspired by the Tibetan MASTER known as K.H.), we are all 'units of CONSCIOUSNESS breathed forth on one of the seven EMANATIONS from God'. These emanations are usually called the seven rays. The spiritual aspect of each each individual or MONAD is determined by the ray it is on. 'These seven subsidiary groups produce a varying outlook, mentality and approach, all equally right, but all presenting a slightly different angle of vision.'[5] The seven rays are: Ray One — Power or Will (typified in statesmanship, diplomacy and politics); Ray Two — Love-Wisdom (typified in true initiation and religion); Ray Three — Active Intelligence (typified in communications, travel and finance); Ray Four — Harmony, Beauty and Art (typified in architecture and planning); Ray Five — Concrete Knowledge and Science (typified in psychology and education); Ray Six — Devotion and Idealism (typified in Christianity and organized religions); Ray Seven — Ceremonial Order or Magic (typified in all forms of white magic and psychic phenomena).

. The notion of seven soul types occurs in other systems. The communications received via the OUIJA BOARD from 'an ancient entity' called Michael divided all souls into king, sage, warrior, artisan, scholar, slave and priest. As with the seven rays the soul-type remains the same throughout all a soul's incarnations.[215]

READINGS When the American psychic, Edgar Cayce (1877—1945), was consulted by or on behalf of someone (present or absent) he went into TRANCE and gave details about the person's health, relationships, life-purpose and even past life experiences. The information given in such a sitting was commonly called a reading, possibly because while in trance Cayce gained access to the information by 'reading' the AKASHIC RECORD. CLAIRVOYANTS who read the TAROT cards also 'give readings', and psychics of all kinds often use the same term to refer to the information they give their clients.

Giving a reading is not fortune-telling. The SENSITIVE should be able to help the individual to see life's challenges in perspective, to recognize a sense of purpose, and to notice both the lessons that have been learned and the direction in which one's life is going. Many people may well be disappointed by a good psychic reading, especially if they were expecting 'fortune-telling', since such a reading shows how much ultimately depends on them. Advice may be given concerning how to come to a decision but not on what decision to come to. Reassurance may be offered where it is needed, but the individual's independence is always respected.

There is a natural tendency for people to want to have readings at periods of difficulty, change and uncertainty in their lives. There is obviously also a danger that one may become dependent on what the psychic says. All reputable psychics will always stress the element of free will in whatever is given, and the importance of action rather than waiting for things to happen. They also advise against having too many readings: it is unlikely that one could benefit from more than one reading a year (assuming it was a worthwhile reading) and some sensitives refuse to see their clients more than once every two years.

REBIRTH The term rebirth is sometimes used synonymously with REINCARNATION, and occasionally with RESURRECTION, although all three terms can have distinct meanings. Reincarnation and resurrection are clearly distinct. Rebirth is usually synonymous with reincarnation, but Buddhists prefer the former since it avoids the notion that something such as a SOUL is given a body. Buddhists consider that each life is a continuation mentally of a previous life in the sense that certain characteristics such as memory are carried over from one life to the next. This life-craving structure of psychic elements is not a conscious self, but a repository of the dispositions that have been generated by experiences and actions on earth.

In Buddhist belief, rebirth can also refer to entering one of several different worlds after death. Most men and women are reborn in PURGATORY, or as animals (TRANSMIGRATION), or as GHOSTS. These worlds are the *kama*-worlds of the senses – purgatory (*kamaloca*), the earth and the angelic DEVACHAN. There are also the higher *rupa*-worlds of form but without senses, and the highest incorporeal *arupa*-worlds of thought.

REGRESSION It is fashionable in some circles to be regressed under HYPNOSIS so as to recall past lives. Bearing in mind the ease with which TELEPATHY can operate between the hypnotist and the subject, combined with the subject's creative imagination and the natural desire to please the hypnotist by complying with even unspoken requests, it would be dangerous to assume that experiences recalled supposedly by FAR MEMORY under such circumstances were true memories without further corroboration, such as a spontaneous dream or intuition without the participation of another person. Even when meditating in the hope of supposedly contacting past lives, it is still easy to be deceived. The meditator may be 'OVERSHADOWED' by a spirit helper or teacher, whose past incarnations may filter through to one's own awareness. It may not be easy to identify a life recalled in this way as actually one of one's own past incarnations. One might also be simply tapping into the AKASHIC RECORD somehow, perhaps because of some strong affinity with the soul whose experiences one is 'remembering'.

People often warn against becoming too interested in past life experiences. Apart from the doubts concerning their authenticity, there is often a tendency to become more interested in the past life than in the purposes of the present incarnation. Generally speaking, knowledge of a past life is useful only if the incompleteness of the former experience is recognized so that one can make sense of the continuity with the present life and further one's development. It is a natural human tendency when learning of a past life, to be fascinated by its exotic nature compared with the present. Dwelling on a past life in such a way detracts from the benefit which such knowledge could bring — the realization that the same tests, temptations and crises tend to recur until one has finally mastered the weaknesses within oneself which gave rise to them.

REINCARNATION The Sicilian Greek philosopher Empedocles (c. 490–430 BC) said 'I have already been a boy and a girl, a bush, a bird, and a dumb sea-fish.' This form of reincarnation, also known as TRANSMIGRATION or metempsychosis, included the notion that SOULS passed not only from one human body to another after death, but also that one could reincarnate in the form of other kinds of living being. Plato regarded education as a recollection of things we already know from having lived on earth before. Both Empedocles and Plato were bequeathed a belief in reincarnation by the PYTHAGOREANS, and Pythagoras himself had probably learned it from his contacts with India. KARMA and rebirth are part of Hindu, Buddhist, Jain, Parsee, and Sikh religions. Even the Druids are thought to have believed in reincarnation, to the extent that they would borrow money from each other promising to return it in the next life.

Among all the major world religions, only Judaism, Christianity and Islam reject reincarnation. Even in Islam and Christianity there are 'unorthodox' sects such as the Druse, ROSICRUCIANS, GNOSTICS, and many Christians in Brazil who have accepted reincarnation, but for orthodox Jews, Christians and Moslems each human conception and birth on earth sees the creation of a new human soul.

Some have claimed that a few references in the New Testament indicate that Jesus and his disciples believed in reincarnation, notably Jesus's statement that 'Elijah has already come' and his question to the disciples 'Who do men say that the Son of Man is?' But these arguments are inconclusive. Elijah's reappearance as prophesied would not have been a case of reincarnation, since he had not died but had been carried bodily into HEAVEN by the chariot of fire. His reappearance as John the Baptist would have been no more nor less miraculous than his ascent into heaven. It was also a common Jewish belief that many other prophets had not died but continued to live on in heaven. (Heaven was not a place for ordinary mortals.) So a belief that a prophet might return to earth by no means implied a belief in reincarnation for all. Even the ESSENE doctrine, as recorded by Josephus, may have been misinterpreted: when they said that after death men were changed into another body, it has been claimed that this was much the same as Paul's 'RESURRECTION of the body' rather than a reference to the doctrine of reincarnation.

There is a popular notion today that Origen (185−254) supported a belief in reincarnation, but many scholars maintain that this is a misreading of his writings. His reference to the previous existence of the soul referred, they say, to its existence in heaven rather than on earth. In *De Principiis* he writes: 'Every soul comes into this world strengthened by the victories or weakened by the defects of the previous life. Its place in this world as a vessel appointed to honour or dishonour is determined by its previous merits or demerits. Its work in this world determines its place in the world which is to follow this.'

Nevertheless, throughout the Christian era there have been many believers who have been convinced that souls do reincarnate. They have usually arrived at the conclusion simply by a process of logic. Given that God is just and loves humanity it would be unjust and illogical for individual life circumstances to be so varied if we were granted one lifetime only, and one lifetime would never be sufficient to make the spiritual progress that would justify salvation. As Rudolf Steiner says, 'If we take a single earth-life ... and look at what emerges from that life alone, it is as though we were to pluck off a flower from a plant and imagine that it can exist by itself. A single life on earth is not comprehensible by itself; the explanation for it must be sought on the basis of repeated earth-lives.'[186] Annie Besant expressed the same idea: 'With reincarnation man is a dignified immortal being, evolving towards a glorious end; without it, he is a tossing straw on the stream of chance circumstances, irresponsible for his character, his actions, his destiny.'[10]

We tend to recapitulate our chief tests, temptations and crises in recurring lifetimes until we have finally mastered the weaknesses which caused them. It is a long self-perfecting process. Zoroastrian scriptures taught the same idea: 'If the soul during earthly life does not purify itself, remains ignorant and cherishes any worldly desires, afterwards it must return and take physical bodies one after another until it is quite pure.'

The Vedantic Hindu belief is that every soul is a spark of divinity, part of ATMAN or BRAHMAN. In the *Bhagavad Gita* Krishna says: 'I myself never was not, nor thou, nor all the princes of this earth; nor shall we ever hereafter cease to be. As the Lord of this mortal frame experienced infancy, youth and old age, we in future incarnations will meet it the same.' In incarnation we become distinct individuals in a state of illusion (MAYA), and through repeated incarnations our soul (*jiva*) eventually evolves to true self-consciousness, liberation (MOKSHA or *mukti*) and ultimate unity and identity with Reality, Brahman. 'As a man casts off his worn-out clothes and puts on other new ones, so does the embodied SELF cast off its worn-out bodies and enters other new ones' (*Bhagavad Gita*). Another branch of Vedanta (Hindu theism) considers that the constant round of rebirths (*samsara*) is a reflection of the exuberance and playfulness (*lila*) of divine creativity, without such a strong sense of purposefulness. Individual souls may still strive and evolve towards liberation and reunion with Brahman, but there will always be an infinite number of souls constantly being reincarnated.

In the nineteenth century reincarnation formed part of the original Spiritualist (or Spiritist) doctrine as represented in *The Spirits' Book*, the first anthology of spirit communications compiled by H.L.D. Rivail under the pseudonym Allan Kardec (1804–69) and published in 1856.[100] But because of the attempt to reconcile SPIRITUALISM with orthodox Christianity a belief in reincarnation was soon driven underground. The references to reincarnation in Kardec's book were channelled through Celina Japhet, a MEDIUM under the supervision of a hypnotist (or 'mesmerist') M. Roustan, who was himself a firm believer in reincarnation, which may or may not have influenced the content of the communications. D.D. Home was among the many who declared themselves opposed to the doctrine. At the time of Kardec's death Home purportedly received a spirit communication from him saying, 'I regret having taught the spiritist doctrine.'

Despite such detractors, communications through mediums continued to proclaim the truth of reincarnation, often in cases where the medium was strongly opposed to the idea. This was the case with Edgar Cayce (1877–1945) whose 'life-readings' often included references to the subject's previous incarnations. The communications described by Bligh Bond in *The Company of Avalon*[15] (See PSYCHIC ARCHAEOLOGY) mention the reincarnation of a Glastonbury monk as the woman through whom the communications were received, and neither she nor Bond originally believed in the doctrine. Arthur Guirdham, an English doctor, was brought together with a whole group of people who it was revealed in dreams and spirit communications had previously incarnated in a community of Cathars in twelfth- and thirteenth-century Languedoc.[72,73,74,75]

One of the most widely publicized accounts of reincarnation in the West was *The Search for Bridey Murphy*.[9] The story was serialized in a Chicago newspaper in the 1950s and published in book form in 1956. Virginia Tighe, the wife of a Chicago insurance salesman was regressed under HYPNOSIS and spoke of her life as Bridey Murphy, born near Cork in 1798. She married a barrister who taught at Queen's University, Belfast, and died in 1864. Under hypnosis Virginia described Bridey's life in great detail and all the facts were later verified.

However, the case was later exposed as a fraud. In her childhood, Virginia had spent a great deal of time with an aunt, who was Irish. It was apparently a case of CRYPTOMNESIA. What has often been overlooked since then is that the exposé itself was exposed. The exposé was in fact pure fabrication by a rival Chicago newspaper, a newspaper which had previously tried to buy the rights to serialize the original Bridey Murphy story but had been outbid.

Much of the empirical evidence for reincarnation comes from children between the ages of three and five who recall details of another existence spontaneously. When they recount such 'memories' in the East they may receive more attention than in the West, particularly if the past life was recent and relatives may be traceable. Detractors have remarked on how often such children seem to have had past lives in wealthier families, with the implication that their parents are hoping for patronage if not outright adoption. But by the same token memories of poorer lives, which probably do occur, are less likely to be followed up with the same enthusiasm, so the apparent disproportion of previously-rich to now-poor cannot be regarded as grounds for discrediting the evidence.

Many cases of past-life memories in children have been recorded and investigated by Dr Ian Stevenson. One such involved an Indian boy, Jasbir, who had apparently died of smallpox but subsequently revived as a completely different person, Sobha Ram, from another village (and another caste) who had died after a fall from a cart. He later met many members of Sobha Ram's family, recognizing them and greeting them by name. He even confirmed the family's suspicions that their deceased relative had in fact been poisoned. This particular case may be more accurately described as POSSESSION, but it seems to point to the possibility that the personality can exist separately from the body and inhabits the body in the way that reincarnationists suggest. Sobha Ram's desire to explain the facts behind his death may have resulted in his immediate return in Jasbir's body, both 'deaths' having occurred at approximately the same time.[187]

Some children's DREAMS and nightmares (e.g. of drowning) are inexplicable in terms of the dreamer's actual experience in this life but can be explained as a traumatic past-life memory, although this is becoming increasingly difficult to validate with the variety of images even toddlers are exposed to on the television screen. Re-incarnation is also claimed to be an explanation for a variety of phenomena ranging from phobias to birthmarks − the sites of earlier wounds − and from child prodigies (learning old skills again) to falling in love. Some seem to carry the idea of a 'soul-mate' too far. Most teachings suggest that we try a variation of family relationships with those we are closest to, but seldom if ever repeat the same one exactly.

People sometimes wonder how long SOULS spend on other PLANES between lives? Christine Hartley was surprised at the frequency of Joan Grant's supposed incarnations.[66,82] It is generally thought that souls with little development on the egoic level return more quickly. With a strengthening link with the individuality, longer is spent between lives.

Rudolf Steiner gave details of previous incarnations of many famous people. Souls that had incarnated as Arabs in the eighth and ninth century, Tarik (after whom Gibraltar was named), Haroun al Raschid and the unnamed astrologer of Mamun, the Caliph of Baghdad, returned respectively as Charles Darwin, Lord Bacon and the astronomer Laplace. Franz Schubert had also been a Moor in ninth-century Spain. Woodrow Wilson had been the caliph Muawiyah, one of the earliest successors of Mohammed as leader of the new faith. Ernst Haeckel had been Pope Gregory VII. Tycho Brahe had been Julian the Apostate. Nietzsche had been a Franciscan ascetic. Madame Blavatsky had been Paracelsus. Annie Besant had been Giordano Bruno. Jesus of Nazareth had been Joshua son of Nun. These and many more Steiner read from the AKASHIC RECORD.[186]

The theosophists Annie Besant and C.W. Leadbeater maintained that Gautama, the Buddha, had previously incarnated as other great spiritual teachers: as Hermes, the founder of the Egyptian Mysteries, as the first Zoroaster, founder of the Zoroastrian religion, and as Orpheus, founder of the Greek Mysteries. Jesus (as distinct from Christ) reincarnated as Apollonius of Tyana in the eleventh century. And the Tibetan MASTER D.K. by whom it was claimed Alice Bailey's writings were inspired had been Pythagoras.

There may be less interest in past lives of the great and famous nowadays, but reincarnation is today enjoying something of a revival among a variety of marginal groups. CLAIRVOYANTS at 'Psychic Fairs' will tell you what your previous incarnations were, with the help of a hypnotist you can undergo a REGRESSION to a previous life-time, and a few modern psychiatrists may even regress their patients to re-experience the cause of an enduring trauma in a previous life-time.[213]

REMOTE DIAGNOSIS SENSITIVES such as Edgar Cayce may go into TRANCE and deliver a diagnosis of a patient who is not actually present. This is sometimes called a PROXY READING or PROXY SITTING. In the case of Edgar Cayce's READINGS such diagnoses were extremely detailed. Mental CLAIRVOYANTS also practise remote diagnosis but seldom give such detailed information, perhaps because the rational mind obstructs the process. When someone is in trance their conscious powers of reason simply do not enter the picture.

Where physical instruments are used in remote diagnosis, such as a PENDULUM, or the more comlex equipment used in RADIONICS, the diagnostic information can again be extremely detailed, probably because the rational faculties of the mind are fully occupied in manipulating the equipment and interpreting the results logically according to the patterns laid down cumulatively by previous practitioners. Whether these patterns are an accurate reflection of what happens physically seems to be of less significance than the fact that the rational mind accepts them as real and therefore employs them to bring to awareness what might otherwise remain unconscious and inaccessible.

REMOTE SENSING This term may refer to DOWSING — sensing the presence of particular substances beneath the ground, or, more remotely, achieving the same with the aid of a map and without actually being present in the place being investigated. It may also mean REMOTE DIAGNOSIS of the sick as a preliminary to HEALING, with or without a PENDULUM or some other equipment used by RADIONICS practitioners. It may also refer to a specific area of ESP, also called travelling ESP, travelling clairvoyance or REMOTE VIEWING, in which subjects give detailed information about a distant place as if they were actually in that place.

REMOTE VIEWING The term 'remote viewing' was coined by the team of investigators at the Stanford Research Institute (SRI) at the University of California in 1972. It is 'a human perceptual ability' by which 'individuals are able to experience and describe locations, events, and objects that cannot be perceived by the known senses, usually because of distance.'[193] In other situations it might have been called travelling clairvoyance, but the researchers wanted to get away from any possible preconceptions regarding the mechanism involved.

In the experiments devised by Targ and Puthoff, volunteer subjects with no previously recognized psychic ability would try to focus on and describe a 'target site', where the other participant, the 'beacon', would stand for about fifteen minutes. Independent assessors were taken to all the sites and actually matched the viewer's descriptions and sketches correctly in, on average, two out of three cases.[192] This sounds like an experiment to test TELEPATHY, but further consideration of the results revealed that various other aspects of the PSI faculty might have been involved. For example, feedback seemed to have a positive and retroactive effect. In other words the viewers who were subsequently told of their success were in retrospect more successful than those who were not given any feedback. Emotional reactions and intensely personal responses to a target site were also usually a sign that psychic contact had successfully been made. Another indication that PRECOGNITION might be involved at a very personal level was the fact that those viewers who later visited the target sites themselves turned out to have been those who had been most accurate in their descriptions. This tallies well with Dunne's ideas on precognition, that in catching glimpses of the future we actually experience something of our own future state of mind. As Targ and Harary say, 'There is something incomplete about our understanding of the space-time coninuum in which we exist.'[193]

Perhaps the most significant conclusions that the SRI team came to were that probably everyone has this remote viewing faculty and that it can be further developed by a simple process of training.

REPEATABILITY The constant complaint of sceptical orthodox scientists is that psychic ability, ESP, and PARANORMAL events can never be demonstrated to order. They claim that the phenomena are not susceptible to experimental investigation since they do not satisfy the criterion of repeatability. Yet orthodox scientists seem to attach far more importance to this criterion in some disciplines than in others. As PSI investigators have pointed out, as we study specific phenomena patterns do emerge, and on the basis of these patterns predictions can be made. This is hardly different from certain other scientific disciplines, such as geology, in which evidence, theories and predictions are never condemned for being 'unrepeatable' in the way that data and theories in PARAPSYCHOLOGY are.

Most examples of psi are events in CONSCIOUSNESS, and even orthodox psychologists do not attempt to describe consciousness in quite the same mechanistic terms which are used to explain the operation of the internal combustion engine or even the biochemistry of a living organism. Lawrence LeShan points out that if something is 'repeatable' where an individual's consciousness is concerned, that individual is almost certainly mentally or psychologically damaged. In other words repeatability would be pathological, just as a fixed response in a word-association test would be regarded as pathological. 'The great error of parapsychology has been to try to solve its problems as if they were physical problems from the sensory realm.'[109] (See also PROOF and RESEARCH.)

RESCUE CIRCLE MEDIUMS in SPIRITUALIST circles have sometimes brought through the confused communications of apparently bewildered individuals, lost in a kind of limbo. A man who was decapitated may be looking for his head, not realizing that he has actually gone through the experience of bodily death. Soldiers may be marching along roads in a wasteland of their own creation, not daring to do anything else without orders from their superiors. It is the earthly conditioning and afterlife expectations of such individuals that hold them back, keeping them in an EARTH-BOUND condition. Usually they do not realize that they are dead, or if they do, they do not expect to experience anything other than the lonely existence that they presently find themselves in. The energies of the circle seem to generate a power which is 'seen' by these souls as a light on the lower ASTRAL PLANE. Communicating with the members of the circle they are then persuaded to turn their attention away from the earth plane, to look for a 'higher' light, where they will be met by helpers who will lead them on to the next stage of their existence.

RESEARCH/PSYCHICAL RESEARCH The British Society for Psychical Research was founded by Frederick Myers and a small group of Oxford intellectuals in 1882. Its first major concern was to investigate TELEPATHY or thought transference. Although the founders hoped that their research would provide the basis for an alternative world view, determining once and for all whether human beings survived death, they maintained a strong desire to be as objective as possible and membership of the Society was not conditional on any belief in the existence of forces as yet unrecognized by science. Even so, Myers hoped that psychical research and spiritualism would effect a reconciliation between science and religion. The American Society for Psychical Research, founded in 1884, accepted a slightly wider brief than its British counterpart from the outset. It counted biologists, physicists, astronomers and psychotherapists among its earliest members, but not experimental psychologists, who were more antagonistic.

The year 1934 was a landmark in academic psychic research as it saw the publication of J.B. Rhine's *Extra-sensory Perception*, in which by means of experiments with students the author tried to show that the average person has telepathic and CLAIRVOYANT ability.[159] Rhine, a researcher at Duke University, gave his area of study a new name, PARAPSYCHOLOGY, in an attempt to give the subject greater respectability, as well as to take it out of the realm of the supernatural and make it more acceptable as another aspect of natural science. In 1946 researchers in England at Cambridge University started talking about PSI and the psi-faculty. Parapsychological research seemed to be shaking off its spiritual associations and achieving a certain begrudging academic respectability, even though it was still regarded askance by mainstream scientists.

Whilst the main organizations for psychical research have had as their main underlying aim to understand the nature of paranormal phenomena and the mechanism behind PSYCHIC faculties, a few have been set up with the opposite intention — to debunk. The Committee for the Scientific Investigation of Claims On the Paranormal (CSICOP), inevitably dubbed 'psi-cop', is an organization of 'psi-busters', dedicated to the eradication of anything supernatural. They do not look for any new laws, and none of their investigations may support anything unconventional. It is their belief that everything must be accounted for by existing scientific understanding, a notion that most leading scientists at the forefront of research in, say, physics or cosmology would think utterly absurd. What grounds do we have for supposing that we have already discovered all the laws of nature and the universe? CSICOP includes a few scientists, but a larger number of journalists and entertainers, including James Randi, the professional stage magician who claims to be able to better any psychic.

CSICOP's record is unflattering. They manipulated the figures to disprove Michel Gauquelin's surprising correlation between occupation and the position of certain planets at the time of birth. They also planted fake psychics in metal-bending experiments organized by James McDonnell's 'MacLab'. These fakes were soon dropped because their results were poor, but CSICOP later 'exposed' the research in a blaze of publicity, claiming that they had duped the MacLab team.

The main problem in psychic research has always been REPEATABILITY, and hard evidence of psi has never been hard enough to convince the orthodox scientist. Nevertheless psi research (specifically REMOTE VIEWING) at the Stanford Research Institute of the University of California was funded by the US government, presumably because Pentagon officials recognized its potential as a tool in espionage. When these funds ran dry, Russell Targ and Keith Harary set themselves up as the Delphi Associates to continue their research, financing their new company by using psi to predict movements on Wall Street.

RESONANCE The principle of FORMATIVE CAUSATION proposes that it is easier to do something that has already been done. It has proved very difficult to induce the formation of certain crystals, but once this has been achieved, other chemists (in other parts of the world) have less difficulty. The biologist Rupert Sheldrake claims that the formation of crystals is facilitated by resonance with the MORPHOGENETIC FIELD, which becomes stronger as more crystals are produced. By the same token, it becomes increasingly difficult to form different crystals of the same substance, even though they may be theoretically possible.

This idea of resonance applies not only in chemistry but also in biology as a factor in biological evolution, speeding up the much slower process that would result from chance mutation alone. It is also invoked in mental terms, with the suggestion that ideas that have been learned by some people are progressively easier for others to learn. This may explain the common notion of an idea 'whose time has come' and the phenomenon of different people claiming to have had similar new ideas at the same time, as if ideas spread by a kind of osmosis, or according to the HUNDREDTH MONKEY effect.

The decline in the incidence of tuberculosis and in the deaths caused by the disease did not begin as one would expect following the improvements in treatment, but seemed to start much earlier, apparently as a result of Dr Robert Koch's announcement of his discovery of the bacillus that causes tuberculosis in March 1882. At least that is the claim of those who believe 'that knowledge, even before it has a chance to be applied, can sometimes have a power and an influence of its own'.[207]

RESPONSIVE XENOGLOSSY When people are victims of POSSESSION they sometimes speak languages of which they have no knowledge. This is known as XENOGLOSSY. In many cases the utterances are repetitive and do not form a coherent piece of communication, or if they do form a coherent whole it is completely one-sided, allowing for no participation by the listeners. If the communication becomes a two-way process, with the speaker apparently understanding and responding appropriately to utterances in the same language, the phenomenon is known as 'responsive xenoglossy'. This is what happens when 'spirit communications' are received through a MEDIUM in TRANCE, or when a person is apparently taken over by another spirit, a phenomenon which orthodox psychologists might describe as 'secondary personality with responsive xenoglossy'. Xenoglossy is often explained by CRYPTOMNESIA or by telepathy with some UNCONSCIOUS GROUP-MIND like Lyall Watson's concept of SAMA. But when it becomes responsive xenoglossy it is more difficult to explain in these terms.

RESURRECTION Christianity has developed two different notions of resurrection, often distinguished as 'resurrection of the flesh' and 'resurrection of the body', flesh being physical, whilst body in this sense is not. Many would say that 'resurrection of the flesh', the revivication of a corpse, is a distortion, even a travesty of the true concept of resurrection. St Paul wrote that 'flesh and blood cannot inherit the kingdom of God', and it is difficult to see how this simplistic view could have endured.

298

The 'resurrection of the body', on the other hand, involves abandoning the physical shell and passing to a new life in a new body: the total personality is raised in a spiritual body, a *soma pneumatikon*. In the words of St Paul, 'There is a natural body, and there is a spiritual body. It is sown a natural body; it is raised a spiritual body.'

Resurrection in a spiritual body would seem to come close to what other teachings tell of the afterlife and existence in other realms, but in Christianity a further theological distinction is made between resurrection and immortality. Immortality implies that the soul does not die but lives on; resurrection is a divine act, raising a person who has died to a new life in a new act of creation. But most occult traditions (e.g. THEOSOPHY) regard the soul as having a mental or causal BODY in accordance with its level of development without the need for an act of grace. This is more in line with the notion of immortality than with resurrection. The Christian resurrection in a spiritual body might better equate with a soul's eventual release from the need to reincarnate, its development to a state of remaining permanently in the spiritual realm.

RETROCOGNITION As paranormally acquired knowledge of future events before they happen is called PRECOGNITION, retrocognition is knowledge of the past acquired in similar ways. In parapsychology it refers to ESP or TELEPATHY in which the information obtained relates to the past, rather than the present, for which the experiment was set up, as when a subject's successful responses in card-guessing experiments seem to be delayed rather than instantaneous. As a catch-all term retrocognition covers DEJA-VU experiences, FAR MEMORY, reading the AKASHIC RECORD, TIME-SLIPS, and even perhaps PSYCHOMETRY, although it is difficult to see the same basic mechanism at work in all these, unless it is a SUPER-ESP faculty (which would not normally be understood as being restricted to sensing the past).

RHABDOMANCY Rhabdomancy is divination or DOWSING by means of a rod or stick.

ROS – See DEW.

ROSICRUCIANISM Rosicrucianism is a blend of ESOTERIC Christianity and MYSTERY-SCHOOL teaching, inherited from the tradition of the ALCHEMISTS. With the Protestant Reformation in the sixteenth century the mystery and symbolism of Christianity were in danger of being lost altogether. A century later the Rosicrucian Brethren were trying to preserve these aspects of religion. They reintroduced much of the symbolism that the Protestant church had lost with its abandonment of the Catholic sacramental liturgy, and added more to it. Deprived of the Virgin, they invoked Pan Sophia, the World Soul, the White Queen of the alchemical union. The Rosicrucians went further than the alchemists of the past by specifically identifying Christ as the PHILOSOPHER'S STONE, by which all humanity could be transmuted and assured of rebirth into spiritual union with God.

The outward origins of the Rosicrucian movement were a mixture of unauthenticated writings and make-believe, but the philosophy at the heart of it was true to a long tradition of esoteric teachings. The Rosicrucian Manifesto contained many instructions that would be equally valid for other spiritual disciplines: Always be true to your inner principles; dress and behave in the manner of the country you live in; do not draw attention to yourselves; do not accept money for your services (since your gifts are not yours to sell); meet periodically with others on the same Path; find at least one other person to whom you can transmit your tradition and the fruits of your learning. Some have gone so far as to say that 'Rosicrucianism survived because it has no visible foundation, no headquarters, no officers, no dogmas and no rules of membership.'[124] It was always stronger on the continent of Europe than it was in Britain, where the same niche was occupied by FREEMASONRY.

SAHASRARA – Sanskrit for crown centre. See CHAKRAS.

SAMA (1) The SUFI practice of achieving a TRANCE state by means of music and dancing, as the DERVISHES do, is known as sama.

(2) Lyall Watson has postulated a form of collective awareness exercised by a group, which people establish and make contact with unconsciously. He has coined the word 'sama' for this group-mind, taking two Sanskrit roots – *sa*: together, and *man*: think. As well as being the force which holds a crowd together psychologically,

it also provides people in trance or slightly altered states of CONSCIOUSNESS with access to the content of other people's minds, providing a theory which might explain phenomena such as XENOGLOSSY and POSSESSION. Watson's definition also resembles Wassermann's M-field and Sheldrake's MORPHOGENETIC FIELD: 'Sama describes those parts of an individual or society which share information, whether they be in the soma, the germ cells or the mind.'[207] Although the name given to this kind of group consciousness is new, the possibility that such collective influence might affect mental and even physical phenomena has quite a history in PSYCHICAL RESEARCH. The French doctor and researcher, Gustave Geley (1868–1924): 'Mediumistic investigations belong to the class of "collective experiments", for the phenomena are the result of subconscious psycho-physiological collaboration between the medium and the experimenters.'[60]

SAMADHI In YOGA the fulfilment of MEDITATION is to achieve the state of ENLIGHTENMENT, knowing or realization, known as samadhi. DHYANA has been described as 'a unification or an outpouring of the mind on the object held in view' when one is meditating on a physical thing or a mental idea. Samadhi is unification with the spiritual focus of meditation, a COSMIC CONSCIOUSNESS, when the MIND unites with Universal Mind. It is akin to the mystic union and ECSTASY which mystics such as Teresa of Avila seek and sometimes achieve in contemplation.

SAMSARA According to Buddhist and some Hindu thought there will never be any discernible spiritual progress in the realm of MAYA. The flux of phenomena, the WHEEL OF REBIRTH, samsara, is unending, purposeless and has no direction or pattern, except that the enlightened, liberated individual can escape from it, by achieving NIRVANA and MOKSHA (also called *mukti*).

SATORI The goal of Zen Buddhism is to achieve the state of ENLIGHTENMENT, an intuitive awareness of truth, known as satori, (Japanese). It is comparable to the YOGI's SAMADHI, although some descriptions of it may seem less mystical and visionary. D.T. Suzuki has described satori as 'an insight into the unconscious' and has identified eight of its characteristics: irrationality, intuitive insight, authoritativeness, affirmation, a sense of the beyond, impersonal tone, a feeling of exaltation, and momentariness.

SCRYING Scrying is a form of divination by means of gazing into a crystal, water (also called hydromancy), or any shiny surface. It has been suggested that the biblical Joseph, famous for his interpretations of pharaoh's dreams, used a particular silver cup filled with liquid for the purposes of divination (lecanomancy), hence his rhetorical 'Wot ye not that such a man as I can certainly divine?' following his subterfuge with the cup at the expense of his brothers (Genesis 44, 15). The object used in scrying is sometimes known as a speculum. The Elizabethan magician, Dr Dee, is said to have used polished coal.

Staring into water or a candle-flame is a common form of mental discipline when meditating: narrowing the field of view on one relatively featureless plane helps to reduce the visual stimuli coming into the brain, which aids meditation. By the same token this focusing on a surface where nothing is in focus, but beyond which images might appear, facilitates the spontaneous evocation of hallucinatory images, which can be interpreted symbolically for divination purposes. In some cases the concentrated gaze could lead to a mild form of self-induced TRANCE, which might be used by MEDIUMS as a method of communication with spirits.

SEANCE The French word 'seance', meaning sitting, was adopted for the gathering of a circle of up to about eight people including a MEDIUM, sitting for the purpose of obtaining communication with spirits or other paranormal phenomena. The term has fallen into disuse, perhaps because of its stereotypical associations, and people more often refer nowadays to a circle or a SITTING.

In the early days of SPIRITUALISM seances were held by all and sundry for TABLE-TURNING (or levitation) and table-RAPPING, the easiest physical phenomena to obtain. This is the origin of the mistaken belief that all seances are held around a table with the participants' hands placed palm downwards on the table, fingers touching. In the majority of sittings with a medium nowadays there is no table and the sitters do not touch.

SECOND SIGHT Originally the term 'second sight' referred to the ability to see beings which were normally invisible such as fairies and DEVAS. This faculty might also permit those so gifted to see a person's AURA. Later it came to mean the ability to see clairvoyantly and foretell the future.

SELF The Self is that part of us which remains above the everyday concerns of the personality (the lower self), yet which seems to guide us along our life-path and lend support when we need it. It is the HIGHER SELF, the SOUL, ATMAN and Paul Brunton's OVERSELF. According to the *Upanishads* everyone must become aware of the unity of Self and God: 'If a man dies without realizing the unity of the Self with BRAHMAN he has not reached the true goal of life.' 'All the powers of life, and the elements of creation are contained deep in his own Self, to be drawn on and experienced. The Self is everything, and everything is the Self.' 'The Self is nearer to us than anything else. If a man worships Brahman, thinking that Brahman is one thing or another, he does not realize the truth. . . . The Self is the source of all virtue.' 'Your own Self lives in the hearts of all. Nothing else matters.' 'The Self is eternal and immortal, the one without a second.'

Just as Hindu teachings emphasize the need to meditate on the Self, so also Jung's psychological process of individuation depended on aligning the ego (lower self) more directly with the Self, building and strengthening the 'ego-Self axis'. Roberto Assagioli's system of Psychosynthesis[3] also employs techniques intended to bring the conscious self or 'I' closer in line with the Higher Self in the SUPERCONSCIOUS.

SELF-HYPNOSIS Under HYPNOSIS people respond to the suggestions of the hypnotist in remarkable ways, adopting 'uncharacteristic' modes of behaviour, demonstrating unusual mental or psychic powers and subjecting themselves to physical effects such as blistering simply through the power of thought. Even after waking from the hypnotic trance the SUBCONSCIOUS mind can still overrule the conscious mind if the appropriate SUGGESTION has been planted there. It is clear therefore that the subconscious mind is in some ways more powerful than the conscious mind.

Self-hypnosis is a deliberate form of auto-suggestion. When in a self-induced TRANCE people may be deluded by hallucinatory images evoked from their subconscious, but the object of self-hypnosis is not to listen to the subconscious but to take charge and give it instructions. A mild hypnotic trance state is achieved by a simple relaxation technique and one tells one's subconscious mind how one wants to change, what one wants to achieve or become. There are many textbooks on 'self-improvement' techniques in which self-hypnosis plays a central role.

A similar form of positive auto-suggestion, which seems to bridge the area between self-hypnosis and SPELLS, is the practice of 'affirmations'. According to many channelled writings (such as the bestseller *A Course in Miracles*),[218] by constantly asserting that something is so, one can not only affect one's perceptions of reality but reality itself, since that reality is ultimately dependent on the consciousness which creates it.

SENSITIVE Someone who is sensitive to impressions that are not normally perceived by the average person is called a sensitive. Such a person is also commonly known as a psychic. Sensitives are aware of other dimensions of reality, sensing for example the quality of a person's AURA and interpreting what is sensed in this way in terms of the subject's physical, emotional and mental state.

Sensitives who gain information from other levels with the help of apparently DISCARNATE beings have more commonly been known as MEDIUMS. Sometimes a distinction has been drawn between sensitives, who rely on their own powers to practise CLAIRVOYANCE, TELEPATHY, PSYCHOMETRY and the like, and mediums, who are guided by discarnate entities in performing such tasks. With this distinction there was often an underlying assumption that the ability and technique of mediumship was somehow better and more reliable than that of the sensitive, and that a 'weak' medium, if also a sensitive, might resort to picking up information independently instead of receiving it from discarnates and might then give confused or inconsistent messages.

It is certainly true that not all mediums have been sensitives, in the sense that they have been unable to pick up information 'as themselves'. But the relative success of a sensitive is more likely to result from varying degrees of sensitivity, rather than from an inability to operate as a medium. Sensitivity to a person's aura on an ASTRAL level will provide much information about that person's emotional state at the moment, and about their hopes and fears for the immediate future. Some future events may even cast their shadow before them on an astral level. The individual may find what the sensitive says as a result of all this quite convincing, but it would not constitute true clairvoyance. Sensitivity on a higher, mental level is necessary for insight into the individual's life-purpose and the possible karmic influences. Furthermore, even deceased spirits will not necessarily be able to give this information if they are themselves confined to the astral level, so mediums may quite easily be less reliable than a sensitive, providing the sensitive is expert enough to judge on what level he or she is operating.

The original distinction between mediums and sensitives has now become rather blurred, perhaps because some who would normally have been designated as mediums have themselves suggested that some of the supposed discarnates communicating through them might not be separate entities. Geraldine Cummins, for example, was quite willing to accept that some of the communicators who gave her the information she passed on were sub-personalities of her own, parts of her psyche which could only be brought to conscious awareness in the guise of separate personalities. (She did not doubt that sometimes these parts of herself actually brought through communications from deceased souls, but she was always aware of the lack of clarity, the uncertain degree of reliability and the risk of possible distortion or contamination by her own subconscious.)

Despite the current popularity of CHANNELS there seems to be a movement away from trance mediumship — the manner in which mediums were originally expected to operate (whether by speaking or with AUTOMATIC WRITING), and towards mental mediumship, which to the onlooker is indistinguishable from the manner of operation of a sensitive. The only difference that a sitter might be aware of is when the mental medium says 'They're telling me ...'. The sensitive seems to know intuitively, without being told, but both are perceiving information and bringing it to awareness without relinquishing their own ego CONSCIOUSNESS. This seems to be the type of sensitivity which is appropriate for our times. It is also an inner sensitivity which more people can develop for themselves, without relying on external agencies, whether they be channels or GURUS.

SEPHIROTH – See TREE OF LIFE, KABBALISM.

SERAPH A seraph (plural: seraphim) is a type of ANGEL, ranking above the cherubim in the heavenly hierarchy. They are among the wisest and most zealous of angels and are said to burn with love for God. In his vision Isaiah saw the six-winged seraphim above the throne of God and one of them carried a burning coal to his mouth to purge his sin.

SERENDIPITY Serendip (or Serendib) is an old name of Arabic origin for the Island of Ceylon, now Sri Lanka. The eighteenth-century essayist Horace Walpole discovered (or invented) a fairy-tale entitled *The Three Princes of Serendip*, in which the heroes kept making chance discoveries, and in 1754 he coined the word 'serendipity' for this desirable faculty. In its weakest form it may be regarded as lucky coincidence. Sometimes it seems related to 'beginner's luck', when the naive ignorance of what *could* go wrong means that perhaps one does not totally share everyone else's CONSENSUS REALITY. In such cases expectation seems to play a dynamic part in events in the same way that SUGGESTION may also make one accident-prone. In its strongest form there may be a feeling that serendipity has taken charge of one's life, such that a need is satisfied as soon as it arises, as if by some mysterious agent of benign SYNCHRONICITY. At the heart of all forms of serendipity is the suspicion that our wishes alone can influence events — the power of mind over matter.

SERPENT SYMBOLISM is much more universal than language and the serpent has symbolized eternity, knowledge, enlightenment and healing in many cultures all over the world. Its (Western) associations with evil are relatively recent and not typical.

The eternal cycle of death and rebirth is represented symbolically in many parts of the world as a snake biting its own tail. This is Ouroboros, one of most universal symbols for ETERNITY. The snake was probably originally chosen to represent the cyclic nature of time and the fecundity of nature because of its habit of sloughing its skin. Death and rebirth is understood not only as the way of nature but also as the way of the soul in terms of *samsara*, the WHEEL OF REBIRTH. For this reason the Hindu god Vishnu, the Preserver, is often portrayed seated on a serpent. The implied understanding of such principles as 'My beginning is my end' and 'the Alpha and Omega' may also have led to the serpent's status as a symbol of wisdom.

The serpent was venerated in ancient Egypt, Greece and Rome. It was worshipped in the temples of Asklepios (Aesculapius), and was depicted wrapped round this god's staff. With two intertwined serpents this image, known as the *caduceus*, is still used as a symbol for healing. Some people have suggested that it is more than coincidental that this entwining of the two snakes seems to foreshadow what we now know of the double helix structure of DNA. The spaces and loops formed by the snakes also seem to mirror the seven main spinal CHAKRAS, and the image of a serpent is also used to

The caduceus

represent the power of KUNDALINI in YOGA. Esoterically the two serpents of the caduceus represent the process of involution and evolution, spirit descending into matter and rising again enlightened into spirit. The serpent was therefore the symbol of wisdom, and thus became associated in Christianity with the invitation to eat of the TREE OF KNOWLEDGE. Although orthodox (exoteric) Christianity sees this as the Fall from grace and a step towards evil, it can be seen esoterically as liberation from unconscious limitation and the dawn of self-consciousness. The serpent is then seen as a necessary precursor of Christ.

SETH The American trance medium or CHANNEL, Jane Roberts (1929–84), wrote several books dictated through her by a DISCARNATE entity who called himself Seth. His communications included a complex philosophical system of consciousness, reality, parallel universes and probabilities. His pronouncements on REINCARNATION included the notion that we live different lives simultaneously, as counterparts of each other in our 'multiperson-hood', working on different aspects of the same problem.[163,164,166]

SHAKTI In Hindu thought shakti is the life-activating principle, the power of creative energy in God. This spiritual power is also the female principle, representing the feminine aspects of the Hindu Trinity (BRAHMA, Vishnu and Shiva) or their partners. Shakti is sometimes personified as the consort of Shiva.

SHAMAN The word 'shaman' comes from the Tungus people in Siberia and may also be related to the Indian *samana* for a monk.
Mircea Eliade's study of 1951 (*Shamanism*) showed shamanism to be a universal phenomenon.[50] Shamanistic practices in China, Japan, Australia and North and South America have much in common with each other. The shaman acts as a middle-man between different levels of reality, a PSYCHOPOMP or leader of souls. By using music and rhythm to go into TRANCE or by taking psychotropic DRUGS he gains access to other levels of reality: his soul can leave the body, rising to the sky or descending to the underworld, and bring back messages to his people. In Siberian practices shamans have been described as rising through heaven after heaven to receive messages from the supreme Creator. While in trance a shaman may also fly through the air or walk through fire. He is a combination of priest, poet, magician and medicine-man.[46,81]
Although shamans are usually male, some tribes have traditionally

assigned such roles to women. The Igorot people in the mountains of Luzon in the Philippines have adopted Christianity but their intermediaries between this world and the world of the spirits are the 'aniteras', the traditional female shamans.

The religious life of a community centres on its shaman as the mediator between it and its gods, as the escort of the souls of the dead, and as a HEALER of the living. In some senses the Old Testament prophets could be regarded as shamans, even though their monotheism was not typical. As societies changed, shamanic practices gradually became fragmented into a variety of arts and crafts, and the shaman was replaced by the smith, magician, astrologer, priest, poet and philosopher. In Europe in the Middle Ages some of these roles were temporarily united again in the person of the ALCHEMIST, who was sponsored by a wealthy patron to pursue the Great Work, but probably only under the guise of ultimately creating great material riches for the patron by transmuting base metal into gold.

SHEN In TAOISM the SOUL is called shen. It consists of *Hun* (spirit) and *Po* (earth). The *Po*, which is YIN in quality, returns to earth at death but may become a ghost. The *Hun* starts its journey to heaven, a transition which is divided into seven periods. This reminds one of the seven PLANES of being in occult tradition.

SHEOL In the Old Testament Sheol is the Hebrew equivalent of the Greek HADES, HELL. Like Hades it was initially a place where the dead existed as shades. Later it was regarded more as a place of torment for the wicked, like the Christian concept of Hell. (See also GEHENNA.)

SIBYL In the ancient world of Greece and Rome there were divinely inspired prophetesses called sibyls. Their prophecies were recorded in the *Sibylline Books*. One of the most famous was the sibyl at Cumae near Naples, whose prophecies were contained in three volumes, kept in the Temple of Jupiter on the Capitol in Rome where they could be consulted by priests when requested by the Senate in cases of national emergency. Cicero, the Roman orator, (106–43 BC) mentions the sibyl's prophecy of a coming great teacher, which many regard as foretelling the life of Jesus.

SIGNATURES The mathematician and alchemist Paracelsus (1493–1541) believed that the medical uses of plants were revealed in their shapes and markings — their signatures. Thus lungwort, useful in treating lung diseases, has leaves which resemble lung tissue. The doctrine of signatures was developed further by Gianbattista della Porta (1538–1615) in his *Physognomonica* published in 1588 in Naples.

SILVER CORD If the astral BODY leaves the physical body, as it is said to during OUT-OF-THE-BODY EXPERIENCES, ASTRAL PROJECTION and astral travel, it remains connected to the sleeping physical body by the silver cord, also known as the psychic cord. Only at the death of the physical body is the silver cord severed. The silver cord is mentioned in the Bible in just this context: '. . . man goeth to his long home, and the mourners go about the streets. . . . the silver cord be loosed, . . . Then shall the dust return to the earth as it was, and the spirit shall return unto God who gave it.' (Ecclesiastes 12, 5–7.)

When people having OBEs have looked for the silver cord they have been surprised to find that it did not fit in with certain preconceptions, e.g. regarding the point at which it is apparently attached to the 'travelling body'. Robert Monroe, one of the most experienced 'astral travellers' of recent years, had expected the silver cord to be attached at the head, but found that it entered between the shoulder blades, branching out rather like the complex of roots entering the ground at the base of a tree trunk.[127] This is surprising, for in other respects the 'astral body' reflects the individual's thought patterns: if you always think of yourself as clothed, your second body will also be clothed. The cord is described as silver because of the pulsating energy which it appears to carry to and fro between the two bodies, in the same way that an embryo receives sustenance via the umbilical cord.

According to Dion Fortune, when people create astral manifestations or 'artificial ELEMENTALS', these too are attached to their parent body, at least initially, by a cord along which energy pulses. It emanates from the person's SOLAR PLEXUS, the CHAKRA which is always most closely associated with physical phenomena in MEDIUMS. Once this line is severed the elemental can carry on an independent existence of its own. 'The life of these creatures is akin to that of an electric battery, it slowly leaks out by means of radiation, and unless recharged periodically, will finally weaken and die out.' Dion Fortune believed that she involuntarily created an elemental in the form of a werewolf, but she was able to reabsorb it via the cord, before it could do any damage.[55]

SITTING A group of people sitting with a MEDIUM or CHANNEL is often called a circle, and their activity, which was formerly known as a SEANCE, is now usually referred to more simply as a sitting. Sittings can also be held by just one or two people with a medium. The purpose of most sittings is to receive information from other levels of awareness. It is usually assumed that this means the sitters expect communications from spirit entities, although not even all mediums automatically assume that what they say while in TRANCE necessarily originates in the mind of another.

Certain conditions are traditionally thought to be favourable for a successful sitting. Assuming a medium is present, the other sitters need not have any particular psychic ability, although the more sensitive they are the better. A certain amount of scepticism or doubt is not necessarily deleterious, although hostility or suspicion are definite obstacles. A completely open mind is most conducive. The atmosphere should be as relaxed, happy and harmonious as possible, and solemnity should be avoided. Calm anticipation is more beneficial than too much eagerness or excitement, and fear can have a very bad effect on results. Worry, depression, fatigue, tension and ill-health are all obstructive.

Music is sometimes used, perhaps with the suggestion that this helps to 'raise the vibrations'. Whatever the truth behind that claim its effectiveness is twofold in that it helps to create a relaxed attitude for the sitters, reducing the tension that undue concentration may cause, and it also reduces possible inhibitions in the medium, who might otherwise find the initial hurdle of breaking the silence too difficult to overcome. Silence is often seen as an obstacle and sitters may usefully be encouraged to indulge in casual conversation.

The onset of phenomena in a circle or trance communications from the medium may be marked by an apparent drop in temperature or a current of cold air. This suggests that energy is being used and sitters often report the feeling that energy is drawn out of them, usually from the SOLAR PLEXUS. Sometimes there is a deliberate attempt to generate this energy by 'passing the power' around the circle. It is unclear whether this is a visualization technique which helps to build up the sitters' belief in what is happening, thus encouraging it to happen, or whether some BIOPLASMIC energy is at work.

SIXTH SENSE There are generally assumed to be five senses through which we are aware of the external world: sight, hearing, smell, taste and touch. These are not as discrete as is commonly supposed.

Sound, for example, can be felt as well as heard, as demonstrated by the musical sensitivity of the deaf, who can feel music reverberating through their bodies to such an extent that they can dance to it and even play musical instruments. In our cheeks and fingertips there are light-sensitive cells, which the blind have sometimes been trained to develop to such an extent that they can identify colour — the faculty of PAROPTIC VISION. And our sense of taste is strongly affected by our sense of smell, from which it cannot be completely separated.

At least two of our senses, seeing and hearing, can operate subliminally, i.e. without our conscious awareness. When we sense someone's presence behind us, this can sometimes be attributed to subliminal hearing. Subliminal sight has been proved by showing films which include a few frames of single words of which the viewer is not aware, but which are seen subliminally and remembered, for they then consistently crop up in free association tests in conjunction with the film.

Under HYPNOSIS our senses are also much more acute than normal. A hypnotized subject can readily distinguish between two 'identical' blank sheets of paper, presumably by recognizing minor blemishes and differences in the grain. This acute form of perception is known as HYPERACUITY or hyperaesthesia.

The term 'sixth sense' is therefore applied to perception or sensing which cannot be explained by what are regarded as the normal five senses, nor by subliminal perception, nor by hyperaesthesia. It is most frequently used as a synonym for INTUITION. The percipient is typically unable to explain how the perceived data have come to awareness and may refer to the experience with words such as 'I had a feeling' or 'I just knew'. The more usual term when someone senses events occurring elsewhere in this way is ESP — EXTRA-SENSORY PERCEPTION or TELEPATHY if it is thought that someone else's mind is also involved as 'transmitter'. Sometimes the sixth sense operates as a warning mechanism, giving rise to PREMONITIONS. Some believe that human beings were once much more aware in this way than they are today, and that the sense has atrophied since the environment in which we live has become more secure. On the other hand, greater awareness of imminent danger when hunting, for example, could have been achieved by more acute sensitivity of hearing, sight, and smell, all of which may have diminished during the process of humanity's civilization.

311

SLEEP – See DREAMS, BRAIN WAVES.

SOLAR PLEXUS CENTRE – See CHAKRAS.

SOLIPSISM From the Latin, 'alone' + 'self', solipsism is the philosophical theory which states that all that can be known to exist is oneself. As an idea this may seem to be something of a dead end as far as philosophical discussion is concerned, but it is a reminder that everything that we regard as being 'out there' in the external world is essentially unprovable, since our experience of it is mediated by our senses, so our picture of the world is mental and may bear little relation to the world as it is. After all, we would regard a whale's view of the world to be seriously flawed if its partiality and bias were not also recognized – its value and justification lie in its usefulness for the whale. So why should our human pragmatic view of the world, which serves our purposes as far as survival is concerned, be any more accurate as a representation or true model than the whale's? The Oxford researcher into parapsychology, Celia Green, contends that scientists have avoided study of certain undeniable psychological phenomena because they remind us of the fact that the mind creates its own view of reality and of the possibility that our 'normal' perception of the external world – our CONSENSUS REALITY – might also be illusory.

When the Irish philosopher and Anglican Bishop George Berkeley (1685–1753) argued for the solipsist view that matter did not exist, Dr Samuel Johnson delivered his famous kick against a large stone saying, 'I refute it thus'. This was rather an oversimplification of Berkeley's system of 'subjective idealism' according to which objects exist only when perceived and God's perception sustains the UNIVERSE. Such a view in fact has a long history all over the world. For Hindus existence is sustained by BRAHMA, and in the Night of Brahma everything ceases to exist. Australian Aboriginals on walkabout have to sing the land into existence before it can emerge over the horizon, an act of re-creation they refer to as 'singing up the country', just as the Ancestors created everything first as a mental concept, and then as physical reality through song. Even physical science has given rise to the view that, 'The universe begins to look more like a great thought than like a great machine'.[91] The agent of creation is therefore CONSCIOUSNESS. 'Our consciousness is not just a passive epiphenomenon carried along by the chemical events in our brains, but is an active agent forcing the molecular complexes to make choices between one quantum state and another. In other words, mind is already inherent in every electron.'[49]

SOMNAMBULISM A somnambulist (literally 'sleep walker') is someone who while asleep engages in various activities regarded as abnormal for someone in that state. Somnambulists usually seem preoccupied or dazed, are less aware of their surroundings than normal and do not respond to what might be going on around them. On waking they have no recollection of their actions while asleep. Although their actions may be purposeful, they are generally fragmentary and suggestive of irrational DREAM experiences being acted out. But electroencephalograms reveal that somnambulism occurs during 'orthodox' sleep and not when the sleeper is dreaming. In spite of this, on the few occasions when people have committed murder while purportedly asleep, their pleas of somnambulism have been accepted by courts in both Britain and the USA and they have been acquitted. We are apparently not to be held responsible for the actions of our SUBCONSCIOUS minds.

There seem to be links between somnambulism and HYPNOSIS. Apart from the dissociation of the conscious mind, sensory stimuli are also similarly affected, with the somnambulist's eyes often being directed upwards towards the forehead, and there is a certain insensibility to taste, smell and even pain. When hypnotism was first practised by the Marquis de Puységur it was classified as a form of somnambulism. Somnambulism was then divided into four types: natural somnambulism, which might occur spontaneously in people of a certain nervous temperament but who were otherwise perfectly healthy; symptomatic somnambulism, associated with certain diseases and occurring at some crisis point in the disease; artificial somnambulism, otherwise known as hypnotism: and ecstatic somnambulism, when people fall into a self-induced TRANCE.

Medical and psychological opinion of what actually happens in somnambulism is matched in its sketchiness by the same experts' accounts of hypnosis. In both instances the subconscious mind seems to assume direct control of the body, but why and how remains a mystery to a science which still tends to disregard the subconscious.

SORCERY Sorcery is the selfish use of magical powers, casting SPELLS for personal gain and advancement, and gaining power over others by the practice of black magic. When people who have been developing psychically have chosen to adopt such practices,

313

they are sometimes said to have taken the LEFT-HAND PATH. In some respects the difference between sorcery and the right use of PSYCHIC gifts is simply one of attitude. What seem overtly to be similar practices may be inherently good or 'evil' depending on whether the motivation behind them is love for humanity and a desire to serve or self-aggrandizement and a desire to control. In such a situation, by 'evil' we mean a retrograde step in the spiritual EVOLUTION of a soul: someone who indulges in such practices will accumulate a considerable amount of 'bad KARMA' which will affect future incarnations. Some actions may even rebound on the perpetrator in this lifetime. The THOUGHT-FORMS and ELEMENTALS which sorcerers create need energy to survive and can ultimately drain their creators of life-energy, reducing them to little more than automata, a phenomenon which is often seen in irrational obsessive behaviour which may have started off as more rational but selfish or cruel activity. Sorcerers are usually considered to be conscious agents of sorcery, but a far greater number of people use the same techniques unconsciously, resulting in suffering for their victims and ultimately perhaps mental illness for the unconscious sorcerers.

SOUL Of the world's major religions only Buddhism denies or is agnostic about the existence of the soul. It goes by many names: *jiva* (Jain), ATMAN (Hindu), MONAD, EGO, SELF, HIGHER SELF, OVERSELF, elusive self, psyche, or even MIND. It is universally eternal and indestructible, although it may undergo various changes. Despite some laxity in the use of the two terms in English, the soul is to be distinguished from SPIRIT: the soul is animated by spirit in the same way that the body is animated by the soul. The soul is individualized spirit, just as we may consider the body to be personalized soul.

In Jain doctrine the soul is known as *jiva*. Souls are present not only in human beings but also in animals, plants, minerals and the elements. This is typical also of American Indian beliefs and animist religions. The Jain view is that souls are imprisoned in matter as a result of KARMA. All souls, including those of the gods, experience REINCARNATION and TRANSMIGRATION until a state of NIRVANA is reached. In order to become purified and dissolve away their karma, souls must shun all violent deeds — hence the doctrine of non-violence, known as *a-himsa*.

From ancient times we can trace the concept of the soul in different cultures:

Egyptian	–	BA	
Hindu	–	atman	
Greek	(Aristotelian)	psyche	(creative reason)
..	(Plutarch)	nous	(uncorrupted, surviving death)
Jewish	–	neshamah	(divine soul, incapable of sin)
medieval Christian		anima divina	

The spiritual origins of the soul are always considered to be in some way timeless. Plato regarded the soul as originating in a world of Being and entering a world of Becoming (in the *Timaeus*). NEOPLATONISTS such as Plotinus described the soul as a stranger on earth, having fallen into matter from a world without space and time (in the *Enneads*). Sometimes the timeless v. trapped-in-time aspects of an individual are tweezed apart with symbolic imagery. In the *Upanishads* the soul (higher Self) and the personality (lower self) are compared to two birds sitting in the same tree: one, the personality, pecks at the fruit, whilst the other, the soul, simply watches. 'There are two birds on a tree. The one in the lower branches is of gorgeous plumage. It eats the fruits of the tree, sings and preens its feathers. Its companion on the higher branches is of sombre plumage, is silent and watches over its companion. The bird on the lower branches is the lower self, absorbed in living and activity. The bird on the higher branches is the higher Self, at one with spirit. The lower self, while still absorbed in living, must at all times recognize its higher Self which watches over it and is at one with pure spirit' (*Mundaka Upanishad*).

Further subdivisions of the soul are sometimes made. According to the Menomini, an American Indian tribe, there is one soul for the head and another for the heart. In the Philippines the Bagobo believe that there is one soul for the left and another for the right, one remaining earth-bound as a ghost after death and the other destined to join the ancestors. This seems to reflect the occult view of various spirit BODIES. The soul has sometimes been called the astral body, although this is simply the form in which the soul expresses itself at a particular time after the death of the physical body but when the personality is still very strong. Even the mental body may retain aspects of the personality, or start to accrue aspects of the next personality, but it is on the mental or manasic PLANE that the soul starts to be more truly itself, with an overview of its many incarnations. At this level the soul is also sometimes called the causal body. It is this soul that incarnates. As incarnate beings we are male or female, whereas the soul is neither male nor female. Jung saw the soul as androgynous, both male and female, and he described it as 'the greatest of all cosmic miracles'.[95]

The causal body is still not necessarily the highest expression of the soul. Many esoteric schools put the number of our bodies at seven, and by 'soul' may be meant any or any combination of what in the *Upanishads* are four separate bodies: the astral body the mental body, the EGO, and the Atman. The seventh level is unity with BRAHMAN, where soul and spirit are truly one.

SPELLS It is clear that the SUBCONSCIOUS MIND can overrule the conscious mind both in determining behaviour, as is seen in post-hypnotic suggestion, and in its effect on the body, as when people have been made to realize that they have said 'You make me sick' or 'You're a pain in the neck' so often to a particular person that the physical affliction becomes a reaction to that person's presence. Affirmations are a more positive use of the power of the subconscious, operating on the same basic principle to help one to fulfil one's potential. One could take the process further with SELF-HYPNOSIS.

Spells are similar to affirmations in that they are overtly voiced statements which are used to direct the power of the subconscious mind, but instead of being directed inwards on ourselves, they are directed outwards to other people. To most people the notion of spells sounds like mumbo-jumbo, but the concept does fit in with what is already accepted about the subconscious mind and HYPNOSIS. It has been shown that TELEPATHY is facilitated by hypnosis. Telepathy can be understood as subconscious minds communicating with each other, perhaps temporarily overlapping or fusing somehow. So at this level of consciousness there are three known processes which appear to operate: telepathy, hypnosis and SUGGESTION. These are the three ingredients of a spell. This can also be understood as the level of CONSCIOUSNESS at which certain forms of ABSENT HEALING work: the difference is simply that spells are usually considered to be less beneficial to the subject concerned and more beneficial to the one who is invoking the powers of the mind – casting the spell.

SPIRIT The divine spark in each human being is known as Spirit (as distinct from 'spirits'). Spirit dwells in the SOUL, the connecting principle between it and the physical body. The ultimate aim of most spiritual disciplines is to achieve unity between this spark and its divine origin and between soul and spirit. When we recognize that we are more than our bodies and our minds, we appreciate that we are souls. Realization that we are spirit is much rarer.

St Paul refers to the gifts of the Spirit. 'For to one is given by the Spirit the word of wisdom; to another the word of knowledge by the same Spirit; to another faith by the same Spirit; to another the gifts of HEALING by the same Spirit; to another the working of MIRACLES; to another PROPHECY; to another the discerning of spirits; to another divers kinds of tongues; to another the interpretation of tongues: but all these worketh that one and the selfsame Spirit, dividing to everyman severally as he will' (1 Corinthians 12, 8−11).

Spirit is also used more widely as a generic term to describe all non-material states of being. So the soul is spirit, even though the two are not identical. When people ask for guidance from a spirit, they may be referring to God or to any number of levels of being or degrees of evolution − ANGELS, GUIDES, MASTERS etc. − from which help may be sought. In this sense people also refer to SPIRITS.

SPIRITS When SOULS become separated from the physical body at death they are commonly referred to as spirits, even though they are active primarily on the ASTRAL level and are probably no more 'spiritual' than they were when in the physical body. All beings which are active in realms other than the physical plane are generally referred to as spirits. These may include non-human spirits too, such as ELEMENTALS, ANGELS, DEMONS.

Other non-human spirits sometimes referred to are 'the Nation Spirit' and 'the Spirit of the Age' (Zeitgeist). These are usually thought of as mere metaphors, empty abstractions, but some OCCULTISTS claim otherwise. If one considers the power of thought and the ability to create THOUGHT-FORMS, then it is not such a great leap to investing such spirits with some degree of objective reality. They are like DEVAS and some SENSITIVES can be aware of them, as they are of PRESENCES like the 'Angel of the House of Commons'. 'Those who have the faculty of spiritual sight perceive such beings and can describe them. ... Such descriptions cannot be faithful reproductions of the reality that underlies them. They attempt to make clear a spiritual reality which can only be represented in this way: that is, by similes. ... They can of course never become visible to the eye of the sense, for they have no material bodies. The superstition does not consist in regarding

317

such beings as real, but in believing that they appear in forms perceptible to the physical senses. Such Beings co-operate in the building of the world and we encounter them as soon as we enter the higher realms that are hidden from the bodily senses.'[183]

In the ancient classical world there were several types of human spirit. The spirits of the dead, *manes*, could apparently be divided into separate parts: while the shades were in HADES, at the same time another earth-bound part of their spiritual being in the form of the *lemures* or *larvae* might haunt places or people known to the dead when they were alive. In a few cases the spirit of someone like Hercules might gain admission to Olympus, but this would not exclude his spirit from also carrying out the other roles. Everyone had a personal guardian spirit called a GENIUS or DAEMON. The *lares* were the spirits of the ancestors who protected the private homes of the living; the *penates* were more public protective spirits, akin to the patron saints in Roman Catholicism.

Emanuel Swedenborg recognized a hierarchy of spirits which can interact with human beings: there are two types — high and low. Allan Kardec held the same view, the low spirits being EARTH-BOUND spirits of the dead. The KAHUNAS have a similar belief. The American psychiatrist, Wilson Van Dusen, believes that the influence which these spirits have on the minds of human beings, which Swedenborg claimed usually remains unconscious, can become conscious in the mentally-ill. He came to this conclusion because so many of the HALLUCINATIONS described by his patients in the Mendocino State Hospital, California, bore a striking resemblance to Swedenborg's HEAVEN and HELL. Only the low spirits made any attempt to 'invade' the individual; they were also often violently anti-religious. (See POSSESSION.) The higher order of spirits showed much more concern for the individual, respecting their individuality and helping with advice rather than taking them over.

Spirit communications have always been regarded with a certain amount of suspicion by most of the major religions, which is slightly paradoxical when one considers how many religious traditions and sects have been based on such inspired writings. Moses received the Law from Jehovah; most of the Old Testament prophets had a direct line to the Lord God; Mohammed received the KORAN from Gabriel; later sects such as the Mormons and Christian Science based their teachings on channelled communications.

Part of the reason for the common religious veto on seeking advice from spirits is the possible temptation to abandon personal responsibility for one's actions and do whatever they say. Nevertheless, Saul consulted the witch of Endor to commune with the spirit of Samuel, even though he was rebuked by Samuel for doing so. (The witch's GUIDE or CONTROL is referred to in the Bible as her 'familiar spirit'. I Samuel 28, 7–11.) Another reason for wariness in such consultations is the lack of reliability in the spirits that do communicate. We have no guarantee that they are any wiser or more enlightened than we are ourselves, and we are also told in the Bible to 'prove the spirits, whether they be of God', meaning that we should ask them and even test them. But more important than any indirect contact with spirits via a medium or channel is the direct awareness of Spirit that can be developed within ourselves. This is what YOGA teaches, that we must be aware of SELF, ATMAN, within and recognize that it is BRAHMAN. The Bible also tells us that the gifts of the SPIRIT in this sense are wisdom, faith, HEALING, MIRACLES, TONGUES, and discernment of spirits.

SPIRIT HYPOTHESIS According to the spirit hypothesis the personalities who appear to speak and write through MEDIUMS or CHANNELS are DISCARNATE SPIRITS, as they usually maintain they are. The psychological theory is that they are sub-personalities of the medium. Although the two theories are often put forward as being totally at variance with each other, there seems to be nothing mutually exclusive about them. In fact, learning to 'hand over' control of the body to a subconsciously created alternative personality might be a preliminary, an easier first step, to surrendering to a discarnate CONTROL.

Apparent spirit interventions to find a lost will or receipt for a payment already made are sometimes cited as evidence for the spirit hypothesis, although these might also be explained by the SUPER-ESP HYPOTHESIS. Other phenomena such as so-called CROSS CORRESPONDENCES and DROP-IN COMMUNICATORS are perhaps more difficult to explain in this way and may be considered to be more supportive of the spirit hypothesis.

William James died in 1910. Before his death he agreed with Professor James Hyslop that whoever should die first would try to get a message to the other. Eventually Hyslop received a letter from a medium in Ireland, who maintained that a spirit calling itself William James had told her to ask Hyslop if he remembered a pair of red pyjamas. When he first read the message it meant nothing to him, but later he remembered a curious incident when the two of them had been in Paris together as young men. Their luggage had been delayed and Hyslop had wanted to buy some pyjamas: the only pair he was able to find in the time available were bright red, and James had teased him for days about his strange taste. It was extremely unlikely that anyone else would have known about this, let alone remembered it. Hyslop was convinced: he concluded that at least in this case the 'spirit hypothesis' was much more logical and economical than any super-ESP theory.

SPIRIT PHOTOGRAPHY This term should not be confused with PSYCHIC PHOTOGRAPHY. Certain people seem to be able to impress an image on a photographic film without the usual procedure of exposing the film to the light from a physical object. This is known as psychic photography or 'thoughtography'. But it has been claimed that physical manifestations of spirits — MATERIALIZATIONS — have been photographed, and this is what is known as spirit photography.

Charles Richet and Baron Schrenck-Notzing conducted experiments independently of each other with the French medium Marthe Béraud. Both reported materializations which were photographed, and the photographs were published.[161,175] Richet was a rigorous experimenter. He was a firm believer in the materialist position and could not accept the SURVIVAL hypothesis, although some say he came close to doing so towards the end of his life. One of Richet's colleagues, G. Geley, who also tested Marthe Béraud in 1910, said of her: 'I do not say there is no trickery. I say there was no possibility of trickery.'[61]

The phenomenon of psychic photography provides a way out for those who without invoking fraud still do not wish to concede that spirit photography represents evidence of survival. If the spirit manifestations are hallucinatory, the result of group HYPNOSIS by the MEDIUM, or if they are exteriorizations generated by the medium, the photographs might be produced psychically rather than in the normal way. Both materializations and photographs are then manifestations of the medium's psychic powers rather than evidence of the presence of DISCARNATE SPIRITS. But since science has no understanding of the process by which exteriorizations, mass HALLUCINATIONS or psychic photographs are produced, the SPIRIT HYPOTHESIS actually seems more economical.

SPIRITISM In Europe, SPIRITUALISM originally went under the name of Spiritism. The doctrine of REINCARNATION occupied a pivotal position in the spiritual teachings communicated to the early members of the spiritist/spiritualist movement, many of whom were deeply antagonistic to the idea because of their Christian faith. This resulted in the anti-reincarnation faction calling themselves spiritualists, whilst those who accepted reincarnation, as presented in the messages assembled by Allan Kardec in *The Spirits' Book*, continued to call themselves spiritists. Spiritism is still the most widely held religious belief in Brazil.

SPIRITUAL BODY The 'spiritual body' is an extremely ambiguous term. St Paul uses it when referring to the RESURRECTION of the faithful in HEAVEN. Others use the same words to refer to the ASTRAL BODY or any level of being after death. The SUBTLE BODY is usually regarded as the ETHERIC body, which is as much a part of physical manifestation as the physical body is. Beyond the physical and etheric bodies five other BODIES have been identified (e.g. in the *Upanishads*) and they might all be considered to be spiritual: astral, mental, EGO, ATMAN and BRAHMAN. So the 'spiritual body' might be any one or a combination of these.

The spiritual body which survives the death of the physical body presumably bears the characteristics and the memory traces of the personality which originally inhabited the physical body. This may seem paradoxical when we consider that many of our character traits are the product of our genetic inheritance, and so are apparently dependent on our physical body. Similarly we seem to depend on our physical brain as the storehouse for our memory. Some have claimed that those experiences when all one's life seems to flash before one's eyes just before the moment of death are in fact instances when the memory was being transferred from the brain to the spiritual body, but this seems far too reminiscent of modern technology and the rapid copying of recordings from one tape to another. We need only to think of all those whose memories are impaired by deteriorating brain function towards the end of life (Do their spiritual bodies retain faulty memories?) to realize that any earthly memories which reside in a spiritual body must have been there during earthly life too.

SPIRITUAL SCIENCE Steiner wrote, 'To the study of the spiritual processes in human life and in the cosmos, the term *spiritual science* may be given.' The term is used by occultists to refer to OCCULT teaching, the ancient wisdom, as for example in THEOSOPHY and ANTHROPOSOPHY.

SPIRITUALISM As a movement, spiritualism is considered to have been born in the middle of the nineteenth century. In 1848 the home of the Fox family in Hydesville, New York, was invaded by a noisy POLTERGEIST. With the help of a neighbour the family devised a code in order to communicate with the supposed spirit: the now familiar one rap for no, two raps for yes. (See RAPPING.) By questioning the poltergeist it was learned that the spirit was that of a murdered pedlar, buried in the basement. (This was unsubstantiated at the time, but fifty years later human remains and a pedlar's tin box were excavated from the basement.) Some time later the two daughters of the family went to stay with relatives and the poltergeist phenomena followed them: in addition to the noises objects were now being thrown around too. This time an alphabetical code was used to communicate with the spirit, which announced 'You must proclaim this truth to the world'. As a result, the first Spiritualist meeting took place in Rochester, the town to which the Fox sisters had moved, on 14 November 1849. The Fox sisters had founded Spiritualism.

The first significant book to proclaim the Spiritualist doctrine (SPIRITISM as it was then called) was *The Spirits' Book*, published in 1856.[100] This was a collection of spirit writings assembled by a French educationalist, Dénizard Hyppolyte Léon Rivail. He had first attended a session of HYPNOSIS in 1855. There he met Madame Plainemaison, who invited him to her house where regular table-rapping SEANCES were held. He met the Baudin daughters who practised AUTOMATIC WRITING. He read many such communications and realized that they had an inner consistency. He published the writings under the name Allan Kardec, names given to him by spirits as names he had had in previous incarnations. The book soon became a classic.

According to the ideas presented in *The Spirits' Book*, life is a union of spirit and matter. Human beings have a body, a 'vital principle' or AURA, an intelligent SOUL and a spiritual soul. (These four BODIES are found in many teachings although they go under various names. The vital principle is more commonly called the etheric body; the 'intelligent soul' may be called the EGO, the mental body or simply the soul; the 'spiritual soul' is often simply referred to as SPIRIT, the divine principle or the divine spark.) It is the destiny of all spirits to evolve towards perfection, and EVOLUTION is the purpose of incarnation. After death a spirit stays in the spirit world for a certain period before returning to earth or to some other world in a new incarnation, the elements of which are chosen by the soul itself.

Quite early on in its development, the spiritualist movement split in two. The reason was that many could not bring themselves to accept the doctrine of REINCARNATION, which was an essential part of 'spiritist' teachings. The spiritism of Allan Kardec crossed the Atlantic and was readily accepted in Brazil, where perhaps the way had already been prepared by familiarity with voodoo, and where it still flourishes. European spiritualism established its own orthodoxy, which for a long time generally rejected reincarnation.

This version of spiritualism presented a cosy if unadventurous view of life and death, concerned above all with satisfying its adherents that their personality survived physical death to live on in the SUMMERLAND, a paradisical domain where one's every wish was granted.

The relative failure of Spiritualism to establish itself as a powerful force in religious and spiritual circles is probably due to its obsession with proving SURVIVAL and its depiction of the AFTERLIFE as a rather boring, albeit happier version of this life; the popularizers of Spiritualism, the platform MEDIUMS and CLAIRVOYANTS have never dwelt sufficiently on the 'bigger questions', spiritual progress, the evolution of the soul, individual responsibility.

It was probably on account of this neglect of the truly spiritual purpose of existence that Rudolf Steiner said, 'The Spiritualists are the greatest materialists of all.' (Steiner had been sympathetic to the views put forward in *The Spirits' Book*.) Far from revealing that life is independent of matter, the spiritualists' concentration on the 'life-after-death' issue reduces cosmic reality and the concept of life itself to a mere three-dimensional shadow of reality, inspired by the material rather than the spirit. Such spiritualists never escape from Plato's cave.

NEO-PLATONISTS had practices which closely resembled spiritualist seances, although what modern spiritualists attribute to DISCARNATE human entities was attributed by neo-Platonists to gods and DAEMONS. In late classical times 'katakoi' exhibited the same PARANORMAL phenomena as those who were burned at the stake for witchcraft in the sixteenth and seventeenth centuries.

In 1936 the Archbishop of Canterbury, Cosmo Lang, set up a commission to investigate Spiritualism and decide whether its teachings were consistent with Christianity. After three years the commission presented its conclusions to the archbishop, who apparently found them so embarrassing that he promptly put them in a drawer and forgot about them. The report was eventually published in the 1970s: the conclusions were that Spiritualism was not opposed to Christianity and that the evidence for 'survival' as taught by Spiritualists was most convincing.

STANDING STONES – See MEGALITHS.

STARSEED TRANSMISSIONS Ken Carey, through whom the *Starseed Transmissions* were channelled over a period of eleven days just after Christmas 1978, describes the communications as having been 'transmitted neurobiologically', by entities that he sometimes regarded as 'informational cells within a Galactic organism of some sort', in an act of 'extra-terrestrial or angelic communion'. 'The messages came first in non-verbal form, on waves, or pulsations, that carried the concise symbolic content of what I term meta-conceptual information.' Humanity is addressed in a decidedly millenarian tone – 'I come with a message that will prove vital to you in these final days of your history' – with authority – 'I bring instructions to your race from the directive organ of Galactic Being' – in the idiom of Christianity – 'Identification with Christ is the key to the time that lies before you' – and of mysticism – 'When you have awakened to the reality of your true being, you will perceive me and all my species as being inside yourself.'[25]

In many respects these communications are typical of inspired writings. However uplifting their effect may be, the content is not particularly new. There is a welcome de-emphasis on the nature of their external originator, later named as 'Raphael', and a strong focus on human spiritual development. 'Ten years from now there will be many working signs and wonders in the name of Christ. Twenty years from now, individual awakenings to the reality of Christ-consciousness will be commonplace. Thirty years from now, there will be a sufficient number of healthy functioning holoids to undertake consciously the final cycle of Creation on this level.' There will follow, we are told, 'a thousand-year Period of Planetary Awakening'. During this period 'from the perspective of Spirit, the Star-Maker will be organically growing through the instrumentality of the human species, a physical body capable of universal exploration. The completed body will resemble a human body in both design and structure. The completed physical body, incorporating much of the Earth's biological life, will depart from this planet in approximately AD 3011. From the outside it will have the appearance of a human baby of about one year of age.'[25]

Is it coincidental that that image is so reminiscent of the concluding frames of the seminal sci-fi cult-movie *2001: A Space Odyssey* by Stanley Kubrick and Arthur C. Clarke? Admittedly the film showed an embryo rather than a one-year-old child, but the combination of a new child, galactic exploration and human evolution is unmistakable. Which was foreshadowing or reflecting the other? Or were they both tuning into some larger truth? Despite their mystico-religious content the mood of *The Starseed Transmissions* contains more than a hint of Olaf Stapledon (*Starmaker*, 1930; *Last and First Men*, 1937) as well as Arthur C. Clarke (*Childhood's End*, 1953). Is there really an EXTRA-TERRESTRIAL link where spiritual matters are concerned, or is this just another demonstration of the way the magpie mind works when in 'receiving' mode. We are reminded that Geraldine Cummins picked up communications about a period of Irish history which turned out to be part of a plot that the poet W.B. Yeats was currently working on. And in 1898 a novelist wrote a novel foreshadowing in many details the sinking of the Titanic in 1912. (See PRECOGNITION.) Inspiration works in mysterious ways.

Ken Carey's CHANNELLED writings are among the most powerful of modern times. Like many mystical writings *The Starseed Transmissions* often speak as if from an inner source, the Divine within, but then authorship is ejected to 'out there' and we seem to be back among the Sky People of UFOs and abductions. Are our concrete minds so concrete that we cannot maintain a belief in pure spirit without conceptualizing extra-terrestrial guides? The undeniable link between the two in the human psyche at least supports the notion that reported encounters with extra-terrestrials are probably symptomatic of some spiritual crisis or development, regardless of whether there is a connection in physical reality.

STIGMATA From the Greek, 'to brand', stigmata are the wounds which appear spontaneously on a person's body, often in imitation of the wounds of Christ. As well as appearing in states of transcendent ECSTASY such wounds can also be symptoms of HYSTERIA. St Francis of Assisi is the most famous individual to have demonstrated this in 1224, following forty days of fasting, prayer and contemplation on the Passion of Christ. Before him, St Paul's reference to bearing the marks of Christ on his own body had been assumed to be metaphorical, although it retrospect it is likely that his were the first stigmata of this kind. There have been many others since. The fact that the marks of the nails have always manifested in accordance with the popular conception of the crucifixion, i.e. in the palms of the hands, and not in the wrists, where the victims of this form of death penalty were actually nailed, has been cited as evidence that the phenomenon is not 'miraculous'. Such wounds do, however, demonstrate the power of the SUBCONSCIOUS MIND. Further demonstration of this is seen when hypnotized subjects are touched with a feather which they are told is a red-hot poker: the skin blisters exactly as if burned.

STONE CIRCLES – See MEGALITHS.

SUBCONSCIOUS MIND Orthodox psychologists tend to use the term 'UNCONSCIOUS' in preference to 'subconscious' nowadays. In *The Oxford Companion to the Mind* there is no entry at all for 'subconscious'.[70] Any difference between the two terms has been all but lost in everyday usage too, although the preferred lay term seems to be 'subconscious'. Part of the modern dislike for both terms is the implication that the MIND is something that can be divided up into separate parts. For psychologists the mind is not an entity at all but a process, and some mental processes are unconscious such as SUBLIMINAL perception. If we refer to ideas, complexes or patterns of behaviour as originating in the subconscious or unconscious mind, this does not mean that we regard the mind as having separate compartments: rather it is a metaphorical way of referring to different aspects of CONSCIOUSNESS.

Despite the modern myth that Freud discovered the unconscious mind, poets, philosophers and scientists had been discussing the concept for a long time and even using the word 'unconscious' since about 1750.[210] When the French neurologist Jean-Martin Charcot (1825–93) started investigating HYPNOSIS there was an added need to refer to the workings of the mind in specific, newly discovered ways. He and his foremost pupil Pierre Janet (1859–1947) used the term subconscious extensively, linking sub-personalities, for instance, to 'subconscious fixed ideas' (*idée fixe subconsciente*). It was also a convenient metaphor to regard the hypnotist as talking to the subject's subconscious mind.

This subconscious mind seems to have not only greater powers of memory and recall than the person in a normal state of consciousness, but also the ability to override both the person's perceptions and sensations while hypnotized and even their conscious wishes and decisions concerning behaviour, after the return to normal consciousness. The placebo effect is a demonstration of the positive usefulness of the subjective mind and its control over the physical organism (via the sympathetic nervous system). Its power can also be put to effective use in the practice of SELF-HYPNOSIS or affirmations. The subconscious mind can apparently go through normal thought processes, solving problems in our sleep and even doing creative work in a contracted time-scale when instructed to do so under hypnosis.

Another reason why the subconscious may still be a useful concept to preserve is that it represents a personal aspect of the unconscious mind. As such it represents the field of activity not only of sub-personalities referred to by Janet, but also of the Shadow and the Animus/Anima as conceived by Jung. These are part of what Jung called the 'personal unconscious', but they are also always visualized by our spatially-oriented mentality as being below consciousness. When Jung himself dreamed about the contents of his own unconscious he saw himself descending to lower and lower levels of a building. Penetrating deeper he came to a level representing the COLLECTIVE UNCONSCIOUS where the archetypes dwelt and interacted with the development of our psyche. Jung believed that it was possible to explore these areas of the mind by means of ACTIVE IMAGINATION. Similar techniques are practised in Psychosynthesis and in Inner Guide Meditation.[182]

Because the collective unconscious seems to be transpersonal it is often associated with a higher aspect of consciousness and is sometimes referred to as the SUPERCONSCIOUS. Consequently access

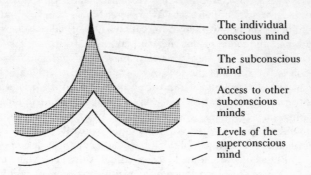

The individual
conscious mind

The subconscious
mind

Access to other
subconscious
minds

Levels of the
superconscious
mind

Model of the mind based on Edgar Cayce's readings

to the superconscious is attained, perhaps paradoxically, via the subconscious. This two-dimensional 'map' of consciousness is expounded by the school of thought that has grown up around the readings of Edgar Cayce.[158] The idea that in the spectrum of consciousness subconscious processes merge into superconscious states of awareness is not as strange as it may first sound. At a subconscious level of awareness we can gain access to the subconscious minds of others (TELEPATHY), so at that level our personal boundaries are already becoming blurred. Whilst we still have some individual identity at the superconscious level (in the form of our HIGHER SELF) we can also be much more aware of unity with something bigger than ourselves, a kind of transcendence or COSMIC CONSCIOUSNESS.

SUBJECTIVE MIND The unrestricted, supernormal powers of the SUBCONSCIOUS MIND and of Myers's SUBLIMINAL SELF, Thomas Jay Hudson attributed to the dormant subjective mind.[86] He believed it registered every single impression of an individual's life and was capable of receiving telepathic impressions. It was also responsible for constructing the delusory scenarios in which people apparently communicated with their dead friends. Although Hudson believed (like Myers) that the subjective mind survived death, he insisted that there was no possibility of communication between the living and the dead.

SUBLIMINAL SELF F.W.H. Myers (1834—1901) saw normal CONSCIOUSNESS as only a fraction of the real EGO. The subliminal self was an unconscious aspect of ourselves which was able to perceive sensations, emotions and thoughts 'beneath the threshold' (Latin: *sub limine*) of conscious awareness. Myers believed that the subliminal self could work in co-operation with normal consciousness to produce the mode of thinking and creativity which we associate with genius, but few were able to achieve this conscious amalgamation of two facets of the self. In most respects the subliminal self was what others have called the SUBCONSCIOUS MIND. It is usually hidden, but in the TRANCE state Myers thought it came to the fore, allowing such phenomena as AUTOMATIC WRITING. Myers had a profound effect on PSYCHICAL RESEARCH by attributing most psychic phenomena to the subliminal self rather than to disembodied spirits. But at the same time he believed that since such phenomena were evidence of the existence of a spiritual component within an individual, the probability of the survival of the spirit consequently increased. The subliminal self, like Hudson's SUBJECTIVE MIND, was an aspect of consciousness which survived death. Unlike Hudson, Myers believed that some instances of psychic phenomena might be attributable to deceased spirits, even if they were only a very small minority.[135]

Many believe that Myers himself communicated with MEDIUMS after his death. It is claimed that he set up the first case of CROSS-CORRESPONDENCES, which no one had apparently thought of until they actually happened. All who knew Myers agreed that the series of fragmentary and apparently disconnected communications, which eventually formed a coherent, albeit cryptic whole, were typical of the kind of thing that Myers might devise. Thirty years after his death the medium Geraldine Cummins received further communications purporting to come from Myers, in which he described progress through seven after-death states.[38]

SUBTLE BODY The 'subtle body' is rather an ambiguous term sometimes applied to the astral body, especially during ASTRAL TRAVEL, sometimes to the etheric body, especially when considering the AURA which can be observed by SENSITIVES, and sometimes to other non-physical BODIES. However, it is misleading to refer to the etheric body as the subtle body. The etheric body is the vital principle behind the physical body, visible to some as the aura, and it dissolves a few days after the death of the physical organism.

In Vedantic theory there are three bodies: the gross body (the physical organism), the subtle body and the causal body. The subtle body is mental and may be synonymous with the mind, but it is more than the intellect, being the seat of the emotions and registering both moral and spiritual attitudes and carrying them over from one incarnation to another. It is known in Vedanta as the *linga sharira*. The Theosophist, Annie Besant, referred to the *linga sharira* as the 'astral double', 'the ethereal counterpart of the gross body of man'. It is considered to be material rather than spiritual, in the same way that thoughts, emotions and desires are energies which exist independently of consciousness. (It is worth noting that the Jains consider KARMA to be a physical substance consisting of very fine, imperceptible material particles.) So the subtle body has shape and size in space; it changes over time, is finite, and is not conscious of itself. It is a structure of mental dispositions, a psychic organism, but lacking in self-consciousness.

SUBUD The *Subud* was a movement which grew up around a SUFI mystic, Mohammed Subuh, when he was invited to Europe by J.G. Bennett and others. The name is derived acronymically from three Sanskrit words *susila* (right living), *budhi* (intuitional wisdom) and *dharma* (duty according to divine law). Subuh was born in Java in 1901 and as a young man he had a mystical experience in which a ball of light appeared to pass through the crown of his head into his body. After this experience Subuh was aware of his own spiritual power and able to pass this awareness on to others simply by touching them when they were in a state of deep relaxation. Bennett maintained that this process of 'opening up', known as *latihan* or divine grace, was an effective way of opening up the higher CHAKRAS. *Latihan* is a kind of ENLIGHTENMENT which comes in a flash, and returning to the state two or three times a week encourages the development of the soul. It may be accompanied by mystical experiences, the development of PSYCHIC faculties and powers of HEALING.

This 'opening up' has been experienced in many other forms of mystical teaching and even by people who are meditating without following any formulated doctrine. In YOGA divine energy is received through the 'Hole of BRAHMAN' in the top of the head, as a counterpart to the process of KUNDALINI. In both the East and the West this is sometimes seen as DEW.

SUCCUBUS A succubus was thought to be a female DEMON which materialized for the purposes of sexual intercourse with a man during sleep. It was the female equivalent of an INCUBUS. It is easy to imagine how some people might have been said to have been fathered by an incubus, just as a few heroic figures in the past claimed to have been fathered by gods. It is slightly more surprising to note the legends that the mothers of Alexander the Great and the eleventh-century Robert, Duke of Normandy were succubi.

Having apparently generated his own succubus, the author Stan Gooch has built a theory in which he claims that the mind, more specifically the cerebellum, creates the whole experience. He sees the cerebellum as 'the seat of an alternative consciousness', the origin of all that is described as coming from the unconscious, and the creator of a wide range of phenomena from DISCARNATE entities to STIGMATA. His conclusion is that, 'Incubi, succubi, demons and POLTERGEISTS are not, after all, visitations from another world. No less amazingly, they seem to be visitations from another brain; we are haunted, it seems, by aspects of ourselves.'[64]

SUFISM Within two centuries of Mohammed's death, Islam was seen by some to have become too strongly focused on outward observance. Various Moslem poets and philosophers tried to restore the mystical nature of their religion, and an ascetic movement arose whose devotees habitually wore garments of white wool. *Suf* is Arabic for 'wool' and these Moslem mystics became known as Sufis.

There are both Sunni and Shiah Sufis. Like mystic sects of other religions Sufis see divinity in the whole of creation. They teach direct communion between God and humanity and aim at ultimate union with God. Sufis acknowledge that there is truth in all religions, and some believe in REINCARNATION. Sufism has much in common with YOGA, particularly in its devotional exercises and the overriding principle of non-attachment. Sometimes more emphasis seems to be laid on developing PSYCHIC powers. FAKIRS and DERVISHES are members of Sufi sects: both words originally mean 'poor' (*faqir* is Arabic, *darvish* is Persian) in the sense of 'poor in spirit' — reducing dependency on the emotions and living a devotional life of contemplation.

SUGGESTION The term 'suggestion' was introduced by A.A. Liébeault (1823—1904), a physician who practised in Nancy and opposed the views on HYPNOSIS of Charcot at the Salpêtrière School in Paris. Whilst Charcot pursued the search for a physical explanation of hypnotism, Liébeault maintained that ideas were crucial. He believed that it was ideas that the hypnotized mind accepted and responded to.

It is perhaps surprising that in an age when so much money is spent by business on advertising on the basic assumption that suggestion is effective, it is an area of psychology about which little is known. There is no entry for 'suggestion' in *The Oxford Companion to the Mind*.[70] It is one of those unquantifiable phenomena which orthodox science seems to prefer to ignore. It is a function of the SUBCONSCIOUS MIND which is demonstrated not only in our susceptibility to advertising, but in the placebo effect, 'affirmations' and SELF-HYPNOSIS as well as hypnosis. Post-hypnotic suggestion affects a subject's behaviour even after the return to normal consciousness: a person can be instructed to perform some meaningless task after a certain period of time has elapsed and the task is performed on time for no obvious reason.

SUMMERLAND When DISCARNATE communicators described their own personal HEAVEN to early spiritualists, it seemed so idyllic that it was called Summerland. The name was first coined by Andrew Jackson Davis (1826—1910), also known as the Poughkeepsie Seer, who was the uneducated son of a drunkard shoemaker, an inspirational speaker and writer, also reputed to have predicted the coming of Spiritualism.

Spiritualists equate their Summerland with the PARADISE referred to by Jesus on the cross: 'And Jesus said unto him, verily I say unto thee, today shalt thou be with me in paradise.' (Luke 23, 43.). The spirit communicators who describe Summerland, as Dion Fortune says, 'have little of value to tell the average well-educated man'.[54] Far from being an eternal paradise, Summerland is simply a subjective creation on the ASTRAL PLANE, part of the Hindu MAYA, a 'world of similarities' as the SUFIS call it, the *kamaloca* described in the Tibetan BOOK OF THE DEAD. The communicator 'Myers' (supposedly the deceased F.W.H. Myers) identified it as the 'Plane of Illusion'.[38] When we cease to be quite so engrossed in ourselves in the astral state, we may start communicating telepathically with others. Some may reach this stage almost immediately on passing over. We may then jointly construct communal dreamworlds with individuals with whom we have a special rapport, common beliefs, attitudes and interests. The longer one needs to spend at this level the more likely it is that one will eventually reincarnate. Sooner or later we discover an urge to move on, to prepare for a new incarnation and gravitate back to earth.

Judging by communications received through MEDIUMS, children who die young seem to experience the astral world of Summerland in a slightly different way from adults, continuing to some extent the learning and maturing process that they started while in the body, under the guidance of those who choose to serve by remaining longer at that level or returning to it. The astral world is probably a blend of objective and subjective existence, since all can be aware of each other at that level, as well as creating their own images of each other. Passage to the next stage of growth and the death of the astral body (the 'second death') comes with the recognition that one's experiences have been illusory, the product of the desires and emotions that one has held on to since the death of the body. With the purging of these emotions the soul can progress to a more mental level of awareness.

SUPER-ESP HYPOTHESIS Communications from DISCARNATE SPIRITS give intimate if often rather trivial details about the earthly lives of the deceased and of the families and friends they have left behind. Some people are prepared to accept the accuracy of such information in so far as it relates to the living, but nevertheless deny that this is evidence of survival and do not believe that the provenance of the communications is so-called discarnate entities as claimed. They cite the facility which the SUBCONSCIOUS MIND has for invention and dramatization, as shown under HYPNOSIS or in cases of MULTIPLE PERSONALITY, as a possible mechanism which the MEDIUM employs unconsciously. Much of the factual information may be gleaned by TELEPATHY, supported by an innate ability to interpret the slightest reaction of the sitter. (See IDEODYNAMICS.) When information is supplied of which the sitter is totally ignorant at the time of the sitting, the anti-survivalists invoke a virtually unlimited power of ESP which they attribute to the medium. This is the super-ESP hypothesis. Although some mediums do claim to be able to read the AKASHIC RECORD when it is appropriate, this super-ESP ability would have to be attributed to a far greater number than actually claim it, and many find it easier to accept that the minds of the deceased are still active and able to link with the medium. DROP-IN COMMUNICATORS are particularly difficult to explain by the super-ESP hypothesis, since there seems to be no logical reason why the medium should pick up information for a recently bereaved widow or widower who once traced is generally extremely sceptical and even antagonistic to the idea that the deceased is still 'around'.

SUPERCONSCIOUS MIND The superconscious or higher unconscious is a region of the UNCONSCIOUS MIND which has been largely ignored by orthodox psychology. Freud's concept of the super-ego as the agency which prolongs the socializing influence of parents by instilling conscience and a sense of shame and guilt is a shrivelled-up judgmental embodiment of one small part of the superconscious. 'From this region we receive our higher intuitions and inspirations — artistic, philosophical or scientific, ethical "imperatives" and urges to humanitarian and heroic action. It is the source of the higher feelings, such as altruistic love; of genius and of the states of contemplation, illumination and ECSTASY. In this realm are latent the higher psychic functions and spiritual energies.'[3] This is the abode of the

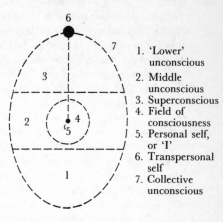

1. 'Lower' unconscious
2. Middle unconscious
3. Superconscious
4. Field of consciousness
5. Personal self, or 'I'
6. Transpersonal self
7. Collective unconscious

Assagioli's map of the psyche

333

real SELF, the HIGHER SELF, the noumenal self, as opposed to the empirical ego or PERSONALITY which is its projection and which drifts along with the ceaseless flow of conscious mind-chatter.

In psychosynthesis the existence of a spiritual self and a superconscious are taken as fact: 'All the superior manifestations of the human psyche, such as creative imagination, intuition, aspiration, genius, are facts which are as real and as important as are the conditioned reflexes, and therefore are susceptible to research and treatment just as scientifically as conditioned reflexes.' Certain techniques in psychosynthesis have as their aim 'the activation of superconscious energies and the arousing of latent potentialities.'[3]

Feeling the effects of the superconscious in one's life does not necessarily mean that one is conscious of the self. Direct awareness of the self may be called spiritual consciousness, 'superconsciousness' or COSMIC CONSCIOUSNESS. But inspiration of many kinds may come without this and without affecting the conscious ego very much at all. Assagioli cites as a supreme example of this the genius of Mozart. There is, however, another class of geniuses 'who have an all-round expansive self-realization ... who have achieved a more or less permanent self-realization with many ways of expression, who are adjusted and who have achieved an inner and outer equilibrium.' Assagioli cites Pythagoras, Plato, Dante, Leonardo and Einstein as examples of such genius. In them the conscious self is more closely aligned with the true self, and they seem to allow greater expression of superconscious energies in all areas of their lives.

The superconscious could also be regarded as a source of much of the inspired writing and speaking that is delivered in trance. Eileen Garrett is reported to believe that her psychic powers are activated by withdrawing consciousness from the outer world and focusing awareness 'in the field of the superconscious — the timeless, spaceless field of the as-yet-unknown'.[214] Wilson describes this as a deep absorption, of a kind that we can experience when concentrating on any activity. Lawrence LeShan also uses the concept of a superconscious mind 'above' everyday awareness to describe what happens in phenomena such as CLAIRVOYANCE.[108]

Although the MIND is usually discussed as if it were an entity in space with spatially conceived areas or regions which can be mapped symbolically, the various subdivisions are not really structural in the sense that the mind might be thought to have an anatomy. It would be more accurate to regard these subdivisions as different functions of CONSCIOUSNESS, different ways of focusing consciousness, different modes of consciousness. The superconscious mode is the one that enables us to perceive without the distractions on the one hand of stimuli from the external world and on the other of psychological eruptions that are symptomatic of our personality. To some extent the superconscious mode is TRANSPERSONAL and transcendent, but the personality's access to it is inevitably individual and much of the content which is thus projected into the personality will also be highly individual whilst at the same time having universal validity.

SUPERNATURAL One thing that both scientists and psychics have in common is an avoidance of the word 'supernatural', since it implies that there are phenomena in which the laws of nature are broken. Those who accept a spiritual dimension to reality accept that there are laws of nature which apply to spiritual forces; physical science is simply as yet unfamiliar with them, but that does not mean that psychic phenomena defy the laws of nature. Scientists who investigate such phenomena refer to them as paranormal, 'beside' or parallel to the natural laws with which we are already familiar, rather than beyond or above them. Their discipline is not the study of the miraculous but PARAPSYCHOLOGY. The supernatural is the domain of the miraculous, with the intervention of supernatural beings.

SURVIVAL Most cultures have never doubted that the SPIRIT which resides in each human being continues to exist after the death of the body. With the development of technology in the eighteenth and nineteenth centuries, the benefits of a scientific attitude in Western society became apparent, and it was perhaps natural that people should want to exercise this materialist attitude further by scrutinizing many commonly held assumptions and testing belief by looking for PROOF. Material values seemed to start to replace spiritual values, as the aims of society were increasingly identified with material progress, and society also became increasingly individualistic. So the concept of survival of death came to acquire a new emphasis, meaning not just the continued existence of spirit, but the continued existence of the individual personality in a relatively comfortable environment. It was at this point that SPIRITUALISM took up the challenge of trying to convince people of survival. The historical period tends to explain the early spiritualists' preoccupations with proving survival in such individualistic and even materialistic terms.

If we consider older traditions of what happens after death, many suggest that the individualized PERSONALITY becomes less important as a SOUL evolves. Ultimately the aim of spiritual EVOLUTION was the loss of self, the *fana* that some SUFIS may experience temporarily in moments of ECSTASY, the non-attachment of YOGA, and the NIRVANA of Buddhists. According to many spiritual teachings there are several stages through which we pass after death. First we enter a kind of dream world where all our experiences are private and self-induced. It is a solipsistic existence in the ASTRAL WORLD. Whatever we have in earthly life been conditioned to expect after death we will now experience; we will produce our own PURGATORY, our own JUDGMENT at the hands of deities we conjure up for ourselves, our own HEAVEN or SUMMERLAND and even our own HELL, but we will accept all this as if it were external to ourselves, rather than a projection from our own minds. It is because existence is so subjective at this stage that the communications supposedly coming from those recently deceased are not only inconsistent and rather fanciful but also relatively insignificant, except inasmuch as they may offer comfort to the bereaved.

Our understanding of the physical world has been built up as an expression of what we see happening around us in terms of physical laws, and we expect the visible universe to obey these laws. But the laws that govern the next world, the state in which we find ourselves after death, if they bear any relation to any of the laws that we have discovered about life in the physical world, will resemble the laws of psychology more than the laws of physics. It is reasonable to assume that our minds without bodies will behave at least initially not very differently from the way they did with bodies. There is unlikely to be any drastic change of character. The realization that 'life goes on' may have some effect, but recognizable personality traits are likely to remain. This view is supported by communications through MEDIUMS. Sitters are on the one hand overjoyed to recognize deceased relatives as described by mediums, even identifying remarks they make as typical of them, but on the other hand there is often a certain amount of dismay that their tendencies to meddle, moan or give bad advice have not been instantaneously cured by passing over. Even this can be regarded as evidence of survival, since if the medium were picking up information telepathically from the sitter, it would be contaminated by the sitter's desires, but the fact is that what is given often comes as a great surprise to the sitter rather than as wish-fulfilment.

What is the evidence for survival from a scientific point of view? Most spirit communications are discounted by IDEODYNAMICS and TELEPATHY. DROP-IN COMMUNICATIONS are explained by the so-called SUPER-ESP HYPOTHESIS. Encounters with the deceased in DREAMS are considered to be memories (CRYPTOMNESIA) or perhaps ESP (when a new will is found, as in the Chaffin case), and such accounts are often affected by retrospective reporting. What individuals accept as evidence of survival is generally regarded as inadequate for science. Its value is subjective. Even CROSS-CORRESPONDENCES are seen by orthodox scientists as being open to fraud, conscious or unconscious, selective reporting and retrospective colouring. But the subjective value of the so-called evidence may acquire a certain objective status when one realizes how many intelligent people have themselves been convinced and often quite reluctantly by such evidence. Ultimately it remains a matter of personal disposition whether one considers that being persuaded by the evidence for survival represents merely a deep inner need to deny the possibility of extinction, or an unconscious knowledge of immortality.

SYMBOLISM Symbolism is as much a means of acquiring knowledge as is logical reasoning. Symbols are international as language cannot be, cross-cultural even though imbued with particular traditions, and relatively timeless. Although symbols may be rooted in well-established archetypes, they are also dynamic, changing as the reality they express changes, and a symbol can express so much more than mere words, which seem limiting in comparison to the inclusive and expansive nature of symbols. Symbols arise out of a much deeper, more fundamental level of human consciousness than words. Symbolism is the language of dreams, where even words often have symbolic rather than literal meaning. DREAMS are just one example of the many ways in which the UNCONSCIOUS communicates with the conscious MIND. All aspects of the unconscious, whether SUBCONSCIOUS or SUPERCONSCIOUS, use symbols to communicate with the conscious mind, and the conscious mind communicates with the external world via the symbols of religion, ritual, and MAGIC. Psychically acquired information such as CLAIRVOYANCE is often presented to the conscious mind in symbolic terms and the expertise of the clairvoyant may well be tested in finding the appropriate interpretation.

Some symbols arise spontaneously through meditation or when people are in slightly altered states of consciousness in the same way that archetypes can be evoked by specific techniques. Many aspects of the SUBTLE BODY, the CHAKRAS and their colours, the mysticism of Light, the heavenly DEW, can be understood and appreciated symbolically, regardless of whether one attaches literal significance to them. Some of the most powerful and most universal symbols are the SERPENT, the tree, the lotus, the rose, the cross, and various other diagrammatic designs and numbers.

The tree appears as the Tree of Knowledge, as the TREE OF LIFE in KABBALISM, as the cosmic tree or world axis, like the World-Ash in Nordic mythology, uniting heaven, earth and water. The lotus or water-lily also unites matter and spirit. Although the flower of the water-lily grows in the air, the stem is in water and the root is in the mud below the water; the flower thus represents spiritual order arising out of chaos. As such the lotus is an important symbol in the religions of many people ranging from ancient Egyptians to Hindus and Buddhists. Osiris floated on a lotus after his birth, BRAHMA is depicted as being born on a lotus, and Gautama, the BUDDHA is often shown seated on a lotus. The chakras are often depicted as lotus flowers. The flower itself can also be regarded as a MANDALA representing the physical universe.

In the West the rose has been more common than the lotus. It grew from the blood of Venus when she was wounded by Cupid's dart. In Christian tradition the Virgin Mary is called the Rose of Heaven, and the wounds of Christ are often represented by five roses on a bush. There is a Moslem legend that when Mohammed rode to heaven the sweat from his brow fell to the earth and produced white roses. The rose is often a symbol of divine perfection but is also associated with the sensual and the passionate. It represents a variety of complementary pairs: life and death, time and eternity, the abundance of fertility and the purity of virginity. The added associations of thorns and the different colours of the flowers make for a very complex symbology. Like the lotus the rose is used to represent the chakras and as a mandala. As such it can, like a lotus or a candle flame, be a focus of tranquility for the purposes of MEDITATION.

The rose garden is often a symbol for paradise. Gardens in general represent another dimension, away from the ephemeral concerns of the everyday world. In meditation we can enter our own inner landscape in the shape of a garden, where we explore another world of symbolic significance, representing psychological and spiritual truth.

There are many geometric designs with symbolic significance. The power of YIN and YANG forces in the universe are represented by the PA-KWA disc. The Pythagoreans built up a system of numerology and proportions related to music, and Plato attached further significance to the Perfect Solids, continued in the Middle Ages in ALCHEMY. But the most universal symbol of an inanimate or abstract nature is the cross in its various forms. The cross is a symbol for the cosmos, the universe of matter, the descent of spirit into matter. As the Egyptian *ankh* it represents life and immortality, the mysteries of life and knowledge, just as the Christian cross stands for the RESURRECTION and eternal life. The cross within a circle can represent the wheel of change, the wheel of fortune, or the WHEEL OF REBIRTH.

SYMPATHETIC MAGIC Sticking pins in a wax doll or effigy is the most common picture people have of sympathetic magic, a process by which desired effects are achieved by symbolic acts, e.g. inflicting harm on an image of a person will cause that person to suffer the same effects. The Hunas would say that the effigy and the person were connected by MANA. The RAPPORT between the two can be increased by something from the subject's body (blood, hair, nail-clippings) or even something from their possession. It is worth noting that this is how many psychics and mediums work in PROXY SITTINGS, and a sample or 'witness' is also used in PENDULUM DOWSING and RADIONICS. PSYCHOMETRY could be regarded as sympathetic magic in reverse: instead of mental processes producing physical effects at a distance, physical effects are somehow perceived mentally at a distance in time. It is no surprise to note that sympathetic magic works best when the victim is aware that the practitioner is operating. The effect can then be put down to SUGGESTION. But suggestion is thought to work via the subject's SUBCONSCIOUS, which must also be the channel for HYPNOSIS and TELEPATHY. So if sympathetic magic is less common and less effective in modern civilized society, it may be as much a result of the practitioner's lack of belief as a consequence of the victim's imperviousness to suggestion.

SYNCHRONICITY Literally: 'together time', synchronicity is another name for the phenomenon of meaningful coincidences with the thinly disguised implication that it also explains them, or perhaps explains that they need no explanation. The idea of 'a synchronistic connective principle' was first proposed in 1930 by C.G. Jung, who subtitled his book on synchronicity 'An Acausal Connecting Principle'.[96] This has been described by Colin Wilson as 'a completely meaningless term meaning a cause that is not a cause', but it can be seen as a law rather than a cause. Just as the law of gravity does not *cause* bodies to be attracted to each other but describes what happens, so the principle of synchronicity is also a description of what seems to happen.

Jung thought he recognized a type of coincidence which was not just the consequence of random events. He was influenced in this by his familiarity with the I CHING, in which 'two Chinese sages, King Wen and the Duke of Chou, in the twelfth century before our era, basing themselves on the hypothesis of the unity of nature, sought to explain the simultaneous occurrence of a psychic state with a physical process as *an equivalence of meaning*.'[96] At any given moment the apparently chance results of tossing coins seem to reflect the psychological situation. The one does not cause the other; they are both simply aspects of a much greater situation. At certain levels of the unconscious, Jung suggested, we are capable of grasping this greater situation which transcends space, time and causality. This is another way of accounting for (or describing) most of PARAPSYCHOLOGY, as well as astrology, and the Hermetic principle of 'As above, so below'.

Despite the 'acausal' label, the notion of synchronicity also points to the possibility that the mind might interact with the rest of the UNIVERSE and somehow affect events. If the links are already there in the interrelated wholeness of the universe, they can probably be used as channels to effect changes. Modern physicists readily admit this, recognizing that it is impossible to exclude the effect of the observer from experiments. And events are likely to be affected as much by expectantly wanting something to happen as by the fearful preoccupation that something might happen. 'So it seems that the ultimate implication of Jung's theory — although it is one that he himself took care never to state — is that it should be possible for us to influence events by our mental attitudes: that people whose attitude is negative "attract" bad luck, while those whose attitude is positive attract "SERENDIPITY".'[214]

TABLE-TURNING/TABLE-LIFTING The lifting of a table in a SEANCE without any visible agency was one of the most widespread psychic phenomena in the early days of SPIRITUALISM. Whilst LEVITATION of the human body was always one of the rarest achievements, it seemed relatively easy for a group of sitters even without a medium to cause a table to tilt and eventually rise. The process resembles the movement of an upturned glass on a OUIJA BOARD, despite the difference in weight and defiance of gravity: in that case each sitter rests a finger on the glass, and in the case of table-turning everyone rests their hands on top of the table. Physical contact seems to help, as does relative darkness.

Assuming there was no fraud, the rational explanation was that involuntary unconscious muscular action was responsible, combined with the added strength that can be induced by slight hypnotic TRANCE. The light-trance state could easily be induced by the usually long expectant wait in subdued lighting. Sometimes, however, the table was reported to have risen so high that the 'sitters', now standing, had difficulty in keeping their hands on it. It seems likely therefore that PSYCHOKINESIS of some kind was operating. Mesmerists claimed that odyllic force (OD) was being used. If this was so it might have been significant that the table-tops had once been trees and were presumably molecularly suited to being reservoirs for such 'vital' energy.

Messages were sometimes received by repeatedly reciting the alphabet and noting at which letters the table tilted. Table tilting of this kind often led to table RAPPING and messages were obtained following the same routine, noting the letters with which the knocks coincided. These effects were facilitated by the presence of a MEDIUM, and people usually became more interested in the presumed spirits held responsible for the effects and what they had to say than in investigating the possibility that they themselves had psychokinetic powers.

F.W.H. Myers was reasonably convinced that at least in cases where physical contact was maintained between the sitters and the table, the SUBLIMINAL SELF was the most likely agency. As for cases when movement occurred independently, he wrote, 'If a table moves when no one is touching it, this is not obviously more likely to have been effected by my deceased grandfather than by myself. We cannot tell how I could move it; but then we cannot tell how he could move it either.'

TALISMAN A talisman is popularly called a good-luck charm, but good-luck charms such as the St Christophers favoured by travellers are mass-produced nowadays, whereas a talisman is specially made for a particular purpose and imbued with the appropriate charge or force. It is the MAGICIAN's belief that the power to ward off certain influences or attract others can reside in an inanimate object. Although magical traditions may dictate specific materials for the making of particular talismans, the material is not as important as the energy with which they are endowed by concentration, meditation or ritual. The belief that objects can be invested with spiritual energy forms part of all animist religions. It was, for example, part of the ancient Egyptians' belief system. The Egyptian hieroglyph for a sculptor was 'he who keeps alive', demonstrating their belief that a person's KA could reside in sculptures of their human form.

It has been suggested that the effectiveness of talismans might be that they act as reminders for the bearer, helping to increase confidence or will-power by means of SUGGESTION in the manner of an 'affirmation'. With the appropriate belief-system, possession of a talisman increases a person's sense of security, and one is consequently less accident-prone. In one sense this is 'mind over matter', and the talisman can be seen to work regardless of whether it has any powers of its own.

On the other hand, crystals are increasingly being seen today as containing energies which can affect the human body, just as copper amulets have long been used to ease rheumatism. DOWSING and PSYCHOMETRY seem to indicate that there may be a psychic information channel between objects and the human mind. Talismans as bearers of energy (or information) could fit into this pattern: they may communicate their nature or purpose to the SUBCONSCIOUS MIND in the way that underground materials betray their presence to the dowser. The individual then acts accordingly by means of suggestion. In this way talismans could work in the same way as SPELLS, being used either positively or for the purposes of sorcery in BLACK MAGIC.

Talismans can also be created as THOUGHT-FORMS. To protect

himself from snakes a SHAMAN creates a thought-form or ELEMENTAL talisman in the shape of a golden snake resembling the one he wants to keep at arm's length. Jung described how a man dreamed that a woman gave him a ring, saying, 'Hold on to it, and don't lose it'. The next day he had to make a speech about which he was extremely nervous. He held the dream image in his mind, concentrated on the ring in his hand, and delivered a speech that exceeded all expectations.

TAO/TAOISM Tao (often pronounced like 'dhow' rather than with an initial 't') means 'the way' or 'the path'. It is the way the UNIVERSE works, the course of life, the order in life, and the relation of life to eternal truth. The Tao is Absolute; it is the Void, ultimate Emptiness. The Tao is central to Taoists, but the notion of 'the way' is also an important part of Buddhist and Confucian philosophy. Chinese Christians have equated the Tao with the LOGOS.

The philosophy of the Tao is presented in the *Tao Te Ching* and in the I CHING in which the dynamic polarities of YIN and YANG are seen to interact throughout the universe. Wisdom is knowing how to conform to the Tao and live in harmony with it by observing and accepting the forces at work in the universe and acting intuitively and spontaneously in accordance with them. The way to achieve this is not by intellectualizing and defining or refining the concept of the Tao, but by living in simplicity and tranquillity.

The mystical approach inherent in Taoism is demonstrated by the almost paradoxical content of some of its aphoristic teachings (taken from the *Tao Te Ching*, written in the sixth century BC).

By non-action everything can be done.

Without stirring abroad
One can know the whole world;
Without looking out of the window
One can see the way of heaven.
The further one goes,
The less one knows.

Be humble and you will remain entire
Be bent and you will remain straight
Be vacant and you will remain full
Be old and you will remain new.

He who knows does not speak.
He who speaks does not know.

He does not show himself; therefore he is luminous.
He does not define himself; therefore he is distinct.
He does not assert himself; therefore he succeeds.
He does not boast of his work; therefore it endures
  for long.
It is precisely because he does not compete that the
  world cannot compete with him.

TAROT The origin of the Tarot cards is uncertain. One popular notion is that they originated in Egypt (as people also thought gypsies did). This idea grew current after Napoleon's military campaigns in Egypt, when many Egyptian relics and ruins were brought to light, such as the temples at Luxor and Karnak, but cards had been in use in Europe since the fourteenth century. Although containing elements of Egyptian and Persian religion, cards from renaissance Italy suggest a more direct line with European mystery schools: the Mantegna pack of about 1465, although divided up differently from the way we now accept as usual, used the familiar symbolism for individual cards and reflected the philosophy and cosmology of the PLATONIST schools.

Today's pack consists of seventy-eight cards in all. There are four suits of fourteen cards each (four of which are court cards — king, queen, knight and knave), also called the minor arcana, and twenty-two cards of the major arcana. The major arcana represent many powerful archetypes and sequentially they depict the individual's search for ENLIGHTENMENT, starting and ending with the unnumbered card known as The Fool. Those intending to work with the Tarot are advised to meditate at length on each of these major arcana, entering into the scene shown in the design and exploring the symbolic world depicted there as another level of reality.

When the Tarot is used for divination the assumption may be that some sort of SYNCHRONICITY is in operation, as when one consults the I CHING. On the other hand, dwelling on the archetypal symbolism of the cards can open up innate CLAIRVOYANT powers and spark off a more intuitive faculty, without direct reference to what this or that card might mean in concrete terms. Most people who express some belief in the practice of Tarot-reading would probably support a combination of both views.

TELEKINESIS 'Telekinesis' is a less common term for PSYCHO-KINESIS often abbreviated to PK, although its implications tended to be slightly different because of its use in the context of alleged spirit activity. It was originally coined by the French researcher Charles Richet (1850–1935). The word was used to denote 'alleged supernormal movements of objects, not due to any known force'[135] and was applied to all unexplained movements in SEANCES, such as TABLE-TURNING, LEVITATION, and APPORTS. When PSYCHICAL RESEARCH seemed too 'contaminated' with spiritual ideas for modern materialist scientists, the field of study relating to PARANORMAL phenomena came to be called PARAPSYCHOLOGY, and 'telekinesis' was replaced by psychokinesis.

TELEPATHY The word 'telepathy' was invented by the researcher F.W.H. Myers in 1882. He defined it as 'The communication of impressions of any kind from one mind to another, independently of the recognized channels of sense.'[135] It was usually applied to cases of thought transference. Myers also coined 'telesthesia' for a wider ability to perceive the sensations and emotions of another at a distance through some kind of rapport, for example feeling a pain at the moment when a close relative suffered a comparable injury.

There is an almost universal belief that minds can communicate with each other independently of the usual five senses. In Bali it is natural if you are unable to contact a person physically that you 'call him on the wind'; sending such telepathic messages is an everyday occurrence to the Balinese. Most people in the West have anecdotal examples, which ever sceptical orthodox scientists put down to coincidence, saying that we remember the cases where our chance thoughts matched someone else's, whilst forgetting thousands of instances where there was no such match. But the founder of modern scientific psychology, Freud, was convinced that telepathy existed. Close colleagues persuaded him that trying to gain acceptance for telepathy would make gaining acceptance for psychoanalysis even more difficult, but he is reported to have said that if he had his life over again he would devote it to research into telepathy and similar phenomena.

Experimenters have often noticed telepathic effects arising in experiments which were not designed to evoke telepathy at all. For example, when hypnotized subjects were told to imagine a UFO abduction they described what was in the minds of the experimenters. Some of the first experimental demonstrations of telepathy were made as demonstrations of HYPNOSIS. In England in the 1860s a schoolmaster, Alfred Russel Wallace (1823–1913), who was later to become famous as a friend and colleague of Charles Darwin, found that some of his pupils when placed under hypnosis could identify the taste of things in the hypnotist's mouth, a phenomenon known as COMMUNITY OF SENSATION. In France in 1885 a Dr Gibert sent his patient, Léonie, into a hypnotic trance simply by thinking of her. They were at opposite ends of the town of Le Havre at the time. On other occasions she was aware that the doctor was trying to hypnotize her at a distance, but she refused to co-operate. These incidents were witnessed by the French psychologist Pierre Janet. A few years later, in the 1890s, Dr Paul Joire also caused hypnotized subjects to follow his telepathic instructions: they obeyed his mental commands. So hypnosis and telepathy appear to facilitate each other.

It may be difficult for many people to accept but the fact that subjects can be put into hypnotic TRANCE telepathically leads fairly logically to the ideas of magic SPELLS and sorcery. The fact that hypnosis facilitates telepathy could have serious implications for REGRESSION, in which a person is hypnotized with the purpose of recalling past incarnations. How can one guarantee that the subject is not influenced by the hypnotist's thoughts and expectations when experiencing a 'past life', especially if the hypnotist is acknowledged to be PSYCHIC and possibly aware of the subject's supposed past lives?

In the 1920s a Russian scientist at the University of Leningrad, Professor L.L. Vasiliev (1891–1966), carried out further experiments in what he called 'distant influence'. In these experiments a subject was sent into a hypnotic trance and brought to normal awareness simply by the mental command of the hypnotist acting at a distance. The experiments were repeated successfully and without reducing either the speed or effectiveness with which the instructions were carried out at distances of up to 1700 kilometres (between Leningrad and Sebastopol). These telepathic instructions were equally effective with screens of iron and lead placed around the subject, disproving the hypothesis (or at least making it highly improbable) that telepathy made use of electromagnetic fields.

The image sometimes conjured up by the words 'thought transference' is that of ideas contained in one mind leaping across space to enter into another mind. But where are those minds? Our internal picture of reality is conceived in such spatial terms that we tend to overlook the fact that mind – if it exists at all – exists outside space, independent of the three-dimensional world. One cannot point and say 'My mind is here, and your mind is there'. So when minds communicate with each other independently of the physical senses, the process is not one by which ideas are beamed out from one mind, projected across space and picked up by another mind, even though the agent in telepathic experiments is often referred to as a 'transmitter'. Mind is nowhere and everywhere. The question could well be put in reverse: not 'how does telepathy work?' but 'how have minds isolated themselves so successfully against automatic information-sharing?' As J.W. Dunne wrote, 'Telepathy, like PRECOGNITION, is a four-dimensional effect, and it occurs between four-dimensional observers.'[48]

Following the publication of J.B. Rhine's *Extra-Sensory Perception* in 1934, a British researcher and mathematics lecturer at London University, S.G. Soal (1890–1975), tried unsuccessfully to repeat Rhine's experiments with ZENER CARDS. The scores achieved by his subjects were no better than chance. But in 1939 Whately Carington discovered the DISPLACEMENT EFFECT. Card-guessing experiments have shown that the percipient sometimes guesses the sequence of cards turned over by the transmitter either with a time-lag, a card or two behind what the transmitter is concentrating on at that moment, or in advance, a card or two before the transmitter has even seen the card. This displacement shows that where telepathy is concerned there is no cause-and-effect as we normally understand it: telepathic awareness may occur paradoxically a few seconds before its cause. Carington brought this to Soal's attention and urged him to take another look at his records. Taking the displacement effect into account, Soal discovered that the results achieved by two subjects, Gloria Stewart and Basil Shackleton, had demonstrated definite ability and they were later recalled for further tests. Shackleton often consistently missed the present target card guessing the next card instead, and in other tests where the agent 'transmitted' at a faster rate, he guessed correctly *two* cards ahead.[181]

As with many statistical results from experiments in PARA-PSYCHOLOGY, other scientists have hotly disputed their validity, suggesting selective recording or outright manipulation by Soal. But in this particular case it seems very strange that the experimenter should go to the trouble of producing what he deemed to be inconclusive results first, and waiting until someone else suggested a way in which evidence of telepathy might be concealed in them. Even if fraud were involved in an unknown proportion of tests in parapsychological research, the question remains, why on earth should the researchers do it? The opprobium in which they have been held by the vast majority of mainstream scientists can hardly be seen as an inducement to falsify the evidence.

In all Soal's tests there was no predetermined sequence of cards: they were randomly selected while the test was proceeding. As they were tests for telepathy there was always an agent as 'transmitter'. In tests for CLAIRVOYANCE (i.e. ESP without the involvement of another mind) Shackleton's results proved to be no better than chance. It is interesting to note that even telepathic precognition does not amount to the same thing as clairvoyance. This also reminds us of the danger that much of what clairvoyants tell their clients might be obtained telepathically if it reflects hopes and fears that are already present in the client's mind. And following a sitting, might the client even transmit information retrospectively to the clairvoyant?

In the 1970s at the Stanford Research Institute in California, Russell Targ and Harold Puthoff developed their REMOTE VIEWING experiments. When the viewers in these experiments were successful, they reported that their state was 'relaxed, attentive and meditative'. This seems to involve quietening the over-active left hemisphere of the BRAIN and allowing the right hemisphere to register intuitive impressions. It is interesting to note that viewers' drawings were on the whole more accurate than their verbal descriptions, which again suggests a deeper involvement of the right hemisphere.

It has often been suggested that telepathy operates below the normal level of awareness. 'Perhaps the most discouraging and perplexing aspect of the extra-sensory process is its unconscious nature. The fruits of the faculty are garnered into consciousness, but the undergrowth of supporting stems is matured in darkness and seemingly inaccessible to introspection.'[181] But is this so surprising? Is the way we recognize a friend's face any more conscious a process? Perhaps the crucial point is that the left hemisphere always finds it difficult to verbalize the methods employed by the right hemisphere.

Whether the right hemisphere is mainly responsible, or the cerebellum as Stan Gooch has suggested, the phenomenon seems to involve an aspect of consciousness which for want of a better term Myers called the SUBLIMINAL SELF, and it is more likely to occur when normal consciousness is partially disengaged, as in the HYPNOPOMPIC state, for example. Rosalind Heywood worked as a nurse in a military hospital during the First World War. When patients were unsettled or in pain, she developed the ability to will them to sleep. One night this was recognized by one of the patients who sat up and said 'It's no use trying to think me to sleep again'; a moment later he died.[84] The English philosopher H.H. Price said, 'Telepathy is more like an infection than knowledge.' Lyall Watson agrees and adds 'once infection has taken place, once information has been transferred, its nature and future is governed by the recipient, who controls the course of the disease.'[207] This is linked with his theory of SAMA and XENOGLOSSY.

Watson's 'sama' theory, in which minds somehow overlap, fuse or infect each other, is supported by the discovery by Targ and Puthoff that during laboratory tests for telepathy, both transmitting and receiving subjects somehow manage to synchronize their alpha BRAIN WAVES. This may have something to do with the link between hypnosis and telepathy: on the one hand hypnosis can be induced telepathically, on the other telepathy is facilitated by hypnosis, but perhaps both are facilitated by synchronized brain waves.

Apart from the mechanism itself two other big questions surround the phenomenon of telepathy. First of all, is it new or old, a future development or a prehistoric faculty? Is telepathy just emerging in humanity, or is it a faculty which predates the development of the cerebral cortex and has now become somewhat atrophied? Some researchers claim that certain animals show telepathic ability, which might suggest that in humans the faculty has become atrophied, but it is always difficult to judge other animals' senses as they are often so much more acute than our own. Whatever the case with animals, in humans the ability such as it is seems universal (not restricted to 'psychics') but relatively dormant, and from the evolutionary point of view we just do not know whether it is developing or being replaced by other faculties.

The other big unknown is how did telepathy arise in the first place? At first sight the obvious answer is that it was a way of being made aware of danger. But the ability demonstrated in the remote viewing experiments seems to bestow no biological advantage on the viewers, the distance being so great that no advantage could be had in recognizing the places. Neither was there any emotional reason for the information to be transmitted, which seems to make it unlikely that the possibility of danger might aid the phenomenon. Furthermore, despite the fact that telepathic impressions and the external events perceived by the person 'transmitting' often occur simultaneously, the transfer of information from one mind to another is by no means limited by time. In fact there is no guarantee that reception of an impression is simultaneous with transmission. Telepathy is unaffected by both distance and time. So what would the biological advantage of such an indeterminate faculty be? There seems to be no logical reason why it should have evolved at all in the form we know it.

TELEPLASTY 'Teleplasty' is a term used by José Martinez Romero in his book *Las Caras de Belmez* (The Faces of Belmez). He defined it as 'the objectivation of forms due to an unknown energy'. These forms are marks or impressions rather than full-blown MATERIAL-IZATIONS. Romero's book relates how faces appeared on the floor of a house in a mountain village in Andalusia, Spain. The faces varied in permanence, some remaining in the same form once they had appeared, others changing or being replaced by others, and others appearing only very briefly before disappearing again.[117]

DIRECT WRITING is a kind of teleplasty. The phenomenon also includes cases of 'psychic imprints' in which impressions of hands or faces have been made in clay while a MEDIUM was in TRANCE. A nineteenth-century American medium, Mrs Blanchard, achieved such effects in clay under water, as did the Polish medium Franek Kluski in wax, as if by projecting PSEUDOPODS.

TELEPORTATION The phenomenon of teleportation, also known as translocation, when someone is transported instantaneously across great distances as if by magic, is familiar in classical mythology and fairy-tales. The sudden appearance of objects from nowhere, the phenomenon of APPORTS, is relatively rare. The translocation of people is even rarer, but there have been a few apparently authenticated cases. When it has happened, it appears to have been involuntary and uncontrolled.[53] The phenomenon is not to be confused with BILOCATION in which a DOUBLE appears in another place, while the 'main' body remains where it is. When translocation is a subjective experience on the part of the apparently teleported person it may be indistinguishable from a TIME-SLIP.

TELERGY 'Telergy' is a word coined by F.W.H. Myers denoting the psychokinetic or paranormal influence exerted on the mind, brain or nervous system of another person. It is a form of energy that has been postulated to account for the 'transmission' of thoughts from mind to mind in TELEPATHY. Others have suggested that this force lies at the root of all paranormal phenomena, and that ECTOPLASM is a condensation of it. However, if telergy exists as a force, as a kind of mental energy, it must exist outside three-dimensional space. As minds are not bound by space, thoughts do not need to cross space to pass from one mind to another, and it is more likely that the minds themselves undergo a change of some kind in order to share their information. It is unclear what role the hypothetical force called telergy would play in this and what form it would take.

TELESTHESIA Myers coined the word 'telesthesia' in 1882 to denote the sensing of distant objects or conditions in a wider sense than TELEPATHY. Even more than the word 'telepathy', 'telesthesia' seems to have been replaced in modern usage by 'EXTRA-SENSORY PERCEPTION'. Whilst telepathy refers simply to mental impressions or ideas, telesthesia refers to the extra-sensory perception of physical sensations or emotions. One may suddenly feel a pain and later learn that someone with whom one has a close RAPPORT suffered a comparable injury at just that moment. Such cases of telesthesia are more likely to occur between twins. The apparent importance of personal rapport between the people involved, as well as the generally subjective and unpredictable nature of the phenomenon, makes it virtually impossible to investigate experimentally. Some form of telesthesia could be considered to be at the root of CRISIS APPARITIONS.

THAUMATURGY Thaumaturgy is the working of miracles by a thaumaturge, or magician. See THEURGY and MAGIC.

THEOSIS This is a Greek term meaning 'divinization' — a process of achieving eventual union with God. This form of deification is not to be confused with the Roman custom of deifying their emperors (apotheosis). Christian mystics maintain that restoration of the perfection of humanity and ultimate reunion with God requires the interaction of human nature and divine grace, and most agree that whilst the process must be begun on earth it can only be completed in the next world. Grace is less significant in Eastern religions and in most Hindu and Buddhist teachings all rests on an individual's works while on earth.

THEOSOPHY Literally theosophy means 'divine wisdom'. It can be applied to a number of ESOTERIC religious systems which profess knowledge of the nature of the Divine and its relation to the cosmos, including a detailed cosmology. GNOSTICISM can be regarded as a theosophical religion.

More often the name is applied to a particular religious movement which began in the 1870s. The promulgation of Theosophy had two major aims: to bring science and religion closer together, showing that they are not incompatible, and to demonstrate that all religions are in fact aspects of the same one basic truth.

Membership of the Theosophical Society, founded by Madame Blavatsky and Colonel H.S. Olcott in New York in 1875, is open to adherents of any of the world's faiths and requires simply that one supports the Society in its three objectives:

1. To form a nucleus of the Universal Brotherhood of Humanity, without distinction of race, creed, sex, caste or colour.
2. To encourage the study of comparative religion, philosophy and science.
3. To investigate the unexplained laws of Nature and the powers latent in Nature.

The core teachings of Theosophy represent a combination of Hinduism, Buddhism, Christianity and SPIRITUALISM. The human spirit is an emanation from the Universal Spirit of God. God is both immanent and transcendent, and all living things are part of the unity that is God. Apart from humanity there is a vast hierarchy of spiritual beings, greater and lesser intelligences. Spirit is eternal and evolves. The human individual learns and develops through a series of incarnations until a state of perfection is reached and incarnation is no longer necessary. Such an enlightened individual is known as a MASTER or Mahatma. Masters may continue to guide others while in a DISCARNATE state, or they may choose to incarnate again in order to teach humanity, as the founders of the major religions have done.

Theosophists believe that when in incarnation we live on three PLANES, the physical, the astral and the mental, even though we are almost totally focused on the physical. This focus shifts to the astral immediately after death, and then to the mental between incarnations. Some people are aware of the astral plane while in the body. A few are also able to read the AKASHIC RECORD, from which they have gained information, for example, about previous races of humanity in ATLANTIS and LEMURIA. Rudolf Steiner adapted many Theosophist teachings to construct ANTHROPOSOPHY.

THETA BRAIN WAVES – See BRAIN WAVES.

THEURGY Literally 'God + work', hence 'the practice of magic', theurgy means the working of miracles either by divine intervention or by human beings who have acquired supernatural powers. If the aim of Theosophy was to achieve wisdom and understanding of the Divine, the aim of theurgy, as demonstrated by some GNOSTICS and the NEO-PLATONISTS, was to be endowed with the god-like power to work miracles. This was a beneficent form of MAGIC, covering the powers to heal, to preserve health, to prolong life, to see distant events, to foretell the future, to overcome enemies, in fact most of the duties expected of Old Testament prophets and SHAMANS.

THIRD EYE The third eye is the popular name for the *ajna* CHAKRA otherwise known as the brow centre. Some people regard the third eye or the 'Eye of Shiva' as a separate manifestation which develops when energies flow through both the crown chakra and the brow centre, creating a new organ of spiritual perception. For this to happen the energies of the lower chakras, the organs of the so-called lower triad of the personality, also have to be purified and channelled through the brow centre.

Sensitives regard the third eye as being the organ of CLAIRVOYANCE, just as our two eyes are the organs of normal sight. In this respect the brow centre is often associated with the PINEAL GLAND, which is also sensitive to light. With the third eye the soul is said to be able to distinguish spiritual light. The third eye is the organ of inner vision and the seat of divine knowledge.

Buddha is often depicted with a jewel set in his brow, representing the divine awareness which the third eye endows. In Greek mythology Minerva, the goddess of wisdom, was born from the forehead of Zeus. All over the world people have adorned themselves by placing marks on the brow in the position of the third eye, often symbolizing spiritual status (such as the Indian caste mark) or clairvoyant powers. Many initiations involve cutting the forehead: Kalahari Bushmen rub a piece of skin from the forehead of a young hunter's first kill into the cut in his forehead to endow him with clearer vision when hunting.

THOUGHT/THOUGHT-FORMS The power of thought was recognized implicitly long before the advent of psychology. 'The thing I greatly feared is come upon me,' said Job (Job 3, 5.). Some would say that focusing mentally on a condition contributes greatly to creating or attracting that condition, and in putting these words into Job's mouth the narrator could well have been drawing attention to this. Just as worries are self-perpetuating and even become self-fulfilling prophecies, so also positive thinking is therapeutic. Western men and women today readily appreciate that thought and belief — from the placebo effect to vertigo — can have a positive or negative effect on the thinker through the power of SUGGESTION via the SUBCONSCIOUS MIND, but can they also have an effect on other people? And when such thoughts are part of an individual's psyche, do they have an objective existence? The Arab philosopher and physician, Avicenna (980—1037) seemed to imply as much when he wrote, 'When ideas and beliefs become firmly fixed in the soul, they necesssarily must exist in reality'. Charles Dickens created characters in his imagination which he said then appeared to him. Through his power of thought he created thought-forms that seemed to him to have objective reality, just as Tibetan magicians create TULPAS through the power known in Tantrism as *kriya-shakti*, creative power. Theosophists sometimes refer to such thought-forms as 'ELEMENTALS' when they appear clothed in matter.

Our belief-system naturally affects the way we see the world. This has been expressed by two leading Theosophists in language which suggests that thoughts have objective reality. 'Each man travels through space enclosed within a case of his own building, surrounded by a mass of the forms created by his habitual thoughts. Through this medium he looks out upon the world, and naturally he sees everything tinged with its predominant colours, and all rates of vibration which reach him from without are more or less modified by its rate. Thus until the man learns complete control of thought and feeling, he sees nothing as it really is, since all his observations must be made through this medium, which distorts and colours everything like badly-made glass.'[11] This reads rather like a very materialistic version of orthodox psychology, attributing physical reality as well as power to thoughts and feelings. Some might argue that such descriptions betray an inability to envisage power without there being some three-dimensional vehicle for it in physical space. But if we exist simultaneously on the physical, astral and mental 'PLANES' while we are in the body, our emotional 'baggage' could be envisaged as having astral reality which could be translated into a description of colours and vibrations for us to appreciate in our physically conditioned language.

A different kind of thought-form is produced by music. C.W. Leadbeater developed his psychic awareness to an unusually high degree and described the fantastic shapes and colours he saw emanating from buildings where music was being played, forms which sometimes towered high into the sky. In the same way that he saw the evidence of particular emotions in a person's AURA, he also saw the effects produced by crowds of people, processions, or an attentive audience at a lecture. Leadbeater had previously been a minister of the church. He was a relatively unimaginative man, not given to exaggeration, and not particularly fond of music, so it was all the more convincing when he substantiated the drawings that others had drawn of the forms they had seen with their inner eye surrounding organ recitals. In their book, *Thought-Forms*, Annie Besant and C.W. Leadbeater reproduce in colour many different forms that they have seen, some evoked by pieces of music, some associated with particular human emotions.[11] These thought-forms are again essentially astral manifestations. The suggestion is that different SENSITIVES will agree on what they see, although to what extent we can visualize or represent visually to others something which is not perceived by the eyes is a moot point.

If thoughts exist anywhere it is on a mental plane of being, fuelled by will but without any particular emotion. That they do exist somehow 'out there' as objective entities is suggested by the notion that thoughts seem to be contagious. A few advanced original thinkers can fill the thought-plane with ideas which the majority will eventually absorb and adopt as their own. This is sometimes understood in another sense: when the time is right for a particular idea we often say, 'Its time has come'. Two or more individuals may then have the same original idea at the same time, sometimes giving rise to unfortunate and unjustified accusations of plagiarism.

All our conscious acts start off as thoughts. Everything that civilization has produced was originally conceived as an idea. Fleeting thoughts that flit through the brain have no cohesive element to make them endure, but thoughts reinforced by the will or the emotions last for a considerable time, even longer than the life of their begetter, and they can act as forces for good or evil. 'The only real things which man creates are his thoughts.' 'A human thought is not an independent being; it is dependent upon the one who issued it, or on ... another human who entertained and nourished it.' 'A thought is a being, conceived by thinking, with a purpose and a plan. It is like an invisible blueprint to be exteriorized as an act or an object. The exteriorized action is physical destiny.' The results of this exteriorization are physical, psychic or emotional, and mental. Eventually the thinker learns that thinking works in accordance with KARMA: all thoughts endure for as long as it takes for them to be 'balanced', a process which requires the thinker to bear the consequences of the thought, whether in this life or the next, and recognize the rightness of the process through conscience.'[147]

The communications CHANNELLED by Jane Roberts from the entity calling himself SETH expound a philosophy based on the notion that our thoughts and beliefs create the reality we see around us. This is not an exercise in SOLIPSISM since so many people share the same belief that their thoughts give substance to the external world as a combined effort. By the same token such belief systems endure from generation to generation, so there is hardly any chance that what we see around us could collapse through lack of sustaining thought-power. On the other hand, according to Seth's view, which is not untypical of channelled philosophies, a simple change in thought pattern and belief system can work miracles.

THOUGHT TRANSFERENCE The term 'thought transference' is sometimes considered to be misleading since it seems to imply that thoughts have to travel across space in order to pass from one MIND to another. Since minds are not bounded by space, they are nowhere and everywhere, so information may be relayed from mind to mind by some change in the minds themselves such as an attuning process of some kind. The preferred term is TELEPATHY.

THOUGHTOGRAPHY – See PSYCHIC PHOTOGRAPHY.

THROAT CENTRE – See CHAKRAS.

TIME/TIME-SLIPS/TIME-WARPS In some APPARITIONS people have seen not only what they might take to be a ghost, but also the environment around the person from the past. Sometimes the observer might also participate in the scene, so that it becomes more like a waking lucid DREAM, walking around a church and seeing it as it was centuries ago. It is as if two streams of reality were flowing so close to each other that despite their separation in sequential time an individual is able to look from one to the other.

A famous case was when two English ladies from Oxford visiting the Trianon Park at Versailles in 1901 saw a scene which resembled a fancy dress ball: all the people were in eighteenth century dress. They also reported feeling slightly depressed and as if in a dream. On a return visit three years later they found that the garden had changed completely. Their subsequent descriptions of their first visit convinced many that they had actually witnessed a court scene at the time of Marie-Antoinette.[30] In another case a bustling fair around the megalithic stones in Avebury was seen by Edith Oliver over sixty years after the custom of holding an annual fair there had been dropped.[136] There have been other cases where people have been so impressed by a chance visit to a particular place, sometimes a church, that they have tried to find it again afterwards, only to discover that it no longer exists and had actually been destroyed or converted long before the time of their first visit.

Such glimpses of the past may be more common when the individual is particularly interested in the past, as in the case of the historian, Arnold Toynbee. Toynbee was visiting the ruins of an open-air theatre in Ephesus, when he suddenly became aware of a near riot taking place, in which he believed he witnessed the protests against St Paul of the silversmiths who made the shrines to Diana (as recounted in Acts 19). He had a similar experience of what he called 'falling into a time-pocket' at Pharsalus in Greece: when bringing to mind a battle which took place there in 197 BC he suddenly found himself watching the battle in progress. It was another such vision of a battle, this time at Mistra, where virtually everyone had been massacred in the Greek wars of independence in the 1820s, that prompted Toynbee to write his *Study of History*. He was convinced that some kind of time-slip was involved in these visions, rather than mere imagination.

Forward-looking time-slips, glimpses of the future, might be facilitated if the individual is eventually going to participate in the scene witnessed. In 1935 Wing Commander Victor Goddard was flying in thick cloud and heavy rain in Scotland. He was in danger of losing his way, so to get his bearings he made for a disused airfield, Drem, that he knew he would recognize. He had visited Drem earlier and knew that it was in a derelict state − fields overgrown, tarmac cracked and buildings falling down. Suddenly he found himself in brilliant sunshine, flying over Drem airfield, but what he saw below was not the derelict site he had expected. Everything on the ground was new, there were aircraft standing by the renovated hangars and RAF mechanics going about their business. None of them looked up as he flew over. Goddard made no mention of his 'vision' in his official report. Four years later war broke out. The next time Goddard saw Drem it was exactly as he had seen it in his vision, even down to the colours of the mechanics' overalls (which had surprised him in 1935 as they had not been standard issue in those days) and an aircraft which he had not been able to identify before. The personal connection with the future event fits in with some of Dunne's ideas of PRECOGNITION: he thought that in premonitions we are made aware not of a future external event so much as our future mental and emotional reaction or state during that event.

Colin Wilson believes that information about the past may be stored somehow and then retrieved by people falling unwittingly or deliberately into the right mode of CONSCIOUSNESS, using what Eileen Garrett calls 'a fundamental shift in one's awareness'.[214] To a certain extent this notion of an 'information universe' may be a reflection of the contemporary focus on information processing generally, but it is reminiscent of the AKASHIC RECORD. And tradition has always maintained that the Akashic Record includes information about past, present and future.

The presence and availability of such information is implicit in David Bohm's theory of the IMPLICATE ORDER: 'The implicate order is there all at once, having nothing to do with time.' Twentieth century scientists have often suggested that our common-sense appreciation of time is a distortion of reality. Albert Einstein (1879–1955) said, 'The distinction between past, present and future is an illusion; although a rather persistent one.' Erwin Schroedinger (1887–1961) agreed: 'The barrier between them cannot be said to have broken down; this barrier does not exist.' With statements like these the Indian concept of MAYA seemed to acquire scientific respectability, but few scientists have chosen to investigate anomalies in the illusory flow of time, probably because this might jeopardize their faith in the physics of cause and effect on which the whole of science is built. Michael Shallis is an astrophysicist who is not afraid to speculate on the 'multi-faceted nature of time'. He admits that somehow sometimes time 'is perceived in a non-linear, maybe subconscious, fashion which intrudes into consciousness'.[177]

Speculating on the nature of time, Dunne wrote, 'We have, unconsciously, got into the habit of regarding as "time" something which is not really time at all.' What we call time is really just one line or even one moving point on the plane of possibilities which become actualizations. 'In real time, ... everything which has established its existence *remains in existence*.'[48] CLAIRVOYANCE simply gives a fuller picture of this plane of possibilities and actualizations. As Eileen Garrett says, 'On clairvoyant levels there exists a simultaneity of time.'

Although time is a quality of the physical universe our sense of time is not so much physical as emotional and mental. We do not feel time with our bodies in the way that we can feel other aspects of the external world. Our minds might tell us that an hour has passed, but not our bodies. Even under 'normal' circumstances our appreciation of time is extremely variable, depending largely on our emotional involvement in what we are doing and how focused and concentrated our attention is. This does not simply mean that time drags when we are bored. Sometimes time seems to stand still: PEAK EXPERIENCES, feelings of TRANSCENDENCE or moments of ECSTASY are often accompanied by a sense of timelessness, as if we were standing outside time. If this way of describing the feeling is a reflection of what actually happens mentally, then it does not require such a great leap of the imagination to recognize that this is how we might sometimes catch a glimpse, perhaps subconsciously, of our own past or future which leads to DEJA-VU experiences, or we may be transported temporarily to other mental viewpoints in time-slips.

TOMOYE This is the Japanese name for the circular PA-KWA symbol representing the YIN and YANG nature of the UNIVERSE. The circle was also divided into four to produce the pattern known as *ogee* from which the straight-lined *swastika* developed.

TONGUES, SPEAKING IN If orthodox psychologists refer at all to the phenomenon of speaking in tongues, they label it as a form of DISSOCIATION with XENOGLOSSY — speaking another language while in TRANCE. But speaking in tongues is usually a particular form of xenoglossy in which an unintelligible or completely unknown language is spoken, rather than one that is simply unknown to the speaker in a normal state of consciousness. This is known as GLOSSOLALIA. It occurs most typically when mystics achieve a state of ECSTASY and their unintelligible devotional utterances are filled with emotion. In this sense it is associated with Pentecostal churches, since the gift of tongues was demonstrated by the apostles on the Day of Pentecost (Acts 2), but on that occasion all listening understood what was said as their own language, which suggests xenoglossy rather than glossolalia. Speaking in tongues is mentioned as one of the gifts of the Spirit by St Paul in 1 Corinthians 12,10, where he also refers to the interpretation of tongues as another gift, implying that he is referring to glossolalia rather than xenoglossy.

TRANCE There are generally thought to be at least five states of CONSCIOUSNESS: normal awareness, dreaming sleep, deep sleep, coma, and trance. But the last category of trance includes various so-called altered states of consciousness: a medium's self-induced trance is different from involuntary POSSESSION, and neither is it the same as a hypnotic trance.

At Oxford in 1934, the medium Eileen Garrett (1893–1970) was investigated by a hypnotist, Dr William Brown, in an attempt to discover whether her trance personality or CONTROL, Uvani, was created by her own mind in the manner of people with multiple personalities. Under HYPNOSIS Eileen Garrett recalled detailed memories of her past, but the hypnotist was unable to contact Uvani. For Dr Brown to speak to Uvani, Eileen Garrett had to go into her usual mediumistic trance, not a hypnotic trance, suggesting that the two kinds of trance were quite distinct.

Psychologists refer to trance states as DISSOCIATION, but dissociation is generally regarded as a pathological condition, which seems to imply a denial of the fact that a trained MEDIUM goes into trance at will. Eileen Garrett described her own trance states as 'mental levels that I could deliberately escape to and from at will'.[58] A medium's trance state is not a hysterical condition, brought on as a means of escape from a difficult situation or some heavy responsibility. Even though the medium's personality withdraws from the external world, this does not constitute an escape from the world: it is a world-affirming act, since it is put to good use to help others.

Just as there were initially conflicting theories regarding the nature of hypnosis — whether the effect was physiological or psychological — so with mediumistic trance there have been various suggestions as to whether the condition is achieved physiologically, psychologically or psychically. From the physiological point of view, the pulse has been seen to increase to 130 in female mediums, and male SHAMANS in trance have had pulse rates of 230 and above when apparently possessed. This may have something to do with the way whirling DERVISHES achieve their trance state. Although a medium in trance feels generally relaxed, there also seems to be a state of muscular tension with occasional eye tremor, both these having been recorded with Eileen Garrett in trance.

The fact that mediums seem to enter the trance state at will suggests that it is a psychological effect. Just as there are degrees of concentration and attention which suggest a spectrum of focused consciousness merging into day-dreaming, dozing and sleep, so trance states also seem to be graded. When a medium or psychic switches into a slightly unfocused state in order to perceive clairvoyant impressions, the sitter may notice no change at all: this would not normally be called a trance state, but some change of consciousness has already taken place. The medium may then start to speak in an inspired way as the trance gets deeper, but this may still be regarded as a 'light trance'. If another personality seems to speak (or write) through the medium, but the medium is still aware of what is happening, this is described as 'light control'. Although there is full awareness of what is happening in such a situation the medium seldom has complete recollection of the events afterwards: conscious memory seems to be disengaged even in light trance.

Full trance occurs when the medium's personality withdraws from the situation completely. On returning to normal awareness there is usually no recollection at all of what has happened. To some the onset of the trance state may be marked by a slight feeling of nausea, to others it is like falling asleep. While in trance the medium may become the mouthpiece for apparently DISCARNATE entities, or may engage in other automatisms such as AUTOMATIC WRITING. (Like inspired speaking, automatic writing is also possible in light trance.)

Everard Fielding (1867–1936) was a researcher who exposed many mediums. He investigated the physical medium, Eusapio Paladino (1854–1918), for the Society for Psychical Research and was convinced that the effects she produced were genuine. He also described three stages of consciousness similar to the degrees of entrancement mentioned above. First, LEVITATIONS of objects were accomplished in a normal state of awareness. Second, in half-trance the medium answered questions with a quieter and more plaintive voice than normal, with her eyes clouded over, and she had no recollection of the events afterwards. Third, there was the deep trance, in which the medium spoke with a new voice, that of her control, who would refer to the medium herself in the third person.

It is dangerous to subject to loud noises or touch a person who is in trance or in any slightly altered state of awareness, such as having an OBE or a visionary experience. Rosalind Heywood described such an occasion: 'While I was staring enthralled at these splendid surroundings my husband thought I looked odd and touched me gently. The effect of this touch was far from gentle: it forced me back sharply and painfully into the body.'[84] Quiet taps are similarly amplified into loud bangs in such circumstances.

People can train themselves to 'leave the body' while in trance, not as a form of ASTRAL TRAVEL but in order to experience soul-consciousness, as mystics experience ECSTASY. Some occultists regard this exercise as escapism: the true aim should be to become attuned to soul-consciousness while still in the body, better to align the body to soul-consciousness and to make it a better instrument for the soul.

TRANCE CHANNEL – See MEDIUM.

TRANCE PERSONALITY – See CONTROL.

TRANSCENDENCE Transcendence is an attribute of God, the Absolute or the Ultimate which is beyond perception and beyond human understanding. The complementary characteristic or opposite emphasis would be immanence – the concept of God's presence within the whole of creation, rather than above and separate from it. Mystics who stress the transcendent nature of God usually aim to achieve mystic union with the divinity by denying the senses, detaching the SOUL from the material world and leading a life of MEDITATION and asceticism.

However, feelings of transcendence are not restricted to mystics and ascetics. Abraham Maslow (1908–70), the founder of what came to be known as humanistic psychology, which focuses on psychologically healthy individuals rather than pathological conditions, is one of the few psychologists who have recognized, studied and described the human experience of transcendence. The experience can take many forms. It can be a form of self-forgetfulness, a loss of self-consciousness, such that the ego is transcended. This may lead to a sense of mystic fusion, either with the whole cosmos or with just one part of it, perhaps another person. There may simply be a feeling of timelessness: time is transcended. Pain may be transcended in some mysterious way. The sense of struggling against the elements may be transcended in an almost TAOIST acceptance of one's harmony with the universe. There may be a transcendence of petty concerns, a feeling of being 'above it all', what Eileen Garrett called 'high carelessness', which verges on a state of grace. Transcendence usually evokes a sense of being rather than of becoming. All these types of transcendence and many more have been considered by Maslow and he notes that whilst they may be induced by meditation, they often occur quite out of the blue as PEAK EXPERIENCES.

Maslow goes on to distinguish between 'merely healthy people' and transcenders. 'For the transcenders, peak experiences and plateau experiences become *the* most important things in their lives, the high spots, the validators of life, the most precious aspect of life.' Such people tend to seek out the kind of work which might encourage such feelings. When Maslow considers the ideal psychological type for his 'Eupsychia', the Good Society, one could almost consider the transcending capacity to represent the next evolutionary development in humanity. 'Transcendence refers to the very highest and most inclusive and holistic levels of human CONSCIOUSNESS, behaving and relating, as ends rather than means, to oneself, to significant others, to human beings in general, to other species, to nature, and to the cosmos.'[123]

The area of humanistic psychology which concentrates on the process and nature of transcendence in this sense is known as transpersonal psychology, sometimes referred to as the 'fourth force' in psychology (following Freud, Adler and Jung). One of the most fully developed systems of transpersonal psychology is psychosynthesis, which helps the individual to contact sources of energy in the SUPERCONSCIOUS and integrate all levels of the psyche.

TRANSCENDENTAL MEDITATION – See MEDITATION.

TRANSFIGURATION If a MEDIUM takes on the physical appearance of the deceased person whose communications are apparently being brought through, the medium is said to have been overshadowed or transfigured. Transfiguration is a much more profound change of appearance than OVERSHADOWING.

Another use of the term applies to a change of appearance accompanying deep meditation, prayer or ECSTASY in certain saints and mystics. In such cases it seems to be the AURA that becomes visible to all, so that the person seems to shine with an inner light. Christ was transfigured in this way when Peter, James and John saw him conversing with Moses and Elijah (Matthew 7, Mark 9).

TRANSLOCATION – See TELEPORTATION.

TRANSMIGRATION The term transmigration may be used as an alternative expression for REINCARNATION, but it is often used to refer to the belief that the human SOUL may also be incarnated in the body of an animal. Although some Hindus accept the possibility of being reborn as a lower life-form, most esoteric religions which accept the doctrine of reincarnation would maintain that this goes against the principle of spiritual EVOLUTION. It would surely need an unimaginably terrible crime to warrant such an enormous step backwards in the slow process of the development of the soul. In Buddhism there is no concept of an individual soul: the life impulse has no independent existence and transmigrates at death to another body, so the word 'transmigration' is more often used, since use of the word 'reincarnation' tends to be accompanied by the notion that the soul spends some time between incarnations in other realms.

TRANSMUTATION – See ALCHEMY.

TRANSPOSITION OF THE SENSES – See PAROPTIC VISION.

TRAVELLING CLAIRVOYANCE Travelling clairvoyance is an old term for EXTRA-SENSORY PERCEPTION which operates at a distance. Like the alternative term, ASTRAL PROJECTION, it suggests that part of the person actually leaves the physical body. The more recent coinage, REMOTE VIEWING, has so far managed to avoid this implication.

TREE OF LIFE According to KABBALISM there are ten attributes of God, emanations known as the *sephiroth* (singular: *sephira*), which together form a vital organism, the Man of Light, Adam Kadmon, or the Tree of Life, linking the terrestrial world with the celestial. 'The Tree of Life extends from above downwards and is the sun which illuminates all.' (The *Zohar*.) The ten attributes are the crown, wisdom, intelligence, love, justice, beauty, steadfastness, majesty, foundation and kingdom. The Tree has its root in the Infinite, the kingdom as the trunk, the foundation as the point where the branches begin to spread, beauty at the centre and the crown at the top.

Kether	the Crown
Chokmah	Wisdom
Binah	Intelligence, Understanding
Chesed	Love, Mercy
Geburah	Justice, Judgment, Severity
Tiphareth	Beauty
Netzach	Steadfastness, Eternity, Victory
Hod	Splendour, Majesty
Yesod	Foundation
Malkuth	the Kingdom

These emanations have archetypal significance, and the progression from one to another can be seen as representing the individual's journey of self-discovery and self-realization. The ten sephiroth are also called Major Paths of Wisdom and there are twenty-two pathways linking them, known as Minor Paths of Wisdom. These are sometimes equated with the twenty-two Major Arcana of the TAROT, as well as with the twenty-two letters of the Hebrew alphabet, particularly by diviners.

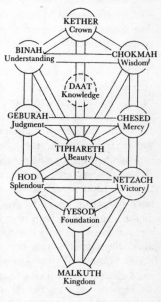

Kabbalist Tree of Life

There is also an eleventh (unnumbered) position, knowledge (*D'aat* or *D'aath*), to which the Kabbalist progresses via the other ten stages. Its position, which is often not marked, is on the line representing The Abyss, which separates the 'Supernal triad' of perfect, ideal states (Kether, Chokmah and Binah) from the seven lower emanations. This additional mysterious sephira, D'aath, represents ultimate Knowledge, a point of profound transformation, a point at which one enters the higher realm of understanding and wisdom, and where identity vanishes and one may experience union with the divine Kether (positioned directly above it on the Tree diagram). Thus in one sense D'aath represents death, the death of the EGO, and entry into timelessness, where revelation and inspiration replace normal thought. Its position below Kether and directly above Tiphareth places D'aath on the central Pillar of Equilibrium, which represents consciousness (the other two Pillars representing force and form). It has been likened to cosmic consciousness, or in Christian terms to the state of being blessed with the Holy Spirit.

TRIAL BY ORDEAL The most common form of trial by ordeal is trial by fire or FIRE-WALKING. Eileen Garrett relates how she was accepted by the people of Haiti as one who could train with their hungan or priest, working with MAGIC and in particular with the power of HEALING. In one ceremony she had to prove that she was worthy by going through the ordeal of fire. 'In this trial one holds one's hands over a flame, and a healing stone is held above them in a silk handkerchief which burns, whereupon one must catch the stone as it falls. Knowing what was coming, I got myself into a TRANCE-like state, and consequently my hands were not burned. The hungan stood by and examined my hands every carefully. ... The assumption is that if one is guilty of human error or the love of power, it would be revealed in the first rite.'[58]

TULPA Tibetan priests are adept at using the power of thought to create phantasms, ELEMENTALS or THOUGHT-FORMS known as tulpas. In this form of MAGIC the thought-form initially serves its creator, but negative thoughts or selfish desires and the exercise of the will without regard for spiritual truth and harmony can lead to the separation of the tulpa from its creator, so that it becomes an independent entity which can be extremely difficult to destroy and can even work against its creator.[40]

Thought-forms of this kind are described by Dion Fortune, who once unwittingly created one herself in the form of a werewolf out of the negative feelings she was feeling towards someone. It had already been roaming around semi-independently when she managed to reabsorb it into herself with considerable pain just in time before it broke free permanently.[55] Such thought-forms can also be used positively. SHAMANS protect themselves from dangerous animals by creating an elemental of the appropriate animal and regarding it as a friend. They believe that the actual animal will then recognize the elemental of the same species and pass by without molesting the human being who is apparently guarded in this way. Elementals of this kind are almost a non-material form of TALISMANS.

UFOs/UNIDENTIFIED FLYING OBJECTS The American astronomer, Donald Menzel, believes that the celestial lights mentioned by Pliny, Seneca and Aristotle would today be described as flying saucers (UFOs).[125] They were called 'chasms' and were thought to be breaks in the heavens which allowed celestial light to shine through. The ancients thought they presaged the end of the world. It is difficult to judge retrospectively whether they were the same phenomenon as today's UFOs — some at least might have been supernovae, but it is interesting to note that prophecies of cataclysmic events are associated with both 'chasms' and UFOs.

Modern Ufologists have surmised that the relatively small stature of most reported aliens might suggest a certain continuity between the fairies of folklore and extra-terrestrials. The aliens described to date have always been so remarkably unsurprising and humanoid that sceptics wonder what the reaction would be if something truly alien were ever encountered. It has even been suggested that they are humans of the future travelling back into the past, or that the sightings are TIME-SLIPS of some kind. As well as their size traditional fairies and modern aliens share a predilection for abduction, which is often associated with an apparent desire to breed with humanity. People who witness the same encounter in which others experience an abduction are not affected as profoundly as those who claim to have been abducted. The abducted are often inexplicably sunburned. It is common for several hours to be unaccounted for in such cases. Something happens, although those not involved can never be sure what, and the sceptics' view that it is all mere imagination and wishful thinking is rendered less likely by the fact that encounters are typically reported by people who initially had no belief in UFOs at all.

Experiences of encounters with extra-terrestrials are commonly accompanied by intuitive feelings, such as the sense that it is a very private experience, 'for my eyes only'. The humans seem to know 'instinctively' that the experience is not of this earth, but it is usually more reassuring than frightening. The extra-terrestrials seem to communicate these ideas telepathically.

Some have commented on certain similarities between NEAR-DEATH EXPERIENCES (NDEs) and UFO encounters. A brilliant light at the end of a tunnel is not unlike the shape and brightness of a flying saucer. The individual is often sucked up or along towards this light and meets or approaches figures who may be familiar or angelic in NDE and 'familiarly alien' in UFO encounters.

People who have experienced either UFO encounters or NDEs always insist that they were 'nothing like a HALLUCINATION', and there is no reason to doubt this. In terms of their after-effects alone these phenomena are obviously much more significant than a mere hallucination. After NDEs and UFO encounters people are never the same again: both types of experience seem to change the individual's whole worldview.

In the case of NDEs the effect is more reliably wholly positive, resulting in a much more relaxed attitude towards death, more exuberance for life, greater tolerance and acceptance, and a general feeling of increased well-being and happiness. UFO encounters *can* have this effect (e.g. Whitley Strieber: *Communion* and *Transformation*), but sometimes the result is less harmonious.[189,190] Those who have been 'chosen' by the extra-terrestrials may become too obsessive about the 'message' they have to tell humanity and too intent on building up their own egos as leaders of a new cult. NDEs almost invariably result in the individual adopting a much more positive attitude towards the future. In UFO encounters, the individuals may be given messages which are apparently intended to prepare them for the future, but too often they become preoccupied with the experience itself. It is quite easy to accept an NDE as a private affair for the individual concerned and no one else. UFO encounters seem to be less readily accepted in this way; they seem so much more material in this materialist age that there is a strong temptation to regard them as being of *universal* significance. Hence the fanatical attitude of some Ufologists.

Jung, considering the UFO phenomenon as 'a mass rumour accompanied by collective visions', looked for psychic explanations. Regardless of whether anything external gave rise to them, he thought that UFOs would not have seized such a hold on the human imagination unless they had psychological significance. 'If the round shining objects that appear in the sky be regarded as visions, we can hardly avoid interpreting them as archetypal images.' Their customary roundness he regarded as a recapitulation of the MANDALA theme as a symbol for the SELF or the SOUL, a symbol of order, a God-image; he noted the old GNOSTIC saying 'God is a circle whose centre is everywhere and whose circumference is nowhere'. According to Jung, the technological construction of UFOs was characteristic of a technological age in which mythological personification would be unsuitable, but the phenomenon was fundamentally a modern myth. 'A myth is essentially a product of the unconscious archetype and is therefore a symbol which requires psychological interpretation.' The root cause which Jung believed evoked the projection of UFOs was emotional tension, and in particular the tension created by the cold war. He cited previous cases in which 'heavenly armies' had been seen on battlefields when all seemed to be lost. In classical times presumably the vision would have been of the gods themselves, but today it is a futuristic machine, but its occupants are just as superhuman as the gods of the ancients, 'technological angels who are concerned for our welfare', coming to warn of impending doom and perhaps to rescue.[93]

UNCONSCIOUS FRAUD THEORY In 1892 a report was written by Richard Hodgson of the Society for Psychical Research on the medium Mrs Piper. Her CONTROL, known as Phinuit, claimed to have lived earlier in the nineteenth century as a French doctor, practising in England, Belgium and France. However, there were no records of the man he claimed to have been in the medical schools where he claimed to have studied and practised, and as Mrs Piper's control, Phinuit displayed no more medical knowledge than the average layman, and was not even very proficient at speaking French. Yet when speaking as Phinuit, Mrs Piper undoubtedly had access to information about the living and the dead which in waking consciousness she did not have.

William James came to the conclusion that Phinuit was not a spirit entity with an independent existence outside the medium, but rather a secondary personality of the medium herself. This 'explanation' of the phenomenon has been called the 'unconscious fraud' theory, although it does not explain how the medium gained access to the information which as Phinuit she disclosed. TELEPATHY is invoked, but the question of how telepathy works remains unanswered.

There have been other cases which seem to support the 'unconscious fraud' theory. Several mediums have while in TRANCE produced the voices of living people, voices which purported to come from those who had departed this earth. One such was a certain Gordon Davis, who 'communicated' through the medium Blanche Cooper (1925) as if he were dead, while he was in fact living and working as an estate agent.

The theory regards mediums as having a subliminal actor who can don the personality of any individual. Experiments with hypnosis have provided plenty of evidence to show that there is a subliminal actor present in the human mind. People who suffer from personality disorders such as 'DISSOCIATION' unconsciously invent for themselves the characters that they act out − a condition popularly known as MULTIPLE PERSONALITY. In a similar way, according to this theory, mediums unconsciously dramatize the personalities to which they gain access telepathically.

It is difficult to invoke straightforward telepathy as a means by which mediums gain the information they use to build up the communicating spirits. These spirits habitually provide accurate information which is unknown to all those present, and this would mean that the medium also had telepathic contact with minds beyond the circle of those sitting and which those present might not even know. This is virtually the same as the SUPER-ESP HYPOTHESIS.

In many cases telepathy between the medium and the sitters has been ruled out for purely logical reasons. Communicating spirits have sometimes been shown to be under misapprehensions which appeared to be incomprehensible at the time to those present. For example, a medium was communicating information from a man who had been killed in a motor accident. The deceased insisted that the collision had been with a lorry, but his family knew that it had been with a car. Only later did they learn from another passenger who had survived the accident that all those in the car had thought at the time that the oncoming vehicle was a lorry. The easiest way to understand such a case is to assume the existence of an independent and newly DISCARNATE spirit communicating through the medium. Apparently the deceased was the last to learn the true circumstances of the accident — after his death. Another possibility might be that the medium linked across time with the mind of the deceased a moment before his death and unconsciously dressed it up as a surviving personality, but the charade becomes even more complicated when the 'spirit' actually modifies what he says in accordance with the new information he receives from the living. To many the SPIRIT HYPOTHESIS seems more economical.

C.D. Broad has gone further in considering the process by which spirit communication operates. He postulates a PSYCHIC factor in the mind of an individual, which survives the individual's physical death, and which can be temporarily united with a medium. This produces what he calls a 'temporary' mind or 'mindkin' which enables the medium to have memories and display characteristics of the deceased individual.[19] This is very similar to the *linga sharira* or SUBTLE BODY of Vedantic belief, which becomes temporarily reincarnated in the mediumistic trance. In the above example the medium was therefore in touch with the subtle body of the deceased, which possessed all the individual's memories up to the time of death, and which continued to exist on the ASTRAL PLANE or in the BARDO world of Tibetan Buddhism.

UNCONSCIOUS MIND Referring to a state of mind the word 'unconscious' describes a condition of not being aware, whether asleep, drugged, drunk, in a faint, in TRANCE, or in coma. The notion of 'the unconscious' is a reflection of the way we tend to convert processes and functions into concrete things: the mind is not a spatial entity and yet the unconscious is regarded as a part of it, as if it could be delineated and as if it were mappable. The unconscious mind is that part of the mind of which we are not aware: it is therefore subliminal, preconscious or SUBCONSCIOUS (a term avoided by psychologists), not accessible by exercising the will, and in fact it seems to be capable of overriding the will — as in Freudian slips. According to Freud, the unconscious is the repressed part of the mind, full of traumatic memories which we prefer to forget, but which continue to affect our perception of the world. Perhaps surprisingly, in view of what is generally accepted as the Freudian view, Freud also regarded the unconscious as 'the part of us that is so much nearer the divine than our own poor consciousness'.[56] In other schools of thought this aspect of the unconscious is called the SUPERCONSCIOUS.

In Jung's view the unconscious has a much wider canvas than suppressed memories. These formed the individual's Shadow, but there are also many intuitive, instinctive and even mystical elements in the unconscious. For example every person has an unconscious aspect of the self which would normally be thought of as belonging to the opposite sex, the animus or anima. The unconscious is also the field in which we experience archetypes and by ACTIVE IMAGINATION we may be able to meet figures arising from our own unconscious. (See also COLLECTIVE UNCONSCIOUS.)

The idea that a trance personality could be part of the medium's unconscious or subconscious personality was being discussed by Myers[135] and other investigators of Mrs Piper some ten years before Freud published his views. Experiments in HYPNOSIS had long since demonstrated the unconscious mind's great ability to dramatize and to remember facts which had been consciously forgotten. Geraldine Cummins was quite prepared to concede that the personality known as Astor, who acted as her CONTROL when she practised AUTOMATIC WRITING, might be a creation of her own unconscious. Another medium, Eileen Garrett, believed that the so-called DISCARNATE entities who spoke through her were formed out of her own spiritual and emotional needs. 'I have never been able to accept them as the spiritual dwellers on the threshold which they seem to believe they are. I rather leaned away from accepting them as such, a fact which is known to them and troubles them not at all.' Nevertheless she allows that they could exist independently of her own mind: 'I suspect they will exist as long as

I do, and perhaps even after I have passed from the scene.' One of her controls, Abdul Latif, even chose to work through another medium in England when Eileen Garrett went to America, so that he could maintain contact with those he had got to know through his first medium. If this personality was simply a modus operandi of Eileen Garrett's UNCONSCIOUS MIND, the fact that the recognizable personality apparently transferred to another medium would have astonishing implications for the scope of our mental activity and the extent to which we might be able to participate in each other.[58]

'Seth', as CHANNELLED by Jane Roberts, without denying the possibility that some communicators are discarnate entities, has expressed similar views to Eileen Garrett, noting that assigning all channelled messages to disembodied personalities creates 'a confusing mass of dogma or superstition'. 'If you understood to begin with that you are a spirit, and therefore free of space and time yourself, then you could at least consider the possibility that some such messages were coming to you from other portions of your own reality.'[166] In other words, via the reality of our own unconscious mental processes our minds can gain access to material of which we are more directly aware as spirits.

UNIVERSE Cosmologists now talk of the possibility of countless parallel universes, each with its own laws. This has also been part of so-called OCCULT SCIENCE. According to the cosmogeny communicated to Dion Fortune in 1923–4, there are many universes in the cosmos, each the creation of its own 'Great Entity'. 'A universe is a THOUGHT-FORM projected by the mind of God, who to it is omnipotent and infinite.' 'The universe may be conceived of as the aura of God.'[54] In this cosmogeny the Creator God of our universe, the LOGOS, is also in a state of evolution in relation to the Cosmos. (This is at variance with the teachings of exoteric religion, in which God is changeless.) Such EVOLUTION is brought about by knowledge of the evolution of its universe, which gradually develops self-consciousness and increasing awareness of the Logos, until the Logos eventually absorbs its universe into itself. 'The goal of evolution is the development of a CONSCIOUSNESS which can unite with the Logoidal consciousness and pass from the phase of a reflected, or a projected existence – a phenomenal existence – to that of a real, actual or noumenal existence in the Cosmic state.' Teilhard de Chardin's views on the evolution of life towards the OMEGA POINT are comparable. When this synthesis of the universe with the Creator Logos has been achieved there follows the 'NIGHT OF GOD', Night of Brahma or *pralaya*.

VERIDICAL The adjective 'veridical' is commonly used in PSYCHICAL RESEARCH in the sense of 'corresponding to external reality'. It was first used in this way by F.W.H. Myers. When an APPARITION is positively identified as being that of a particular person, in the right clothing and so on, and about whom the percipient knew nothing beforehand, or when a DROP-IN COMMUNICATOR gives information through a MEDIUM with which no one present was familiar but which is later confirmed as true, it is concluded that the phenomenon is *veridical*.

VIDYA In Hindu Vedanta teaching *vidya* is wisdom or spiritual knowledge. A similar direct knowledge of God, GNOSIS, forms the basis of Christian GNOSTICISM, but otherwise the two doctrines have little in common. The Gnostic belief is based on dualism, and only the elect are granted gnosis, whilst Vedanta teaches that all may aspire to spiritual knowledge, since there is a fundamental unity between BRAHMAN (God, the Ultimate) and ATMAN (the human soul).

VISHUDDHA – Sanskrit for throat centre. See CHAKRAS.

VISIONS HALLUCINATIONS, APPARITIONS, visions – is there any difference between them? Some might argue that they are all hallucinations – illusory experiences in which we apparently perceive something without any external stimulus. But when we talk of apparitions and visions, we make no judgment as to whether the experience has an external cause or not. The inference may often be that there is an external agent, as in the case of ghosts, but using the term apparition or vision need not necessarily imply this. For example, many would say that CRISIS APPARITIONS are a mental device by which we are able to bring information acquired telepathically to conscious awareness: nothing actually appears.

In a sense, the word 'vision' may seem more appropriate for the more ambiguous meaning: the emphasis is on seeing, rather than appearing. But people have tended to refer to visions in a religious context, or at least when the apparition, even if not of something on a religious theme, has had an effect which affects the perceiver's subsequent attitudes or belief system in a way that religious experiences might. Within a year of experiencing such a 'vision of light' Thomas Aquinas died, having immediately stopped writing and declaring 'All I have written is like straw'.

The most obviously religious visions have been of saints or the Virgin Mary: the most famous being at Lourdes in France (1858), Knock in Ireland (1879), Fatima in Portugal (1917) and more recently Medjugorje in Yugoslavia (1981). Sacred images and statues have been seen to weep, bleed, move or even speak, as when St Francis was instructed to 'rebuild my church' by the figure on the crucifix at Assisi in 1208. All these sites and many more still attract thousands of pilgrims every year, and the phenomena themselves are still being reported: in 1985 residents of Ballinspittle in Ireland saw a statue of the Virgin move and crowds again flocked to wait and watch.

It has often been noted that the first sightings of such visions (for example of the Virgin at Lourdes and Fatima) are commonly made by young girls. Are their minds more open to seeing the unexpected, which others older and more set in their ways would be less willing to consciously acknowledge? Or are they more prone to hallucinate, being at a time of life when they are suddenly more conscious both of their religious devotion and of their own female nature? A third possibility, which contains something of both these viewpoints, is that they can more easily attune mentally with each other, unconsciously uniting their minds as a group (in the manner of Lyall Watson's 'SAMA') to produce an idea and perhaps even to project a THOUGHT-FORM. This could be an explanation for mass sightings, as were reported at Fatima.

Visions of a religious nature are often associated with DREAMS, both of which can be revelatory experiences. Mohammed saw the ARCHANGEL Gabriel in a dream, and angels appeared to Joseph in dreams as recorded in the first two chapters of St Matthew's gospel. Using this description may simply be a way of saying that those who saw the visions knew that the experiences were not to be equated with normal sight. It might have been their way of saying that they knew they were in an altered state of awareness. Although Teresa describes her famous vision of an angel 'in bodily form, such as I am not in the habit of seeing except very rarely,' she adds, 'Though I often have visions of angels, I do not see them.'[29] This spiritual awareness is not the same as seeing with the eyes. This seems to be another common (though not universal) difference between visions and apparitions: people who see visions are often aware that they are in a different mental state at the time, whilst apparitions may be more likely to take one by surprise without any apparent altered state of CONSCIOUSNESS.

Jung had several visions while in unusual physical states: while being given injections, after a heart attack, and while unconscious. He denied that there was anything pathological about them. On the contrary. 'It was not a product of the imagination; there was nothing subjective about them; they all had a quality of absolute objectivity. We shy away from the word "eternal", but I can describe the experience only as the ECSTASY of a non-temporal state in which present, past and future are one.' He also wrote, 'It is impossible to deny the beauty and intensity of emotion during these visions. They were the most tremendous things I have ever experienced.'[97]

Similar visions occur in NEAR-DEATH EXPERIENCES with similarly profound after-effects. Jung's 'ecstasy of a non-temporal state', when time seems to stand still, is a common characteristic of experiences of TRANSCENDENCE. People also seem to lose a sense of time in UFO encounters, and sometimes the sighting of a UFO is also described as a vision, with the likely implication that the experience was accompanied by feelings of awe, comparable to those felt in a religious context. There seems to be a mode of consciousness in which our everyday sense of time disappears, regardless of whether the experience would be described as visionary in the transcendental sense. Entering such a mode of consciousness enables some people to catch glimpses of the past or future, as in the 'time-pockets' or TIME-SLIPS experienced by Arnold Toynbee and in premonitive dreams. Experiences of this kind which transcend time also seem more likely to occur in the HYPNOPOMPIC and HYPNAGOGIC state.

VISUALIZATION As a means of self-healing visualization techniques have come to the fore in recent years as one of the ways in which people are recognizing the enormous power the mind has over the body. Visualization is a form of mental imagery. Someone with a tumour may imagine the body's natural defences surrounding the cells that have grown out of control and dissolving them: the tumour may be visualized as a wild animal or an invading army which the body's cavalry of white blood cells engage in battle and wipe out. The effectiveness of this technique has been shown by patients at the Bristol Centre for Cancer Treatment.[142] Spiritual HEALERS often ask their patients to visualize too while they are receiving HEALING in order to focus or amplify the effect.

VITALISM This is the belief that living organisms contain a vital force (Bergson's *élan vital*) which distinguishes them from non-living matter, and that this indwelling force or spirit is gradually establishing greater control over matter. In imbuing matter with life, spirit endows it with ever more freedom. T.E. Hulme said that the amoeba represents a tiny 'leak' of freedom, fishes are bigger leaks, animals bigger leaks, and man the biggest leak so far. The main exponents of the theory in the twentieth century were the German biologist Hans Driesch (1867–1941) and the French philosopher, Henri Bergson (1859–1941). Bergson regarded CONSCIOUSNESS and free will as operating in complete contrast to the rigid determinism of cause and effect in the physical world. The EVOLUTION of life in this sense can be seen as counteracting the process of entropy in the physical universe. Teilhard de Chardin also saw life as establishing ever greater order on the UNIVERSE, evolving towards the OMEGA POINT, but in his view every atom already possesses a certain degree of consciousness, so for him the whole spectrum of the physical universe from non-living matter to living organisms was more of a continuum than for the vitalists.

VOICES – See CLAIRAUDIENCE, DIRECT VOICE, RAUDIVE VOICES.

VRIL In the middle of the nineteenth century Louis Jacolliot coined the term *vril* to refer to a concentration of cosmic ETHER which certain individuals could use to develop and enhance their PSYCHIC powers. It seems to have been comparable to the Melanesian concept of MANA and to Reichenbach's OD and Reich's ORGONE energy.

WALK-IN The term 'walk-in' refers to cases of mild POSSESSION, when someone with mediumistic powers involuntarily allows another entity to enter the body. With experienced MEDIUMS this should never happen, since only those who are invited by the medium or the medium's CONTROL are permitted to communicate. But when people are starting to develop PSYCHIC faculties they are warned about being 'too open' and allowing entities to come in. These entities are usually thought to be DISCARNATE spirits of an EARTH-BOUND type, which are obviously not welcome. For this reason, when working psychically people are always told to 'close down properly' at the end of any circle or psychic exercise. With individuals who are themselves not well-integrated personalities psychologically, the apparently invading entities could well be sub-personalities or repressed complexes of their own, which are suddenly given free rein to express themselves through the relaxing of the person's conscious inhibitions while focusing on psychic work. (Walk-ins are not to be confused with DROP-IN COMMUNICATORS, who are un-expected and unpredictable but never undesirable or unwelcome.)

WEREWOLF Eliphas Levi suggested that the ASTRAL BODY (which he called the 'sidereal' body) could leave the physical body during sleep and assume the form of an animal. Presumably such a creation would only occur in a very disturbed personality. The same astral phenomenon could also account for vampires. Shamans believe that when they leave the body, perhaps to view the scene in another location or to harm an enemy, they too can take the shape of an animal. 'The SHAMAN projects his consciousness into an animal form on an imaginal level and it is in this "body" that he goes forth on his spirit-journey.' If werewolves are astral forms, this explains why they are reportedly almost impossible to kill by normal physical means: astral beings can only be destroyed astrally. 'Sometimes shamans fight each other on the inner planes in their magical bodies. If a shaman "dies" during this encounter, it is often said that he will die in real life as well, for his "essence" will have been destroyed.'[46]

WHEEL OF REBIRTH The eternal round of birth, death and rebirth, sometimes called SAMSARA, is commonly called the 'Wheel of Rebirth' or the Wheel of Brahman. The *Upanishads* declare that 'The world is the Wheel of God, turning round and round with all living creatures upon its rim. ... On this ever-revolving wheel of being the individual SELF goes round and round through life after life, believing itself to be a separate creature, until it sees its identity with the Lord of Love and attains immortality in the indivisible whole.'

WITCHCRAFT The modern practice of witchcraft, Wicca or the Old Religion, as it is also called, is a system of animistic beliefs and rituals in which the individual aims to harness natural magical powers and use them constructively whilst also living harmoniously with nature. The Earth Mother is regarded as just as important as the traditional Father-figure Deity, if not more so. Although the history of witchcraft was associated with devil-worship, SORCERY and BLACK MAGIC, this was largely due to the propaganda of the Christian church. Witches were probably never as important in their societies as SHAMANS, nor their duties so varied, although their beliefs and practices were undoubtedly along similar lines, including the use of DRUGS for HEALING and TRANCE. Most modern practitioners of witchcraft have managed to cast off the old image and have successfully convinced the public of their harmlessness and good intentions. Modern witches use SPELLS and affirmations and invoke spiritual forces, ELEMENTALS and DEVAS in their work. They also approve strongly of developing one's PSYCHIC faculties since not to do so would be a denial of humanity's potential.

WITCH-DOCTOR – See SHAMAN.

WORLDS – See PLANES.

XENOGLOSSY/XENOGLOSSIA The ability to use a foreign language of which the speaker has no conscious knowledge is known as xenoglossy or xenoglossia (literally 'foreign tongue'). The phenomenon of 'speaking in tongues', when the utterances are in no known language, but may or may not be understood by speakers of different languages, is a particular kind of xenoglossy which is usually known as GLOSSOLALIA. The phenomenon which is normally referred to as xenoglossy can be divided into two types: recitative xenoglossy, in which phrases or even long chunks of language are recited and perhaps repeated without any two-way communication taking place, and responsive xenoglossy, in which the speaker actually engages in conversation with another speaker of the foreign language.

Recitative xenoglossy is most often explained by invoking CRYPTOMNESIA, 'latent memory'. Lyall Watson has put forward another theory for some cases in which an apparently possessed person somehow gains access to the memory store of someone close by and repeats phrases from that source. This overlapping or fusing of minds he calls SAMA. Other cases in which few words are actually spoken can sometimes be put down to misperception on the part of the audience: we naturally recognize most readily what we half-expect to hear. The RAUDIVE VOICES have also been dismissed because of hearer error.

Responsive xenoglossy is characteristic of MEDIUMS, who apparently become a CHANNEL for SPIRITS who speak other languages, and of people who assume a different personality, either under HYPNOSIS or spontaneously, suggesting either POSSESSION or regression to a past life. Mrs Piper's French control, Dr Phinuit, usually spoke in English, although he was able to understand some French and spoke in set phrases and clichés. Some mediums have claimed to bring in spirit communications in ancient Egyptian, and although Egyptologists have verified the possibility that the language was accurate, it is of course impossible to authenticate it absolutely.

Xenoglossy is not restricted to mediums and pathological cases of MULTIPLE PERSONALITY. A few instances when someone has suddenly seemed to become another person, speaking a different language, are extremely difficult to explain. In 1974 Uttara Huddar, a lecturer at Nagpur University in India, suddenly started behaving like a very religious married Bengali woman. She said her name was Sharada and spoke perfect Bengali. Uttara spoke Marathi and had had no contact at all with Bengali speakers. Eventually Uttara was herself again, but Sharada would return periodically and sometimes stayed for several weeks. The psychologists refer to this as 'a case of secondary personality with xenoglossy' (Ian Stevenson in *American Journal of Psychiatry* 1979), but such labels go no way towards explaining the phenomenon. The perfect Bengali speech cannot even be explained by TELEPATHY, which is sometimes invoked to explain xenoglossy, unless we accept such a broad definition which would allow Uttara somehow to link mentally with someone called Sharada, living hundreds of miles away and having no other connection with Uttara. It is cases such as this that are seen as evidence of REINCARNATION, although some might say they are indicative of possession too.

XENOPHRENIA Literally 'strange mind', xenophrenia is a scientific term for an altered state of consciousness. A xenophrenic state was formerly referred to as DISSOCIATION, which covered TRANCE phenomena and MULTIPLE PERSONALITY, but xenophrenia covers a wider range of possibilities. For example, there is usually no conscious memory of what has taken place during a period of dissociation, but the events in some xenophrenic states are recalled. Some say that temporary xenophrenia occurs when we fall asleep or become unconscious, when we yawn, when we experience an orgasm, and when we die.

In America, Masters and Houston developed a cage-like 'ASC Induction Device' and J.C. Lilly used sensory deprivation tanks to investigate the ways in which the brain responded to an absence of stimuli by creating pseudo-sensory input. The Oxford researcher, Celia Green, has studied and compared the characteristic signals which seem to mark the onset of a xenophrenic state and the external conditions which may give rise to it. The visual field often narrows before telepathic impressions are received, and the same happens as a prelude to visionary experiences, many of which begin with the image of being sucked along a tunnel towards a light — a common trait in NEAR-DEATH EXPERIENCES and UFO encounters. Driving down a road at night with few visual stimuli is also a typical scenario for UFO sightings.

YANG — See YIN/YANG.

YANTRA A *yantra* is a complex geometrical design, a mystical diagram, traditionally incorporating some Sanskrit letters and representing in abstract form certain attributes of a particular Hindu deity. It is a pictorial equivalent of a spoken MANTRA. It is used as an aid to contemplation in Tantric Hindu worship and is believed to radiate influences for good or evil. Yantras are often recognizable by the use of triangular motifs in their

A Buddhist yantra

design. If framed in rectangular and circular borders such a design may be a MANDALA. Using a yantra in MEDITATION one usually starts at the outer edge of the design, focusing the mind gradually towards the central point which represents the source of Being.

YIN/YANG In Chinese philosophy as presented in the I CHING and TAOISM, there are two balancing forces at work in the phenomenal universe, two dynamic polarities, the principles of yin (female) and yang (male). These negative (yin) and positive (yang) polarities should not be understood in a value-judgment sense, nor is their interaction an equivalent of the Western dualism of the PYTHAGOREANS or the GNOSTICS, but they should be seen rather as complementary qualities: dark and light, ebb and flow, contraction and expansion.

陰　陽

YIN	YANG
negative	positive
passive	active
female	male
receptive	creative
dark	light
shadow	sun
night	day
winter	summer
cold	heat
soft	hard
wet	dry

The balancing relationship between the two forces is demonstrated visually in the PA-KWA symbol.

YOGA The Sanskrit root of the word 'yoga' is also the root of the English word 'yoke' and means 'union' or 'harnessing'. The aim of yoga, as with all MYSTIC systems, is the achievement of true union with one's true SELF, union of the individual with the universal spirit, of the one with the All, of the human with the divine, or the loss of ego and the attainment of MOKSHA or NIRVANA. Those who attain the desired state perceive themselves in all things and all things in the Self; they lose the lesser self and find the greater Self in God or BRAHMAN. This is achieved by self-discipline, control over desires and varying degrees of asceticism. The practice of yoga techniques is open to people of any religion. Although it is most closely associated with Hindu and Buddhist teachings, there is also a clear affinity between yoga and certain Christian and Moslem sects (e.g. Hesychasts and SUFIS) and many writings of Western mystics reflect the same experiences, feelings and attitudes as those of YOGIS.

Yoga was already being practised in the second millennium BC, but its main scripture, the *Bhagavad Gita*, was probably written about 300 BC. One of its foremost exponents was Patanjali, a historical person whom some identify with a Sanskrit grammarian who lived about 330 BC. Meditation techniques lie at the heart of all forms of yoga, but there are several routes that the training and self-discipline may follow, according to their suitability for the individual. The main four of these are:

1. *karma yoga* — the approach to the Divine through good works and the right attitude to work;
2. *jnana yoga* — the approach to the Divine through knowledge, as in Brahmin THEOSOPHY;
3. *bhakti yoga* — the approach to the Divine through personal devotion, which the *Bhagavad Gita* taught was a higher form of yoga, and which some might consider to be closer to Christianity;
4. *raja yoga* — (= the 'royal' way) the use of mental process, of the mind and the will.

The first three of these are presented fully in the *Bhagavad Gita*. Raja yoga concentrates on developing the mind and achieving mastery of it. This 'royal' route is expounded in the sutras of Patanjali, and is the natural way for those who have already advanced all they can in other forms of yoga. These are:

1. *hatha yoga* — (*ha* = sun, *tha* = moon) the attainment and preservation of physical well-being, the yoga of the body and health, through posture (*asana*), breathing (*pranayama*) and sense control (*pratyahara*);
2. *mantra yoga* — the use of MANTRAS as prayers and incantations as an aid to MEDITATION;
3. *laya yoga* — 'the yoga of latency', concerned with arousing the KUNDALINI, using the techniques of both *hatha yoga* and *mantra yoga*.

According to Patanjali these other forms of yoga can be seen as part of an individual's development in *raja yoga* which can be divided into eight stages, each corresponding to specific aspects of renunciation and self-discipline:

1. *yama*: non-violence, speaking the truth, continence, no coveting, stealing or even receiving gifts;
2. *niyama*: contentment, cleanliness, abstinence from desire, concentrated study, recognition of God;
3. *asana*: body posture, using individual body postures (*asanas*) and hand positions (*mudras*);
4. *paranyama*: control of breathing;
5. *pratyahara*: introspection and control of the senses;
6. DHARANA: concentration and mind control;
7. DHYANA: a higher state of mind control;
8. SAMADHI: ecstasy.

YOGIS Often yogis are famous for their supernormal or PARANORMAL powers, including LEVITATION, walking through fire, burial alive, invisibility, flying through the air. They achieve greater mental control over the body. They can control the heart and blood vessels, varying blood circulation and pulse at will. Hereward Carrington reported a yogi, Hamid Bey, whose pulse was measured in different parts of his body at different rates: 102 at his left wrist, 84 at his right, and 96 at the heart. He was also buried for three hours after entering a cataleptic state with his heart beating only a few times a minute. Houdini achieved a similar feat for an hour and a half in a coffin under water with enough air to last normally for only four minutes. The mental abilities of yogis are not restricted to bodily control. They can acquire the ability to read the minds of others, and to remember past INCARNATIONS.

However, none of these abilities is the true aim of YOGA. They may develop naturally as the yogi or *chela* (pupil) advances spiritually, but they are also seen as a distraction from the true purpose of yoga.

Z

ZEN The word Zen came from a Chinese word *ch'an,* derived from the Sansrit DHYANA meaning MEDITATION. Zen is a combination of Taoist and Buddhist thought. TAOISM taught simplicity, and tranquility, living in harmony with nature and with the TAO. Zen attaches supreme importance to meditation: it is the means to ENLIGHTENMENT, SATORI. But Zen meditation is different from the DHARANA and dhyana of YOGA: it is essentially a receptive state, an emptying of the mind, rather than a focusing of it. A Zen teacher does not argue and discuss with his pupil: the teaching is acquired through INTUITION. The teacher may present a KOAN to the pupil, a paradoxical question with no logical answer, which serves to subvert the dominance of the rational process by as it were paralysing the mind and make the pupil more receptive to enlightenment through intuition.

ZEN ARCHERY The basic idea behind Zen archery is that in the right state of mind one can hit the bull's eye without needing to take aim. It is as if a higher sense takes over and guides one's hand: focusing attention with the conscious mind would only spoil the aim. This is not simply a question of nerves and apprehension, although such feelings are obviously disruptive. It is as if we have learned that certain tasks are difficult and we consequently plot a difficult route to fulfil them, whereas in fact there is a more direct route. So we have to unlearn what we have learned, banish our preconceptions about the task and behave to a certain extent more instinctively.

The influence of such preconceptions or mental conditioning can be tested in a very simple way. Imagine that you have a rather awkward lock which there is a certain knack in opening. When presented with the key a child is much more likely to succeed in opening the lock than an adult would be, even if the adult did not know beforehand that the lock was tricky. The adult already has set ways of turning a key which are very difficult to modify. The child is much more open, less rigid, and more likely to turn the key in the appropriate way automatically. The phenomenon of 'beginner's luck' is another example of a natural knack for doing something in the right way taking over when one is unaware of the difficulties involved.

ZENER CARDS Zener cards, named after a pyschologist who suggested the idea, were devised by J.B. Rhine for use in his experiments into ESP (EXTRA-SENSORY PERCEPTION). They are used in packs of twenty-five, consisting of five of each of the following symbols: a star, a circle, a cross, a square, and three wavy lines. In TELEPATHY experiments they are shuffled and then turned over one by one by the sender. The percipient, sitting in a position from which the cards cannot be seen, sometimes even in another room, tries to guess the cards as they are turned over.

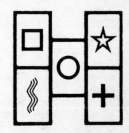

Zener cards

Bibliography

1. Alexander, P.P.: *Spiritualism: a Narrative with a Discussion*, W.P. Nimmo, Edinburgh, 1871.
2. Allison, Ralph: *Minds in Many Pieces*, Rawson Wade, New York, 1980.
3. Assagioli, Roberto: *Psychosynthesis*, Turnstone Press, Wellingborough, 1965
4. Backster, Cleve: *Evidence of a primary perception in plant life*, International Journal of Parapsychology 10: 329, 1968.
5. Bailey, Alice: *A Treatise on White Magic*, Lucis, New York and London, 1934.
6. Bailey, Alice: *Esoteric Psychology*, New York and London, 1942.
7. Behe, George: *Titanic: psychic forewarnings of a tragedy*, Thorsons, Wellingborough, 1988.
8. Bernheim, H.: *De la Suggestion dans l'état hypnotique et dans l'état de veille*, Doin, Paris, 1884: *De la Suggestion et de ses applications à la thérapeutique*, Doin, Paris, 1886; tr. New York, 1888.
9. Bernstein, Morey: *The Search for Bridey Murphy*, Doubleday, New York, 1965.
10. Besant, Annie: *The Ancient Wisdom*, London Theosophical Publishing House, 1897.
11. Besant, Annie and C.W. Leadbeater: *Thought-Forms*, Theosophical Publishing House, London, 1905.
12. Blavatsky, H.P.: *The Secret Doctrine*, London, 1888.
13. Bohm, David: *The Enfolding-Unfolding Universe*, 1978, in Wilber, Ken (ed.): *The Holographic Paradigm and Other Paradoxes*, Shambhala, Boulder & London, 1982.
14. Bond, F.B.: *The Gate of Remembrance*, Blackwell, Oxford, 1918; Thorsons, Wellingborough, 1978 reprint.
15. Bond, F.B.: *The Company of Avalon*, Blackwell, Oxford, 1924.
16. Bowles, Norma and Hynds, Fran: *Psi Search*, Harper & Row, New York, 1978.
17. Boyd, Doug: *Rolling Thunder*, Random House, New York, 1974.
18. Bramwell, J.M.: *Hypnotism: its history, practice and theory*, 3rd edition, London, 1913.
19. Broad, C.D.: *The Mind and its Place in Nature*, Kegan, Paul, Trench & Trübner, London, 1925.
20. Brown, Rosemary: *Immortals at my Elbow*, Bachman & Turner, London, 1974.

21. Brunton, Paul: *The Wisdom of the Overself*, Rider & Co. London, 1943.
22. Buchanan, J.R.: *Manual of Psychometry*, Holman, Boston, 1885.
23. Bucke, R.M.: *Cosmic Consciousness*, (1901) Dutton, New York, 1923; University Books, New York, 1961.
24. Burr: *Blueprint for Immortality*, Neville Spearman, Jersey, 1972.
25. Carey, Ken: *The Starseed Transmissions*, Starseed Publishing Company, Edinburgh, 1986.
26. Carrington, Hereward: *Higher Psychical Development*, (1918) reissued Newcastle Publishing Co., California, 1983.
27. Cayce, Edgar Evans: *Edgar Cayce on Atlantis*, Warner, New York, 1968.
28. Coates, James: *Photographing the Invisible*, L.N. Fowler, London, 1911; The Advanced Thought Publishing Co., Chicago, 1911.
29. Cohen, J.M. (trans.): *The Life of Saint Teresa*, Penguin, Harmondsworth, 1957.
30. Coleman, Michael A. (ed.): *The Ghosts of the Trianon*, Wellingborough, Aquarian, 1988. (Originally published as *An Adventure* by C.A.E. Moberly and E.F. Jourdain, 1955.)
31. Collin, Rodney: *The Theory of Eternal Life*, Watkins, Boston Mass., 1974.
32. Cooke, Maurice B.: *Dark Robes, Dark Brothers*, Marcus Books, Toronto, 1981.
33. Cousins, Norman: *Anatomy of an Illness*, New York, 1979.
34. Crabtree, Adam: *Multiple Man: Explorations in Possession and Multiple Personality*, Collins, Ontario, Canada, 1985; Holt, Rhinehart & Winston, London, 1985.
35. Crookall, Robert: *The Mechanisms of Astral Projection*, Darshana International, India, 1968.
36. Crookall, Robert: *Out-of-the-Body Experiences*, University Books, New York, 1970.
37. Cummins, Geraldine: *The Scripts of Cleophas*, Psychic Press, London, 1928.
38. Cummins, Geraldine: *The Road to Immortality*, Psychic Press, London, 1932; reprint, 1967.
39. Cummins, Geraldine: *Mind in Life and Death*, Aquarian, London, 1956.
40. David-Neel, Alexandra: *Magic and Mystery in Tibet*, Souvenir Press, London, 1961.
41. Davies, Paul: *The Cosmic Blueprint*, William Heinemann, London, 1987.
42. Denton, William: *The Soul of Things*, (1863) Thorsons, Wellingborough, 1988 reprint.
43. Desoille, Robert: *The Directed Daydream*, Presses Universitaires de France, Paris, 1945.
44. Dingwall, Eric J. (ed.): *Abnormal Hypnotic Phenomena: a survey of 19th century cases*, Churchill, London, 1968.

45. Dower, A.L.G.: *Healing with Radionics*, Thorsons, Wellingborough, 1980.

46. Drury, Nevill: *The Elements of Shamanism*, Element Books, Dorset, 1989.

47. Dunne, J.W.: *An Experiment With Time*, Faber & Faber, London, 1927.

48. Dunne, J.W.: *The New Immortality*, Faber & Faber, London, 1938.

49. Dyson, Freeman: *Disturbing the Universe* Harper & Row, New York, 1979.

50. Eliade, Mircea: *Shamanism: Archaic techniques of ecstasy*, (1951) tr. Routledge, London, 1964; Arkana, London, 1989.

51. Evans, Hilary: *Alternate States of Consciousness*, Thorsons, Wellingborough, 1989.

52. Faria, Abbé de: *De la Cause du Sommeil Lucide*, Paris, 1819.

53. Fodor, Nandor: *Mind over Space*, Citadel Press, London, 1962.

54. Fortune, Dion: *The Cosmic Doctrine*, (1924) re-issued Aquarian, Wellingborough, 1976, 1982.

55. Fortune, Dion: *Psychic Self-Defence*; re-issued Aquarian, Wellingborough, 1984.

56. Freud, Sigmund: *On Creativity and the Unconscious*, Harper, New York, 1958.

57. Garrett, Eileen: *Adventures in the Supernormal, A Personal Memoir*, 1949; Paperback Library, New York, 1968 reprint.

58. Garrett, Eileen: *Many Voices*, Allen & Unwin, London, 1969.

59. Gauld, A. and Cornell, A.D.: *Poltergeists*, Routledge & Kegan Paul, London, 1979.

60. Geley, Gustave: *De l'Inconscient au Conscient*, Librairie Felix Alkan, Paris, 1919; *From the Unconscious to the Conscious*, Collins, London, 1919.

61. Geley, Gustave: *Clairvoyance and Materialisation*, Unwin, London, 1927.

62. Gooch, Stan: *Total Man*, Allen Lane, London, 1972.

63. Gooch, Stan: *The Secret Life of Humans*, Dent, London, 1981.

64. Gooch, Stan: *Creatures from Inner Space*, Rider, London, 1984.

65. Goodman, Jeffrey: *Psychic Archaeology*, Panther, London, 1979.

66. Grant, Joan and Kelsey, Denis: *Many Lifetimes*, Doubleday, New York, 1967.

67. Graves, Tom: *The Elements of Pendulum Dowsing*, Element Books, Shaftesbury, 1989.

68. Green, Celia and McCreery, Charles: *Apparitions*, Hamilton, London, 1975.

69. Greenhouse, H.B.: *Premonitions: A Leap into the Future*, 1971; Turnstone Press, Wellingborough, 1972.

70. Gregory, R.L. (ed.): *The Oxford Companion to the Mind*, OUP, Oxford, 1986.

71. Grof, Stanislav: *Realms of the Human Unconscious: Observations from LSD Research*, E.P. Dutton, New York, 1976.

72. Guirdham, Arthur: *A Foot in Both Worlds*, Neville Spearman, Jersey, 1973.

73. Guirdham, Arthur: *The Lake and the Castle*, Neville Spearman, Jersey, 1976.

74. Guirdham, Arthur: *The Great Heresy*, Neville Spearman, Jersey, 1977.

75. Guirdham: Arthur: *We Are One Another*, Turnstone, Wellingborough, 1982.

76. Gurney, Edmund, Myers, F.W.H. and Podmore, Frank: *Phantasms of the Living*, Trübner, London, 1886.

77. Haldane, J.B.S.: *The Inequality of Man*, Chatto, London, 1932.

78. Hardy, Alister: *The Living Stream*, Collins, London, 1965.

79. Hardy, Alister: *The Spiritual Nature of Man*, OUP, Oxford, 1979.

80. Hardy, Jean: *A Psychology with a Soul*, Routledge & Kegan Paul, London, 1987.

81. Harner, Michael: *The Way of the Shaman*, Harper & Row, San Francisco, 1980.

82. Hartley, Christine: *A Case for Reincarnation*, Robert Hale, London, 1972.

83. Hawken, Paul: *The Magic of Findhorn*, Souvenir Press (UK), Harper & Row (USA), 1971.

84. Heywood, Rosalind: *The Infinite Hive*, Chatto & Windus, London, 1964.

85. Hoyle, Fred: *Galaxies, Nuclei and Quasars*, Heinemann, London, 1965.

86. Hudson, T.J.: *The Law of Psychic Phenomena*, (1893) G.P. Putman's Sons, London, 1902.

87. Huxley, Aldous: *The Perennial Philosophy*, Harper & Row, New York, 1944; Chatto & Windus, London, 1946.

88. Huxley, Aldous: *The Doors of Perception*, Chatto & Windus, London, 1954.

89. James, William: *Varieties of Religious Experiences: a study in human nature*, Longmans Green, London, 1902.

90. Jaynes, Julian: *The Origin of Consciousness in the Breakdown of the Bicameral Mind*, Houghton Mifflin, Boston, Mass., 1976.

91. Jeans, James: *The Mysterious Universe*, Cambridge University Press, Cambridge, 1930.

92. Johnson, Raynor C.: *The Imprisoned Splendour*, Hodder & Stoughton, London, 1953.

93. Jung, C.G.: *Flying Saucers*, Routledge & Kegan Paul, London, 1959.

94. Jung, C.G.: *The Structure and Dynamics of the Psyche*, Routledge & Kegan Paul, London, 1960.

95. Jung, C.G.: *The Soul and Death*, Routledge & Kegan Paul, London, 1960.

96. Jung, C.G.: *Synchronicity*, (in *The Interpretation of Nature and the Psyche*, 1955) Routledge & Kegan Paul, London, 1972.

97. Jung, C.G.: *Memories, Dreams, Reflections*, Collins, London, 1963.

98. Jung, C.G.: *VII Sermones ad Mortuos (Seven Sermons to the Dead)*, Stuart & Watkins, London, 1967.

99. Karagulla, Shafica: *Breakthrough to Creativity*, De Vorss, Los Angeles, 1969.

100. Kardec, Allan: *The Spirits' Book*, privately published, 1856; Trübner, London, 1857; Lake-Livraria Allan Kardec Editora Ltd., Sao Paulo, Brazil, 1972.

101. Keyes, Daniel: *The Minds of Billy Milligan*, Random House, New York, 1981.

102. Kilner, Walter: *The Human Atmosphere*, Kegan Paul, London 1911 and 1920.

103. Knight, Gareth: *A History of White Magic*, Mowbrays, London, 1978.

104. Koestler, Arthur: *The Roots of Coincidence*, Hutchinson, London, 1972.

105. Koestler, Arthur: *Janus*, Hutchinson, London, 1978.

106. Küng, Hans: *Eternal Life?*, (*Ewiges Leben?*), R. Piper, Munich, 1982; tr. Collins, London, 1984.

107. Laski, Marghanita: *Ecstasy*, Cresset Press, London, 1961.

108. LeShan, Lawrence: *The Medium, the Mystic and the Physicist*, (also published as *Clairvoyant Reality*) Turnstone, London & USA, 1974.

109. LeShan, Lawrence: *From Newton to ESP*, Turnstone Press, Wellingborough, 1984.

110. Lethbridge, T.C.: *Ghost and Ghoul*, Routledge & Kegan Paul, London, 1961.

111. Lethbridge, T.C.: *The Monkey's Tail*, Routledge & Kegan Paul, 1969.

112. Lethbridge, T.C.: *The Power of the Pendulum*, Routledge & Kegan Paul, 1976.

113. Lombroso, Cesare: *After Death — What?*, (1909) modern reprint Thorsons, Wellingborough, 1988.

114. Long, Max Freedom: *Recovering Ancient Magic*, Rider, London, 1936.

115. Long, Max Freedom: *The Secret Science Behind Miracles*, De Vorss, Santa Monica, California, 1948.

116. Lovelock, James: *Gaia*, Oxford University Press, Oxford, 1979.

117. Mackenzie: *The Seen and the Unseen*, Weidenfeld & Nicolson, London, 1987.

118. Manning, Matthew: *The Link*, Colin Smythe, Gerrards Cross, 1974.

119. Manning, Matthew: *In the Minds of Millions*, W.H. Allen, London, 1977.

120. Manning, Matthew: *The Strangers*, W.H. Allen, London, 1978.

121. Marais, Eugène: *The Soul of the Ape*, Blond, London, 1969.

122. Markides, Kyriacos: *The Magus of Strovolos*, Routledge & Kegan Paul, 1985.

123. Maslow, Abraham: *The Farther Reaches of Human Nature*, Viking Press, London & New York, 1971.

124. Matthews, Caitlin & John: *The Western Way*, Arkana, London, 1986.

125. Menzel, Donald: *Flying Saucers*, Cambridge, USA, 1953.

126. Mitchell (ed.): *Psychic Exploration*, Putnam, New York, 1974.

127. Monroe, Robert A.: *Journeys Out of the Body*, Doubleday, New York, 1971.

128. Moody, Raymond: *Life After Life*, Bantam, New York, 1975.
129. Moody, Raymond: *The Light Beyond*, Bantam, New York, 1988; Macmillan, London, 1988.
130. Moore, W.U.: *The Voices*, Watts, London, 1913.
131. Moses, Revd Stainton: *Psychography*, Psychological Press Association, W.H. Allen, London, 1882.
132. Muck, Otto: *The Secret of Atlantis*, William Collins, London, 1978.
133. Muldoon S. & Carrington H.: *The Projection of the Astral Body*, Rider & Co., London, 1929.
134. Muldoon S. & Carrington H.: *The Phenomena of Astral Projection*, Rider & Co., London, 1951.
135. Myers, F.W.H.: *On Human Personality and its Survival of Bodily Death*, Longmans, Green & Co., London, 1903.
136. Oliver, Edith: *Without Knowing Mr Walkley*, London, 1938.
137. Ornstein, Robert E.: *The Psychology of Consciousness*, W.H. Freeman & Co., USA, 1972.
138. Ostrander & Schroeder: *Psi: Psychic Discoveries Behind the Iron Curtain*, Sphere Books, London, 1973.
139. Ouspensky, P.D.: *Tertium Organum*, Manas Press, 1920; Random House, New York, 1970 reprint.
140. Ouspensky, P.D.: *A New Model of the Universe*, Knopf, USA, 1931; Random House, New York, 1971 reprint.
141. Ouspensky, P.D.: *In Search of the Miraculous*, Harcourt Brace Jovanovich, New York & London, 1949, 1977.
142. Pearce, Ian: *The Gate of Healing*, Spearman, Jersey, 1983.
143. Pearce, J.C.: *The Crack in the Cosmic Egg*, Julian Press, New York, 1971.
144. Pearce, J.C.: *Exploring the Crack in the Cosmic Egg*, Julian Press, New York, 1974.
145. Pelton, Robert: *The Devil and Karen Kingston*, Pocket Books, New York, 1977.
146. Penfield, Wilder: *The Mystery of Mind*, Princeton University Press, Princeton, 1975.
147. Percival, Harold Waldwin: *Thinking and Destiny*, The World Foundation Inc., Dallas, 1946.
148. Playfair, Guy Lyon: *The Flying Cow*, Souvenir Press, London, 1975.
149. Playfair, Guy Lyon: *The Indefinite Boundary*, Souvenir Press, London, 1976.
150. Playfair, Guy Lyon: *If This Be Magic*, Jonathan Cape, London, 1985.
151. Playfair, G.L. & Hill, Scott: *The Cycles of Heaven*, Souvenir Press, London, 1978.
152. Polge, Coral & Kay Hunter: *The Living Image*, Regency Press, London, 1984.
153. Popper, Karl: *Objective Knowledge*, OUP, Oxford, 1971.
154. Quanjer, J.H.: Lectures given on 5 July, 1974 in Caxton Hall, London, published by The New World Movement, and on 28

September 1974 at the Royal Overseas League for the Human Development Trust. The concept of *pneumatocracy*, has subsequently been discussed at length in the journal *New Humanity*, starting with its first issue in February 1975.

155. Randles, Jenny: *The Sixth Sense*, Hale, London, 1987.

156. Raudive, Konstantin: *Breakthrough: an amazing experiment in electronic communication with the dead*, Smythe, Gerrards Cross, 1971.

157. Reed, G.: *The Psychology of Anomalous Experience*, Hutchinson, London, 1972.

158. Reed, Henry: *Edgar Cayce on Mysteries of the Mind*, Warner, New York, 1989; Thorsons, Wellingborough, 1990.

159. Rhine, J.B.: *Extra-sensory Perception*, SPR/Brandon, Boston, 1934. Rev. ed. 1971.

160. Rhine, J.B.: *The Reach of the Mind*, Morrow, New York, 1947; Penguin, Harmondsworth, 1954.

161. Richet, Charles: *Thirty Years of Psychical Research*, William Collins, London, 1923.

162. Ring, Kenneth: *Life at Death: A Scientific Investigation of the Near-Death Experience*, Coward, McCann and Geoghagan, New York, 1980.

163. Roberts, Jane: *Seth Speaks*, Bantam, New York, 1974.

164. Roberts, Jane: *The Nature of Personal Reality*, Prentice-Hall, Englewood Cliffs, 1974.

165. Roberts, Jane: *Adventures in Consciousness*, Prentice-Hall, Englewood Cliffs, 1975.

166. Roberts, Jane: *The 'Unknown' Reality*, Prentice Hall, Englewood Cliffs, Vol. I, 1977; Vol.II, 1979.

167. Robins, Don: *Circles of Silence*, Souvenir Press, London, 1985.

168. Robins, Don: *The Secret Language of Stone*, Century Hutchinson, London, 1988.

169. Rogo, D. Scott: *The Infinite Boundary*, Dodd, Mead & Co., New York, 1987.

170. Roll, W.G. (ed.): *Research in Parapsychology*, (1973) Scarecrow Press, Metuchen, 1977.

171. Russell, Peter: *The TM Technique*, Routledge & Kegan Paul, London, 1976.

172. Ryle, Gilbert: *The Concept of Mind*, Hutchinson, London, 1941/1949.

173. St Clair, David: *Drum and Candle*, Macdonald, London, 1971.

174. Schatzman, M.: *The Story of Ruth*, Duckworth, London, 1980.

175. Schrenck-Notzing: *Phenomena of Materialisation*, Dutton, London, 1920.

176. Scott, Cyril: *An Outline of Modern Occultism*, (1935) Routledge & Kegan Paul, London, 1950.

177. Shallis, Michael: *On Time*, Hutchinson, London, 1982.

178. Sheldrake, Rupert: *A New Science of Life*, Blond & Briggs, London, 1981.

179. Sidgwick H. (and SPR committee): *Report on the Census of Hallucinations*, Proceedings of Society for Psychical Research, 10, 1894.

180. Sinclair, Upton: *Mental Radio. Does it work, and how?*, Werner Laurie, London, 1930.

181. Soal, S.G. & Bateman, F.: *Modern Experiments in Telepathy*, Faber, London, 1954.

182. Steinbrecher, Edwin C.: *Inner Guide Meditation*, Samuel Weiser Inc., York Beach, Maine, 1988.

183. Steiner, Rudolf: *Theosophy*, Kegan Paul, London, 1910.

184. Steiner, Rudolf: *Cosmic Memory*, Rudolf Steiner Publications, New York, 1959.

185. Steiner, Rudolf: *The Course of My Life*, Anthroposophical Press, New York, 2nd edition 1986.

186. Steiner, Rudolf: *Karmic Relationships*, (Lectures delivered in 1924). Rudolf Steiner Press, London, 1955 & 1972. `

187. Stevenson, Ian: *Twenty Cases Suggestive of Reincarnation*, American Society for Psychical Research, New York, 1966.

188. Stewart, R.J.: *Music and the Elemental Psyche*, Thorsons, Wellingborough, 1987.

189. Strieber, Whitley: *Communion – a true story*, William Morrow, New York, 1987; Century, London, 1987.

190. Strieber, Whitley: *Transformation*, William Morrow, New York, 1988; Century, London, 1988.

191. Tansley, David V.: *Subtle Body*, Thames & Hudson, London, 1977.

192. Targ, Russell & Harold Puthoff: *Mind Reach*, Delacorte, New York, 1977; Cape, London, 1977.

193. Targ, Russell & Keith Harary: *The Mind Race*, Villard, New York, 1984.

194. Taylor, John: *Superminds*, Macmillan, London, 1973.

195. Taylor, John: *Science and the Supernatural*, Granada, London, 1981.

196. Teilhard de Chardin, P.: *The Phenomenon of Man*, (*Le Phénomène Humain*, 1955) William Collins, London, 1959; Harper & Brothers, New York, 1959.

197. Temple, William: *The Shining Brother*, Psychic Press, London, 1941.

198. Thalbourne, Michael A.: *A Glossary of Terms used in Parapsychology*, Heinemann, London, 1982.

199. Thigpen, C.H. and Cleckley, H.M.: *The Three Faces of Eve*, Secker & Warburg, London, 1957.

200. Thouless, R.H. and Wiesner: *On the Nature of Psi Phenomena*, in *The Journal of Parapsychology*, 10, 1946.

201. Tompkins, Peter and Bird, Christopher: *The Secret Life of Plants*, Harper & Row, New York, 1973.

202. Tromp, S.W.: *Psychical Physics*, Elsevier, New York, 1949.

203. Tyrrell, G.N.M.: *Science and Psychical Phenomena*, London, 1938; University Books, New York, 1961 reprint.

204. Vasiliev, L.L.: *Experiments in Distant Influence* (1962), London, 1963.
205. Walter, William Grey: *The Living Brain*, Duckworth, London 1953.
206. Watson, Lyall: *Lifetide*, Hodder & Stoughton, London, 1979.
207. Watson, Lyall: *Beyond Supernature*, Hodder & Stoughton, London, 1986.
208. Webster, Ken: *The Vertical Plane*, Collins, London, 1989.
209. Whitehead, A.N.: *Science and the Modern World*, Macmillan, London, 1925.
210. Whyte, L.L.: *The Unconscious before Freud*, Julian Friedmann, London, 1978.
211. Wilber, Ken: *Up From Eden — a transpersonal view of human evolution*, Anchor Press, Doubleday, New York, 1981; Routledge & Kegan Paul, London, 1983.
212. Wilbur, C.: *Sybil*, Doubleday, New York, 1975.
213. Williston, Glenn: *Soul Search*, Turnstone, Wellingborough, 1983.
214. Wilson, Colin: *Beyond the Occult*, Bantam, London, 1988.
215. Yarbro, Chelsea Quinn: *Messages From Michael*, Playboy Press, Chicago, 1979.
216. Yarbro, Chelsea Quinn: *More Messages From Michael*, Berkley Books, New York, 1986.
217. Zhirov, N.F.: *Atlantis*, 1970.
218. Anon: *A Course in Miracles*, (anonymous because channelled by Helen Cohn Schucman, a New York psychologist). Foundation for Inner Peace, Tiburon, California, 1975.

Index

Index